Race, Nation, and Religion in the Americas

Race, Nation, and Religion in the Americas

EDITED BY HENRY GOLDSCHMIDT
AND ELIZABETH McALISTER

OXFORD
UNIVERSITY PRESS

2004

OXFORD
UNIVERSITY PRESS

Oxford   New York
Auckland   Bangkok   Buenos Aires   Cape Town   Chennai
Dar es Salaam   Delhi   Hong Kong   Istanbul   Karachi   Kolkata
Kuala Lumpur   Madrid   Melbourne   Mexico City   Mumbai
Nairobi   São Paulo   Shanghai   Taipei   Tokyo   Toronto

Published by Oxford University Press, Inc.
198 Madison Avenue, New York, New York 10016

www.oup.com

Oxford is a registered trademark of Oxford University Press

Library of Congress Cataloging-in-Publication Data
Race, nation, and religion in the Americas / edited by Henry Goldschmidt and Elizabeth
McAlister.
p.   cm.
Includes bibliographical references and index.
ISBN 0-19-514918-1; 0-19-514919-X (pbk.)
1. America—Race relations—History.   2. America—Religion.   3. Blacks—America—
Religion.   4. African Americans—Religion.   5. Indians—Religion.   6. Jews—America—
History.   I. Goldschmidt, Henry.   II. McAlister, Elizabeth A.
E29.A1R33 2004
305.6'0973—dc22   2003066225

9 8 7 6 5 4 3 2 1

Printed in the United States of America
on acid-free paper

For Koukou and Goog

Acknowledgments

We are deeply indebted to all of the individuals and institutions who supported our work over the years it took to bring this project to fruition.

This collection was first conceived following a panel on similar themes we organized at the 1998 annual conference of the American Anthropological Association, then further developed through a panel we organized at the 2000 annual conference of the Association for the Sociology of Religion. Thanks to all of the panelists who contributed to these productive dialogues: Karen McCarthy Brown, Kamari Clarke, Cheryl Townsend Gilkes, Sharmila Rudrappa, Nina Schnall, and Jennifer Wojcikowski.

Our work on the collection found an institutional and intellectual home through our affiliations with the Institute for the Advanced Study of Religion at Yale University. Our heartfelt thanks to Jon Butler, Ken Minkema, Harry Stout, the IASRY staff, and all of the participants in their warm and wonderful conferences and colloquia.

Thanks, as well, to all of the friends and colleagues who commented on or contributed to this project along the way, including (but by no means limited to): Algernon Austin, Christine Ayorinde, Michael Barkun, Ron Cameron, Eric Canin, Mattias Gardell, Eddie Glaude, Jr., David Shorter, Derek Williams, and our anonymous reviewers from Oxford University Press. Henry would also like to thank Ben Chesluk and David Valentine (the Writer's Bloc), and Jillian Shagan. Liza would also like to thank Holly Nicolas, her colleagues in the Wesleyan University Faculty Seminar on Intersexionality, and her students in the course "Religion and the Social Construction of Race." Liza is particularly grateful to Robin Nagel, for years of rich and sustaining dialogue and friendship.

It was a pleasure to work with the authors who contributed to the collection. As is the case with any true collaboration, our understanding of the project was both enriched and challenged through our engagement with their work. Thank you all. And thanks, in particular, to Judith Weisenfeld, whose research and teaching on race and religion helped us imagine this project in the first place.

Finally, many thanks to everyone at Oxford University Press. Thanks, above all, to our editor Cynthia Read, for her unflagging support and unerring savvy.

Contents

Contributors, ix

Introduction: Race, Nation, and Religion, 3
Henry Goldschmidt

SECTION I "Heathens" and "Jews" in the Colonial Imagination

1. Race and Religion on the Periphery: Disappointment and
   Missionization in the Spanish Floridas, 1566–1763, 35
   Daniel Murphree

2. The Jew in the Haitian Imagination: A Popular History of
   Anti-Judaism and Proto-Racism, 61
   Elizabeth McAlister

SECTION II Constructing and Critiquing White Christianities

3. A Great Racial Commission: Religion and the Construction of
   White America, 85
   Daniel B. Lee

4. The Catholic Afro Mass and the Dance of Eurocentrism in
   Brazil, 111
   John Burdick

SECTION III   Race and Nation in the Mission Field

5. "Marked in Body, Mind, and Spirit": Home Missionaries and the
   Remaking of Race and Nation, 133
   Derek Chang

6. "In Search of Souls, in Search of Indians": Religion and the "Indian
   Problem" in Northern Mexico, 157
   Julia Cummings O'Hara

SECTION IV   Segregation, Congregation, and the North American
              Racial Binary

7. Catholics, Creoles, and the Redefinition of Race in New Orleans, 183
   James B. Bennett

8. Beyond the Binary: Revisiting Father Divine, Daddy Grace, and Their
   Ministries, 209
   Danielle Brune Sigler

SECTION V   Policing the Racial and Religious Boundaries of "Civilization"

9. Legislating "Civilization" in Postrevolutionary Haiti, 231
   Kate Ramsey

10. The Civilization of White Men: The Race of the Hindu in *United States v.
    Bhagat Singh Thind*, 259
    Jennifer Snow

SECTION VI   Sense and Sensuality in Rituals and Representations of Race

11. The House of Saint Benedict, the House of Father John: Umbanda
    Aesthetics and a Politics of the Senses, 283
    Lindsay Hale

12. Projecting Blackness: African-American Religion in the Hollywood
    Imagination, 305
    Judith Weisenfeld

Index, 329

Contributors

James B. Bennett is Assistant Professor of Religious Studies at Santa Clara University, Santa Clara, California. He holds a Ph.D. in Religious Studies from Yale University. He is completing a book on Protestant and Catholic responses to segregation in New Orleans.

John Burdick is Associate Professor of Anthropology and Associate Director of the Program on the Analysis and Resolution of Conflicts at Syracuse University. He is the author of *Legacies of Liberation: The Progressive Catholic Church in Brazil at the Turn of a New Century; Blessed Anastacia: Women, Race and Popular Christianity in Brazil;* and *Looking for God in Brazil: The Progressive Catholic Church in Urban Brazil's Religious Arena;* and co-editor (with Ted Hewitt) of *The Church at the Grassroots in Latin America: Perspectives on Thirty Years of Activism.* He is currently conducting research on the black evangelical movement in Brazil.

Derek Chang is Assistant Professor of History and Asian American Studies at Cornell University. He received his Ph.D. in history from Duke University in 2002. He is currently completing a manuscript on African American and Chinese interactions with the American Baptist Home Mission Society.

Henry Goldschmidt is Assistant Professor of Religion and Society at Wesleyan University. He received his Ph.D. in anthropology from the University of California at Santa Cruz, and has taught cultural anthropology and diaspora studies at Rutgers University and Dickinson College. He is currently completing a book on race, religion, and Black-Jewish difference in the Brooklyn neighborhood of Crown Heights. His work on Crown Heights has been published in the journal *Diaspora* and a number of edited collections.

Lindsay Hale is presently a lecturer at the University of Texas at Austin (where he earned his Ph.D. in anthropology in 1994) and at the University of Texas at San Antonio. His research explores the contested fields of race, gender, class, and power among Umbanda practitioners in Rio de Janeiro, Brazil, focusing especially on the aesthetic, sensual, autobiographical, and poetic dimensions of ritual performance and religious narrative. His work has appeared in *American Ethnologist,* and in several edited volumes. He is presently completing an ethnographic account of Umbanda integrating phenomenological, sociological, and historical perspectives.

Daniel B. Lee is Associate Professor of Sociology at the Pennsylvania State University. He received his Ph.D. in 1995 at the Maxwell School for Citizenship and Public Affairs at Syracuse University. His current research interests include social systems theory, organizational culture, and the sociology of religion. He is the author of *Old Order Mennonites: Rituals, Beliefs, and Community* and is writing a book on communication and social systems theory.

Elizabeth McAlister is Associate Professor in the Department of Religion and in the programs in American Studies, African-American Studies, and Latin American Studies at Wesleyan University. She is the author of *Rara!: Vodou, Power, and Performance in Haiti and its Diaspora* and of various articles on religion, race, gender, and transnationalism.

Daniel Murphree is Assistant Professor of History at the University of Texas at Tyler. In 2003 he received the Arthur W. Thompson Best Article award for his essay titled "Constructing Indians in the Colonial Floridas: Origins of European-Floridian Identity, 1513-1573." He is currently working on a book manuscript that deals with similar themes in relation to the Gulf South borderlands.

Julia Cummings O'Hara is Assistant Professor of History at Xavier University in Cincinnati, Ohio. She received her Ph.D. in History from Indiana University in 2003 and has held fellowships from the Erasmus Institute at the University of Notre Dame, the Institute for the Advanced Study of Religion at Yale, and Fulbright-Hays. Her archival and ethnographic research has focused on the cultural history of indigenism and religion in twentieth-century Mexico. She is currently working on a book on Indians and Catholic missionaries in the state of Chihuahua, Mexico.

Kate Ramsey received her Ph.D. in anthropology from Columbia University in 2002. She is currently a Mellon Postdoctoral Fellow at the University of Pennsylvania's Humanities Forum, teaching in the anthropology department and writing a book on the politics of law and religion in Haiti.

Danielle Brune Sigler received her Ph.D. in American Studies from the University of Texas at Austin in 2002 and is a participant in the Young Scholars Program of the Center for the Study of Religion and American Culture at Indiana and Purdue Universities. She has received support for her research from the Social Science Research Council and the John Nicholas Brown Center for American Civilization. Her book *Sweet Daddy Grace: The Making of A Modern Day Prophet* is forthcoming.

Jennifer Snow received her Ph.D. in Religion from Columbia University in 2003 and is currently a postdoctoral research fellow at the Center for Religion and Civic Culture at the University of Southern California. Her essay is part of a larger research project examining the response of Protestant missionaries to early Asian immigration and the ways their interaction contributed to American racial ideology and religious identity.

Judith Weisenfeld is Associate Professor of Religion at Vassar College. She is the author of *African-American Women and Christian Activism: New York's Black YWCA, 1905–1945;* co-editor (with Richard Newman) of *This Far By Faith: Readings in African American Women's Religious Biography;* and the founder and editor of *The North Star: A Journal of African-American Religious History*. She is currently at work on a project on African American religion in American film, 1929–1950, from which her essay is drawn.

Race, Nation, and Religion in the Americas

Introduction: Race, Nation, and Religion

Henry Goldschmidt

Writing, as I am, in New York City in the summer of 2003—at the dawn of a thus far violent millennium—it is difficult to overlook, or overstate, the sociopolitical significance of religious discourses and identities. The horrific terrorist attacks of September 11, 2001, continue to haunt the individual and collective imaginations of New Yorkers and other Americans.[1] The growth of militant religious movements throughout the world would seem, at least, to shake the once popular faith in the inevitable secularization of "modern" society. We who watched in shocked disbelief as plumes of acrid smoke rose from the streets of lower Manhattan—and the walls of the Pentagon and the fields of Pennsylvania, then the streets of Kabul and Muzar-e-Sharif, then Basra and Baghdad, and who knows where next—need not be reminded of the enduring power of religion to shape the social world.

Or perhaps we do. Perhaps, at the very least, we in the United States, and throughout the Americas, need to be reminded of our *own* complex relationships to this world-shaping power. For our reactions to the events of 9/11 have all too often reinscribed the most misleading and dangerous assumptions of secularization theory and modern self-identity. As Americans have responded to changing world events, many have continued to assume a stark opposition between "the West" and "the Rest"—the former imagined as modern, rational and secular, while the latter is thought to languish in a fantastical world of tradition, superstition, and religion. Against all evidence to the contrary, we tend to believe that religious politics and identities thrive only—or at least primarily—on the *other* side of a civilizational divide. When a small group of Islamic militants conspires to commit mass murder, or when popular movements in predominantly Muslim countries denounce the global hegemony of American culture, their actions are attributed to "religious extremism." But when a small number of Americans respond to these real and imagined threats with hate crimes against immigrants of Middle Eastern and South Asian descent, their actions are attributed to "racial profiling." And when the United States government targets members of the same communities for interrogation and deportation—or targets their homelands for military occupation—its actions are attributed to the interests of "national security." Religion, we feel, has nothing to do with it. The lines are all too clearly drawn: religion is distinguished from, and set against, both race and nation.

Even when racism is condemned in unambiguous terms, and nationalism subjected to searching critique (as in most popular reactions to racial profiling, and some progressive responses to the war on Iraq and the rhetoric of homeland defense) a troubling conceptual divide remains. Non-Western others are thought to act in terms of "religion"—to base their identities and politics on beliefs about the supernatural world that we in the West implicitly, or explicitly, deem unfounded or irrational. Yet Americans are thought to act in terms of "race" and "nation"—to base our identities and politics, for better or worse, on rational analyses of social or scientific facts. Our belief in a secular modern world thus remains largely secure, despite our growing fear of nonmodern religious others.

This faith is rarely shaken by the insights of scholars and pundits. Indeed it remains secure, in part, because it is echoed and affirmed by a long history of scholarly research that has argued—or assumed—that religion is no longer a significant marker or determinant of identity and community in the "modern" world.[2] As Mark C. Taylor puts it, the "prophets and analysts" of modernization have proclaimed for over a century that "the progressive advance toward modernity is . . . inseparable from a gradual movement away from religion."[3] Though the self-identity of medieval "Christendom" was defined in opposition to the "Hebrews" and "heretics" within its borders, the "Mohammedans" next door, and the "heathens" everywhere else, in the eyes of many scholars these "traditional" religious identities have been superseded by "modern" ones based on race and nation.

There is, of course, some truth to this analysis. In many social contexts, religious identities are, in fact, less significant today than they seem to have been in the past. And the world has, in fact, been wracked, over the past few centuries, by the birth of racial and national differences. But if we imagine that race and nation have supplanted religion, what are we to make of the words of George W. Bush—our self-avowed evangelical Christian president—whose unscripted reaction to the horror of 9/11 was to call for a "crusade" against terrorism, to protect the "civilized world" from "barbarians" and "evildoers"?

And how are we to respond when the president's rhetoric is echoed, a year and a half later, in the accusations of Islamic militants that a "crusader coalition" of "infidel colonizers" has invaded Iraq? How are we to understand the murder of Balbir Singh Sodhi, a Sikh who was shot to death in Arizona in the week after 9/11 because his beard and turban cast him as a vaguely defined "other" in the eyes of a bigoted White—and at least nominally Christian–American? And how, by contrast, are we to appreciate the inclusive vision of American society articulated on September 14, 2001, our "National Day of Prayer and Remembrance," when for the first time in American history, a Muslim imam, Dr. Muzammil H. Siddiqi, offered a prayer from the pulpit of the National Cathedral?[4]

In each of these cases and countless others—in the United States and throughout the Americas, from the fifteenth century through the twenty-first—religion has been inextricably woven into both racial and national identities, to such an extent that "race," "nation," and "religion" have each defined the others. These seemingly distinct discourses of difference have at times borrowed and at times contested each other's rhetorical authority, reinforcing and undercutting each other's social hierarchies, mixing and mingling in unresolved dialectics irreducible to any one term. If we fail to appreciate the relationships among these categories of collective identity, we will be unable to grasp the contours of our own histories—that of the United States, and those of the Americas more broadly. We will misunderstand our increasingly diverse societies. And we are likely to misinterpret the sweeping social changes propelling us toward an increasingly global future.

This, then, is the immodest goal of this collection: to shed new light on the societies of the Americas by exploring the coarticulation of race, nation, and religion—and, more broadly, to develop a theoretical and methodological understanding of the complex ways such categories intersect in the construction of collective identity, difference, and hierarchy. Through research in a range of fields, the authors of the essays to follow examine how race, nation, and religion have helped to define the identities of "Blacks," "Whites," and "Indians," "Americans," "Haitians," and "Christians," and the countless other inhabitants of our not-so-New World; how these cultural and conceptual categories have been linked to global relations of power; and how they have shaped the everyday lives and political projects of individuals and communities.

The authors' attention will be focused, by and large, on these communities—on detailed analyses of the relationships between racial, religious, and (in some cases) national identities in specific social and political contexts. But we, as editors, must first sketch a number of broad historical trends and theoretical arguments that inform their work. In the following section, we will outline our understanding of the co-constitutive relationships among race, nation, and religion (and other categories of identity) in relatively abstract terms, and point out some of the ways our understanding differs from those of other scholars who have examined similar themes. We will then examine some of the ways this understanding reframes scholarly analyses of racial, national, and religious identities. And finally, in conclusion, we will sketch the scope and structure of the collection as a whole.

Race, Nation, and Religion: The Co-constitution of Collective Identities

Much like scholars and theorists of modernity, scholars of collective identity have generally paid scant attention to religion. This conceptual blind spot is, unfortunately, just as pronounced in recent research in cultural studies and critical theory—the loosely defined fields from which the authors in this collection draw theoretical inspiration—as it was in previous scholarship on similar themes. The thriving debates now surrounding race, ethnicity, class, gender, sexuality, and nation have tended to overlook the links between these identities and others based on religious discourse and practice.[5]

Yet there are, of course, a number of significant—and at times inspiring—exceptions to this broad critique. Scholars of African-American and Afro-Caribbean history and culture, for example, have long been concerned with the religious dimensions of racial identities.[6] And their concerns have been echoed, more recently, in research on such diverse topics as transnational migration;[7] American Jewish identities;[8] Pentecostal Christianity in Latin America;[9] White supremacist movements in the United States;[10] the longstanding links between Christian missionary work and European colonialism;[11] the ethnic, national, and communal conflicts that have divided South Asia, the Balkans, the Middle East, and other parts of the world;[12] and the recent rise of militant Islam and other religious "fundamentalisms."[13] Taken together, these small but vibrant literatures, and others, have offered subtle portraits and analyses of the religious lives of racial, ethnic and national communities in the Americas and elsewhere, and have thus laid invaluable foundations for our work in this book.[14]

Unfortunately, however, most authors on these subjects have not, in our view, done justice to the depth and complexity of the relationships between race, nation, and religion. Their work has too often been limited by a fundamental misunderstanding of the nature of collective identity—and above all by a misunderstanding of the relationships among the diverse categories of identity (race, nation, religion, gender, sexuality, etc.) that coalesce to define individuals and communities. Most of the scholarship just referenced—including, let us repeat, a great deal of invaluable research—has started from the assumption that race, nation, and religion are fundamentally distinct, clearly bounded categories, and then traced the ways these categories may "interact" or "intersect." Scholars have shown, for example, how religious rhetoric and ritual have been used to build solidarity within racial and national communities, how racial ideologies and nationalist sentiments have shaped the development of religious sects and denominations, and so on. But these intersections between race, nation, and religion have typically been accorded a kind of *secondary* historical and ontological status—secondary, that is, to the presumed boundedness and integrity of the primary categories themselves. However fluidly they may interact in the course of social life, in the eyes of most scholars, race, nation, and religion nevertheless manage to retain their analytical clarity and autonomy.

Yet a great deal of recent research has also shown that the seeming clarity—and in some sense, the very existence—of such collective identities is, in fact, the contingent result of ongoing processes of reification, or social construction, that are intimately linked to structures of power and domination.[15] This book builds on such critiques of the reification of identity, and departs from much of the scholarship referenced above, by working to disrupt the supposed boundedness of race, nation, and religion; by showing how these categories of identity are always already inextricably linked; by demonstrating that they are, in fact, *co-constituted* categories, wholly dependent on each other for their social existence and symbolic meanings.

Although these theoretical assumptions and analytical strategies mark a relatively new direction in scholarly research on the relationships between race, nation, and religion, the contributors to this collection have hardly invented them from whole cloth. We are deeply indebted to recent research on the social construction of collective identities, and on the relationships among diverse categories of identity. Perhaps above all, our work builds on a history of research on the complex relationships between race and gender in the loosely defined field that Maxine Baca Zinn and Bonnie Thorton Dill have termed "multiracial feminism."[16] Though multiracial feminist scholars (like other scholars of collective identity) have rarely examined religious identities, their work has focused attention on what Zinn and Dill describe as the "simultaneity of systems [such as race, class, gender and sexuality] in shaping women's experience and identity."[17] By questioning the ostensibly universal—yet often implicitly White—accounts of gender that animated a great deal of previous feminist theory, contemporary feminist scholars have come to realize, as Sandra Harding has argued, that "in societies stratified by race, class, or culture . . . there are no gender relations per se but only gender relations as constructed by and between classes, races, and cultures."[18] Somewhat similarly, we argue, in the societies of the Americas there are no such things as race, nation or religion, per se—only race, nation, and religion as they are constructed in and through each other, and through other categories of difference.

Yet the question remains: How exactly are we to describe the intersections of these diverse, and seemingly distinct, identities? Like many scholars of race, nation, and religion, multiracial feminist thinkers have often assumed an "additive" relationship between gender and other identities—in which the identities and experiences of Black women, for example, might be understood by simply "adding up" the social realities of race and gender, while maintaining a clear distinction between the two. The philosopher and social theorist Judith Butler has critiqued this reductive approach to intersectional identities in an essay on the fraught relationships between race, gender, and sexuality. Butler writes:

> Though there are clearly good historical reasons for keeping "race" and "sexuality" and "sexual difference" as separate analytic spheres, there are also quite pressing and significant historical reasons for asking how and where we might read not only their convergence, but the sites at which the one cannot be constituted save through the other. This is something other than juxtaposing distinct spheres of power, subordination, agency, historicity, and something other than a list of attributes separated by those proverbial commas (gender, sexuality, race, class), that usually mean that we have not yet figured out how to think the relations we seek to mark.[19]

Here again is the subtle, yet far-reaching, distinction we are working to draw: while previous scholars of race, nation, and religion have tended to examine the "convergence" of these identities, the contributors to this book focus instead on sites where these categories of identity "cannot be constituted save through [each] other."

Another example of such an analysis may be found in the work of Evelyn Brooks Higginbotham, a historian of (among other things) the gender politics of Black Baptist churches. In her provocative essay, "African-American Women's History and the Metalanguage of Race," Higginbotham shows how racial difference has been linked to differences of gender, class, and sexuality in the United States. She argues that:

> Race serves as a "global sign," a "metalanguage," since it speaks about and lends meaning to a host of terms and expressions, to myriad aspects of life that would otherwise fall outside the referential domain of race. By continually expressing overt and covert analogic relationships, race impregnates the simplest meanings we take for granted. It makes hair "good" or "bad," speech patterns "correct" or "incorrect." . . . Race not only tends to subsume other sets of social relations, namely, gender and class, but it blurs and disguises, suppresses and negates its own complex interplay with the very social relations it envelops.[20]

Higginbotham's discussion of race as a "metalanguage" for other differences offers a vitally important tool for understanding the relationships between seemingly distinct categories of identity. Like Higginbotham, the authors in this collection are working to reveal "analogic relationships" between diverse arenas of sociocultural life—relationships that have been "disguised, suppressed and negated" in the process of constructing hierarchical difference.

At times, however, our analyses may differ from Higginbotham's in one crucial way. Higginbotham argues that in the United States, at least, race is *uniquely* able to "subsume other sets of social relations," and although this is undoubtedly true in some social contexts, this collection shows that it is not the case throughout the history of the Americas as a whole. At times, in American societies, race has emerged as the preeminent category of difference and identity, lending meaning to both nation and religion (as well as gender, class, and other identities). At other times, however, nation or religion (or other identities) have taken center stage. And at times one finds more volatile or contested situations, in which race, nation, religion, and other forms of identity struggle to assert conceptual and political preeminence, to act as metalanguages for each other.

The essays that follow chart these complex dynamics in subtle detail. But it may nevertheless be helpful, at this point, to illustrate our fundamental argument concerning the co-constitution of collective identities with a brief concrete example. We may do so by examining one of the most significant and enduring tropes of racial, national, and religious identity in the history of the United States: the identification of many Americans, of various "races," with the biblical people of Israel and the narrative of Israel's exodus from Egypt.

A close identification with the chosen people of the scriptures was central to the self-understanding of the Puritans, who saw their colonization of New England as an "errand into the wilderness" like Israel's journey to the Promised Land. And as Sacvan Bercovitch, Werner Sollors, and other scholars have shown, this religious mythmaking helped to define the national identity of the United States.[21] Sollors quotes, for example, from the 1799 Thanksgiving Day sermon of a Massachusetts minister, who told his congregation: "It has often been remarked that the people of the United States come nearer to a parallel with Ancient Israel, than any other nation upon the globe. Hence, 'OUR AMERICAN ISRAEL,' is a term frequently used; and common consent allows it apt and proper."[22]

In fact, however, the "common consent" of the time did not agree on the identification of "America" with "Israel." For as Albert Raboteau, Theophus Smith, and other scholars have shown, a great many African-Americans—brought to the Americas in chains, and converted to Christianity during the Great Awakenings of the eighteenth and nineteenth centuries—saw the United States as a modern-day Egypt, holding Israel in bondage on its southern plantations.[23] Black Christians in the antebellum South often read and preached the biblical narrative of Israel's exodus as the story of their own inevitable redemption, and this identification with Israel has formed a central strand of African-American racial identity—as could still be seen, for example, in Martin

Luther King Jr.'s renowned 1968 sermon on Moses' trip to the mountaintop. Yet while Black Americans have struggled to reach the "Promised Land" of racial equality, a number of their White neighbors—both Jews and Gentiles—have staked their own racialized claims to the identity of "Israel." As Michael Barkun, James Aho, and other scholars have shown, narratives of Israelite descent lie at the heart of the White supremacist Christian Identity movement, and help to define the movement's views of Blacks and Jews as "mud people" and "Satan's spawn," respectively.[24] These competing claims to the privileged status of God's chosen people have all taken shape at charged intersections of race, nation, and religion in the Americas.

But how, once again, are we to understand these intersections? How should we interpret these claims to Israelite identity? What might they tell us about Black, White and American identities? A scholar convinced of the essentially—or eventually—secular nature of American society would probably grant little weight to such claims. Though he or she might concede that they form useful political rhetorics, he or she would nevertheless insist that they do not touch on the identities of the people who make them in any fundamental way. Though race and nation may be shaped, he or she would acknowledge, by the empirical realities of class and gender, these prototypically modern identities have little to do with mythical narratives of Israelite descent or millennial fantasies of divine redemption. This, in essence, is the unstated assumption of many contemporary scholars of collective identity.[25]

But the path-breaking work of scholars like Bercovitch, Raboteau, and Barkun has debunked this (equally mythical) narrative of secular modernity, by showing the profound effects of religious discourses on racial and national identities. Raboteau argues, for example, that:

> By appropriating the story of Exodus as their own story, [antebellum] black Christians articulated their own sense of peoplehood. Exodus symbolized their common history and common destiny. . . . Identification with Israel, then, gave the slaves a communal identity as special, divinely favored people. This identity stood in stark contrast with the racist propaganda depicting them as inferior to whites, destined by nature and providence to the status of slaves. The Exodus, the Promised Land, and Canaan were inextricably linked in their minds to the idea of freedom.[26]

Yet even as he explores their intimate connections, Raboteau continues to assume a relatively clear analytical and empirical distinction between "race" and "religion"—between Blackness and Christianity, slavery and chosenness. He charts an ideological contest between "identification with Israel" and "racist propaganda" over the meaning and politics of Blackness, yet he seems to suggest that Blackness itself—like Whiteness, its twin—exists independently of the struggles raging around it. And of course, in a certain sense, it does. Black,

White and American identities have been formed by a broad range of social and discursive forces, of which the Exodus story is but one. Yet along with the economics of chattel slavery, the politics of segregation, the pseudoscience of biological race, and countless other forces, the biblical narrative of God's chosen people has helped to *produce* race in America, rather than simply *inflect* its symbolic meanings and political valences. The Exodus story, in this case, is "inextricably linked" not only to "the idea of freedom," but to the fact of Blackness itself.

This is, no doubt, a subtle distinction. The essays collected in this book are deeply indebted to the work of Raboteau and others, who have framed the fundamental questions about race, nation, and religion we are trying to address. But as we have argued, our work builds on—and departs from—theirs by exploring the co-constitutive relationships between these seemingly distinct categories of difference and identity. This shift in perspective has a number of profound implications, which we will explore in the following sections.

Rethinking the Historiography of Race and Modernity

As we have noted, recent scholarship in a broad range of fields has demonstrated quite clearly that the "racial" identities typically attributed to immutable biological differences are, in fact, historically contingent products of social and political forces.[27] Though "race" remains all too brutally real as a social and historical phenomenon—continuing to structure hierarchy and inequality in the Americas and elsewhere—it is, quite simply, a biological fiction. There are no clear biophysical divisions within the human species. The widespread belief in such divisions is a historical product of prejudice, crafted in the course of colonial domination and chattel slavery, then cloaked in the mantle of spurious science.

This volume contributes to the critique of "race" and racial identity formation by demonstrating the parallels and links between race and religion—between a constellation of politics and identities thought to be grounded in "natural" fact, and another thought to be grounded in "supernatural" belief. It furthers the denaturalization or deconstruction of race by demonstrating that a culturally constructed belief in one's "Whiteness" or "Blackness" makes no more or less sense, on a basic conceptual level, than a belief in one's divine "chosenness," one's "possession" by an ancestral spirit, or one's mystical participation in "the body of Christ." Yet by drawing such parallels between race and religion, this volume also casts doubt on a number of assumptions that have structured the scholarly critique of race. Perhaps above all, it calls for a reconsideration of the historical emergence of racial discourse in the early modern era, and of the complex ties between race and modernity.

Historians and others have shown that the concept and politics of "race" are relatively recent historical phenomena. "Racial" identities and differences as we now know them did not truly take shape until the late eighteenth century, and only became a dominant form of social identity and hierarchy in the mid- to late nineteenth century.[28] But how are we to understand the relationships between these emergent racial identities and the diverse forms of identity that preceded them? Inspired, in part, by a desire to critique the common-sense understanding of race as an immutable biological fact, scholars have tended to highlight the radical newness of race, and the *discontinuities* between race and prior forms of social identity. Audrey Smedley, for example, argues that over the course of the nineteenth century, in the United States and perhaps elsewhere, race "supersed[ed] all other aspects of identity."[29] She writes:

> Because of the cultural imperative of race ideology, all Americans were compelled to the view that a racial status, symbolized by bio-physical attributes, was the premier determinant of their identity. "Race" identity took priority over religion, ethnic origin, education and training, socioeconomic class, occupation, language, values, beliefs, morals, lifestyles, geographic location, and all other human attributes that hitherto provided all groups and individuals with a sense of who they were.[30]

Smedley is entirely correct to point to the increasing significance of "race" in the nineteenth century, and its contemporary status as a dominant form—in many contexts, *the* dominant form—of human identity. And yet, we would argue, the hegemony of race was not constructed by "superseding all other aspects of identity." Race did not simply "[take] priority" over, for example, religion. Rather, discourses of race were constructed through the incorporation of preexisting differences, by resignifying prior forms of human identity in terms of racial biology, lending racialized meanings to religion, ethnicity, class, language, values, and so on, and thus folding these differences into the hierarchical orders of racialized societies. "Race" was undoubtedly *superimposed* on these different differences, but it hardly *superseded* them. Indeed, the enduring presence of previous differences within the discourse of race was, and remains, essential to its status as "the premier determinant of [human] identity."

The racial biology of the nineteenth century clearly drew, for example, on preexisting understandings of kinship, descent and procreation. Racial inequalities were built on, yet transformed, the inherited social inequalities at the heart of European feudalism. Perceptions of racial phenotype may have drawn, as Colette Guillaumin has argued, on prior perceptions of clothing as a visible mark of social status.[31] And the concept of race, in nearly all its forms, was inseparably tied to the religious identities and differences that had structured European society for centuries. The boundaries of Christendom shaped the boundaries of Whiteness, and longstanding perceptions of heathenism shaped emerging perceptions of racial difference. The very idea of a social group defined by biological ties must have resonated, in subtle ways, with the narratives of peoplehood and descent found in the Bible's "Table of Nations" (Genesis 10). Indeed, as a number of scholars have shown, the biblical narrative of Noah's three sons lent a degree of scriptural authority to the popular tripartite scheme of "Negroid," "Caucasoid," and "Mongoloid" races.[32] And as Sander Gilman has suggested, the legendary "stubbornness" of the Jews—whom Christians often accused of willful disbelief in their own messiah—may have contributed to developing perceptions of the intractable, inherited differences supposedly separating these biologized communities.[33] The common preoccupation of nineteenth-century racial discourse with "blood" as a marker of difference and determinant of character probably drew on centuries of popular speculation about the bodily fluid's magical properties—speculation that fed the "blood libels" European Christians occasionally leveled against Jews, accusing them of using Christian blood for nefarious purposes.[34] Indeed, the popular perception that "Christian blood" was somehow different from that of Jews and others was codified in the "purity of blood" statutes of fifteenth- and sixteenth-century Spain—a system of social hierarchy and exclusion targeted not at Jews and Muslims per se but at Christian converts and their descendants, thought to be tainted by the blood of their Jewish and Muslim ancestors. As George Fredrickson has recently and persuasively argued, this late medieval prejudice—defined by "blood" rather than belief—may have been the "first real anticipation [of modern racism]."[35]

The concept of race that emerged in the eighteenth and nineteenth centuries undoubtedly transformed these religious discourses of difference in a number of far-reaching ways. Perhaps above all, as Fredrickson argues at length, the imagined biological basis of racial difference tended to foreclose the possibility of conversion that had usually been open, at least in theory, to the religious others of medieval Christendom. While the difference between Jew and Christian could supposedly be washed away in the baptismal font, the difference between Black and White was rendered, in Fredrickson's terms, "innate, indelible and unchangeable" by the concept of race.[36] And yet, when we examine the relationships between race and religion, we find significant continuities between "modern" and "medieval" discourses of difference. The birth of biological race thus marks, as Ann Stoler has argued, following Michel Foucault, "not the end of one discourse and the emergence of another, but rather the refolded surfaces that join the two."[37] Or again, as Winthrop Jordan argued in his magisterial White Over Black, "the shift [between religious and racial perceptions of Blackness] was an alteration in emphasis within a single concept of difference, rather than a development of a novel conceptualization."[38]

Why, then, do scholars tend to emphasize the newness of the concept of race, and the discontinuities separating race from religion? Even historians like Jordan and Fredrickson—who each offer subtle analyses of the links between race and religion, and thus trace the history (or perhaps prehistory) of race to the fifteenth century rather than the eighteenth—ultimately conclude, in Fredrickson's terms, that "for an understanding of the emergence of Western racism in the late Middle Ages and early modern period, a clear distinction between racism and religious intolerance is crucial."[39] Why such insistence upon a "clear distinction" that is, as this collection shows, so often transgressed in the everyday lives and hierarchical structures of racialized societies? As we have suggested, this sociological and historiographic judgment may be attributed, in part, to the vitally important project of denaturalizing race—debunking its claims to reflect an immutable natural order by demonstrating its rather brief social and intellectual history. However, as we have also suggested, these distinctions between race and religion may ultimately rest on the popular equation of modernity with secularization, and a reductive contrast between "modernity" and "tradition."

For race has often been described as a prototypically "modern" form of identity—the illegitimate child of secular humanism and scientific rationality, dark underbelly of Enlightenment universalism, and ideological grease on the wheels of industrial capital. Jordan famously argued, for example, that the "growing interest in the physical distinctions among human beings" at the heart of the eighteenth-century concept of race "was one aspect of the secularization of Western society."[40] And to some extent, of course, he was right. Similarly, Fredrickson argues that "modernization or 'becoming modern' was a precondition for the [development of] overtly racist regimes" that have thrived "in an age of heavy industry, big cities, increased social and economic mobility, and the consolidation of nation-states."[41] Indeed, a number of scholars have shown the fateful ties that bind discourses of race to the sweeping social trends—such as capitalism, colonialism, industrialization, urbanization, and the birth of the nation-state—that have restructured much of the world over the past few hundred years.[42]

But we must take care to specify the scope, and limits, of these trends. Have they, in fact, displaced every element of "traditional" society? Have they transformed every aspect of "modern" life? Have they, for example, cut the societies of the Americas loose from the moorings of religious faith—or the power of religious discourse? To paraphrase Karl Marx, has all that was once solid in fact melted into air?[43] By demonstrating the enduring significance of religion in the social and political life of the Americas, as well as the co-constitutive links between racial, national, and religious identities, the essays in this collection suggest that the answer to these questions is no. They suggest instead, as Talal Asad recently has, that the social world may not be so easily "divided into modern and nonmodern, into West and non-West . . . that the world has *no* significant binary features, that it is, on the contrary, divided into overlapping, fragmented cultures, hybrid selves, continuously dissolving and emerging social states."[44]

In so doing, these essays give us a new appreciation of the historical roots of the concept and politics of race—roots that run deeper in Western thought and society than we might have hoped. More broadly, they suggest a new historiography of modernity, and a subtler analysis of the social transformations this term denotes. And perhaps above all, by interrogating the boundaries between "secular" and "religious," they demonstrate the internal complexities of contemporary racial discourses. These complexities are essential to the hegemonic order of "race," and a richer understanding of them may thus suggest new strategies for its undoing.

Imagining National and Religious Communities

As many readers will no doubt recognize, the title of this section alludes to Benedict Anderson's path-breaking analysis of the nation-state, *Imagined Communities: Reflections on the Origin and Spread of Nationalism*.[45] As much as any other single text, Anderson's work has fundamentally reshaped scholarly research on nations and nationalism. Perhaps above all, Anderson makes clear that nations must be seen as *cultural* phenomena rather than—or prior to—*political* ones. "What I am proposing," he writes, "is that nationalism has to be understood by aligning it, not with self-consciously held political ideologies, but with the large cultural systems that preceded it, out of which—as well as against which—it came into being." It must be analyzed "as if it belonged with 'kinship' and 'religion,' rather than with 'liberalism' or 'fascism.' "[46] This critical shift in perspective has fostered innovative analyses of the nation-state as a culturally and historically specific form of social organization, rather than a necessary fact of geopolitical life, and has encouraged comparative research on the diverse imaginations that underwrite diverse communities.[47] This is precisely the shift in perspective that allows us to examine the intersections of national and religious identities, and we are thus very much in Anderson's debt.

Yet our debt is somewhat ambivalent, for although Anderson himself explores the conceptual and historical *parallels* between nation and religion, he explicitly forecloses discussion of the concrete and ongoing *connections* between these forms of imagined community. He argues, in brief, that "in Western Europe the eighteenth century marks not only the dawn of the age of nationalism but the dusk of religious modes of thought." Like other theorists of secular modernity, Anderson argues—or simply assumes—that the "rationalist secularism" of the European Enlightenment was linked to "the ebbing of religious belief" and thus to the decline of religion as a vibrant force in sociopolitical life. The nation-state, in his view, may or may not be causally linked to this decline, but it fills the cultural void—the absence of meaning—left by the "disintegration of paradise" and the "absurdity of salvation."[48] As is already quite clear, we disagree with Anderson's basic assumptions concerning secularization. Where he sees the historical divergence of nation and religion, we see their ongoing and inextricable connections. But his secularization narrative nevertheless highlights important aspects of national and religious identities, and is thus worth exploring in some detail.

Anderson argues, in essence, that the emergence of the modern nation-state marked the "relativization" and "territorialization" of universalistic religious communities, like Christendom and the Islamic Ummah, that had previously attempted to monopolize absolute truth—through the medium of a sacred language tied directly to the structure of creation—and to inhabit a potentially infinite territorial expanse.[49] While "Christendom" had staked an exclusive claim to both heaven and earth, the "United States" and other nations staked more limited claims to local truths, vernacular languages, bounded territories, and finite populations. With the birth of the nation-state, according to Anderson, "the sacred communities integrated by old sacred languages were gradually fragmented, pluralized, and territorialized."[50] He points out that "No nation imagines itself coterminous with mankind. The most messianic nationalists do not dream of a day when all the members of the human race will join their nation in the way that it was possible, in certain epochs, for, say, Christians to dream of a wholly Christian planet."[51] And in a sense, of course, he is right. In the limited terms of juridical citizenship, nation-states do not seek "converts" across their borders. Indeed, they tend to build fences to keep such converts out.

But when the United States, above all, seeks to instill "American values" and market American consumer goods in societies around the world, can we really say that "messianic nationalists" like George W. Bush do not "dream of a wholly [American] planet"? When evangelical Christian missionaries follow United States marines into Afghanistan and Iraq, can we even distinguish clearly between an "American" planet and a "Christian" one?[52] And when American strategic interests define the contours of a "New World Order," does America not, in some sense, "imagine itself coterminous with mankind"? In the broad terms of cultural citizenship—and cultural imperialism—have nation-states truly eschewed the absolutism and universalism that Anderson locates in epochs prior to our own? Unfortunately, we think not. Indeed, they often seem to have inherited the exclusivist truth claims and evangelical ambitions of the religious communities that preceded—and helped to define—them.

Of course, one might object that our analysis applies only to powerful states with imperial ambitions, like the United States at the turn of the twenty-first century and the great powers of Europe at the turn of the twentieth. Do the universalist pretensions of "American values" in fact reflect broader truths about the nation-state, or just the excesses of a nation enthralled with its own power? We would argue the former. It is important to keep in mind that Anderson's analysis of religious universalism also applies primarily to sociopolitically powerful imagined communities—and perhaps above all to European Christianity.[53] The diasporic networks and particularist concerns of medieval rabbinic Judaism, for example, had little in common with the territorial sprawl and triumphalist fantasies of Christendom and the Islamic Ummah. The global reach of today's United States may thus represent the universalist tendencies inherent within the structure of the nation-state in much the same way that the global reach of the Catholic Church represented—and continues to represent—the universalist tendencies inherent within Christianity and many, but not all, other religions.

These tendencies are nowhere more evident than at moments, in the United States and elsewhere, when national and religious identities are defined in each other's terms. Consider, for example, the oft-quoted (and nearly as often mocked) 1925 response of the Texas governor Miriam "Ma" Ferguson to a proposal for bilingual education in Texas's public schools: "English was good enough for Jesus Christ," she noted, "and it's good enough for the children of Texas."[54] Though ridiculous on its face—a Bible scholar Governor Ferguson was not—her conflation of vernacular and scriptural language reflects the intimate bonds between national and religious identity that run through the entire history of the United States, and through the histories of many other nations, in greater or lesser degrees.[55] Confounding Anderson's secularization narrative, Ferguson enlisted the ostensibly universal truth of Christianity in the service of an aggressively particular nationalism—in defense of the boundaries of America (or maybe just Texas). In so doing, she elevated her nationalism to the status of universal truth, deftly removing the "harsh wedge between cosmology and history" that Anderson considers a constitutive principle of national identity.[56] Like nationalists in many other contexts, Ferguson imagined her national community as the privileged representative of God's will on earth.

The United States may differ from the other nations of the Americas in the *degree* to which its national identity has been defined in such religious terms. It was founded, after all, by settlers and revolutionaries who saw themselves as modern-day Israelites—a divinely chosen people fulfilling the mandates of biblical prophecy. Yet it does not differ from other American nations in *kind*. The history of the Americas has unfolded, from the fifteenth century through the present day, under a far-reaching—though never quite complete—Christian hegemony. It is hardly surprising, then, that the nations of the Americas have inherited the universalist tendencies of a religion that set out to "make disciples of all peoples, baptizing them in the name of the Father and of the Son and of the Holy Spirit" (Matthew 28:19).

This collection thus examines the bonds between nation and religion—and the concomitant play between particularism and universalism—in a number of American societies. It shows how the nations of the Americas have been built out of raw materials provided by preexisting religious communities, rather than built on these communities' ruins. This analysis speaks to fundamental questions of national identity and to the shifting contours of the nation-state in an increasingly globalized world. The American cultural imperialism alluded to earlier is but one example of the complex ties between national and global social formations. As politicians and pundits link the interests of nations to a worldwide "clash of civilizations," transnational migrants link the social and political lives of their native and adapted homes, and global flows of culture and capital link us all to global structures of power and inequality, we would do well to remember the enduring ties between the nation-states of today and the religious communities that preceded them.[57]

Blurring the Boundaries of Religion and Society

In the preceding sections we have focused, above all, on the ways that scholarly understandings of "race" and "nation" may change if we question the oft-assumed secularity of these modern collective identities. But we have yet to examine the flip side, as it were, of this coin. How might scholarly understandings of "religion" change if we chart its role in the constitution of race and nation? What might the ties between these categories of difference tell us about the nature of religious discourse and practice?

These questions speak to ongoing debates in religious studies and related fields over the history and utility of the very concept of "religion." It seems quite clear that many, if not all, societies—now and in the past, in the Americas and throughout the world—have developed complex systems of thought and practice oriented around perceptions of supernatural, superhuman, or nonempirical entities of some kind. But in recent years, an increasing number of scholars have argued that "religion"—the conceptual category thought to embrace *all* of these diverse systems—is a culturally specific product of Western, if not Christian, social and intellectual history. Jonathan Z. Smith has argued, for example, that "religion is solely the creation of the scholar's study. It is created for the scholar's analytic purposes by his [or her] imaginative acts of comparison and generalization. Religion has no independent existence apart from the academy."[58] Even among scholars who accept or celebrate this self-reflexive critique, its implications for the study of those social phenomena we tend to describe as "religious" are hardly clear. As Mark C. Taylor has noted, "just at the moment when it seems urgent to develop a more sophisticated understanding of religion [at the moment, that is, when it takes center stage in global politics and culture], there appears to be little consensus about precisely what religion is and how it can best be studied."[59] This book does not aim to reach such a consensus—let alone offer its own comprehensive definition of religion—but it will help clarify certain issues at stake in these debates.

Above all, this book makes clear that one cannot understand "religion" as an autonomous sphere of individual experience and belief set apart from everyday social life, from underlying social structures, or from hierarchical relations of power. Religious discourses may be distinguished from many other discursive forms—though by no means all—by their profound engagement with beings and truths thought to transcend the social world. But this sense of transcendence, however deeply felt by many religious people, is not sufficient, in itself, to account for the role of religion in these people's lives. Nor can religious doctrines, narratives, and symbols be interpreted outside of their social, historical, and political contexts. As Talal Asad has argued, in his critique of Clifford Geertz's influential essay "Religion as a Cultural System," the common tendency to describe religion as a matter of "faith" and "meaning" rather than practice and power—of cosmic rather than social order—reflects the limited role allotted to religion by theorists of Western modernity. This is, as Asad suggests, "a modern, privatized Christian [conception of religion] because and to the extent that it emphasizes the priority of belief as a state of mind rather than as a constituting activity in the world." In place of this focus on personal faith and transcendent meaning, Asad argues that "religious symbols . . . cannot be understood independently of their historical relations with nonreligious symbols or of their articulations in and of social life, in which work and power [and, we would add, identity and difference] are crucial."[60]

If, for example, as Winthrop Jordan has shown, seventeenth- and eighteenth-century English colonists in North America tended to "[employ] the terms *Christian, free, English,* and *white* . . . indiscriminately as metonyms," then analyses of colonial Christianity must account for the complex relationships between religious rituals and symbols, the economics of chattel slavery, and the politics of national and racial identity.[61] These seemingly "nonreligious" social forces are, in fact, intrinsic to the history of American Christianity—every bit as much as, say, the doctrine of the trinity, the symbol of the cross, the experience of conversion, or the ritual of baptism. Needless to say, these more strictly "religious" phenomena remain central to an analysis of Christianity. They may not be reduced to epiphenomena, or simple reflections, of other social forces. But in the Americas, and elsewhere, their significance must be reevaluated in terms of their co-constitutive links to racial and national politics and identities—just as these politics and identities must be reevaluated in terms of their links to religion.

This fundamentally social analysis will hardly be surprising or controversial to most anthropologists, sociologists, and social historians of religion—drawing, as it does, on established scholarly traditions, stretching back to pioneering figures like E. B. Tylor, Emile Durkheim, and Max Weber. It may, however, be somewhat more controversial within the field of religious studies itself. In a recent series of polemical essays, collected in the book *Critics Not Caretakers*, Russell McCutcheon has charted the tensions between two divergent approaches to the study of religion, one of which sets out to explore "essential meanings and values . . . derived from experiences of God, the gods, the sacred, the wholly other, the numinous, or the mysterium," while the other situates the study of religion within "the wider cross-disciplinary study of how human beliefs, behaviors, and institutions construct and contest enduring social identities."[62] Clearly, this collection follows the latter approach. By demonstrating the links between religion and other aspects of social life, our analyses illustrate McCutcheon's "naturalist" or materialist argument that "it is only when we start out with the presumption that religious behaviors are ordinary social behaviors—and not extraordinary private experiences—that we will come to understand them in all of their subtle yet impressive complexity."[63] And yet, by demonstrating the links between religion, race, and nation, more specifically, our analyses also cast doubt on any strictly—or reductively—materialist view of "ordinary social behavior." In so doing, they suggest new understandings of both religion and society.

Strictly materialist analyses of religion, like McCutcheon's, tend to rest on a naively positivist understanding of social life, and aspire to a scientistic clarity that rarely, if ever, exists in the social world itself. They generally appeal to an outsider's "objective" view of sociohistorical fact, in an effort to debunk—rather than contextualize or historicize—religious discourses and perceptions. McCutcheon suggests, for example, that the political ambitions of the 1995 Million Man March invalidate many marchers' own experiences of the event as a religious "pilgrimage," and that the cost of a hotel room at the 1993 Parliament of World Religions renders its participants' religious discourses little more than "rhetorical flourishes."[64] He argues, more broadly, that scholars of religion must "develop a coherent, theoretically based vocabulary capable of placing religion firmly within the social world, with no leftover residue that prompts supernaturalistic speculations," a conceptual and methodological framework that explains religion as a "thoroughly human activity, with no mysterious distillate left over."[65] Yet this collection demonstrates clearly that the social world is founded, in part, on just such "supernaturalistic speculations" and "mysterious distillates." The brutally real, material foundations of the racial and national identities that structure "human activity" in the Americas rest, in turn, on a cultural bedrock of metaphysical fantasy—on fevered speculations about the origins of humanity, mythical narratives of apocalyptic destiny, ritualistic definitions of sacred territory, and spectral presences that go bump in history. These "ghostly matters," in Avery Gordon's phrase, are the very stuff of race, nation, and religion in the Americas, and of other collective identities in other social contexts.[66] A refusal to take such matters seriously thus marks a betrayal, rather than a defense, of "ordinary social behavior."

This collection, by contrast, works to blur the boundaries between religion and society without reducing either to a pale reflection of the other—to demonstrate the concrete, empirical foundations of religious discourse and experience, as well as the otherworldly, metaphysical foundations of social order and identity. We thus hope to offer a productive middle ground in the current debate over the nature of "religion," as well as an innovative method for the social analysis of our still-enchanted world.

The Scope and Structure of the Collection

We have outlined an extremely ambitious project for a collection of just a dozen essays. We hope to explore the intersections of race, nation, and religion throughout the Americas, on a hemispheric scale. And in so doing, we hope to suggest new understandings of each of these categories of difference and identity, as well as a new understanding of the underlying social and discursive processes through which diverse categories of identity come to define each other's most fundamental meanings. Moreover, as the essays themselves make clear, we hope to expand the scholarly discourse on race by examining the role of religion in constructing a broad range of racialized identities, rather than assuming, as scholars often have, that racial politics and identities are the province of "Black" religions alone.

An ambitious project indeed. We must therefore acknowledge, at the outset, that our work toward these analytical goals will inevitably be incomplete. This is, of course, the fate of all scholarly research. But given the scope of our project, we are particularly—at times painfully—aware of the limits of our accomplishment. We simply cannot hope to survey *all* of the complex intersections of racial, national, and religious identities in the centuries-long history, and diverse societies, of the Americas. Indeed, we have not tried to do so. There are a number of particularly significant aspects of this history that are not represented in this collection. There are, for example, few discussions of the historic "Black Church"—the Protestant churches founded by African-American and Anglophone Afro-Caribbean communities over the course of the nineteenth century. There are no detailed discussions of the Jews and other "White ethnic" immigrants who came to the Americas in the late nineteenth and early twentieth centuries. There are no discussions of Islam, among African Americans or in more recent immigrant communities. There are no discussions of the Andes, or parts of the Caribbean basin, or Canada, or a number of other regions of the Americas. The list of omissions is longer than we care to contemplate. Some of these topics have been explored in great detail elsewhere (see the literatures referenced in the notes to this introduction) while others, unfortunately, have not. None, however, are explored in detail in the essays that follow.

In what sense, then, can this collection hope to address the "New World" as a complex whole? In the absence of any pretense to a comprehensive social, historical, or geographic survey, we have tried to do so by examining a series of themes—or raising a series of issues—that run through the entire history of racial, national and religious identity formation in the Americas. The essays that follow are organized in pairs, each of which examines one of these central themes. In the first thematic pair, Daniel Murphree and Elizabeth McAlister trace the roots of American racial categories in European colonial fantasies of religious difference. In the second pair, Daniel Lee and John Burdick chart the construction and critique of a symbolic association between Whiteness and Christianity. In the third, Derek Chang and Julia Cummings O'Hara explore the role of Christian missionary work in the definition of racial differences and national identities. In the fourth, James Bennett and Danielle Brune Sigler examine the battles fought within religious communities over segregation, integration, and the North American racial binary. In the fifth, Kate Ramsey and Jennifer Snow show how nation-states have tried to police the racial and religious boundaries of "civilization." And in the sixth, Lindsay Hale and Judith Weisenfeld explore how experiences and representations of religious ritual have helped to define racial differences. (We will outline the significance of each theme, and the arguments of each essay in greater detail in brief introductions to each pair.) Taken together, these twelve essays on six themes offer a provocative—and preliminary—introduction to the intersections of race, nation, and religion in the Americas.

We have tried to shed new light on these intersections by juxtaposing historically and geographically disparate case studies within each thematic pair. The sixteenth century will be read against the twentieth, manifest destiny against liberation theology, Hollywood films against Umbanda temples, and so on. In most of the pairs, we have juxtaposed one essay focused on the United States with another focused on Latin America or the Caribbean. The resulting emphasis on the racial and religious diversity of the United States reflects our own social positions (and those of many of our readers) as North American scholars, while our broader comparative approach reflects the pressing need to situate the United States within the diversity of the Americas as a whole. Ideally, these thematically defined juxtapositions of historically disparate materials will reveal the underlying similarities, and far-reaching differences, that unite and divide American societies.

Finally, and perhaps above all, these thematic pairs—and the collection as a whole—might achieve the denaturalizing effects of what Michael Taussig (following Walter Benjamin and the Surrealists) has called "montage." That is, in Taussig's terms, "the juxtaposition of dissimilars such that old habits of mind can be jolted into new perceptions of the obvious." Taussig argues forcefully that scholars working to address, and ultimately redress, "the legacy of conquest" in the Americas must interrogate the seductive clarity of social context and historical narrative, and work instead to "jump-cut and splice space and time, abutting context with context," self with other, past with present, hegemony with resistance, reality with fantasy—until the patterns of identity and community we have learned to take for granted dissolve in a space of emergent possibility.[67] This is, ultimately, the most ambitious goal of this collection: by exploring the ties between race, nation, and religion, we hope to unsettle all three of these time-hardened categories, and thus clear a space for new American selves and new American histories.

NOTES

Though I am the sole author of this essay, more or less, its arguments have taken shape in dialogue with my coeditor, Elizabeth McAlister. Liza has commented insightfully on the entire text, contributed original material at a number of key points, and—above all—helped shape my thinking on these issues through years of generous dialogue and productive debate. I speak in the first person plural at various points in the essay, in what might seem an odd sort of "royal we." At times I am speaking for the contributors to the collection as a whole, and at times—at risk of hubris—for "we Americans" or "we of the Americas." Most often, however, I am simply speaking for Liza and myself, in a usage that reflects the depth of our collaboration.

1. At times we will use "Americans" and "American" as colloquial terms—or native categories—denoting the people and culture of the United States. At other times, however, we will use the same terms to refer to the peoples and cultures of the Americas as a whole. This double usage may be somewhat confusing, but it reflects the social reality of these terms' semantic range.

2. For a range of perspectives on the contested relationship between modernity and secularization, see the essays collected in Steve Bruce, ed., *Religion and Modernization: Sociologists and Historians Debate the Secularization Thesis* (New York: Oxford University Press, 1992); William Swatos and Daniel Olson, eds., *The Secularization Debate* (Lanham, Md.: Rowman and Littlefied, 2000). The argument that secularization is a necessary aspect or outcome of modernization generally draws on Max Weber's classic analysis of the "disenchantment" of the modern world. See Weber's 1918 lecture "Science as Vocation," in *From Max Weber: Essays in Sociology*, edited by H. H. Gerth and C. Wright Mills (New York: Oxford University Press, 1946), 129–156. For a particularly subtle, and conditional, rearticulation of the secularization thesis see Jose Casanova, *Public Religions in the Modern World* (Chicago: University of Chicago Press, 1994). For innovative analyses of "the secular," as well as culturally specific ideologies of secularism, see Talal Asad, *Formations of the Secular: Christianity, Islam, Modernity* (Stanford: Stanford University Press, 2003).

3. Mark C. Taylor, introduction to *Critical Terms for Religious Studies*, edited by Mark C. Taylor (Chicago: University of Chicago Press, 1998), 1.

4. For more details on these quotes and events see: R. W. Apple Jr., "A Clear Message: 'I Will Not Relent,'" *New York Times*, September 21, 2001, A1; Associated Press, "Purported Bin Laden Letter Urges Unity Against 'Crusader Coalition,'" *Washington Post*, January 20, 2003, A20; Tamar Lewin and Gustave Niebuhr, "Attacks and Harassment Continue on Middle Eastern People and Mosques," *New York Times*, Sep-

tember 18, 2001, B5; Robert McFadden, "After the Attacks: Bush Leads Prayer," *New York Times*, September 15, 2001, A1; Todd Purdum, "After the Attacks: Bush Warns of a Wrathful, Shadowy and Inventive War," *New York Times*, September 17, 2001, A2; Susan Sachs, "Shiite Leaders Compete to Govern and Iraqi Slum," *New York Times*, May 24, 2003, A18. For a broader theoretical perspective, see Bruce Lincoln, *Holy Terrors: Thinking about Religion after September 11* (Chicago: The University of Chicago Press, 2003).

5. The loosely defined fields of "cultural studies" and "critical theory" are far too large and diverse to summarize here. For useful introductions, see the essays collected in: Nicholas Dirks, Geoff Eley and Sherry Ortner, eds., *Culture/Power/ History: A Reader in Contemporary Social Theory* (Princeton: Princeton University Press, 1994); Patrick Fuery and Nick Mansfield, eds., *Cultural Studies and Critical Theory* (New York: Oxford University Press, 2000); Lawrence Grossberg, Cary Nelson, and Paula Treichler, eds., *Cultural Studies* (New York: Routledge, 1992). One of the central themes of these literatures has been a far-reaching critique of essentialism in racial and other identities, and a fundamental reevaluation of the process of collective identity formation. For useful introductions to these issues, see the essays collected in: Homi Bhabha, ed., *Nation and Narration* (New York: Routledge, 1990); Brett Beemyn and Mickey Eliason, eds., *Queer Studies* (New York: New York University Press, 1996); Diana Brydon, ed., *Postcolonialism: Critical Concepts in Literary and Cultural Studies* (New York: Routledge, 2000); Judith Butler and Joan Scott, eds., *Feminists Theorize the Political* (New York: Routledge, 1992); Geoff Eley and Ronald Suny, eds., *Becoming National: A Reader* (New York: Oxford University Press, 1996); Henry Louis Gates Jr., ed., *"Race," Writing and Difference* (Chicago: University of Chicago Press, 1986); David Theo Goldberg, ed., *Anatomy of Racism* (Minneapolis: University of Minnesota Press, 1990); Steven Gregory and Roger Sanjek, eds. *Race* (New Brunswick, NJ: Rutgers University Press, 1994); Stuart Hall and Paul du Gay, eds., *Questions of Cultural Identity* (London: Sage, 1996); Wahneema Lubiano, ed., *The House That Race Built* (New York: Vintage, 1998); Jonathan Rutherford, ed., *Identity: Community, Culture, Difference* (London: Lawrence and Wishart, 1990). For an introduction to the small but growing dialogue between religious studies and cultural studies, see the essays collected in Susan Mizruchi, ed., *Religion and Cultural Studies* (Princeton: Princeton University Press, 2001).

6. Religion has been a major focus of research on African-American and Afro-Caribbean communities since at least the pioneering work of W.E.B. Du Bois, whose writing on the subject has been collected by Phil Zuckerman in *Du Bois on Religion* (Walnut Creek, Calif.: AltaMira Press, 2000). The scholarly literatures on Black religions in the Americas—in history, sociology, anthropology, religious studies, theology, and other fields—are far too large and diverse to summarize here. For useful introductions, see the essays and documents collected in: Barry Chevannes, ed., *Rastafari and Other African-Caribbean Worldviews* (New Brunswick, N.J.: Rutgers University Press, 1998); Timothy Fulop and Albert Raboteau, eds., *African-American Religion: Interpretive Essays in History and Culture* (New York: Routledge, 1997); Joseph Murphy, *Working the Spirit: Ceremonies of the African Diaspora* (Boston: Beacon Press, 1994); Milton C. Sernett, ed., *African American Religious History: A Documentary Witness*, 2nd ed. (Durham, N.C.: Duke University Press, 1999); Patrick Taylor, ed., *Nation*

Dance: Religion, Identity, and Cultural Difference in the Caribbean (Bloomington: Indiana University Press, 2001); Gayraud Wilmore, ed., *African American Religious Studies: An Interdisciplinary Anthology* (Durham, N.C.: Duke University Press, 1989).

7. See for example the essays collected in: Jose Casanova and Aristide Zolberg, *Religion and Immigrant Incorporation in New York* (forthcoming); Helen Ebaugh and Janet Chafetz, eds., *Religion and the New Immigrants* (Walnut Creek, Calif.: AltaMira Press, 2000); R. Stephen Warner and Judith Wittner, eds., *Gatherings in Diaspora: Religious Communities and the New Immigration* (Philadelphia: Temple University Press, 1998). Current scholars of religion and migration are deeply indebted to Will Herberg's classic analysis of religion, ethnicity and nationalism, *Protestant-Catholic-Jew* (New York: Doubleday, 1956). Herberg, however, was largely blind to issues of race.

8. See for example: Karen Brodkin, *How Jews Became White Folks* (New Brunswick, N.J.: Rutgers University Press, 1998). Matthew Jacobson, *Whiteness of a Different Color* (Cambridge: Harvard University Press, 1998), chap. 5. Daniel Itzkovitz, "Secret Temples," in *Jews and Other Differences*, edited by Jonathan Boyarin and Daniel Boyarin (Minneapolis: University of Minnesota Press, 1997), 176–202. Ann Pellegrini, "Whiteface Performances," in Boyarin and Boyarin, *Jews and Other Differences*, 108–149. Much of the literature on Jewish racial identities draws on Sander Gilman's influential work *The Jew's Body* (New York: Routledge, 1991). Some (but by no means all) the extensive literatures on Black-Jewish relations touch on fundamental questions of Jewish racial identity. See for example Jack Salzman and Cornel West, eds., *Struggles in the Promised Land* (New York: Oxford University Press, 1997).

9. See for example: Diane Austin-Broos, *Jamaica Genesis* (Chicago: University of Chicago Press, 1997); John Burdick, *Looking for God in Brazil* (Berkeley: University of California Press, 1993); André Corten and Ruth Marshall-Fratani, eds., *Between Babel and Pentecost: Transnational Pentecostalism in Africa and Latin America* (Bloomington: Indiana University Press, 2001); Stephen Glazier, ed., *Perspectives on Pentecostalism: Case Studies from the Caribbean and Latin America* (Washington, D.C.: University Press of America, 1980).

10. See for example: James Aho, *The Politics of Righteousness: Idaho Christian Patriotism* (Seattle: University of Washington Press, 1990); Michael Barkun, *Religion and the Racist Right: The Origins of the Christian Identity Movement* (Chapel Hill: University of North Carolina Press, 1994); Ann Burlein, *Lift High the Cross: Where White Supremacy and the Christian Right Converge* (Durham, N.C.: Duke University Press, 2002).

11. See for example: James Axtell, *The Invasion Within: The Contest of Cultures in Colonial North America* (New York: Oxford University Press, 1985); Jean and John Comaroff, *Of Revelation and Revolution: Christianity, Colonialism and Consciousness in South Africa*, vol. 1 (Chicago: University of Chicago Press, 1991); Robert Hefner, ed., *Conversion to Christianity: Historical and Anthropological Perspectives on a Great Transformation* (Berkeley: University of California Press, 1993); Vincente Rafael, *Contracting Colonialism: Translation and Christian Conversion in Tagalog Society under Early Spanish Rule* (Ithaca, N.Y.: Cornell University Press, 1988); Peter Van Der Veer, ed., *Conversion to Modernities: The Globalization of Christianity* (New York: Routledge, 1996).

12. See for example: Paul Brass, ed., *Riots and Pogroms* (New York: New York University Press, 1996); Fred Halliday, *Nation and Religion in the Middle East* (Boul-

der, Colo.: Lynne Rienner, 2000); Liisa Malkki, *Purity and Exile: Violence, Memory and National Cosmology Among Hutu Refugees in Tanzania* (Chicago: University of Chicago Press, 1995); Martin Marty and R. Scott Appleby, eds., *Religion, Ethnicity, and Self-Identity: Nations in Turmoil* (Hanover, N.H.: University Press of New England, 1997); Peter Van Der Veer, *Religious Nationalism: Hindus and Muslims in India* (Berkeley: University of California Press, 1994).

13. The literatures on religious fundamentalism rarely engage with questions of race but often reflect on ethnicity and nationalism and explore the role of religion in collective identity formation. For an introduction see the essays collected by Martin Marty and R. Scott Appleby in the five large volumes of *The Fundamentalism Project* (Chicago: University of Chicago Press, 1991–95). Discussions of Islam have long been central to discussions of religious fundamentalism (perhaps inordinately so). For a range of recent perspectives see: Bruce Lawrence, *Shattering the Myth: Islam Beyond Violence* (Princeton: Princeton University Press, 1998); Ahmed Rashid, *Jihad: The Rise of Militant Islam in Central Asia* (New Haven: Yale University Press, 2002); Bassam Tibi, *The Challenge of Fundamentalism: Political Islam and the New World Disorder* (Berkeley: University of California Press, 1998).

14. In addition to the specific literatures already cited see Craig Prentiss, ed., *Religion and the Creation of Race and Ethnicity: An Introduction* (New York: New York University Press, 2003). The contributors to this book develop analyses of race and religion that resonate, in many ways, with our own. Unfortunately, however, the collection was published just as ours went to press, so we cannot engage with its contents in detail.

15. For discussions of the "social construction" of identity see the collections on race and other identities referenced in note 5. Although these analyses are sometimes dismissed as an academic fad, they rest on a long history of scholarship—ranging, for example, from Emile Durkheim's concept of the "social fact" through Michel Foucault's theories of power and subjectivity.

16. Maxine Baca Zinn and Bonnie Thorton Dill, "Theorizing Difference from Multiracial Feminism," in *Race, Identity and Citizenship: A Reader*, edited by Rodolfo Torres, Louis Mirón, and Jonathan Xavier Inda (London: Blackwell, 1999), 103–111. For further feminist analyses of the relationships between race and gender see, among others, Kimberle Crenshaw, "Mapping the Margins: Intersectionality, Identity Politics, and Violence Against Women of Color," *Stanford Law Review* 43 (1991), 1241–1299; Patricia Hill Collins, *Black Feminist Thought: Knowledge, Consciousness, and the Politics of Empowerment* (Boston: Unwin Hyman, 1990); Angela Davis, *Women, Race and Class* (New York: Random House, 1981); Chadra Mohante, Ann Russo, and Lourdes Torres, eds., *Third World Women and the Politics of Feminism* (Bloomington: Indiana University Press, 1991).

17. Zinn and Dill, "Theorizing Difference," 107.

18. Sandra Harding, *Whose Science? Whose Knowledge? Thinking from Women's Lives* (Ithaca, N.Y.: Cornell University Press, 1991), 179.

19. Judith Butler, *Bodies That Matter: On the Discursive Limits of "Sex"* (New York: Routledge, 1993), 168. Also see Butler's *Gender Trouble: Feminism and the Subversion of Identity* (New York: Routledge, 1990), especially her critique of the "metaphysics of substance" in understandings of identity.

20. Evelyn Brooks Higginbotham, "African-American Women's History and the Metalanguage of Race," *Signs*, 17, 2 (1992), 255. Higginbotham draws the term "metalanguage" from Roland Barthes, *Mythologies*, translated by Annette Lavers (New York: Hill and Wang, 1972), esp. 111–117.

21. See for example: Sacvan Bercovitch, *The American Jeremiad* (Madison: University of Wisconsin Press, 1978) and *The Puritan Origins of the American Self* (New Haven: Yale University Press, 1975). Werner Sollors, "Typology and Ethnogenesis," in *Beyond Ethnicity* (New York: Oxford University Press, 1986), 40–65.

22. Abiel Abbot, *Traits of Resemblance in the People of the United States of America to Ancient Israel*, cited in Sollors, "Typology and Ethnogenesis," 44.

23. See for example: Albert Raboteau, "African-Americans, Exodus, and the American Israel," in *A Fire in the Bones: Reflections on African American Religious History* (Boston: Beacon Press, 1995), 17–36; Theophus Smith, *Conjuring Culture: Biblical Formations of Black America* (New York: Oxford University Press, 1994); Sollors, "Typology and Ethnogenesis." For the more recent histories of the Black Hebrew Israelites and other Black Jews, see the essays collected in Yvonne Chireau and Nathaniel Deutsch, eds., *Black Zion: African-American Religious Encounters with Judaism* (New York: Oxford University Press, 2000). Similar forms of Jewish identity or Israelite identification run through the histories of Black Pentecostalism, Rastafarianism, and secular Black nationalism.

24. Aho, *The Politics of Righteousness*, esp. 83–113; Barkun, *Religion and the Racist Right*, esp. 103–196.

25. It is, admittedly, difficult to prove this "unstated" secularist bias in unambiguous or incontrovertible terms. Our critique rests, in large part, on the *absence* of any substantive discussion of religious discourse and practice in the vast majority of scholarly research on race, nation, and other collective identities. This silence speaks volumes, but it is hard to determine precisely what it says. We are certainly not suggesting that *all* research on race and nation must account for the role of religion. But there are, undoubtedly, a number of recent analyses of racial identity formation that have clearly suffered for their failure to do so. For example, Karen Brodkin's suggestive discussion in *How Jews Became White Folks* (see note 8) is severely limited by a lack of engagement with religious definitions of Jewishness, a tendency to simply equate race with class, and a resulting reduction of American Jewish identities to ethnic varieties of class consciousness.

26. Raboteau, "African-Americans, Exodus and the American Israel," 33–34.

27. For recent critiques of racial essentialism, see the collections on "race" referenced in note 5. These contemporary authors inherit a legacy of antiracist scholarship that stretches back over a century to the work of the anthropologist Franz Boas and his students. See, for example: Ruth Benedict, *Race: Science and Politics* (New York: Viking, 1943); Franz Boas, *The Mind of Primitive Man* (New York: Macmillan, 1911); Ashley Montague, *Man's Most Dangerous Myth: The Fallacy of Race* (New York: Columbia University Press, 1942).

28. On the social and intellectual history of the concept of race see: George Fredrickson, *Racism: A Short History* (Princeton: Princeton University Press, 2002); Thomas Gossett, *Race: The History of an Idea in America*, new ed. (New York: Oxford University Press, 1997); Winthrop Jordan, *White over Black: American Attitudes Toward the*

Negro, 1550–1812 (Chapel Hill: University of North Carolina Press, 1968); George Mosse, *Toward the Final Solution: A History of European Racism* (New York: H. Fertig, 1978); Audrey Smedley, *Race in North America: Origin and Evolution of a Worldview,* 2nd ed. (Boulder, Colo.: Westview Press, 1999). These scholars often differ, of course, in their specific analyses. As we will discuss hereafter, Fredrickson dates the origins of "race" to the fifteenth century rather than the eighteenth (although he continues to stress the wholesale transformation of the concept in the eighteenth and nineteenth centuries). Despite the critique of her work we will develop hereafter, an excellent overview of this history may be found in Audrey Smedley, " 'Race' and the Construction of Human Identity," *American Anthropologist,* 100, 3 (September 1998), 690–702.

29. Smedley, " 'Race' and the Construction of Human Identity," 695.

30. Smedley, " 'Race' and the Construction of Human Identity," 695.

31. Colette Guillaumin, "Race and Nature: The System of Marks," translated by Mary Jo Lakeland, *Feminist Issues* 8, 2 (fall 1988), 25–43. See esp. 30–32.

32. See for example Benjamin Braude, "The Sons of Noah and the Construction of Ethnic and Geographical Identities in the Medieval and Early Modern Periods," *William and Mary Quarterly* 54, 1 (1997), 103–142. Speculation concerning the racial identities of Noah's three sons has often centered on the "Curse of Ham," which has been invoked, at times, to justify African slavery. See for example: William McKee Evans, "From the Land of Canaan to the Land of Guinea: The Strange Odyssey of the 'Sons of Ham,' " *American Historical Review* 85, 1 (1980), 15–43; Fredrickson, *Racism,* 43–45; Stephen Haynes, *Noah's Curse: The Biblical Justification of American Slavery* (New York: Oxford University Press, 2002); Jordan, *White Over Black,* 17–20, 35–37.

33. Gilman, *The Jew's Body,* 19.

34. George Fredrickson suggests the same connection between popular medieval discourses of "blood" and the modern concept of "race" (see *Racism,* 53). On the blood libel see: Alan Dundes, ed., *The Blood Libel Legend* (Madison: University of Wisconsin Press, 1991); Joshua Trachtenberg, *The Devil and the Jews* (1943; reprint, Philadelphia: Jewish Publication Society, 1983), 124–155.

35. Fredrickson, *Racism,* 31. For a more detailed discussion of the Spanish "purity of blood" statutes and the concept of race, see also Yosef Hayim Yerushalmi, *Assimilation and Racial Anti-Semitism: The Iberian and German Models,* Leo Baeck Memorial Lecture no. 26 (New York: Leo Baeck Institute, 1982).

36. Fredrickson, *Racism,* 3. Again, see also Yerushalmi, *Assimilation.* And for a comparable discussion of conversion and gender, see Steven Kruger, "Becoming Christian, Becoming Male?" in *Becoming Male in the Middle Ages,* edited by Jeffrey Cohen and Bonnie Whaler (New York: Garland, 1997).

37. Ann Stoler, *Race and the Education of Desire* (Durham, N.C.: Duke University Press, 1995), 72. In the passage quoted, Stoler is outlining Foucault's genealogy of race, as developed in his unpublished 1976 Collège de France lectures on the subject.

38. Jordan, *White over Black,* 96.

39. Fredrickson, *Racism,* 6.

40. Jordan, *White over Black,* 217.

41. Fredrickson, *Racism,* 104. Fredrickson distinguishes the "overtly racist regimes" of the Jim Crow South, apartheid South Africa and Nazi Germany from other

societies with "significant racist dimensions"; 100–101. But he nevertheless associates the development of racism, as such, with "modern" society.

42. For influential recent analyses of race and modernity, see Zygmunt Bauman, *Modernity and the Holocaust* (Ithaca, N.Y.: Cornell University Press, 1989), and Paul Gilroy, *The Black Atlantic: Modernity and Double Consciousness* (Cambridge: Harvard University Press, 1993).

43. The quote is from Karl Marx and Frederick Engels, "Manifesto of the Communist Party," in *The Marx-Engels Reader*, edited by Robert Tucker (New York: Norton, 1972), 476. See also Marshall Berman, *All That Is Solid Melts into Air* (New York: Penguin Books, 1988).

44. Asad, *Formations of the Secular*, 15. Asad is, we should note, somewhat less insistent on this point than we have been. He poses this image of a nonbinary social world as an open question, and places it in tension with analyses of the ways the world has, in fact, been divided into "modern" and "nonmodern." For a comparable critique of binary thinking about modernity see Bruno Latour, *We Have Never Been Modern*, translated by Catherine Porter (Cambridge: Harvard University Press, 1993).

45. Benedict Anderson, *Imagined Communities: Reflections on the Origin and Spread of Nationalism* (1983; rev. and extended ed., London: Verso, 1991).

46. Anderson, *Imagined Communities*, 12, 5. Anderson was not the first to make this fundamentally anthropological argument about the nation-state. See for example Clifford Geertz's analyses of nationalism, collected in *The Interpretation of Cultures* (New York: Basic Books, 1973), 193–341. But Anderson drew significant connections between cultural and political life that Geertz and others had not fully recognized.

47. For examples, see the edited collections on national identity referenced in note 5.

48. The preceding quotes and paraphrased arguments are from Anderson, *Imagined Communities*, 11. Quite a few authors have argued that nation-state formation is, in fact, causally linked to secularization. See for example Ernest Gellner, *Nations and Nationalism* (Oxford: Blackwell, 1983). For arguments to the contrary that resonate with our own, see Peter Van Der Veer and Hartmut Lehmann, eds., *Nation and Religion: Perspectives on Europe and Asia* (Princeton: Princeton University Press, 1999). A number of the essays in Van Der Veer and Lehmann's collection also touch on racial identities, and develop analyses of race, nation, and religion that parallel ours.

49. Anderson, *Imagined Communities*, 12–19. The terms "relativization" and "territorialization" are on 17.

50. Anderson, *Imagined Communities*, 19.

51. Anderson, *Imagined Communities*, 7

52. On evangelical missionaries' presence in (and plans for) postwar Afghanistan and Iraq, see Deborah Caldwell, "Should Christian Missionaries Heed the Call in Iraq?" *New York Times*, April 6, 2003, The Week in Review, 14; Laurie Goodstein, "Seeing Islam as 'Evil' Faith, Evangelicals Seek Converts," *New York Times*, April 27, 2003, A1.

53. Anderson includes Christianity, Islam, Buddhism, and (perhaps) Confucianism among the "great sacral cultures" of the premodern world (*Imagined Communities*, 12). Christianity may be unique among these, however, in the central role of an explicitly universalist ethic in its self-definition as a community. For insightful con-

trasts between Christian universalism and Jewish particularism see Daniel Boyarin, *A Radical Jew: Paul and the Politics of Identity* (Berkeley: University of California Press, 1994).

54. As a quick search of the World Wide Web shows, this quotation has actually been attributed to a wide range of Americans—from Governor Ferguson to an anonymous priest in Arkansas, to a congressman (who may or may not have been Sonny Bono) testifying in 1988 before the Joint National Committee on Language. The consensus holds with Ma Ferguson, however.

55. For American examples see: Bercovitch, *The American Jeremiad*; Frances Fitz-Gerald, "The American Millennium," *New Yorker*, November 11, 1985, 88–113; Susan Harding, *The Book of Jerry Falwell* (Princeton: Princeton University Press, 2000), esp. 153–183, 228–246; Sollors, "Typology and Ethnogenesis"; Ernest Tuveson, *Redeemer Nation: The Idea of America's Millennial Role* (1968; reprint, Chicago: University of Chicago Press, 1980). For examples from other nation-states, see Van Der Veer and Lehmann, *Nation and Religion*.

56. Anderson, *Imagined Communities*, 36.

57. On the so-called clash of civilizations, see Samuel Huntington, *The Clash of Civilizations and the Remaking of World Order* (New York: Simon and Schuster, 1996). On transnational migration and the contested boundaries of the nation-state, see for example: Arjun Appadurai, "Patriotism and Its Futures," *Public Culture* 5, 3 (1993), 411–429; Peggy Levitt, *The Transnational Villagers* (Berkeley: University of California Press, 2001); Nina Glick Schiller and Georges Fouron, *Georges Woke Up Laughing: Long Distance Nationalism and the Search for Home* (Durham, N.C.: Duke University Press, 2001). The broader literatures on transnationalism and globalization are far too large to summarize here. For an introduction one might see the essays collected in: Mike Featherstone, ed., *Global Culture: Nationalism, Globalization and Modernity* (London: Sage, 1990); Frank Lechner and John Boli, eds., *The Globalization Reader* (Malden, Mass.: Blackwell, 2000); Jonathan Xavier Inda and Renato Rosaldo, eds., *The Anthropology of Globalization: A Reader* (London: Blackwell, 2002).

58. Jonathan Z. Smith, *Imagining Religion: From Babylon to Jonestown* (Chicago: University of Chicago Press, 1982), xi. See also Jonathan Z. Smith, "Religion, Religions, Religious" in *Critical Terms for Religious Studies*, edited by Mark C. Taylor (Chicago: University of Chicago Press, 1998), 269–284.

59. Mark C. Taylor, introduction to *Critical Terms*, 6.

60. Talal Asad, "The Construction of Religion as an Anthropological Category," in *Genealogies of Religion* (Baltimore: Johns Hopkins University Press, 1993), 27–54. The passages quoted are on pages 47 and 53. See also Clifford Geertz, "Religion as a Cultural System," in *The Interpretation of Cultures*.

61. Jordan, *White over Black*, 97; emphases in original.

62. Russell McCutcheon, *Critics Not Caretakers: Redescribing the Public Study of Religion* (Albany: State University of New York Press, 2001), 16.

63. McCutcheon, *Critics*, 14–15. See 6–10 for McCutcheon's delineation of the "naturalistic tradition" in religious studies.

64. McCutcheon, *Critics*, 67 (on the Million Man March) and 85–101 (on the Parliament of World Religions).

65. McCutcheon, *Critics*, 24 and xi.

66. Avery Gordon, *Ghostly Matters: Haunting and the Sociological Imagination* (Minneapolis: University of Minnesota Press, 1997). On ghosts and social theory see also: Jacques Derrida, *Specters of Marx*, translated by Peggy Kamuf (New York: Routledge, 1994); Frederick Jameson, "Marx's Purloined Letter," *New Left Review* 209 (1995): 75–109.

67. Michael Taussig, "Violence and Resistance in the Americas: The Legacy of Conquest," in *The Nervous System* (New York: Routledge, 1992), 37–52, passages quoted from 45–46. See also Michael Taussig, *Shamanism, Colonialism and the Wild Man* (Chicago: University of Chicago Press, 1987), esp. 440–446 on montage.

SECTION I

"Heathens" and "Jews" in the Colonial Imagination

The earliest voyages of European exploration—and colonial expansion—marked the beginning of an ongoing process of racialization that has helped define the identities of "Blacks," "Whites," "Indians," and countless others throughout the Americas. In some sense, however, these racial identities began to take shape (perhaps in protoracial forms) long before Christopher Columbus set foot in Aiyti-Kiskeya, or Hispaniola, in 1492. They were born in the religious imaginations of late medieval Christendom—in fantasies of difference that were projected, over the years, onto the indigenous and enslaved populations of the New World.

Some in Europe wondered if the indigenous peoples of the Americas might not be descendants of the "Lost Tribes" of ancient Israel. Some speculated that Africa might be home to fabled races of giants and dogheaded men. But as efforts to Christianize and conquer these peoples proceeded, most European colonists settled on somewhat more familiar—and far less flattering—tropes of religious difference. In European eyes, native Americans and enslaved Africans were "heathens" in need of the Christian gospel. In their stubborn opposition to the mandates of the Church they might even be compared to those archenemies of Christ, the "Jews." Colonial expansion was fueled, in part, by European efforts to save the souls of these subject populations. And as the relatively fluid social space of colonial encounter gave way to the rigid hierarchical orders of settler colonialism and chattel slavery, these religious imaginations of redeemable difference gradually evolved into innate and indelible racial identities.

The essays in this section chart this complex and ongoing process of historical change, by examining how European categories of religious difference have shaped the racialization of American societies. Daniel Murphree explores an early stage of this process in "Race and Religion on the Periphery: Disappointment and Missionization in the Spanish Floridas, 1566–1763." He demonstrates how Spanish colonial missionaries attempted to account for their failure to Christianize the indigenous peoples of the Floridas by linking their perceptions of native heathenism and barbarity to perceptions of native bodies. The Indians, they argued, simply could not be Christianized because their heathenism was an innate, physical characteristic—like their dark skin and "simple" minds. The discourses of bodily heathenism born of these missionaries' frustration established a template, as Murphree suggests, for racialized hierarchies that shape the lives of native Americans, and others, to this day. And yet, as Elizabeth McAlister shows in "The Jew in the Haitian Imagination: A Popular History of Anti-Judaism and Proto-Racism," the contemporary legacies of colonial religious discourses are not always so clear. McAlister examines how participants in Haiti's annual Rara festival at once inherit and transform the anti-Jewish sentiments of the clergy in colonial Saint Domingue. Through an active identification with the Jews who "killed Jesus," disenfranchised Haitians reinvent the European demonization of Jews and Africans—deconstructing colonial religious categories from within, in order to craft rituals of resistance to their country's predominantly Catholic and mulatto elites.

Taken together, these essays demonstrate the ongoing cultural significance of the founding moments of colonial contact in the Americas. Five hundred years later, racialized communities throughout the hemisphere are still haunted—though not circumscribed—by the religious imagination of colonial Christendom.

I

Race and Religion on the Periphery: Disappointment and Missionization in the Spanish Floridas, 1566–1763

Daniel Murphree

The middle decades of the sixteenth century proved to be a defining time for Spanish settlement efforts in the colonial Floridas.[1] After a fifty-year period characterized by Hernando de Soto's exploration attempts and a brief, but bloody, struggle with French-Protestant interlopers during the early 1560s, Spanish officials envisioned the dawning of a new era in the region. No longer preoccupied with discovery expeditions or the ousting of European adversaries, Spain could devote its efforts to developing the peninsula and cultivating a new strategic jewel in the empire's crown. The first, and most important, step in this process, according to many imperialists, involved Christianizing the local native peoples. Proponents of this strategy concluded that widespread Spanish immigration to the Floridas and exploitation of the colony's resources could begin only after the peoples of the region, and by extension, the region itself, embraced the Catholic faith and all it had to offer.[2]

Yet, by the 1760s, when Spain lost political control of the Floridas to Great Britain, the province remained largely un-Christianized. External conflicts and internal misadventures undermined Spanish attempts to convert the native population and establish Catholicism as the dominant religion of the land. Settlement efforts languished as well. Few Europeans immigrated to the region, and neither the Crown nor its subjects enjoyed significant monetary profit. In almost every regard, Spanish goals in the Floridas remained unfulfilled. Despite expectations to the contrary, this potential jewel of the empire never materialized, and colonists ultimately determined that the Indians' inability or unwillingness to embrace Catholicism had impeded overall Spanish designs in the region.

Spain's inability to Christianize the Floridas intensified a previously established European process of racializing Indians in the region.[3] Since the earliest encounters of sailors and natives on the peninsula's margins and hinterlands, Spaniards, Frenchmen, and Britons had understood indigenous peoples in terms of their perceived aberrations in character, behavior, spirituality, intellectual capacity, and physical appearance. But over the course of the seventeenth and eighteenth centuries, in response to their failed conversion attempts, Spaniards and others racialized local Indians on a far greater scale than they had in the past. Supply problems, church-state disputes, and foreign interventions could well have explained their unfulfilled missionary goals, but none of these factors existed in a form that could be easily and consistently reproached. Seeking more amenable explanations and justifications for their lack of success, Europeans focused on the apparent peculiarities of the Floridas' Indians—blaming native heathenism and barbarity for the failure of evangelization, and increasingly, as time went on, linking this heathenism and barbarity to perceptions of native physical abnormality.

Racialization differed from other modes of population "othering" because of the centrality of physical appearance in the construction of images. In racializing natives, colonists wedded native habits, customs, and ways of life to physique, skin color, and adornment. Ethnocentric value judgments gained greater validity and reinforcement among settlers when fused with commonly perceived physical markers. In the early period of contact, racialization enabled colonists to progressively categorize bodily heathenism via the malleable term "Indian" or one of its derivatives. As the process evolved over the decades, European linkages of native heathenism and native bodies morphed into linkages of native bodies and philosophical, ceremonial, and behavioral deviation. Once these characteristics were fused together, colonists perceived native activities, much like native appearance, to be intractable and unalterable. By the end of the colonial period, "Indian" represented a generalized colonist understanding of native peoples based on a preconceived and rarely changing physical image. Often used with little precise meaning or definition, the term itself commonly was interpreted with negative connotations.

The process of racialization established during the early period of European-Indian contact influenced intercultural relationships in the region into the modern era. While quite distinct from modern definitions of "race" and "racism," this process served as the basis for later hierarchical divisions that would predominate in the area during the nineteenth and twentieth centuries.[4] Racialization helped precipitate a wide range of armed conflicts between natives and settlers for over three hundred years, culminating in a series of wars involving the U.S. government and Seminole Indians. As African slaves were brought to the Floridas in ever-increasing numbers during the seventeenth century, racialized terminology and value systems constructed by the early colonists helped predetermine the nature of emerging slave-settler hierarchies. At the same time, racialization fostered the creation of a unique form of pan-European identity in the region that transcended temporal, ethnic, and political boundaries.

While I focus solely on the Floridas, this model, when applied to other areas of intercultural contact in the Americas, provides an alternate perspective for viewing societal development during the colonial period. Racialization in the Floridas established a template for population interaction in other New World settings. Later European-Indian encounters in areas such as Jamestown and Santa Fe adhered to similar patterns. Disputes over labor and servitude in locales such as Charleston and Mexico City originated along corresponding lines. The identities eventually labeled as "Southern" and "American" took shape through comparable processes. Utilized as a perspective for viewing the New World as a whole, racialization in the colonial Floridas opens a unique window into the formation of racial identification in the early modern world and reveals the cultural foundations of race and racism in the United States.

Initial Spanish Enthusiasm and Optimism for Conversion

Racialized viewpoints in the Floridas only emerged over time, however. From the early years of the sixteenth century, Spaniards' motivations for missionization in the region stemmed from concerns over the natives' religious activities, uncivilized behavior, and threat to colonial defenses. Governor Menéndez de Avilés believed that missionaries could help transform the Indians from "great traitors and liars" and thereby help protect the region from foreign intervention.[5] Without conversion efforts, he feared the natives' savage nature and naiveté would enable French Protestants to regain a foothold in the peninsula. Because the Indians "neither know nor fear God . . . the Lutherans would most easily dominate all the provinces of the land . . . since the natives are barbarous and devoid of the light of faith."[6] King Charles V instructed one of the region's first European explorers, Pánfilo de Narváez, "to teach the Indians in good ways . . . in order to lead them from their sins and particularly from sodomy and cannibalism." This was important so that the natives could "be educated and taught good ways and habits . . . [and] live in an orderly way." Indicating the depth of his concern for the interrelated goals of conversion efforts, the monarch also declared that natives should not be taken as slaves *except* in cases "where these Indians are not prepared to allow these monks and priests to come among them and teach them good ways and habits, and preach to them Our Holy Catholic Faith."[7] Other Europeans focused on reforming the uncivilized setting in which the natives lived. Describing a helpful

Indian encountered by Hernando de Soto's expedition, the chronicler Garcilaso de la Vega lamented that the native "did not deserve to have come into the world and lived in the barbarous paganism of Florida."[8]

Some early European immigrants believed that native paganism and its associated evils should and would soon be eradicated.[9] Most colonizers insisted that irrespective of the prospects for success, duty to the monarchy and church necessitated that conversion efforts be attempted. In response to the request of King Philip II that he expel the French from the Floridas and colonize the region for Spain, the future governor of the province, Pedro Menéndez de Avilés, said that because the Floridas were "entirely peopled by savages, without faith and law, unenlightened by the law of Our Lord Jesus Christ, his Majesty was in duty bound . . . for the conquest and settlement of that land."[10] Jesuit missionaries entering the region during the mid–sixteenth century agreed and initially viewed conversion efforts with optimism. In 1568 Father Juan Rogel wrote:

> they [Indians] are rational animals well prepared for saving them-
> selves. Keeping them in hand, they are a harvest so ripe that one
> can swing the sickle on whatever side one chooses, as they see in
> the minister one who is looking out for their spiritual and temporal
> welfare and who preaches life and doctrine to them.[11]

A century later, Catholic officials in the New World continued to promote missionary work among the Floridas' Indians. Contending that the natives "are of a docile character," Don Juan García de Palacios, the Bishop of Santiago de Cuba, asserted

> that in doing this [Christianization], they [missionaries] will do a
> great service to God our Lord and to his Catholic Majesty . . . be-
> cause of what will be achieved in the salvation of the souls and con-
> version of so many heathens as there are in the aforesaid provinces,
> in which there is no doubt but that they would gain great and emi-
> nent merit before the divine Majesty and from whose powerful hand
> they would receive temporal and spiritual rewards.[12]

Members of the clergy promoted the merits of missionary work in correspondence to royal officials. Father Alonso de Posada, a lieutenant of New Spain's viceroy, believed that "the conversion of such a great multitude of Indian barbarians" in the Floridas carried out God's will. Consequently, the deity would "make easy all the means for its attainment and will provide ministers . . . for this purpose . . . since all must assist with equal obligation in such a high and sovereign ministry."[13] These efforts promised to ensure divine rewards for both the missionaries and Spanish empire. As late as 1690, a church official declared that few activities offered more remuneration than "the conversion of more than ten thousand souls whom the Devil holds in tyranny . . . We for our part must . . . advance as much as possible a business of such seriousness and importance."[14]

Regardless of Spanish attitudes toward the potential rewards of missionization, however, ideas of native distinctiveness influenced expectations and evaluations of success. Racialized images constructed during the previous fifty years of European interaction with Indians in the Floridas helped set the stage for later condemnations resulting from conversion failures. Rarely uniform or officially endorsed, these descriptions nevertheless helped Spaniards rationalize their less-than-expected achievements in terms of Christianization.

While generally fluid and all encompassing, the language that settlers used to denote native characteristics adhered to three major patterns. Initially, European immigrants pointed out the lifestyles and ceremonies that typified the perceived savage nature of the Indians. Soon thereafter, colonists began emphasizing the varied displays of native abnormality as represented in regalia and body painting. Ultimately, settlers utilized tales of failed conversion efforts to synthesize previous denunciations and portray native resistance to colonial designs as consequences of irreversible racialized differences. Words and inferences differed over time and place, but the impact was the same. The rhetoric of racialization soon took on greater meaning.

Savagery: Behavior and Rituals

Actual racialized depictions originated from ideas on native barbarity. Europeans throughout the Americas frequently singled out the Indians they encountered on the basis of their seemingly unbridled activities and undisciplined ways of life. Deviation from European norms indicated aberrant mores and defective character. Of all the criteria by which settlers racialized the Indians, barbarity was the most widely encompassing. According to Gary Nash, Europeans consistently viewed natives as "primitive . . . bestial, cannibalistic, sexually abandoned, and, in general moved entirely by passion rather than reason."[15] Such broadly defined parameters, and the elasticity of qualities identified as "barbaric," allowed colonists to condemn any and all aspects of Indian society and culture at will.

Perceptions of native barbarity often affected European views of native spirituality. Colonists in the Floridas encountered an array of indigenous spiritual belief systems. The Calusa, Timucua, Tequesta, Apalachee, and other native peoples with whom missionaries interacted maintained varied rituals, theologies, and value systems. While scholars still know relatively few specifics about these systems, most contend that native societies in the Southeast were theocratic in nature. Caciques (headmen/leaders) who presided over political and war-related matters also orchestrated religious worship due to their ancestral ties to an assemblage of deities, the principle one being the Sun. Their universe consisted of Upper and Lower Worlds, distinct from that in which the natives lived, and all levels had to be kept balanced at all times. Native Floridians worked to achieve balance through a variety of ceremonies and rituals, many involving various forms of inebriation, banishment, dancing, fasting, purging, self-mutilation, and on occasion, animal and human sacrifice. Commonplace among Indians in North America for centuries, such activities and beliefs astounded, and frequently offended, colonists dedicated to European-Christian ideals.[16]

Links between Indian heathenism, racialized distinction, and European misfortune first appeared during the earliest contacts. Gonzalo Fernández de Oviedo, a chronicler of Juan Ponce de León's 1521 incursion into the Floridas, remarked on the natives' resistance to Christianity during initial encounters. Despite "the determination of the monks and priests" the Indians failed to understand Christian teachings. The missionaries met with little success, "even though they preached as much as they wished," primarily because the natives were "very barbarous and idolatrous savages laden with sins and vices."[17]

The pagan ceremonies in which Indians participated elicited lengthy commentary from later colonists. In 1539, Juan Ortiz, a member of Pánfilo de Narváez's exploratory campaign, commented that the "Indians are worshippers of the Devil, and it is their custom to make sacrifices of the blood and bodies of their people, or of any people they can get."[18] At times, Europeans viewed native ceremonies with horror, on other occasions they reacted to them with humor. In 1560, while accompanying Tristán de Luna's expedition in the northwestern Floridas, Father Agustín Dávila Padilla, a Dominican friar, commented on one such instance. According to Padilla, eight Indians entered the camp of the Spaniards, "running and without uttering a word." They removed their cacique from his horse, placed him on their shoulders, and "ran with great impetuosity back the same way they had come." Throughout the process, the Indians "emitted very loud howlings, continuing them as long as their breath lasted, and when their wind gave out they barked like big dogs until they recovered it [enough] to continue the howls and prolonged shouts." These events amused the soldiers on the expedition. Forgetting the hardships of their journey, the soldiers, upon "observing the ceremonious superstitions of the Indians, upon seeing and hearing the mad music with which they honored their lord, could not contain their laughter." Not all Spaniards present viewed the situation with such merriment, however. While the soldiers laughed, Father Domingo de la Anuciación, a missionary accompanying the expedition, "mourned over it, for it seemed sacrilege to him and a pact with the demon, those ceremonials which these poor people used in their blind idolatry."[19]

Most of the early explorers in the Floridas shared Father Domingo's evaluation of native ceremonies. The evil and debauchery they saw in Indian rituals overshadowed any humorous aspects. Before he departed in 1565, the Frenchman René Laudonnière wrote that Indians living near the St. John's River "have no knowledge of God, nor any religion except what is visible to them as the sun and moon. They have their priests, in whom they firmly believe, as they are great magicians, great soothsayers, and invokers of the devils."[20] Europeans especially objected to rituals involving human sacrifice. An anonymous Spanish colonist asserted that certain Indians in the Floridas annually killed "a Christian captive to give him to the Idol, whom they worship, to eat." He disapproved of rituals in which the Indians wore "certain horns on the head" and "made noises like mountain animals." Unnerved by the proceedings, the Spaniard concluded that the ceremonies "never cease night or day for four months and run with such fury into such bestiality that cannot be told."[21]

In 1570, Jesuit priests arrived in the Floridas to explore and initiate conversions in the region's northern tier. Eventually traveling as far north as present-day Virginia, the friars lived among the natives of Jacan near Chesapeake Bay.[22] One of these missionaries, Father Rogel, noted with disdain the lengths to which Indians would go to defend their customs. He recorded that a cacique, discovering that the missionaries hoped to destroy his idols, "wrapped himself in a shroud [and] was determined and prepared, so that if we should burn them, he would throw himself into the fire together with his wife and children so that they might be burned along with them." Rather than an indication of the Indian's faith in his religion, the Spaniard viewed his actions as unrestrained barbarity. Summarizing his observations, Father Rogel asserted the need for extraordinary conversion efforts to help rectify the Indians' "many careless acts and the many failings they have."[23] Like the friar, most Spaniards involved in missionization initially reacted to perceived native paganism by expressing the need for additional clergy. In the 1560s, Governor Menéndez de Avilés complained to officials in Spain that he needed more friars because the Indians sacrificed people "to their idols, even their own children, in funerals, feasts and rejoicings, because they are great idolaters and worshipers of the Devil."[24]

Europeans in the Floridas attributed native uprisings and rebellions, at least in part, to spiritual deviance and associated activities. In this regard, no single event proved to be more devastating to Christianization efforts than the Guale uprising of 1597. Disgruntled Indians living in present-day northeastern Florida and southeastern Georgia revolted against the Spanish when missionaries attempted to stifle traditional marriage practices. Lasting less than a year, this rebellion resulted in the deaths of at least five Franciscan priests and the closing of all missions in the area for almost two decades.[25] To Spanish missionaries, the revolt highlighted the minimal progress they had made with the Indians, and more important, the inherent flaws of the natives. Images of the Guale uprising served as symbolic reminders of Spanish failure in the Floridas and new foundations for the racialization process.

Father Luis Jerónimo de Oré, a chronicler of missionary activity in the

Floridas, blamed the Indians' depraved customs for initiating the Guale uprising. According to his description of the event, a converted native took offense
when a missionary told him he could no longer have more than one wife. In
response, "this cacique and two other Indians, like him, given to the same
immoral practice, went into the interior among the pagans, without saying
anything or without obtaining permission as they were wont to do on other
occasions." A few days later, the natives returned, killed the offensive friar, and
resumed their wicked activities; "[they] began to exchange women in order to
give rein to their sensuality and unlawful pleasures."[26] Other missionaries believed that rebellions stemmed from Indian fears that Christian teachings undermined the power of traditional spiritual leaders. Writing about events related to the Guale uprising, Father Rogel recorded that certain natives
"conceived a great hate against . . . [another friar] . . . because he had revealed
their secrets and profaned their religion." As a result, a local cacique sought
to capture the missionary, "bring him to the temple and to sacrifice him there,
giving his people to understand that, however much it might disturb us, they
would make us adore their idols."[27]

As these events transpired, concerns over native spirituality led to colonist
denunciations of native behavior and practices in general. Near the end of the
sixteenth century, Juan la Cruz, a soldier manning the fort at St. Augustine,
claimed that throughout the Floridas, "in all the Indians they had seen and
dealt with, they had found only wickedness and cruelty."[28] Juan Menéndez
Marquéz, treasurer of the colony at the time, continued to support missionary
efforts while acknowledging the multiple flaws of the Indians. In his words
the natives were "idolaters and savages, hesitating at no crime however horrible."[29] The trustworthiness of the natives also became an issue of concern for
some colonists. One traveler along the Floridas' eastern coast asserted, "the
Indians are great storytellers and when there is the prospect of their being
given something [for it], they will invent tales."[30]

During the mid–seventeenth century, missionary efforts began in earnest
among the Apalachee peoples of the northwestern Floridas. Negative Spanish
portrayals of these Indians resembled earlier descriptions of natives in the east.
Franciscan friars living in the Apalachee missions believed that the Indians
"are easily swayed to come to an agreement on an opinion, not to mention,
that, as they are so fickle, what pleases them today, they detest tomorrow."[31]
Native spiritual predilections continued to serve as the root cause for European
condemnation of native activities. In the 1650s, friars in the northeastern Floridas complained to the king about their worsening standing among the Indians:

the most serious concern was the continuous bodily anguish that
the said religious endured, for they found themselves reviled by the
majority of Indians, deprived of the necessary provisions, and many

times forsaken and alone in their convents because the Indians gave their attention solely to their dances and preparations for war to which they devoted their time, living like pagans during that period.[32]

Missionaries among the Apalachees agreed. They employed physical coercion to prevent the natives from participating in heathen practices. These friars believed it was "necessary to punish the Indians so that they do not return to their pagan ways" or resurrect "the superstitions that they had in them in pre-Christian times."[33]

Additional Indian uprisings worsened European impressions. In 1675, natives rose up against the mission of La Encarnación a la Santa Cruz near the confluence of the Flint and Chattahoochee rivers.[34] Those responsible included the Chacato Indians and their neighbors the Chiscas; "rebellious people, living in the woods and brought up licentiously without the subjection of culture or other conventions."[35] Missionaries continued to enter the region, though few exuded confidence. Describing his initial impressions of the natives upon arriving in the Floridas in 1697, Father Feliciano Lopez commented that the Indians near his mission amounted to "about one thousand, all idlers from what I have seen; I do not know how I shall accommodate myself with them."[36] While attempting to convert Calusa Indians, the friar visited a structure used in native ceremonies. According to his description,

> One can imagine the purpose it serves. They dance around it. The walls are entirely covered with masks, one worse than the other. The cacique [has] given his word to me that we may destroy the house, but by my poor understanding, they are opposing it. May God help me and give me his divine assistance as, at this date, I am much afflicted . . . Fray Feliciano finds himself among these lambs that are stronger than lions.[37]

Government officials feared the impact of native paganism on settlers. The same year, Governor Laureano de Torres y Ayala asked the king for more soldiers to pacify the "heathen natives" in the southern peninsula "before their fickleness moves them to" commit barbarities among the Christianized peoples.[38]

Colonists generally contended that heathen Indians carried out the more "savage" acts. According to Governor Zuniga, the "inhumanities and atrocities which the pagan Indians inflict" severely disrupted daily life among the Christian natives of the Floridas.[39] Paganism played a major role in fostering native indolence in the view of some missionaries. In 1728, Father Joseph de Bullones described the village of Jororo in correspondence to the king. He believed that its native inhabitants "were all idolaters and heathens except two or three." Missionary activity languished, in part, because the Indians refused to work.

The villagers "wander about all year, women as well as men, searching for marine life with which they sustain themselves, killing alligators and other unclean animals, which is delectable sustenance to them." Indians living nearby also were "vile by nature" and hampered conversion efforts because of the "uselessness of the nation."[40] Father Bullones lamented the impact of these factors on converted populations. Providing reasons for why the mission system languished, he focused on the natives' base tendencies:

> the Indians . . . were in the habit of rising up and rebelling, killing
> the doctrineros, subjecting them to notable and harsh extortions and
> torments . . . and when the one reduced were not wont to become
> angry, they were attacked by the heathens, with the latter always
> coming out winners and ours desolated. And if in one or another
> case this took some time to happen, those nations are so fickle and
> unstable that for any whatsoever slight motive that they arrive at
> from their divination, they change their sites and camps to the re-
> gion or territory that their omen indicates.[41]

By the dawn of the eighteenth century, European condemnation of native spirituality had become a recurrent theme in missionary correspondence. Incivility, lying, stealing, murdering, double-dealing, and unrestrained licentiousness indicated Indian paganism to settlers generally dedicated to Christian ideals.[42] Lack of self-control along with worship of idols and resistance to biblical instruction further marked the indigenous peoples' deviant existences. After years of failed missionary attempts and native indifference, many European Floridians began to regard heathenism as a consequence of innate conditions. Though most settlers did not perceive the Indians to be inherently evil, the belief that natives could not or would not embrace Christian theology pointed to "ineradicable qualities of savagery."[43]

Paint and Feathers: Distinctions in Appearance

In the minds of the colonists, barbaric and heathen behavior eventually became tied to Indian physical appearance. Settlers began to view native dress, form, and skin color as, in Audrey Smedley's terms, "surface manifestations of inner realities." Indian physical appearance signaled "behavioral, intellectual, temperamental, moral, and other" defects to colonists. This realization enabled Europeans to racialize natives on a continual basis, regardless of actual activities or lifestyles. Perceived links between physical appearance and behavior also served as the primary factor leading to the establishment of entrenched racial classifications in subsequent centuries.[44]

Significantly, references to native appearance almost always highlighted elements of dress and adornment rather than physical phenotype. Headdresses and war paint dominated descriptions and fascinated colonists. But the language used to describe these features tended to portray artificial adornment as permanent differences. Over the years, settler commentary essentialized such attributes and increasingly described them as manifestations of inherent deficiencies. Feathers and tattoos symbolized native distinction and intransigence to colonists who were progressively disappointed with the Floridas and its indigenous inhabitants.

Most references to native skin color or appearance consisted of vague comments, general in nature and absent of speculation as to meanings. According to an account of Hernando de Soto's journey, the explorer and his companions met Indians who were "brown of skin," though little else on the subject is mentioned.[45] While surveying missionary activity in the Floridas' northern regions, Father Rogel commented on one occasion that "there is great neglect in this village in looking to the salvation of the dark skinned people," again, with little elaboration as to what "dark skinned" meant to him or other Europeans.[46] Father Cancer, one of the earliest Spanish missionaries in the Floridas, offered the first substantial reference to Indians being "red." After greeting a group of natives in 1529 he wrote: "I was getting covered in their red dye from all the embracing that was going on, although I managed to get the worst of it on my habit to leave the skin untouched."[47]

As the decades passed, perceived native skin color, whether artificial or natural, became a marker of distinction between those who had been converted and those who continued to resist Christianity. Describing a meeting of Floridas' Indians and Spaniards, Rodrigo Rangel, a chronicler of Hernando de Soto's campaign, noted:

> and Thursday they [Spanish soldiers] came to another plain where
> the Indians had taken the position, having made a very strong barricade, and within it there were many Indian braves, painted red and
> decorated with other colours which appeared very fine (or rather,
> very bad, at least it meant harm to the Christians).[48]

Europeans rarely applied color-based designations to Indians who did accept Catholic teachings, whereas non-Christian Indians subsequently received labels based on their appearance. According to friars working in the northern Floridas,

> we religious find it necessary to become the defenders and protectors of the *Hanopiras* among the Christian Indians. This term signifies a painted man because the pagans in greater part go about
> smeared and painted with a bright reddish color, and when this is
> lacking they paint themselves with soot and charcoal. In this the Indians of Florida are similar to those pagans and barbarous Indians
> who live in the cordilleras of Peru.[49]

Color-based designations took on added meaning when applied to Indians who participated in uprisings. In his explanation of the previously mentioned Guale uprising of 1597, Father Oré emphasized native appearance when describing the activities of recalcitrant natives. Having already disputed the Spaniards' authority and departed without permission, "after a few days they returned at night with many other pagan Indians, painted and smeared with red paste, and with feathers on their heads. This among them is a sign of cruelty and slaughter." Unconventional appearance indicated savagery to the friar. Describing other natives involved in the rebellion, Father Oré wrote: "we encountered a great number of painted Indians, their faces smeared with red earth, and fitted out with bows and arrows. They seemed to be numberless and looked like demons."[50]

By the early seventeenth century, Europeans commonly used terminology that highlighted appearance or physical form to describe Indians, regardless of the state of hostility that existed between the groups. One church official claimed that Indians in the northwestern Floridas were "fleshy, and rarely is there a small one, but they are weak and phlegmatic as regards work." Styles or lack of clothing seemed to play a part in the Indian's perceived barbarism; "they go naked, with only the skin [of some animal] from the waist down, and, if anything more, a coat . . . without a lining, or a blanket."[51] Missionaries and their superiors in the church hierarchy associated examples of native barbarity with aspects of their appearance. At the beginning of the eighteenth century, a high-ranking church official in St. Augustine believed that neighboring natives were "so bloodthirsty, that if some Indian from their village is killed by one from another, they do not rest until they revenge the killing either on the one who did it or on someone else from the village." He emphasized that in order to carry out these barbaric activities, natives went forth "painted all over with red ochre and with their heads full of multi-colored feathers."[52] By 1760, two Franciscan priests, Father Monaco and Father Alana, explicitly applied negative connotations to native appearance, pointing out that one Indian spiritual leader they encountered in the Floridas stood out because of his appearance, "adorning himself with feathers and painting himself horribly." Noting that this was normal behavior for the Indians, they concluded that "the men paint themselves variously almost every day."[53]

At times, European colonists in the Floridas depicted native appearance and activities via the use of animal imagery. As with other references to natives and their overall appearance, these depictions often implied little European condemnation or hostility. Nevertheless, such characterizations added to racialized impressions. Dehumanization reinforced the idea that Indians, because of their lifestyles, emotions, appearance, skin color, and non-human characteristics, could, and perhaps should, be regarded and treated as inferior.

Garcilaso introduced this imagery in his writings about Hernando de Soto. While assessing Spanish viewpoints toward the Indians, Garcilaso wrote: "in

general these people are looked upon as simple folk without reason or understanding who in both peace and war differ very little from beasts and accordingly could not do and say things . . . worthy of memory or praise."[54] Nicholas
le Challeux, a French visitor to the Floridas, echoed these feelings in his evaluation of Indian behavior. In 1566, he pointed out French mistreatment of
natives at Fort Caroline, a settlement located north of St. Augustine, and explained the consequences as follows.

> This caused the natives to turn from good feelings towards the
> French and since the desire for vengeance is planted in men's
> hearts by nature, and as it is also the common instinct of all animals
> to defend life and limb, and to remove the source of trouble, it can-
> not be doubted that the natives conspired and intrigued with the
> Spaniards to free themselves from us.[55]

While not singling out the Indians as possessing more animal-like characteristics than other groups, Challeux does accentuate the idea that decision-
making by natives was based on animal instinct as much as anything else, thus
validating Garcilaso's assertion.

A more blatant example of dehumanization surfaces in the accounts by
Governor Menéndez de Avilés of warfare with the Floridas' Indians. Recorded
half a century after the first explorations, these writings convey just how far
this idea had progressed:

> when the soldier has fired, the Indian rises at a place different from
> the spot aimed at, as if he had been swimming underwater. So
> adept, and clever at this maneuver are they, that one can only be
> astonished. They fight by skirmishing, and jump over the brush like
> little deer. . . . They are unencumbered by clothes, and swim like
> fish. . . . Once on the opposite bank they shriek and mock the Chris-
> tians.[56]

Menéndez de Avilés directly compared natives to both deer and fish. In his
eyes, their abilities were identical. Along with their nakedness and ridicule of
Europeans (Christians), the Indians themselves had proven through their natural capacities that they were very different from typical humans.

Though few missionaries openly agreed with these assessments, on occasion some did make similar comments. By the early years of the seventeenth
century, friars living among the Floridas' natives began to doubt the capabilities
of those they were trying to convert. Unnerved by native digressions from
European behavior, most sought greater security from Spanish troops. Franciscans serving in the region specifically asked government officials that soldiers be used to control the natives, since Indians, in the friars' words, "can
act as wild animals and would kill our people."[57]

Catalysts: Failure and Discouragement

Differences between Europeans and Indians became more prominent as mis-sionization and colonization efforts faltered. Foreign invasions, inconsistent support from Spain, and questionable conversion successes diminished en-thusiasm among Spaniards.[58] Increasingly, the Indians' paganism, and its per-ceived manifestations, became more pronounced in the writings of Europeans in the Floridas. Facing mounting difficulties, colonists emphasized native cer-emonies, barbarous practices, and physical differences as they related to hea-then behavior. Within these descriptions, characteristics of regional natives were portrayed as fixed obstacles, unchanging abnormalities, and signs of in-herent inadequacy. Settlers collectivized these factors into one general image of natives, thereby forming a single entity on which to blame a variety of im-pediments. The Indians' real and imagined distinctions and resistance to Christianity both excused European failures and reinforced settler understand-ings of native inferiority. By the eighteenth century, Spanish allusions to the Indians, especially those made by missionaries and church officials, consis-tently included racialized imagery.

The transformation of Father Rogel's perspective vividly illustrates the evo-lution of European attitudes. Initially, he believed that Indians listened to what he said and would "take it well with a strong will."[59] Occasionally, his patience seemed to pay off. Father Rogel claimed to have reached success among In-dians along the eastern coast, and some converts even appeared to adopt "civ-ilized" lifestyles.[60] Nevertheless, he always approached the natives cautiously, not wanting them to "return to the vomit of their idolatries." Father Rogel believed that the conversion process would take some time because the Indians were "simple folk and of scant understanding."[61] He also pointed out that natives failed to attend catechism lessons after he condemned their "idolatries and evil customs and wicked laws." In addition, conversions seemed to flourish only when the priest offered the Indians food and gifts but diminished "when the handouts ended." At that point, "they all took off."[62]

Other missionaries reinforced these ideas. Father Oré became disillu-sioned because he believed that the Indians often rebelled and would go about "busily in despoiling the clothing, chalices, patens and sacerdotal vestments which they divided among themselves, profaning the vases and sacred objects in an abominable manner." Describing an Indian who rejected Christian teach-ings, he wrote:

> despite these and other gentle words which . . . the other religious
> spoke to him, they could not soften him, but rather they were the
> occasion of spiritual hardening of the heart, for the devil reigned in

his heart as he did in the heart of Judas. He forged the treachery in
his breast.[63]

The perceived deviant activities of the natives captured the attention of
other missionaries. Father Escobedo, writing in the 1580s, stressed the Indians'
amoral behavior. He believed "it difficult to predict which [sic] idolatrous pagans
might do" and suspected that they planned to expel the missionaries. The
natives he encountered on the peninsula's eastern coast were "evil intentioned"
and "fiendish." Father Escobedo claimed that the "wickedness of the Indian"
caused the natives to reject conversion efforts. At least one group of Indians
he met was a "ferocious nation which wallowed in destructive vices."[64] In this
environment, he could envision Christianization efforts making little headway.

Government officials began to share these sentiments. In a letter to a Jesuit
priest, Governor Menéndez de Avilés explained his continual efforts to reform
the natives despite ongoing resistance. Though he told the natives "that Our
Lord is in Heaven and He is Chief of all the chiefs of the earth and of all
creation, and that he is angry with them for making war and killing each other
like wild beasts," they continued to practice their pagan ceremonies because
"they are highly treacherous and unreliable."[65] Members of the Jesuit order
who sailed to the region in the 1560s could do little to rectify the situation.
Shortly after the missionaries arrived in St. Augustine, church officials decided
"that it is neither useful nor is it convenient" to convert the natives. They based
their conclusions on the difficult living conditions of the missionaries and the
fact that they were scattered among the "heathen Indians, without hope of
converting them due to the barbarousness and rudeness of that nation."[66]

By the second half of the sixteenth century, Franciscan missionaries in the
Floridas held equally pessimistic opinions about the natives they encountered.
Upon arriving on the eastern coast in the 1560s, friars expressed dismay that
the majority of the native villages continued to have substantial heathen populations, despite over thirty years of Christianization efforts.[67] Even those Indians who seemed receptive to Catholicism frequently slipped back into their
pagan ways. An observer of the conversion process, Hernando D'Escalante
Fontaneda, wrote in 1575 that two Floridas' Indians brought to Havana, Cuba,
for conversion indicated that "baptism was not lawful for them,—they were
heretics." After the natives departed for their homeland, the chronicler recorded, "it appears they have returned to their old ways, and are more wicked
than they were formerly."[68] Fontaneda determined that the Indians' paganism
could not be overcome through Christianization, and other measures should
be employed to reduce their threat to the Spanish empire.

Let the Indians be taken in hand gently, inviting them to peace; then
putting them under deck, husbands and wives together, sell them
among the Islands, and even upon Terra-Firma for money as some

old nobles of Spain buy vassals of the king. In this way, there could
be management of them, and their number become diminished.
This I say would be proper policy.[69]

Notwithstanding recently enacted laws prohibiting the enslavement of Indians,
failure and disillusionment made the idea acceptable to many Spaniards dis-
enchanted with the Floridas. Similarly, immediately after the Guale rebellion,
Governor Méndez de Canzo ordered that Indian participants in the uprising
were "to serve as slaves to the soldiers who might capture them . . . inasmuch
as the crime committed by the said Indians was so grave, and deserving of an
equally heavy penalty and punishment."[70] Though this order was later rescinded, it demonstrates the heightened level of anxiety and frustration.

The remaining missionaries in the Floridas continued to do their work,
but most were "very demoralized to see how little progress they are making."
Many believed that if the government's administration of the Indians did not
change, "it will be pointless for the friars to waste their time there."[71] The
failure of conversion efforts came more and more to be seen as a consequence
of native inferiority to Europeans. In 1600, missionaries in the northern Floridas reported:

> there are more than eighty churches which have been built in the
> different missions and others [are] under construction. We are
> moved to do this to encourage the Indians who are incapable of
> good conceptions and obedience. They have always had their minis-
> try so that they listen with little appreciation to what we preach and
> teach, in grave detriment to the poor newly converted Indians, not-
> withstanding that our teaching and converting accrues to their own
> good, as we aid and provide for them in their time of hunger, as
> when crops have failed. The Indians are so lazy, and improvident
> that if we did not take care of the crops after planting they would
> have nothing.[72]

In correspondence to King Philip III, Franciscan missionaries admitted that
the Indians attacked the friars, "making fun of them, turning Christian more
as a gesture than because they were Christian."[73] Partially as a result, government officials in Spain again questioned the viability of Christianization efforts.
In 1657, the Council of the Indies informed the king that if missionization and
administrative problems were not resolved, "the total loss of Florida is to be
feared, whose conversion has cost so much wealth and concern."[74]

As the years passed, Europeans concerned with missionary endeavors in
the Floridas began to consider total conversion of local natives unlikely. Governor Diego de Quiroga y Losada wrote that by 1688, "entire [Christian Indian]
settlements fled to the woods, living in them like barbarians without attending
to any of their obligations as Christians." He warned the king that many convert

villages were "disappearing in this fashion and becoming depopulated."[75] Church officials repeatedly questioned the feasibility of continuing conversion attempts in the Floridas. According to Diego Ebelino de Compostela, the bishop of Santiago de Cuba, even if the Catholic Church possessed the resources to accomplish this endeavor, he "was convinced it was not possible." The bishop based his decision on the assumption that Indians in the Floridas were "numberless," were widely dispersed, and possessed "evil tendencies." In addition, the natives had "launched some uprisings and some treacherous actions implying little fidelity because while they persevere with humility as long as they recognize benefit and subjection," overall they exhibit "damned wickedness."[76]

Additional native rebellions led to greater disillusionment. In 1696, Timucua Indians destroyed the Jororo mission in the southern peninsula, forcing its abandonment by the Spanish.[77] According to one friar, Indians involved in the uprising took the position that "if they [the missionaries] are not going to give them clothes and [food] to eat, what use was it for [Indians] to become Christians"? When the missionaries refused to provide anticipated gifts, the natives "began to subject the religious to some harassment, mistreating them by words and deeds and stealing from them repeatedly." Eventually the Indians declared "that they did not wish to become Christians and that the religious should leave or they would kill them."[78] Afterward, Governor Laureano observed that "it was a pity, because they [the missionaries] were off to a great beginning for the extension of our holy faith. But their [the Indians'] barbarism is great."[79] Even those Indians who seemed to adopt Catholicism remained suspect due to their decadent qualities. In 1698, the Council of the Indies reached the following conclusion regarding conversion attempts.

> What is apparent from . . . the statements of the religious is that as
> long as the religious gave provisions to the Indians and some things
> of those that they brought from Havana, they showed some inclina-
> tion or appearance of becoming converts. And from what happened
> afterward [Indian uprisings] one can certify that they were moved
> solely by self-interest.[80]

The imperial establishment, much like clergy involved in conversion efforts, blamed failure in the Floridas on the region's indigenous inhabitants and their inherent defects.

By the beginning of the eighteenth century, Spanish frustration led to further condemnation of the Indians. St. Augustine's curate rector determined in 1700 that "the pagans . . . even though they [the missionaries] have urged them to accept the Catholic faith and to become Christians, do not want to."[81] The combined efforts of heathen Indians and English colonists to the north undermined Spanish Christianization efforts. The priest concluded that the missions "were depopulated and demolished," the two hostile groups having

"annihilated four parts out of the five that comprised the number of the reduced and converted."[82] As Spain's power in the region slowly declined and
the Americas began experiencing a succession of independence movements,
dreams of a Christianized Florida remained unfulfilled.

Conclusion

Decades of unmet goals and perceived Indian recalcitrance transformed the
perspectives of Europeans in the Floridas who were involved in both missionary work and colony expansion. Between the early days of exploration during
the sixteenth century and the crumbling of the mission system two hundred
years later, the idea that most natives were heathens had changed very little
among settlers and imperial officials. What did change was how Europeans
evaluated this heathenism. After years of tying native religious belief systems
and behaviors to physical appearance, most settlers in the Floridas supported
the notion that native heathenism, and thus resistance to Christianization,
stemmed from ineradicable racial deficiencies. Justifying their lack of success,
this realization led colonists to perceive additional Indian attributes as byprod-
ucts of inherent defects as well. The end result was the transformation of
European attitudes toward natives in the Floridas and the adoption of more
repressive policies in their regard.

The evolution of colonist views surfaced in a report on the Floridas' Indians that was written and submitted to King Charles III in 1760. Authored
by Father Alana and Father Monaco, this assessment reflected the opinions of
numerous settlers who had labored in the Floridas over the decades. Throughout the report, the priests highlighted the many native deficiencies commented
on by missionaries since 1521. They confirmed the widely held belief that "the
idolatrous errors and superstitions of this people [the Floridas' Indians] are of
the crudest sort. But what is surprising is the very tenacious attachment with
which they maintain all this and the ridicule they make of beliefs contrary [to
theirs]." The two Spaniards singled out one village's Indian spiritual leader in
particular, writing: "he is considered to be the doctor for the place. His remedies are great howls and gestures that he makes over the one who is ill. . . .
And he is indeed a man who has in his appearance I do not know just what
traces of [being] an instrument of the Devil." The observers added that most
deviant aspects of native lifestyles stemmed from customs "they practice, we
have learned, for the honor of the principal idol that they venerate."

Dissatisfied with ongoing conversion techniques, the two Franciscans advocated a dramatic change in policy, though one promoted by earlier commentators in the Floridas. Their primary goal was to convince the governor to use
military force in controlling the Indians of the region.

In order to shorten [this litany] by omitting many other individual cases by which they [the Indians] have shown us their bad faith and other numerous superstitions to which we found them blindly devoted like all the American Indians, in view of the special duplicity, audacity, and obstinacy, that these [people] carry to an extreme, we consider it necessary that the conquest of their souls be supported on the same means as it has been over almost all of America, that is, that this mission be secured for some years escorted by 20 or 25 soldiers of excellent customs, with whose protection the necessary rigor can be employed in order to root out even the relics of their superstition.

They further contended that armed measures were essential for the civilization of the Indians:

for the restraining of some Indians for their own good, who with manifest deceit make a mockery of our holy religion, maintaining the adoration of some crude [idols] almost in plain view. The time has passed on permitting some naked creatures to frustrate everything with a stubborn "We do not want it," after their having occupied the time of your Excellency and the rest of the ministers of His Majesty, and after their having caused expenses for the royal coffers. With the measures proposed, or those that your Excellency may find more appropriate, their idolatry will be abolished and the true religion will be established among this people, and in spite of the obstinate ones, who, with punishments, will come to understand what they were not able to grasp with reasonings.[83]

Despite their general condemnation of the natives' behavior, spirituality, and appearance, Alana and Monaco continued to adhere to one of the primary tenets of Spanish missionization in the New World: improving the lives of the heathens. In their minds,

this [military] aid is necessary for the preservation of the Indians. These diminutive nations fight among themselves at every opportunity and they are shrinking as is indicated by the memory of the much greater number that there were just twenty years ago, so that, if they continue on in their barbarous style, they will have disappeared within a few years.[84]

After decades of missionary efforts, the Spanish in the Floridas believed that the only way to Christianize the land and its peoples, and therefore literally preserve both, was through martial coercion.

In their report, Father Alana and Father Monaco encapsulate the major factors used by missionaries and other colonists in the Floridas to racialize natives for three centuries. Primarily concerned with Indian heathenism and rituals from the outset, the Spaniards quickly forged connections between religious deviance and overall behavior considered barbaric according to European standards. Unacceptable behavior and unconventional native adornment subsequently become symbiotic in the missionaries' writings. Eventually, the observers question the Indians' intellectual capacity and potential for self-preservation. In the end, they determine that because of the lack of conversion success among the natives, the indigenous population is inherently deficient and can only be controlled through armed force.

Regardless of their intentions, missionaries and settlers involved in the Christianization of the Floridas enhanced the racialized images of natives held by many Europeans. Emphasizing the paganism of the Indians and its associated barbarous behavior, these individuals supplemented ideas on native physical abnormality and intellectual insufficiency established by the initial explorers in the region. Less overt and all-encompassing than the allusions of the explorers, references made by priests and other colonists involved with missionization proved equally influential on general European attitudes. Unsuccessful Christianization endeavors bolstered ideas that colonization of the Floridas, in its various forms, had failed in large part because of indigenous peoples and their unchangeable differences from Europeans. Consequently, the racialization process in the Floridas gained further justification among settlers in the region, while additional barriers between Indians and new colonists emerged in the late eighteenth and early nineteenth centuries.

NOTES

1. The plural term "Floridas" is used throughout the text to take into account the varied meanings of "Florida" during the colonial period. At different times between the sixteenth and nineteenth centuries, Europeans used derivations of "Florida" to describe specific areas, such as "West Florida," or broader geographic locales, such as the entire present-day southeastern United States. Unless otherwise indicated, the "Floridas" refers to the territory immediately south of the 32° 28' latitude encompassed by the Atlantic Ocean, Mississippi River, and Gulf of Mexico.

2. For detailed examinations of Spanish Christianization efforts in the Floridas see Amy T. Bushnell, *Situado and Sabana: Spain's Support System for the Presidio and Mission Provinces of Florida* (Athens: University of Georgia Press, 1994); Michael V. Gannon, *The Cross in the Sand: The Early Catholic Church in Florida, 1513–1570* (Gainesville: University of Florida Press, 1965); Barbara G. McEwan, ed., *The Spanish Missions of La Florida* (Gainesville: University of Florida Press, 1993); Jerald T. Milanich, *Laboring in the Fields of the Lord: Spanish Missions and Southeastern Indians* (Washington, D.C.: Smithsonian Institution Press, 1999).

3. Most attempts to investigate racial distinctions in the colonial Floridas pertain exclusively to "white-black" relationships. See David Colburn and Jane Landers, eds.,

The African American Heritage of Florida (Gainesville: University of Florida Press, 1995).

4. Recent historical investigations dealing with the concept of race and its application to European-Indian encounters in colonial North America include Kathleen M. Brown, "Native Americans and Early Modern Concepts of Race," in *Empire and Others: British Encounters with Indigenous Peoples, 1600–1850*, edited by Martin Daunton and Rick Halpern (Philadelphia: University of Pennsylvania Press, 1999); Joyce E. Chaplin, *Subject Matter: Technology, the Body, and Science on the Anglo-American Frontier, 1500–1676* (Cambridge: Harvard University Press, 2001); Robert H. Jackson, *Race, Caste, and Status: Indians in Colonial Spanish America* (Albuquerque: University of New Mexico Press, 1999); Ronald Takaki, "The Tempest in the Wilderness: The Racialization of Savagery," *Journal of American History* 79 (1992), 892–912.

5. Pedro Menéndez, Letter to a Jesuit Friend at Cadiz, 15 October 1566, quoted in Eugene Lyon, *Pedro Menéndez de Avilés* (New York: Garland, 1995), 324.

6. Bartolomé Barrientos, "Of the Reasons Furnished His Majesty by Pedro Menéndez for Not Allowing Florida to Fall into the Hands of Lutherans or Other Foreigners," 1567, in *Pedro Menéndez de Avilés, Founder of the Floridas*, translated by Anthony Kerrigan (Gainesville: University of Florida Press, 1965), 27–28.

7. "Capitulations Between Charles V and Pánfilo de Narváez for the Conquest of the Land Between the Rio de las Palmas and Florida, 11 December 1526," in David B. Quinn, ed., *New American World: A Documentary History of North America to 1612*, 5 vols. (New York: Arno Press, 1979), 2:7–10.

8. Garcilaso de la Vega, *The Florida of the Inca: A History of the Adelantado, Hernando de Soto, Governor and Captain General of the Kingdom of Florida, and of Other Heroic Spanish and Indian Cavaliers, Written by the Inca, Garcilaso de la Vega, An Officer of His Majesty, and a Native of the Great City of Cuzco, Capital of the Realms and Provinces of Peru*, translated and edited by John G. Varner (Austin: University of Texas Press, 1962), book 2, chap. 4, 73–74.

9. For European views on native paganism and heathenism, see Robert F. Berkhofer Jr., *The White Man's Indian: Images of the American Indian from Columbus to the Present* (New York: Random House, 1978), 34–38; Thomas D. Matijasic, "Reflected Values: Sixteenth-Century Europeans View the Indians of North America," *American Indian Culture and Research Journal* 11 (1987), 32–36; James H. Merrell, *Into the American Woods: Negotiators on the Pennsylvania Frontier* (New York: Norton, 1999), 129; David J. Weber, *The Spanish Frontier in North America* (New Haven: Yale University Press, 1992), 20–24.

10. "Gonzalo Solis de Mera's Account of Pedro Menéndez de Avilés' Attack on the French Fort in Florida, 1565," in Quinn, *New American World*, 2:426.

11. Father Juan Rogel to Father Jerónimo Ruiz del Portillo, 25 April 1568, in *Missions to the Calusas*, translated and edited by John Hann (Gainesville: University of Florida Press, 1991), 28–29.

12. "Autos of Don Juan García de Palacios, Bishop of Santiago de Cuba, August–December, 1682," in Hann, *Missions*, 52, 56.

13. Alonso de Posada, "Account of Father Fray Alonso de Posada, Representative of Viceroy of New Spain, Report of 14 March, 1686," in *Alonso de Posada Report, 1686: A Description of the Area of the Present Southern United States in the Late Seventeenth*

Century, translated and edited by Barnaby Thomas (Pensacola, Fla.: Perdido Bay Press, 1982), 49.

14. Don Diego Ebelino de Compostela, Bishop of Santiago de Cuba, to the Dean and Chapter of Holy Cathedral Church of Santiago de Cuba, 2 January 1690, in Hann, *Missions*, 87–88.

15. Gary B. Nash, "The Image of the Indian in the Southern Colonial Mind," *William and Mary Quarterly* 29 (1972), 201.

16. James Axtell, "The Invasion Within: The Contest of Cultures in Colonial North America," in *The European and the Indian: Essays in the Ethnohistory of Colonial North America*, edited by James Axtell (New York: Oxford University Press, 1981), 72–76; Charles Hudson, *The Southeastern Indians* (Knoxville: University of Tennessee Press, 1976), 120–184, 317–376; Randolph J. Widmer, "The Structure of Southeastern Chiefdoms," in *The Forgotten Centuries: Indians and Europeans in the American South, 1521–1704*, edited by Charles Hudson and Carmen Tesser (Athens: University of Georgia Press, 1994), 146–152.

17. "Oviedo on Juan Ponce de León's Second Voyage, 1521," in Quinn, *New American World*, 1:247.

18. Luis Hernández de Biedma, *Narratives of the Career of Hernando de Soto in the Conquest of Florida, as Told by a Knight of Elvas and in a Relation by Luys Hernández de Biedma, Factor of the Expedition*, 2 vols., edited by Edward G. Bourne, translated by Buckingham Smith (New York: Allerton, 1922), 1:29–30.

19. "Padilla's Account of Coosa, 1560," in Quinn, *New American World*, 2:243.

20. René de Laudonnière, *Histoire Notable de la Floride. A Foothold in Florida: The Eyewitness Account of Four Voyages Made by the French to that Region and Their Attempt at Colonization, 1562–1568*, translated by Sarah Lawson (East Grinstead, England: Antique Atlas, 1992), 8.

21. "Customs of the Indians in Florida, 1566," in Quinn, *New American World*, 2:539; "Memorial of Juan Lopez de Velasco, 1569?" in Hann, *Missions*, 316.

22. Eugene Lyon, "Settlement and Survival," in *The New History of Florida*, edited by Michael Gannon (Gainesville: University of Florida Press, 1996), 56–57.

23. Father Juan Rogel to Father Jerónimo Ruiz del Portillo, 25 April 1568, in Hann, *Missions*, 235–236, 250, 258–259.

24. Pedro Menéndez, "Florida Indians Customs" (n.d.), quoted in Lyon, *Pedro Menéndez*, 327.

25. Milanich, *Laboring in the Fields*, 112–114.

26. David H. Thomas, ed., *Spanish Borderlands Sourcebooks: The Missions of Spanish Florida* (New York: Garland, 1991), 121–122, 136.

27. "Report on the Florida Missions by Father Juan Rogel, 1608–1611," in Hann, *Missions*, 287.

28. "Inquiry by Gonzalo Méndez de Canzo into the Indian Uprising of 1597 and His Actions in Regard to the Indians Who Took Part in It, 7 October 1597 to 12 January 1598," in Quinn, *New American World*, 5:78.

29. "Report of Juan Menéndez Marquéz to the King, 5 January 1608," in *The Unwritten History of St. Augustine, Copied from the Spanish Archives in Seville, Spain*, edited by Abbie M. Brooks (St. Augustine, Fla.: *The Record*, 1909), 77.

30. Letter of Alonso de Alas to the King, 23 November, 1609, quoted in "Transla-

tion of the Ecija Voyages of 1605 and 1609 and the Gonzalez Derrotero of 1609," in *Spanish Translations: the History of Florida's Spanish Mission Period*, edited by John H. Hann (Tallahassee, Fla.: Bureau of Archaeological Research, 1986), 20.

31. "Letters of Apalachee Friars, 10 May 1657," in *Visitations and Revolts in Florida, 1656–1695*, edited by John H. Hann (Tallahassee, Fla.: Florida Bureau of Archaeological Research, 1993), 17.

32. Letter of the Religious of the Province of Santa Elena to H. M. in Complaint About the Evil Conduct and Affronts Done to Those Natives by the Governor of Florida Don Diego de Rebolledo, 10 September 1657, in Hann, *Visitations*, 13.

33. Letter of the Apalachee Friars, 15 July, 1657, in Hann, *Visitations*, 23.

34. Milanich, *Laboring in the Fields*, 166.

35. Governor Hita Salazar to Queen, 24 August 1675, in Hann, *Visitations*, 42.

36. Fray Feliciano Lopez to Fray Pedro Taybo, 1697, in Hann, *Missions*, 158–159.

37. Fray Feliciano Lopez to Fray Pedro Taybo, 1697, in Hann, *Missions*, 159–161.

38. Governor Laureano de Torres y Ayala to the King, 3 February 1697, in Hann, *Missions*, 143.

39. Governor Zuniga to the King, 15 September 1704, in *Here They Once Stood: The Tragic End of the Apalachee Missions*, edited by Mark F. Boyd, Hale G. Smith, and John W. Griffin (Gainesville: University of Florida Press, 1952), 68.

40. Fray Joseph de Bullones to the King, 5 October 1728, in Hann, *Missions*, 377.

41. Fray Joseph de Bullones to the King, 5 October 1728, in Hann, *Missions*, 374–375.

42. Audrey Smedley, *Race in North America: Origin and Evolution of a Worldview*, 2nd ed. (Boulder, Colo.: Westview Press, 1999), 61.

43. Takaki, "The Tempest," 906.

44. Smedley, *Race in North America*, 28.

45. Hernández de Biedma, *Narratives of the Career of Hernando de Soto*, 1:66–67.

46. Father Juan Rogel to Father Jerónimo Ruiz del Portillo, 25 April 1568, in Hann, *Missions*, 235–236, 250, 258–259.

47. "The Mission of Fray Luís Cancer to Florida as Told by Beteta, 1529," in Quinn, *New American World*, 2:192.

48. "The Official Narrative of the Expedition of Hernando Soto, by Rodrigo Rangel, His Secretary, as Rendered by Gonzalo Fernández de Oviedo, 1539–1541," in Quinn, *New American World*, 2:160.

49. Thomas, *Spanish Borderlands Sourcebooks*, 72, 91–92.

50. Thomas, *Spanish Borderlands Sourcebooks*, 121–122, 136.

51. Gabriel Díaz Vara Calderón, "Characteristics of the Christianized Indians," in *A Seventeenth-Century Letter of the Gabriel Díaz Vara Calderón, Bishop of Cuba, Describing the Indians and Indian Missions of Florida*, translated and edited by Lucy L. Wenhold, Smithsonian Miscellaneous Collections (Washington, D.C.: Smithsonian Institution, 1936), 95 (16), 12–14.

52. "Memorial to the King Our Lord and His Royal and Supreme Council of the Indies, 1700?" in Hann, "Translation of the Ecija Voyages," 199–200.

53. "Report on the Indians of Southern Florida and Its Keys by Joseph Maria Monaco and Joseph Javier Alana presented to Governor Juan Francisco de Güemes y Horcasitas, 1760," in Hann, *Missions*, 424–425, 430–431.

54. Garcilaso, *The Florida of the Inca*, book 2, chap. 27, 2:157–158.

55. "Discours de l'histoire de la Floride, 1566," in Quinn, *New American World*, 2:374.

56. "Of the Adelantado's Departure from Guale to San Mateo and St. Augustine," in Barrientos, *Pedro Menéndez*, 107.

57. The Franciscans of Florida to Phillip III, 16 October 1612, in Quinn, *New American World*, 5:138–140.

58. Comparable situations emerged in other areas colonized by the Spanish. See Miguel Leon-Portilla, *Endangered Cultures*, translated by Julie Goodson-Lawes (Dallas, Tex.: Southern Methodist University Press, 1990), 55–64, 81–83.

59. Father Juan Rogel to Father Didacus Avellaneda, November 1566 to January 1567, in Hann, *Missions*, 280–281.

60. Father Juan Rogel to Father Jerónimo Ruiz del Portillo, 25 April, 1568, in Hann, *Missions*, 239.

61. Father Juan Rogel to Father Didacus Avellaneda, November 1566 to January 1567, in Hann, *Missions*, 280–281.

62. Father Juan Rogel to Father Jerónimo Ruiz del Portillo, 25 April 1568, in Hann, *Missions*, 239.

63. Thomas, *Spanish Borderlands Sourcebooks*, 70.

64. James W. Covington and A. F. Falcones, eds., *Pirates, Indians, and Spaniard: Father Escobedo's "La Florida"* (St. Petersburg, Fla.: Great Outdoors, 1963), 22, 28.

65. Pedro Menéndez de Avilés to a Jesuit, 15 October 1566, in Quinn, *New American World*, 2:536–537.

66. "Letters from the Licenciado Gonzalo de Esquivel to Cardinal Espinosa about the Florida Mission of the Jesuit Order," in Lyon, *Pedro Menéndez*, 411.

67. Thomas, *Spanish Borderlands Sourcebooks*, 91–92.

68. Hernando D'Escalante Fontaneda, *Memoir of D'Escalante Fontaneda Respecting Florida, Written in Spain About the Year 1575*, edited by David O. True, translated by Buckingham Smith (Coral Gables, Fla.: University of Miami Press, 1944), 17.

69. D'Escalante Fontaneda, *Memoir*, 21.

70. "Inquiry by Gonzalo Méndez de Canzo into the Indian Uprising of 1597 and His Actions in Regard to the Indians Who Took Part in It, 7 October 1597 to 12 January 1598," in Quinn, *New American World*, 2:85–86.

71. "Bartolomé de Argüelles' Reports to the King and to the Council of the Indies on the Situation in Florida, 3 August 1598," in Quinn, *New American World*, 2:90.

72. Patron Letter from Fray Francisco Parga of the San Franciscan Order to the King, 1600, in Brooks, *The Unwritten History of St. Augustine*, 49.

73. The Franciscans of Florida to Philip III, 16 October 1612, in Quinn, *New American World*, 5:138–140.

74. "Council of the Indies, 15 June 1657," in Hann, "Translation of the Ecija Voyages," 133–134.

75. Governor Diego de Quiroga y Losada to the King, 1 April 1688, in Hann, *Missions*, 79–80.

76. Diego Ebelino de Compostela, Bishop of Santiago de Cuba, to the King, 10 February 1689, in Hann, *Missions*, 7976.

77. Milanich, *Laboring in the Fields*, 168.

78. "Testimony about the Calusa Mission's Failure, 1698; Notes by the Council of the Indies, 8 August 1698," in Hann, *Missions*, 165–167, 209–210.

79. Governor Laureano de Torres y Ayala to the King, 3 February 1697, in Hann, *Missions*, 144.

80. "Notes by the Council of the Indies, 8 August 1698," in Hann, *Missions*, 210–211.

81. "Memorial to the King Our Lord and His Royal and Supreme Council of the Indies, 1700?" in Hann, "Translation of the Ecija Voyages," 177–178.

82. Fray Joseph de Bullones to the King, 5 October 1728, in Hann, *Missions*, 374–375.

83. "Report on the Indians of Southern Florida and Its Keys by Joseph María Monaco and Joseph Javier Alaña presented to Governor Juan Francisco de Güemes y Horcasitas, 1760," in Hann, *Missions*, 424–425, 430–431.

84. "Report on the Indians of Southern Florida and Its Keys by Joseph María Monaco and Joseph Javier Alaña presented to Governor Juan Francisco de Güemes y Horacasitas," 1760, in Hann, *Missions*, 422–424, 427.

2

The Jew in the Haitian Imagination: A Popular History of Anti-Judaism and Proto-Racism

Elizabeth McAlister

Each year in Haiti, the Holy Week of Easter sets the stage for carnivalesque street theater all throughout the country. While Catholics reenact the Passion of Christ, some practitioners of the Afro-Haitian religion called Vodou take to the streets in enormous musical parades called Raras. There they conduct the spiritual warfare that becomes possible when the angels and saints remove to the underworld, along with Jesus, on Good Friday. The cast of characters who have a hand in the week's events include the deities of Vodou, the *zonbi* (spirits of the recently dead), as well as Jesus, the two thieves crucified with him, a couple of Haitian army officers who secretly witnessed the resurrection, Pontius Pilate and the Romans, Judas, and "the Jews." The week's events combine the plots and personae of the Christian narrative with the cosmology of Afro-Creole religion, and perform them in local ritual dramas. Throughout the week, Haitians perform rituals generated from various moments in the history of the Atlantic world, from the European Christian Middle Ages to the contemporary racialized Americas.

The most boisterous of all the performances, the Rara festival begins right after Carnival, on Ash Wednesday, and builds throughout Lent until Easter weekend. Occurring in multiple localities, Rara represents the largest popular gatherings of Haitian *pèp-la* (the people, the folk). Groups numbering from fifteen to several thousand people play drums and bamboo horns, dance along the roads, and stop traffic for miles in order to perform rituals for Vodou deities at crossroads, bridges, and cemeteries. Rara can be read as an annual ritual period when the religious work of Vodou is taken into public space. In this sense, Rara is a peripheral branch of this Afro-Haitian religion—a fluid, inherited, oral tradition of relationships with deities from various African societies, as well as relationships with ancestors.

Rara festivals remember the religious and racial history of American conquest. Said by some Haitians to be "an Indian festival," the Raras provide a fleeting yearly remembrance of the 250,000 Tainos who died in the first two years after Christopher Columbus's fateful 1492 arrival in Haiti, known as Aiyti-Kiskeya, the "mountainous land."[1] But this is only the first of many fragmented historical memories. The Raras also recall and activate religious principles from the African kingdom of Kongo that lost untold numbers to the slave trade. The festival carries Creole memories of the Americas as well. Rara parades come to their climactic finish on Easter Week precisely because Holy Week was mandated (in 1685, under the Code Noir) to provide a respite from labor for enslaved Africans of the colony. Undergirding all of these memories are rituals and references from the Spanish Inquisition. Families and villages make straw dummies of a "Jew" (who is sometimes the apostle "Judas") and drag him through the streets, beat him, and finally burn this "Jew" in effigy. Yet at the same time, Rara bands also enact the role of "the Jews" as they were portrayed in the Gospels and celebrate the crucifixion with music and dance.

This essay explores these images of "Jews" in Haitian Rara in order to illustrate a broader argument: that race is inextricably bound together with religion, especially in the nascent phases of racial discourse in Europe, but also in lasting examples in the contemporary Americas. It is possible to discern historical connections between religious and racial thought at the start of American history by unpacking these seemingly obscure, ongoing religious dramas in Haiti. This case suggests that anti-Black racism in the Americas—like modern anti-Semitism—had its genesis in the anti-Judaism of medieval Europe.[2]

The seeds of both white supremecy and anti-Semitism lay in medieval European Christianity, particularly in the religious thought of the Spanish Inquisition. Inquisition mythology and practices would be transported to the Americas, and serve as a blueprint for the structures of racialization that would develop so tragically there.

The first agent of such thought in the Americas was Christopher Columbus himself. After all, Columbus and the early colonists were products of the religious worldview of the late Middle Ages, when the Inquisition was in full force. In a telling coincidence of history, Columbus set sail for what he would call the *outro mondo* (other world) in August 1492, only three days after the final departure of the Jews from Spain.[3] This was the era during which Spain expelled its entire Jewish population, and the Inquisition reserved special tribunals for any *anusim*, or *conversos*, converted Jews, who were suspected of "Judaizing."[4]

"The Jews," as Sander Gilman argues, were the original "Other" of Europe, the very first object of projection, marginalization, and demonization for Christendom.[5] Flexible popular tropes about "the Jews" hinged on the figure of the devil and linked the devil with "the Jews."[6] And the imaginary initially reserved for European "demonic" Jews was portable and easily transferred onto the Native peoples and Africans in the Americas.[7] I argue here that many of the negative images of Africans in the colonial Americas draw from and elaborate medieval European images of Jews. Europe's demonization of the Jews became a mythological blueprint for the encounter with Native peoples and Africans in the Americas. The ideologies and practices that developed in this encounter ultimately became a full-blown system of race and process of racialization. We can thus discern a process of domination that married Christianization and anti-Semitism to the formation of racialized capitalist expansion in the Americas.

But the subjects of Othering tell their own stories, and build their own identities. The story is never simply about a one-directional process of demonizing a conquered people. So this essay is also about the agency of the disenfranchised, in their expressions, reactions, and representations. It looks at how some in the African diaspora have inherited, used, and manipulated European Christian anti-Judaism to contest their class position in a racialized society. In contemporary Haiti, local dramas represent the symbolic presence of Judas and of "the Jews" in complicated and ambiguous ways. In the course of Easter week, "Jews" are demonized and burned in effigy by some—but they are also honored and claimed by others as forefathers and founders of the Rara bands. Various Rara leaders embrace the identity of "the Jew" and claim a sort of mystical Jewish ancestry. In accepting the label of "Jew," these Rara leaders take on a mantle of denigration as a kind of psychic and social resistance. In carving out a symbolic territory as "Jews," these Black Haitians symbolically oppose the powers that historically have sought to exploit them—the mulatto Haitian Catholic elite. Myths, by their nature, create imminent and shifting imaginaries, not easily controlled by orthodoxy. Exploited peoples embraced the image of "the Jew" and creatively perform oppositional dramas in which they critique the morality of Christianity and their own place in a racialized class structure.

The Intersections of Religion, Race, Nation, and Class in Haiti

It has long been routine to speak of Haiti as being a "divided society" consisting of two major classes: the rural Black "peasants" and the French-identified mulatto urban "elite." This cliché oversimplifies a complex historical process and the resulting heterogeneities of the various class actors in that country. It *does*, however, refer to a stark divide in Haitian society between a politically and economically enfranchised minority and a disenfranchised, exploited majority. But class by itself is not the only dynamic at work in creating this divide. Class is articulated together with gender, race, and religion. Religious affiliation with Catholicism or Vodou, as well as phenotype and complexion color, with all their racial connotations, are part of the articulation of class position.

The roots of Haitian inequality began in colonial plantation slavery, under European, Christian, and capitalist dominance. Independence in 1804 overthrew France and slavery but ushered in devastating economic policies. Agricultural goods produced with the simplest technology by a growing peasantry were and still are taxed at customs houses and provide the bulk of government revenues. This basic scenario of an overtaxed, unrepresented, nonliterate peasantry exploited by an urban bourgeoisie remains unchanged to the current time.[8]

Social patterns in Haiti are typical of other postcolonial societies, where social status is refracted through class, lineage, color, gender, religion, literacy, and language. The educated urban population—historically called "the mulatto elite"—typically has been French-speaking, Catholic, and with lighter complexions and has carried a sense of aristocracy, or consciousness of old family lineage. Meanwhile, the peasantry is overwhelmingly made up of relatively dark-complexioned people of African descent who are nonliterate, speak Creole, and tend to affiliate with the Afro-Creole religion of Haiti called Vodou. This simple picture must be elaborated by the many gradations of status within these groups.[9]

But social thought about race, color, and nationalism in Haiti complicates this scheme. We must keep in mind that race is a form of fluid and changing thought that understands inconsequential physical differences between peoples to be innate and unchangeable and attaches these differences to intellectual or moral capacity. Europeans' ideologies of race and white supremacy were gaining dominance in the early nineteenth century, just as Haitians revolted against France and abolished slavery. Consequently, Haitians have broadly shared a national identity that has viewed Haiti as a symbol of the redemption of the "Black race." In speaking about Haiti in an international context, Haitian nationalists have long underscored Haiti as the first Black nation to fight white supremacy, where the descendants of Black Africans united together with the descendants of mulatto freed people to form a racially Black nation.[10]

Yet, paradoxically, as social actors inside Haiti's borders, Haitians inhabit an elaborate status hierarchy coinciding with color and phenotype distinctions that were formed in the colonial era. Such a racialized understanding of difference can operate just as easily within "all-Black" nations like Haiti as in white-majority societies elsewhere. So, as David Nicholls notes, "as ethnic solidarity on the basis of race declined in Haiti, ethnic divisions based on color assumed a new importance."[11] In their nationalism, then, Haitians have historically identified as racially "Black." Yet at the same time, Haitians reproduced racial hierarchies based on color and class that, like race, took visible difference, education, and religious affiliation and debated whether they were signs of unbridgable difference.

Much Haitian intellectual thought has argued for the equality of all the races and consequently for the equality and dignity of the Blacks and the peasantry. However, forces of foreign investment and drastic economic disparity have continued to divide Haitian society.[12] The enfranchised classes denied the peasantry political representation, economic resources, and education, using arguments that often replicated the racist anti-Black arguments in other parts of the hemisphere. The historically mulatto classes understood their own French lineage to result in greater intelligence and refinement. Some argued that the Black peasantry shared only "African blood" and that its unbridgeable, innate inferiority held the peasantry back from development. Yet Haitian nationalism insisted on a shared "Haitian blood" when speaking as national subjects.[13] These contradictions have remained salient throughout Haitian history, and the Haitian public sphere has continuously debated diverse positions on race, Blackness, religion, development, language, and education.

Now, the peasantry and urban poor are not unlike other peoples of the so-called developing world, and they occupy a local structural position embedded in the postmodern context of racialized global capital. The Haitian nation-state is a virtually powerless entity on the international stage, and the peasantry and urban poor are caught in a system that constitutes them as the lowest link in a globalized capitalism.[14] The majority of these classes are affiliated with Vodou, and they make up the majority of Rara participants.

These social divisions also follow racialized *religious* cleavages. In Haitian cultural politics, Catholicism has positioned itself against Vodou as an official, European, legitimate, orthodox tradition associated with civilizing power and authority. Vodou occupies an oppositional space that is creole, home-grown, racially Black, unorthodox, diverse, and by extension illegitimate, impure, evil, and satanic. Politically, then, the two traditions have been constructed as polar opposites. The Lenten period becomes an interesting and tense time when Catholic and Vodou practices clash.

Given the drastic disparity of wealth in Haiti, the appearance of thousands of peasant-class people in public space is inherently a deeply charged moment, considered dangerous both culturally and politically by dominant groups. For members of the educated enfranchised classes, hundreds of noisy people celebrating in the streets conjure up nightmarish fantasies about mass popular uprising. As a large-scale popular festival, Rara is structurally oppositional to

FIGURE 2.1. A Rara *kolonel* and his horn players pause for a photo. Artibonite Valley, 1993. Photograph by Elizabeth McAlister.

the dominant classes who make up the Haitian enfranchised minority: the literate, monied classes, in their various aspects, who have historically depended on the Haitian army and United States support to maintain power.

Bwile Jwif: "Burning the Jew" in Effigy

It was Holy Thursday night, and my research team and I were out recording and filming a Rara band in the narrow back streets of Port-au-Prince. We were dancing along down the dark hilly streets at a good clip, on our way to a small cemetery to try to get some zonbi to *chofe* ("heat up") the band for the season's climax on Easter. We stopped while the band paid a musical salute to the invisible guardian of the cemetery gates in Vodou. I looked up and noticed a straw dummy sitting on the roof of the house across the street. It was a "Jew."

He was sitting in a chair in the open air, on top of this one-story tin-roofed house. Made of straw and dressed in blue jeans, a shirt, suit jacket, and sneakers, this "Jew" wore a tie and had a pen sticking out of his shirt pocket. His legs were crossed, and over them sat what looked to be a laptop computer fashioned out of cardboard. A cord seemed to run from the computer down into a briefcase that sat by his chair.

I asked around for the mèt Jwif-la, its owner. An older man missing a few teeth came forward, offering a callused, muscular handshake that revealed a life of hard

FIGURE 2.2. Effigy of a "Jew" waiting to be burned in a Port-au-Prince neighborhood, 1993. Photograph by Elizabeth McAlister.

physical labor. He was from the countryside in the south of the island, a migrant to Port-au-Prince. I found myself in the ridiculous position of having to compliment him on his work. "Nice Jew you've got there," I said ("Ou gen yon bèl Jwif la, wi"). "Oh yes, we leave it up for the Rara band to pass by. Tomorrow afternoon we'll burn it," he said. "Aha . . . well . . . great . . ." said my research partners and I, flaring our eyes at each other. I guess nobody told the guy that Jean-Claude Duvalier banned the practice in the 1970s, around the time of a rush of tourism and foreign industrial investment. I bet other people still do it, here and there.

The Easter ritual of burning "the Jew" or burning "Judas" in effigy was practiced until recently by all classes in Haiti. There were many local variations, but usually by Maundy Thursday an effigy was erected in some central location, and at three o-clock on Good Friday it was burned by the local community.[15] This was done in a ritual retaliation against Judas, who betrayed Jesus, or against "the Jews" who "killed Jesus."

Local peasant communities enacted this carnivalesque theater, and so did wealthy plantation households. Thérèse Roumer, a writer from the provincial city of Jérémie, remembered the "Juifs errants," the "wandering Jews" of her childhood. Her father owned expansive tracts of land in the region and maintained a large family home. A "Jew" was erected at the beginning of Lent. He had stuffed pants and shirt, with a pillow for a head, and he sat in a chair on the veranda by the front door. The idea, said Madame Roumer, was to kick the

Jew whenever you went in or out of the door, "say any bad words you had," and scold him for killing Jesus. On the Saturday morning before Easter, all of the children from town would find wooden sticks, come to the house to beat him, and burn him up in a bonfire.[16] Children were exhorted by the grownups to "pray for the conversion of the Jews."[17] The family would then go off to church for some holy water and wash down the verandah.[18]

Most people I interviewed remembered that the Jew in effigy was part of a child's game, in which the "Jew" represented Judas himself and was hidden by the adults in the neighborhood. William Seabrook, whose book *The Magic Island* has sustained many critical blows since its publication in 1929, wrote this tongue-in-cheek account, worth reproducing in its entirety.

On the last bright Easter morning which I spent in Port-au-Prince—this was only a year ago—the Champs de Mars, a fashionable park adjacent to the presidential palace and new government buildings, resembled an untidied battlefield on which scenes of wholesale carnage had been recently enacted.

It was impossible to drive through it without swerving to avoid mangled torsos; it was impossible to stroll through it without stepping aside to avoid arms, legs, heads, and other detached fragments of human anatomies.

It was impossible also to refrain from smiling, for these mangled remains were not gory; they exuded nothing more dreadful than sawdust, straw and cotton batting. They were, in fact, life-sized effigies of Judas and Pontius Pilate's soldiers—done to death annually by naive mobs bent on avenging at this somewhat late day an event which occurred in Palestine during the reign of Tiberius. . . .

I had made the acquaintance, so to speak, of one Judas before he betrayed our Lord and fled to the woods. All the little community had contributed toward his construction. He sat propped in a chair outside the doorway. They had stuffed an old coat, a shirt, and a long pair of trousers with straw, fastened old shoes and cotton gloves, also stuffed, to the legs and arms, and had made ingeniously a head of cloth, stuffed with rags, with the face painted on it and a pipe stuck in its mouth. They introduced me to this creature very politely. They were rather proud of him. He was Monsieur Judas, and I was expected to shake hands with him. You see—or perhaps you will not see unless you can recall the transcendental logic which controlled the make-believe games you used to play in childhood—that Judas had *not yet* betrayed Jesus. He was, therefore, an honored guest in their house, as Peter or Paul might have been.

And so their righteous wrath will be all the more justified when they learn on Saturday morning that Judas has turned traitor. Then it is that all the neighbors, armed and shouting, the men with ma-chetes and *cocomacaque* bludgeons, the women with knives, even more bloodthirsty in their vociferations, invade the habitation where Judas has been a guest, demanding, *"Qui bo' li?"* (Where is the trai-tor hiding?)

Under the bed they peer, if there is a bed; behind doors, in clos-ets—I happened to witness this ceremony in a city suburb, where they do have beds and closets—while members of the household aid in the search and make excited suggestions. But nowhere can Judas be found. It seems that he has fled. (What has really occurred is that the head of the house has carried him off during the night and hid-den him, usually in some jungle ravine or thicket close on the city's edge. Judas usually takes to the forest as any man would, fleeing for his life. But this is not always predictable. A Judas has been known to hide in a boat, in a public garage yard, even under the bandstand in that Champs de Mars whither so many of them, wherever found, are dragged for execution.)

So tracking Judas becomes a really exciting game. A group col-lects, shouting, beating drums, marching in the streets, racing up side-alleys; meeting other groups, each intent on finding the Judas planted by its own neighborhood, but nothing loath to find some other Judas and rend him to pieces *en passant*. Crowds may be heard also crashing and beating through the jungle hillsides. It is rather like an Easter-egg hunt on a huge and somewhat mad scale.[19]

Other cultures practice the tradition of burning Judas in effigy at Easter week, notably in Mexico and other parts of Latin America.[20] The practice prob-ably stems from the liturgical dramas, or "evangelizing rituals," produced by early Jesuit missionaries. The Jesuits are known to have staged elaborate dra-mas in the communities where they worked, playing out scenes from Jesus' life.[21] Passion plays spread the idea of Jews as "Christ-killers." According to this ritual logic, Judas, who betrayed Jesus, is conflated with "the Jews" who "mistreated Jesus," making all Jews into "Judases."[22] The role that the Jews supposedly played in the crucifixion, as described in the New Testament, em-bellished in legend, and portrayed on the stage, was familiar to both cleric and layman. It was a logical starting point for moral teaching.

The idea that "the Jews killed Jesus" is rooted, of course, in the New Tes-tament, which can be read as a polemic that displays the anti-Judaism of the early Church. Sander Gilman has argued that the negative image of difference of the Jew found in the Gospels (and especially, we might note, the figure of Judas) became the central referent for all definitions of difference in the West.[23] During the medieval period, European Christianity produced the image of "the demonic Jew," an inhuman creature working directly for Satan. Joshua Trachtenberg writes in his classic work *The Devil and the Jews* that "the two inexorable enemies of Jesus, then, in Christian legend, were the devil and the Jew, and it was inevitable that the legend should establish a causal relation between them."[24] By the medieval period, the devil was cast as the master of the Jews, directing them in a diabolical plot to destroy Christendom.

In the medieval Passion plays that set the tone for the popular Christianity of Christopher Columbus's Europe and the colonial Jesuit missions, the Jews are handed the entire weight of blame for Jesus' death, and Pontius Pilate and the Roman participants in the narrative fade into the background.[25] Medieval European Mystery plays were popular liturgical dramas, reenacting various scenes from scripture. They grew into village festivals performed in market-places and guildhalls, taking on the "secular, boisterous, disorderly and exu-berant life of the folk."[26] In *Le Mystère de la Passion,* a fourteenth-century French play depicting the crucifixion, the Jews are the villains of the piece, egged on by devils. In the climax, the devils instigate Judas to betray his master and howl with glee when they are successful.[27] The idea of Jews as demonic "Christ-killers" was elaborated throughout the medieval period, forming a central theme of the anti-Judaism that authorized the persecution of Jews during the Inquisition.

The clergy of Spanish Hispaniola, like the French that followed them, were few in number and faced the overwhelming project of planting and maintain-ing Christianity. It is likely that the island's Jesuit, Dominican, and Franciscan missionaries made use of the theatrical tactics deployed by their colleagues in New Spain to convert the Native Americans. In that colony, large-scale popular dramas were modeled after the Mystery plays of Spain and France, depicting the winners and losers in the Christian story and making clear parallels to the colonists and the conquered. Judas, "the Jews," Jesus, and the apostles made for a cast of characters that would illustrate the larger drama of power relations at the start of the colonial enterprise.[28] The Christian story and theatrical public rituals generated narratives that were meant to authorize and display the tech-nologies—chains and whips—of servitude. European Christendom dramati-cally performed itself as a sole civilizing force, against the barbaric and de-monic forces of Jews, Native Indians, and Africans.[29]

The historical antecedents of the Haitian *bwile jwif* ("Jew burning") rituals may well be in these sorts of Passion Plays that referenced the events of the Spanish Inquisition. In the late fifteenth and sixteenth centuries—as the Span-ish were establishing the slave trade to the colonies—conversos believed to have secretly practiced Judaism were sentenced to be burned alive in Spain. Conversos in hiding were sentenced in absentia and burned in effigy.[30] These auto-da-fé practices were probably the model on which the Latin American rituals are based. Although the Inquisition was never organized in Hispaniola, the Easter effigy burnings are most probably rooted in Inquisition symbolism and its attendant public ritual terror.[31]

Anti-Jewish sentiment was an implicit part of the ruling process of the French colony of Saint-Domingue. The church itself was among the largest of the slave-owning landholders in the colony, and it won an advantage with the establishment of the Code Noir.[32] This edict by King Louis XIV mandated the planter class to baptize and Christianize the slaves, just as it simultaneously outlawed the exercise of any religion other than Catholicism. The Jesuits, working as an order before the official establishment of their mission in 1704, manifested a marked dislike of Jews and their religion. In 1669 they appealed to the Crown representative to take actions against "tavern keepers, undesirable women and Jews."[33] In 1683 the Church induced King Louis XIV to expel all Jews from the colony and to impose a religious test on new immigrants.[34]

It would have been only logical, then, for the colonial clergy to take the image of the Jews as an evil, anti-Christian force and hold them up in comparison with early forms of Vodou—the real threat to Christianity in the colony. Although the Christianization of the Africans in colonial Saint Domingue was a halfhearted and badly organized enterprise, enslaved people were mandated by the Code Noir to be baptized, and they sporadically attended Mass, married, and were directed in catechism.[35] In their efforts to control the enslaved, the clergy preached Paul's letters to the Ephesians and other biblical passages exhorting slaves to obey their masters. Most of their practical worries revolved around the "superstition" of the Africans, their magical abilities, and their knowledge of poison, for greater than the fear of diabolism was the more imminent threat of uprising and rebellion. Numerous regulations were passed in the colonial period and after making various religious and magical practices illegal.

Underlying anti-Vodou sentiment was the notion that Africans, like the Jews before them, were acting in consort with the devil. And in both cases, European Christians debated whether Jews and Africans were even capable of true conversion and thus capable of entering the Church—and society—as equals. Under the Spanish doctrine of *limpieza de sangre* (purity of blood), even converted Jews were tainted with "impure blood." This religious doctrine marked and excluded an ethnic population on the basis of supposedly unbridgeable differences that could not be converted or assimilated. It was a defining moment of religious racism, or protoracism. By the fifteenth and sixteenth centuries, European popular thought held that Jews were evil by nature—and not only because of their refusal of Christianity.[36] This racializing logic would be transferred to colonial Africans, embedded in the same popular mythology.

The litany of charges that had been leveled against Jews in medieval Europe was transferred wholesale onto the Vodouist. The list of devilish crimes attributed to European Jews was an elaborate series of evil activities aimed at destroying Christendom. Jews were accused of a range of magical crimes, from superstition, sorcery, and desecration of the host all the way to ritual murder, the drinking of Christian blood, the eating of human flesh, and poisonings.[37] It is striking that this list was replicated in the colony, targeting Africans and Creoles of Saint Domingue. Like the Jews, the Africans were subjects of a religious protoracism, since even the Christians among them were under suspician for being "of African blood."

Like the converted Jews constantly under suspicion of "Judaizing," African converts to Christianity were suspected of sorcery. Joan Dayan writes of the eighteenth-century San Domingue that "it seemed as if the more Christian you claimed to be, the more certainly you could be accused of conniving with the devil."[38]A decree passed in 1761 complained that slaves' religious meetings at night in churches and catechizing in houses and plantations were actually veiled opportunities for prostitution and *marronage*. Slaves who had taken on roles of "cantors, vergers, churchwardens, and preachers" were charged with "contamination" of sacred relics with "idolatrous" intentions.[39] Africans asked to be baptized over and over, believing in the mystical properties of the rite.[40]

The legal codes of the colony, from then till now, have criminalized numerous practices known as "sorcery," linking the devil with the Africans and Creoles. A decree passed in 1758, for example, prohibited the use of "*garde-corps* or *makandals*."[41] Still in use today as *pwen* (lit: "points"), these "body-guards" were objects infused with spiritual force, directed to protect their wearers. Makandal was also the name of the famous Maroon leader in the Haitian revolution. An adept botanist as well as a revolutionary, Makandal was convicted of instigating a campaign of poisoning planters' wells in 1757, during which more than six thousand Whites were poisoned.[42] Besides being labeled superstitious, sorcerers, poisoners, and false Christians, Africans and Creoles were accused of stealing and desecrating the host, drinking blood, and cannibalism, thus rounding out and replicating the litany of Christian charges against Jews.

However, the doctrine of limpieza de sangre was never successfully applied in San Domingue, and in fact there was a great deal of intermarriage and *mélange de sang* ("mixed blood") in the colony. George Frederickson has noted the paradox that Spain and Portugal were "in the forefront of European racism or protoracism in their discrimination against converted Jews and Muslims, but that the Iberian colonies manifested a greater acceptance of intermarriage and more fluidity of racial categories and identities than the colonies of other European nations."[43] Still, Frederickson is absolutely right that late medieval Spain is critical to the history of racism because its ideologies serve as "a kind of segue between the religious intolerance of the Middle Ages and the naturalistic racism of the modern era."[44] Emerging ideas about race remained tied to religion, with the idea that people with certain "blood" were suspect in their relationship to Christianity, their morality, and their ability to govern themselves. To see how such ideas have been elaborated in the history of the Americas, we can look at later periods in Haiti.

Satan's Slaves: Vodouists in the Catholic Imaginary

The Catholic clergy in Haiti consistently placed Africans and Creoles with "African blood" under suspicion because of their affiliation with the evolving religious system known as Vodou. The Catholic clergy quickly cast Vodou as a cult of Satan, a complex of African superstitions to be purged from the beliefs of the Haitian majority. In cycles of violent repression throughout Haitian history, Vodou practitioners have been jailed, tortured, and killed and sacred objects burned. Using the image of slavery so salient to a population once enslaved and perpetually negotiating its sovereignty, the church's antisuperstition campaigns figured Vodouists as slaves of Satan, who is himself working to contaminate and destroy Christianity. As I've shown, these images came straight from popular Inquisition-era conceptions of "the Jews." Consider this rhetoric from a Haitian catechism of the antisuperstition campaigns of the 1940s:

—Who is the principle slave of Satan?
    The principle slave of Satan is the oungan [Vodou priest].
    —Why do the oungan take the names of the angels, the saints and the dead for Satan?
    The oungan give the names angels, the saints and the dead to Satan to deceive us more easily.
    —Do we have the right to mix with the slaves of Satan?
    No, because they are evil-doers and liars like Satan.[45]

Yet in a sense, institutional Catholicism in Haiti *depended* on its opposition to Vodou, since it was the opposition of the Church to the impure and illegitimate that strengthened Catholic virtue—and authority—in Haiti. Cultural complexes that evolve in unequal relations of power take on a process similar to the culture wars between "high" and "low" culture articulated by Stallybrass and White:

a recurrent pattern emerges: the "top" attempts to reject and eliminate the "bottom" for reasons of prestige and status, only to discover, not only that it is in some way frequently dependent upon the low-Other . . . but also that the top includes that low symbolically, as a primary eroticized constituent of its own fantasy life. The result is a mobile, conflictual fusion of power, fear, and desire in the construction of subjectivity; a psychological dependence upon precisely those others which are being rigorously opposed and excluded at the social level.[46]

The trope of the Jew was used by the enfranchised classes as a fantasy "low-Other" that authorized Catholic mulatto superiority. The equation of non-

Christians with Jews gave these bourgeois Haitians one more cultural differ-ence between themselves and the nonliterate Vodouists. Besides being dark-complected, nonliterate, Creole-speaking peasants, they also were pagans and anti-Christians. Symbolically, they were Jews. And like the Jews of medieval Spain, the moral capacity of these Vodouists was debatable. Haitian Catholics came to depend, in a sense, on the trope of the Vodouist-Jew as a force to oppose and exclude, a way to define the Catholic self through a negative ref-erent. Although they shared the same "African blood," the ongoing practice of Vodou made the peasants a class—some argued, a caste—apart.[47] These dis-tinctions were both religious and quasi-racial. And at no time were (and are) these social divisions more pronounced than at Easter.

Theologically, Easter is the most important holiday in the Catholic calen-dar, celebrated in Haiti both in official church mass and popular ritual. All classes practice the reenactment of Les Chemins de la Croix, the stations of the cross, after church on Good Friday. For this Passion play, a series of ritual stations are set in place, and barefoot pilgrims, some dressed in burlap, visit each station, fasting, without water, and reciting prayers before each spot. A local man plays the role of Jesus, and other actors portray other figures in the story. The Passion play was honed as a genre in medieval Europe, and this somber drama drawn from the four Gospels is still enacted in numerous lo-cations on Good Friday all over the Christian world.

Yet at the same time that Catholics engage in these Easter rituals, Rara bands are busy parading through public thoroughfares. In fact, some Raras deliberately plan to walk past churches on Sunday to annoy the Christians. In the early 1990s, I heard a priest in Pont Sonde end mass with the admonish-ment "Don't go in the Rara," worried he might lose some parishioners to this "devil's dance." In the imaginary of the Haitian bourgeoisie, Vodouists have been cast as evil slaves in Satan's army. As anti-Christians, they became sym-bolic Jews.

"If You Go in the Rara, You Are a Jew."

A Rara band called "Ya Sezi" ("They will be surprised") walked for miles all day on the Good Friday of 1993, along the banks of the Artibonite River. They were on their way to the compound of Papa Dieupe, a wealthy landowner in the region, and also the "emperor" of a Shanpwèl society. My team and I had chosen Papa Dieupè's as the best place to be for Rara; we figured we could comfortably stay put in one place and watch the bands come to salute the "big man."

Ya Sezi's entrance was spectacular for a sleepy country day. We could hear the banbou blowing for miles, and children would run through and breathlessly an-nounce that the band was coming to salute the emperor. They came up the path, and did the ritual salutes for the Vodou spirits living in the trees in the compound, and then turned to salute Papa Dieupe's "children" in the society. Finally, after they'd played until about midnight, Papa Dieupe himself emerged from his small house and received them.

After playing music in the compound for much of the night, the group slept, and awoke early Saturday morning to play and "warm up" before they left. While the musicians played, each of the dancers (who were all women) took turns holding the whip belonging to the leader, and ran in circles through the compound. The other dancers set off in hot pursuit, their dresses streaming out behind. Papa Dieupe told me they were taking turns being Jesus, running from the "Jewish soldiers." Pilate's Roman soldiers were nowhere in evidence but rather had been collapsed into a new bloodthirsty figure of "Jewish soldiers." Comically enacting Jesus' suffering on his walk to Calvary, the Rara members were amusing themselves by taking turns portraying both Jesus and his "killers," "the Jews."[48]

Catholic Haitians make a clear connection between the exuberant celebrations of Rara on the anniversary of Jesus' death and "the Jews who killed him." A popular expressions says "If you go in the Rara, you are a Jew" ("Ou al nan Rara, se Jwif ou ye"). Even some university-educated Haitians have a vague concept that "Rara is a Jewish festival." At a fancy cocktail party in the wealthy enclave above Petionville, I was introduced to a young Haitian architect from the "mulatto elite." "Studying Rara?" he asked incredulously. "Well, you'll find that it's a Jewish thing." Pressed on how a Jewish festival could have found its way through history to be adopted by the Haitian peasantry, the man shrugged his shoulders and reached for his rum punch.

Every Rara band member I interviewed, on the other hand, remembered that Rara "came from Africa," with the slaves. This seems a clear historical fact: Rara continues and extends a number of African cultural principles, including the centrality of community enterprise, relationships with the ancestors and the deities, the use of natural sites for spiritual work, as well as the African-based drumming, call-and-response singing, and dance in public festival.

After establishing the African roots of the festival, however, Rara leaders would invariably go on to articulate the idea that Rara was linked to the Jews. Many of them cited the precise origin of Rara as the celebration of the crucifixion itself. "It was the Jews who crucified Christ who made the first Rara." One oungan explained it this way: "long ago, after they finished nailing Jesus to the cross, the soldiers who did that saw that it would be even more satisfying to put out a Rara to show that they were the winners. They put out a Rara, they made music. They were rejoicing, singing and dancing."[49]

This idea that "the Jews who crucified Christ" rejoiced and made the first Rara was expressed to me over and over by Rara members. The historical genealogy of the notion is obscured here, as is the cultural history of most dispossessed groups. Yet one returns to the Passion plays of the colonial church, modeled after the ones in medieval France, England, and Germany. The Jews are the central villains of these stories and are directed by demons and devils hovering in the background. Together the devils and the Jews convince Judas to betray his master and celebrate when they are successful. Joshua Trachtenberg describes it thus: "around the cross on which Jesus hangs the Jews whirl in a dance of abandon and joy, mocking their victim and exulting in their achievement." This explicit scenario of a crucified Christ surrounded by joyful, dancing Jews celebrating their victory seems to have made its way from the popular European imaginary to become a memory of former African slaves.[50] Another Rara president reiterates: "Rara is what they did when they crucified Jesus, on Good Friday. At that point, all the Jews were happy. They put the Rara out, they masked, they danced, they dressed in sequins, they drank their liquor and had fun."[51]

The link between Rara and "the Jews who killed Christ" was strong enough in the Haitian imagination that Rara members became Jews in their own re-memberings. A oungan told me: "it was the Jews who came with this tradition. Now it's become our tradition."[52] Another oungan provided an explanation that implicitly described how the Africans could have inherited this celebration of the ancient Hebrews. "Rara is something that comes from the Jewish nation. So, mystically speaking, Haitians are descended from Africa. The Africans always kept their mystical rites."[53] In this logic, Africans are equated with the ancient Israelites, and it is this linkage that explains how Haitians have inherited Rara from the Jews. Through Rara, these Haitians embraced the subversive identity of "the Jew" and thus see the Jews as forerunners, somehow, of their African ancestors. "The Jews" became a kindred religious and racial group.

When Rara members embrace the negative cultural category of "the Jew," the mythology they generate may be understood as a repressed people's subversion of the ruling order. This class- and race-based resistance to Catholic hegemony is a form of theatrical positioning on the part of the peasants that says "We are the Jews, the enemy of the French Catholic landowners." Like other groups that take on the negative terms ascribed to them by the powerful, Haitians take on a mantle of denigration in the face of a hostile dominant class. Just as "high culture" includes "low culture" symbolically in its self-construction, so here does the "popular culture" include the "elite" in its turn.

Vodouists' interpretations of biblical stories can be understood as creative subversions of official discourse. Like the Rastafari of Jamaica, Vodouists are adept orators and creative interpreters of myth and scripture. Every imaginative Vodou practitioner may offer a new visionary interpretation of the Bible and of history. These versions allow Vodouists and Rara members to authorize their own history while positioning themselves, for themselves, in terms of the dominant class and its religious ideology.

Jesus Christ is the subject of much theorizing on the part of Vodouists. In one myth, God created the twelve apostles just after he created the earth and the animals. The apostles were rebellious and challenged God. In punishment, God sent them to Ginen, the mythical Africa of Vodou's past and future. The apostles and their descendants became the *lwa*, while a renegade apostle who refused to go to Ginen became a sorcerer and took the name Lucifer.[54] Throughout the oral mythologies of Vodou is a clear theme of morality and a distinction between working with the Ginen spirits and working with the forces of sorcery. Usually the sorcerer is also a slave master of captured spirits and souls, and so themes of morality are bound together with philosophical issues of slavery and freedom.

One story I was told creatively posits Jesus as the first *zonbi*, or soul that has been captured and sold in order to work for its owner. This myth creatively positions Jesus and God as the innocent victims of two unscrupulous Haitian soldiers who secretly witnessed the resurrection. It was related to me by a sorcerer who confided that he knew the techniques of capturing the spirit of the recently dead (zonbi) and ordering it to work:

> "the whole reason that we are able to raise people after they die goes back to when they crucified Jesus Christ. Christ was sent by Gran Jehovah, by *Gran Mèt* [lit.: "Great Master"]. He also sent Mary Magdalene. Along with two bodyguards for Jesus from the Haitian Armed Forces. When Jehovah gave the password to raise up Jesus from the dead, the soldiers stole the password, and sold it. It's been handed down from father to son, which is how I could get it."[55]

Vodou takes what it can use theologically and constantly re-creates itself with fresh material. The Vodouist fits biblical figures into an already existing Afro-Creole scheme. Jesus is problematic for the Vodouist: the heavy catholicizing of the French and later, the Haitian elite, makes him the god of the dominant classes. This story subtly acknowledges the teller's opposition to Christianity: a worker (a Haitian foot soldier) stole something from Jesus (the god of the whites and elite). The stolen knowledge now becomes a tool for the subordinates, since it is Vodouists who now control the resurrection secrets of God. This tale illustrates how the Vodouist uses oppositional mythology as one of the ongoing weapons in everyday Haitian class and color warfare.

Rara leaders I interviewed accepted the Catholic label of *pagan, African, satanist,* and *Jew* and theorized their position in a specific Vodou theology. This view agrees that Rara is anti-Christian. As one leader explained, "Rara is basically against the power of God. Because Rara is what they did when they crucified Jesus, on Good Friday."[56]

Conclusion

Rara may be "against the power of God." But on some level God has abandoned poor Black Haitians. The president of Rara Mande Gran Moun in Léogane explained: "God made the King Lucifer. God commands the sky, and the King Lucifer commands the earth. Everybody who is poor on this earth is in hell."[57] In this interpretation, God rules the heavens but has given Lucifer control over the earth, so humans—especially the poor—are actually the political subjects of King Lucifer. In the face of a class structure divided by access to the means of production but marked, in many ways, by color and religious affiliation, the response of the Vodouist is to embrace and creatively rework the identity given them by Catholics. Commenting directly on the suffering generated by extreme economic exploitation, the figure of Lucifer stands as a kind of moral commentary on the state of Haitian government and its history of class and color inequality.

Rara leaders construct theology through the appropriation of "high" cultural elements into allegories of empowerment. The stories of the "Jewish Rara" and the "zonbi Christ" construct a sort of engagement with the texts of the Catholic mulatto classes in which the power of the Vodouists or Rara members is hidden inside the images of demonization. Haitian sorcerers construct themselves as active enemies of the Catholic order, as Jews, or as allies of thieves who stole from God. The narratives support Hurbon's statement that "in the eyes of the Voodooist, his mysticism is his power. Thus it may be correct to say that the Voodoo cult, since its inception with a creole coloration, is used by Voodoo believers as a power base from which to deal with the power elite."[58]

These myths can be seen as antihegemonic counternarratives that reconfigure histories and genealogies to cast power with the Black peasantry. In Haiti, and many other repressive contexts, cultural expression generates double-voiced, allegorical strategies so that the dominant culture is turned back on itself, transformed by the subordinate. The myths generated and performed in Rara reveal how "high" Catholic culture and the "low" Vodou culture are constructed in relation to one another, each mystically exoticizing the other in the ongoing performance of class and color in Haitian society. Each end of the class spectrum reaches for the figure of "the Jew" to authorize its own power in the religious imaginary of Haitian class and color warfare.

NOTES

This chapter is indebted to many. First and foremost to my friend and constant interlocutor Robin Nagle at New York University; also to Jeremy Zwelling and my colleagues in the Religion Department at Wesleyan University; to Betsy Traube and the Wesleyan Center for the Humanities; and to Deborah Dash Moore, and the Pew Young Scholars in American Religion: Ava Chamberlain, Tracy Fessenden, Kate Joyce, Laura Levitt, Leonard Norman Primiano, and Jennifer Rycenga. Thanks also to Al Raboteau and the Northeastern Seminar on Black Religions at Princeton University, and to Phyllis Mack and the Rutgers Center for Historical Analysis. Thanks also to Jon Butler, Leslie Desmangles, Joel Dreyfuss, Henry Goldschmidt, Leon-François Hoffmann, Glen Ingram, Alan Nathanson, and Judith Weisenfeld. Thanks also to my research partners, Chantal Regnault, Phenel Colastin, Blanc Bazle, Bob Corbett, and his many Haiti listserve members. And finally to my partner in this research and in life, Holly Nicolas.

1. Bartolome de las Casas, *History of the Indies* (New York: Harper and Row, 1971), cited in Catherine Keller, "The Breast, the Apocalypse, and the Colonial Journey," in *The Year 2000: Essays on the End*, edited by Charles B. Strozier and Michael Flynn (New York: New York University Press, 1997), 42–58. Haiti has had various name changes: The Amerindian "Aiyti–Kiskeya" was changed by Columbus to Hispaniola, "Little Spain." Later, in 1697, the French named their colony Saint Domingue, and in 1804, newly independent slaves and people of color returned the land to its original name of Haiti.

2. This is also argued with much more historical breadth in the new work by George M. Fredrickson, *Racism: A Short History* (Princeton: Princeton University Press), 2002.

3. Ronald Sanders, *Lost Tribes and Promised Lands: The Origins of American Racism* (1978; New York: Harper Perennial), 1992, 90.

4. Cecil Roth, *A History of the Marranos* (Philadalphia: Jewish Publication Society of America, 1932). *Anusim*, Hebrew for "forced ones," has now replaced the English "Crypto-Jews" or the Spanish *conversos*, or "converted Jews," and the more derogatory *marranos*, or "swine," in Jewish Studies literature. See also David M. Gitlitz, *Secrecy and Deceit: The Religion of the Crypto-Jews.* (Philadelphia: Jewish Publication Society, 1996).

5. Sander Gilman, *The Jew's Body* (New York: Routledge, 1991).

6. Joshua Trachtenberg, *The Devil and the Jews: the Medieval Conception of the Jew and Its Relation to Modern Antisemitism* (1943; reprint, New York: Harper Torchbooks, 1966), 20.

7. See Fernando Cervantes, *The Devil in the New World: The Impact of Diabolism in New Spain* (New Haven: Yale University Press, 1994), for work on the ways Christendom linked the Jews, the devil, and native peoples in New Spain.

8. Linda Basch, Nina Glick Schiller, and Cristina Szanton Blanc, *Nations Unbound: Transnational Projects, Postcolonial Predicaments and Deterritorialized Nation-States* (Langhorne, Pa: Gordon and Breach, 1994), 159.

9. It is important to note that using "light" and "dark" terminology for complexion color is problematic, since a moral valence is attached to the terms. "Light" connotes "truth" and "darkness" is related to sin and other negative categories; this language is embedded in Christian symbolism. "Melanin-rich" and "melanin-poor" are terms used by some scholars, yet this discourse of melanin is also problematic and politically charged.

10. Nicholls calls this "the mulatto myth" in *From Dessalines to Duvalier: Race, Colour and National Independence in Haiti* (New Brunswick, N.J.: Rutgers University Press), 1996, 100–101.

11. Nicholls, *From Dessalines to Duvalier*, 254. He goes on to note that foreign intervention in periods of Haitian history have resulted in the abatement of such color conflicts and in the development of ethnic solidarity based on race.

12. Nicholls, *From Dessalines to Duvalier*, 103.

13. Nina Glick Schiller and Georges Eugene Fouron, *Georges Woke Up Laughing:*

Long-Distance Nationalism and the Search for Home (Durham, N.C.: Duke University Press), 2001, 103.

14. Perhaps the most crucial factor in upward mobility today is access to family and resources from *lòt bò dlo* (the other side of the water)—New York, Miami, or other points in the Haitian diaspora. Haitian transmigrants send home an estimated one hundred million dollars a year to families and small businesses.

15. This is the time of Jesus' death noted in scripture.

16. Thérèse Roumer, interview, by the author. Petionville, Haiti, February 16, 1993.

17. Georges Fouron, personal communication, New Haven, Conn., November 1997.

18. Thérèse Roumer, interview, Petionville, Haiti, February 16, 1993.

19. W. B. Seabrook, *The Magic Island* (New York: Literary Guild of America, 1929), 270–272.

20. See, for example, Muriel Thayer Painter, Edward H. Spicer, and Wilma Kaemlein, eds., *With Good Heart; Yaqui Beliefs and Ceremonies in Pascua Village* (Tuscon: University of Arizona Press, 1986), and James S. Griffith, *Beliefs and Holy Places: A Spiritual Geography of the Primeria Alta* (Tuscon: University of Arizona Press, 1992), 95.

21. See Marilyn Ekdahl Ravicz, *Early Colonial Religious Drama in Mexico: From Tzompantli to Golgotha* (Washington, D.C.: Catholic University of America Press, 1970), and Richard C. Trexler, "We Think, They Act: Clerical Readings of Missionary Theatre in Sixteenth-Century New Spain," in Steven L. Kaplan, *Understanding Popular Culture: Europe from the Middle Ages to the Nineteenth Century* (New York: Mouton, 1984), 189–227.

22. In *Judas Iscariot and the Myth of Jewish Evil* (New York: Free Press, 1992), Hyam Maccoby points out the consistent use of Judas by Christian myth as a symbol for all Jews. "Of all Jesus' twelve disciples, the one whom the Gospel story singles out as traitor bears the name of the Jewish people."

23. Gilman, *The Jew's Body*, 18.

24. Trachtenberg, *The Devil and the Jews*, 20.

25. Trachtenberg, *The Devil and the Jews*, 20.

26. Painter, Spicer, and Kaemlein, *With Good Heart*, 352.

27. Trachtenberg, *The Devil and the Jews*, 22.

28. Trexler, "We Think They Act."

29. For a discussion of the conflation of British, Protestant, and civilized into one identity against Native American "heathens," see James Axtell, *The Invasion Within: The Contest of Cultures in Colonial North America* (New York: Oxford University Press, 1996).

30. See Roth, *A History of the Marranos.* The anti-Judaism taught by the Catholic clergy in Haiti bears the characteristics of a classically premodern Jew-hatred centering on the betrayal of Judas. In this logic, Jews are primarily polluters and traitors; there is little reference to the modern anti-Semitic tropes of a Jewish conspiracy of exploitation hinging on issues of capital or usury. See Gavin I. Langmuir, "From Anti-Judaism to Anti-Semitism," in *History, Religion and Antisemitism* (Berkeley: University of California Press, 1990), 275–305.

31. On the Inquisition and the Jews in Mexico, see Seymour B. Liebman, *The Jews in New Spain: Faith, Flame and the Inquisition* (Coral Gables, Fla.: University of Miami Press, 1970).

32. Carolyn E. Fick, *The Making of Haiti: The Saint Domingue Revolution from Below* (Knoxville: University of Tennessee Press, 1990), 278.

33. George Breathett, *The Catholic Church in Haiti (1704–1785): Selected Letters, Memoires and Documents* (Salisbury, N.C.: Documentation, 1982), 4.

34. Anne Grene, *The Catholic Church in Haiti: Political and Social Change* (East Lansing: Michigan State University Press, 1993), 76.

35. Debien, "La Christianisation des esclaves des Antilles francaises aux XVIIe et XVIIIe siecles," *Revue d'histoire de l'Amerique francaise* 22 (1967), 99–11.

36. Fredrickson, *Racism*, 32–33.

37. See Trachtenberg, *The Devil and the Jews*.

38. Joan Dayan, *Haiti, History and the Gods* (Berkeley: University of California Press), 1995, 252.

39. Dayan, *Haiti, History and the Gods*, 253.

40. Moreau de Saint Mery, Description topographique, physique, civile, politiqueet historique de la partie français [1797] 1958, 1:55.

41. Dayan, *Haiti, History and the Gods*, 252.

42. Dayan, *Haiti, History and the Gods*, 252.

43. Fredrickson, *Racism*, 39.

44. Fredrickson, *Racism*, 40.

45. Cited in Laënnec Hurbon, *Dieu dans le Vaudou Haïtien* (Port-au-Prince: Editions Deschamps, 1987), 21.

46. Peter Stallybrass and Allon White, *The Politics and Poetics of Transgression* (Ithaca, N.Y.: Cornell University Press, 1986), 3.

47. Nicholls, *From Dessalines to Duvalieres*, p. 201.

48. The band Ya Sezi can be heard playing in Papa Dieupe's compound on track 19a of the recording compiled by me: *Rhythms of Rapture: Sacred Musics of Haitian Vodou*, Smithsonian/Folkways Recording SF 40464, 1995.

49. Interview with Papa Mondy Jean, Port-au-Prince, April 1992.

50. A few Rara presidents told me that there was a game, a noisemaker, that the Jews held in their hands and spun at the crucifixion. This made a noise that came to be called "Rara." One notices the possible connection with the noisemakers of Purim.

51. Rara costumes are elaborately sequined in parts of Haiti. Interview with Simeon, by the author, Bel Air, Port-au-Prince, July 30, 1993.

52. Interview with Simeon, by the author, Bel Air, Port-au-Prince, March 20, 1993.

53. Interview with Simeon, by the author, Bel Air, Port-au-Prince, July 30, 1993.

54. Alfred Metraux, *Voodoo in Haiti* (1959; reprint, New York: Schocken Books, 1972), 326.

55. Interview with Papa Dieupe, by the author, Artibonite, Easter Sunday, April 11, 1993.

56. A smiliar symbolics works in Afro-Cuban religion, Lukumi. Unbaptized ritual objects and "working" charms are called *"judeo,"* "Jewish."

57. Interview with Mayard, by the author, Rara Mande Gran Moun, Leogane,

March 20, 1993. David H. Brown reports an interesting parallel in the Kongo-derived Palo Monte practices in Cuba. As he constructs a *prenda*, a "working" object, on Good Friday, a Mayombero comments to Brown, "on the day of the week, the week of the year when they are quiet—Good Friday—we are doing our thing." Says Brown, "As spiritual opposites of Christ and the Saints of Olofi and the orichas, they are "driving nails" on the day of the Crucifixion." David H. Brown, "Garden in the Machine: Afro-Cuban Sacred Art and Performance in Urban New Jersey and New York" (Ph.D. diss., Yale University, 1989), 375.

58. See Laënnec Hurbon, *Culture et Dictature en Haiti; l'imaginaire sous controle* (Paris: L'Harmattan, 1979), 133.

Constructing and Critiquing White Christianities

Throughout the Americas, from colonial contact through the present day, one of the structuring principles of racial hierarchy and identity has been the imagined—and often enough brutally enforced—superiority of "White" people, or peoples of European descent, over all others. Although the nature and boundaries of "Whiteness" have been defined in extraordinarily diverse ways in different social contexts, the sheer fact of White supremacy has run, like an open sore, through the history of the hemisphere—and indeed, through the history of the modern world.

And in many sociohistorical contexts, the superiority of White over Black (or native, or Creole, or Asian, or what-have-you) has been established, in part, through the symbolic association of Whiteness with Christianity—by grafting the developing racial hierarchies of the New World on to the longstanding religious hierarchies of the Old. White folks in the Americas have all too often attempted to lay exclusive claim to the Christian gospel and its social institutions, and thus to monopolize the promises of salvation and civilization. In the early years of colonial settlement, many Whites were reluctant to convert native Americans and enslaved Africans, fearing that spiritual equality might imply social equality. Over the course of the nineteenth and twentieth centuries most non-Whites in the Americas were ultimately converted to Christianity, but often enough conversion meant incorporation into the racialized hierarchies of White-dominated churches and communities. The hegemonic articulation of Whiteness and Christianity has thus endured despite—and at times because of—the long histories of non-White Christianities throughout the Americas.

The essays in this section explore the making and (attempted) unmaking of this White Christianity. In "A Great Racial Commission: Religion and the Construction of White America," Daniel Lee examines how Whites in the United States in the mid- to late nineteenth century forged a sense of racial and national identity around the unifying cause of evangelical Protestantism—a sense of identity strong enough, they hoped, to withstand the challenges to White supremacy posed by Black emancipation, increased immigration, and other social forces. For many White Americans of that day, Christianity provided a means to incorporate non-White others into the hierarchical order of White society. In today's Brazil, by contrast, many Afro-Brazilians and antiracist activists hope that the incorporation of non-White cultural and religious practices into Catholic doctrine and liturgy will break the link between Whiteness and Christianity and undermine the hierarchical order of White society. In "The Catholic Afro Mass and the Dance of Eurocentrism in Brazil," John Burdick examines the efforts of the progressive Catholic Church to craft an antiracist, "inculturated" Christianity. He argues, however, that these efforts have foundered on an essentialist (mis)understanding of cultural difference—an impoverished multiculturalism that reduces the rich African heritage of Brazilian society to drumbeats, distinctive clothes, and dancing bodies.

Unfortunately, then, for both Burdick and Lee, it seems that the incorporation of racial and religious difference has only strengthened the bonds between Whiteness and Christianity. Taken together, however, their essays clearly show that these bonds are the products of history and society—products of human hands that may ultimately be broken by them.

3

A Great Racial Commission: Religion and the Construction of White America

Daniel B. Lee

For the development of an enduring racial self-description, the late nineteenth century was a particularly innovative period for White people in America. The decades after the Civil War significantly changed the racial and religious landscape of the country. For the first time, Native Americans, emancipated Blacks, and new immigrants from all over the world challenged the cultural hegemony of Anglo-Saxon Christians with their undeniable presence. In the midst of an increasingly diverse population, many White Americans turned to religion as a source of racial and national unity.[1]

As an ideological instrument for constructing social identity, religion was used in a variety of ways during different periods of American history. Religion was effectively used to unify or separate people, with or without reference to racial boundaries. In the colonial era, for instance, religion differentiated Puritans, Quakers, Catholics, Mennonites, and other sects from one another. Yet religion was also used to consolidate all Christians against the "savage" Native Americans. On the plantations of the antebellum South, masters and slaves were "united in Christ." Nonetheless, racially segregated congregations developed exclusive modes of religious expression. Blacks and Whites were clearly aware that they worshiped the same God in different ways. Toward the end of the nineteenth century, White Americans rallied around their common Christianity in a desperate attempt to organize themselves against the growing population of non-Christian, non-White Americans. If people of all races were going to live together in America, then religion seemed to be the only concept that could unify the country. According to the literary historian Werner Sollors, many Whites believed that Christianity had the power to transcend descent. He quoted an article that appeared in 1833 in *American Ladies Magazine*:

> the efforts to obtain personal liberty and the influence of the Christian religion have been the chief means of perfecting the faculties of the white man.
>
> Let him then, as far as possible, plant the seeds of freedom and Christianity in the hearts of every people; and then the brown, the red, the black, and the tawny man will assimilate with each other, and with the more favored white race, till they learn to feel as well as to acknowledge, that "God hath made of one blood all nations of men."[2]

By equating the Anglo-Saxon race with Christianity and by converting non-Anglo-Saxons to Christ, White Americans hoped to make veritable Anglo-Saxons of all of the people in America.

How did "White people" in nineteenth-century America use religion to develop and articulate a socially meaningful racial identity? How was religious discourse employed by Whites to communicate alleged differences between themselves and Americans of other races? In this essay, I use a variety of late nineteenth-century texts (personal narratives, news articles, short stories, sermons, and public speeches) to illustrate how Whites used religious discourse to construct and observe themselves as a race. The majority of the texts I will cite and discuss were published in the most popular "family house magazines" of the period: the *Century*, the *Atlantic*, *Harper's*, *Scribner's*, and the *National Repository*. These magazines featured articles about the "great destiny" of the Anglo-Saxon race in America, the role of Christianity, the dangers of unassimilated immigrants, and the menace of working-class radicalism. Widely read by middle-class, educated, White Protestants, the family house magazines helped, as sociologist Matthew Schneirov argues, to "shape the thinking and tastes of a whole generation of readers."[3]

My analysis of these texts begins with the theoretical assumption that there is no natural way to be White, act White, or communicate as a White person. There is no a priori metaphysical bond or primordial solidarity between Whites or between the people of any other racial or religious group. White society first emerges when people communicate about sharing "Whiteness." Communities of people construct themselves and their others as they communicate.[4] A society, such as Whites exchanging race talk, forms itself *and* its environment in an entirely self-referential, autological manner.

Racial formation, as observed by the students of ethnic relations Michael Omi and Howard Winant, "is the process by which social, economic, and political forces determine the content and importance of racial categories, and by which they are in turn shaped by racial meanings."[5] As social, economic, and political conditions change over time, the forms of racial and religious rhetoric and observations also change. One cannot predict the future forms of racial or religious categories, the forms of inclusion and exclusion. Sollors has stressed that "the same ligament constructions that spelled consensus among Americans could also be adapted to formulate secessionist and separatist people-hoods."[6] Once a form emerges in social discourse, its meaning can be continually tweaked, tested, and applied in different situations.[7] The specific form produced by a distinction is arbitrary; it is a contingency that might be drawn differently by another observer or by the same observer at another time. The racial and religious discourse of White Americans, as found in popular literature of the late nineteenth century, was an intricately connected set of shifting, evolving distinctions.

Even though racial and religious distinctions do not exist in a fixed, objective sense, they structure our everyday interactions in a very real manner. For, as the historian Sander Gilman has asserted, "the structure of our universe is the basis of our actions in this universe. We view our own images, our own mirages, our own stereotypes as embodying qualities that exist in the world. And we act upon them."[8] Gilman continued:

> a comparative study of images, an understanding of the subtle shad-
> ings present in their codification (or, indeed, in their homogeneity),
> can bring to light differences, parallels, and patterns of action. Texts
> provide us with a rich bounty of materials upon which to base these
> observations. But the texts must not be perceived as separate from
> the world that generated them. They also give us the key to decod-
> ing courses of action based upon the presuppositions inherent in
> our mental representation of the world.[9]

White Americans in the nineteenth century were able to use religious and racial concepts to make meaningful social distinctions because the concepts were completely plastic and self-referential, having no particular objective meaning. Once racial discourse began, the meaning of concepts evolved to fit the changing psychological and social needs of White discussants. Old racial and religious distinctions collapsed into new distinctions. What was once used to divide served later to unite, and vice versa.

In the pages that follow, I emphasize how changing social conditions in America influenced the evolution of racial and religious distinctions. Successfully communicating with concepts such as "White," "Christian," or "American" depends on a flexible and creative use of language. To make sense, discussants must continually readjust and reformulate their constructions, adapting meanings to the current, but fleeting, concerns that emerge and disappear with the flow of history. The self-identity of White Christian Americans during the Victorian era was markedly different from that of the Colonial and Reconstruction periods. It changed again in response to the massive influx of immigrants before World War I. With limited attention to chronological order, I provide a colorful set of citations that demonstrate this flexibility in response to social change.

Anglo-Saxons and Others

British colonialists in the New World assumed that they shared a common racial and religious identity. America, in the words of Benjamin Franklin, was to be a "lovely white" nation reflecting its dominant Anglo-Saxon, Christian heritage.[10] In 1882, Edward Eggeleston articulated the same belief when he wrote an article entitled "The Beginning of a Nation" for the monthly magazine the *Century*:

> under every guise of sect and opinion there was present the wonder-loving, credulous, and aggressive Englishman of that age of seething religious and intellectual reaction. The mutually repellant Church-men, Puritans, Papists, and Quakers, who spread themselves into separate communities along the wilderness coast of North America in the seventeenth century, had really more in common than they had of difference.[11]

This view led many influential writers, ministers, and political leaders to voice concern about the ability of Americans to preserve their common "English-ness."

About the time of the Revolutionary War, both American and European writers began to observe that Whites in the New World were quickly evolving into a new race. Compared to Europeans, White people in America had deficient "vital capital": bad teeth, small bodies, weak constitutions, and slower working brains. With Americans in mind, the British Lord Kames suggested in 1774 that races degenerate when transplanted. Unless "continual recruits did not arrive from Europe to supply the places of those that perish," Lord Kames asserted, "the (colonies) would soon be depopulated." In 1787, the Reverend Samuel Stanhope Smith, president of the College of New Jersey, noted that the typical American's complexion no longer "exhibits so clear a red and White as the British or German."[12]

Americans began to view themselves as an emerging new race, willing to struggle to realize traditional Anglo-Saxon ideals that had lost their value in Britain. In his famous pamphlet *Common Sense*, distributed in 1776, Thomas Paine wrote that freedom "hath been given her warning to depart from England."[13] America would be the new "asylum for mankind." In 1823, the former president Thomas Jefferson said:

> America—North and South—has a set of interests distinct from those of Europe, and particularly her own. She should therefore

have a social system of her own, separate and apart from that of Europe. While the last is laboring to become the domicile of despotism, our endeavor should be to make our hemisphere that of freedom.[14]

For Ralph Waldo Emerson, the various nationalities in America would "construct a new race, a new religion, a new state, a new literature," which would be as vigorous "as the new Europe which came out of the smelting-pot of the Dark Ages."[15] In Charles Dudley Warner's opinion, America was uniquely qualified to produce an even stronger race than the "smelting-pots" of the past:

> the mingling of the races, traditions, religions, varied civilizations, which we see here, is not new in the world . . . but it is unique in this, that the field of operation is fresh, that the meeting elements represent the youth and adventure of many people, the restless spirit of aspiration, of dissatisfaction with the present, of willingness to cut loose from the past; and the moving energy of the whole is the old Teutonic passion for acquisition and achievement.[16]

The idea that White people in America had become a different race than their Anglo-Saxon cousins achieved a lasting place in the national consciousness. In 1875, an anonymous contributor to the *Atlantic Monthly* wondered, "Why are we so different from the English? Why is it that when a representative American is spoken of, nobody thinks of a creature in the least resembling an Englishman?"[17] In the same year, Oliver Wendell Holmes maintained that it is a "generally recognized fact that an American is different in physiognomical and physiological qualities, after a very few generations, from the European race that gave birth to his ancestors."

Differences between American and British people went beyond simple appearances—the two races supported alternative ideals. For instance, only the American justice system was thought to genuinely champion freedom. In his essay comparing English and American courts, Oakey Hall concluded:

> no one who is familiar with the appearance, carriage, demeanor, and address of lawyers in the United States, and who has also been an attendant upon English courts, can fail to admit and recognize the superiority in those respects of the American advocate. . . . The average American lawyer attains eloquence which is seldom reached by the English barrister. The latter is a martyr to decorum. . . . He talks as if feeling the weight of his wig upon his brain. . . . In fine, the schooling of the English bench and bar tends toward monotony and artificiality, while the schooling of the American bar tends toward freedom and naturalness in thought and speech, and to a general behavior, that is fettered only by the innate dignity of the gentleman, and plainly impressed by a high sense of duty.[19]

Assuming that they originated from common Anglo-Saxon stock, what distinctions were used to create the new race of White people in America? How did White Americans construct an independent racial identity? Isolated on its island fortress, the English race had spawned a "truly divine civilization." In 1882, Charles Dudley Warner asserted that England's superior status as a nation was due to the racial qualities of her people:

> it is a mixed race, but with certain dominant qualities, which we call, loosely, Teutonic; certainly the most aggressive, tough, and vigorous people the world had seen. . . . Here we have the two necessary traits in the character of a great people: the love and the habit of civil liberty; and religious conviction and independence. . . . Christianity stood for England and English honor and civilization.[20]

Despite its marvelous past, the "mixed" race of Britain had become tired, decadent, and unable to continue its exalted cultural mission. "It must be owned," Warner argued, "that England has pursued her magnificent career in a policy often insolent and brutal, and generally selfish. Scarcely any considerations have stood in the way of her trade and profit."[21] With the "moral corruption" of England, God turned to America to take charge of spreading civilization throughout the world. In an article entitled "Manifest Destiny," the American philosopher John Fiske exclaimed in 1885:

> the work that the English race began when it colonized North America is destined to go on until every land on the earth's surface that is not already the seat of an old civilization shall become English in its language, in its religion, in its political habits and traditions, and to a predominant extent in the blood of its people. . . . I believe that the time will come when such a state of things will exist upon the earth, when it will be possible to speak of the United States as stretching from pole to pole. . . . Indeed, only when such a state of things has begun to be realized can civilization, as sharply demarcated from barbarism, be said to have fairly begun. Only then can the world be said to have become truly Christian.[22]

Only Americans were qualified to accept the White man's burden from the English. The challenge of carving out a place to exist in the fresh wilderness, the healthy air of the frontier, a unique political lifestyle, and, last but not least, as Warner asserted, "fortunate crosses of blood" had combined to produce a superior new race.

Not all crosses of blood were considered fortunate! In 1885, T. U. Dudley, the Episcopal Bishop of Kentucky, wondered how it could be possible for a White American to "forget the mother who bore him, and to pollute the pure stream of our Caucasian blood" by engaging in wanton "race-fusion." Citing the scientific research of Professor Gardiner, Bishop Dudley laid down the hard facts about race mixing between Blacks and Whites: "a general amalgamation would produce a mulatto stock in which the negro physique and physiognomy would predominate. Whites would be absorbed by negroes, not negroes by Whites, and the brain capacity of the mixed race would be little superior to that of the pure negro."[23] Other learned authorities had discovered empirical evidence of the "nonunity of the races" in anatomical differences, such as in the relative sizes of crania, bottoms, and sexual organs.[24] According to Gilman, the most respected Victorian scientists and philosophers had, in their opinion, accumulated ample proof of the inferior racial qualities of Blacks:

> the late nineteenth-century perception of the prostitute merged with
> that of the Black. Aside from the fact that prostitutes and Blacks
> were both seen as outsiders, what does this amalgamation imply? It
> is a commonplace that the primitive was associated with unbridled
> sexuality. This hypersexuality was either condemned, as in Jeffer-
> son's discussions of the nature of the Black in Virginia, or praised,
> as in the fictional supplement written by Diderot to Bougainville's
> voyages. Historians such as J. J. Bachofen postulated it as the sign
> of the "Swamp," the earliest stage of human history. Blacks, if both
> Hegel and Schopenhauer are to be believed, remained at this most
> primitive stage, and their presence in the contemporary world
> served as an indicator of how far humanity had come in establishing
> control over the world and itself.[25]

To guarantee the quality of their blood, White Americans were conscious of the need to be selective in their breeding habits. In 1897, several delegates to the First National Congress of Mothers in Washington, D.C., emphasized their maternal duty to preserve their Anglo-Saxon racial heritage. In her address, Sally S. Cotton quoted from the father of social Darwinism:

> Herbert Spencer says that "Americans may reasonably look forward
> to a time when they will have produced a civilization grander than
> any the world has ever known"; and all the significant portents point
> to America as the field of the activities of the next century of pro-
> gress, and to the Anglo-Saxon as the dominant spirit of that pro-
> gress. This high destiny involves the responsibility of preparing for
> its fulfillment.[26]

Writing in 1886, John Johnston exclaimed: "whites are Anglo-Saxons, and in one sense that race dominates all others with which it comes in contact—red, black, or white. By virtue of its superior energy and force of character they remand the other people to a secondary and subordinate position."[27] Yet if they "polluted their blood stream" by freely mixing with other races, how could White Americans hope to hold on to the divinely instilled "historic vital energy and power" of Anglo-Saxons?

The "noble character" of Anglo-Saxon blood was even contrasted to that of other White races. The Celtic blood of Scotch and Irish Americans was, in particular, deemed to be of inferior quality, producing a culturally weak, spiritually backward, and socially irresponsible race of people. In the Northeast, Anglo-Saxons of good racial stock associated the Celtic immigrants who occupied the urban slums with "Rum, Romanism, and Rebellion."[28] In the southern states, according to the social historian D. R. Hundley, writing in 1860, Celtic paupers and criminals deported from Britain evolved into an untouchable race known as Crackers. Though its etymology is uncertain, use of the term "cracker" spread widely after the Civil War. The term seems to have originally signified illiterate country folk who spend their time cracking jokes and boasting about themselves, but it was later associated with poor White whip-crackers driving slaves and oxen. The historian W. J. Cash suggested that the term may be "properly applied" to the "weakest elements of the old back country population," those who were collectively "barred off from escape or economic and social advance . . . the 'white-trash' and 'po-buckra' of the house-niggers."[29]

As Hundley observed, the physical appearance and corresponding character of the typical cracker, whether in the North or South, may be summarized as "lank, lean, angular and bony, with flaming red, or flaxen, or sandy, or carroty-colored hair, sallow complexion, awkward manners, and a natural stupidity or dullness of intellect that almost surpasses belief."[30] Hundley contrasted the physiognomy of the cracker with that of the "gentleman of the South," whose six-foot "physical perfectness" was the blooded legacy of "those mailed ancestors who followed Godfrey and bold Coeur de Lion to the rescue of the Holy Sepulchre . . . who always signed their names with a *cross*."[31] Clare de Graffenried noted in 1891 that "crackers are an impressive example of racial and religious degeneration caused partly by climate, partly by caste prejudices due to the institution of slavery. Though sprung from the vigorous Scotch-Irish stock so firmly rooted on the Atlantic slope, they have lapsed into laziness, ignorance, and oddity." According to de Graffenried, the term "cracker" is a "scientific designation" applied to hundreds of thousands of the descendants of non-slave-holding Whites. Concentrated in Georgia, crackers transplanted themselves into Tennessee, Kentucky, Louisiana, Missouri, and other states. De Graffenried considered crackers to be members of an independent cultural and racial community:

> rarely intermarrying with the gentry, breeding in for generations,
> the cracker grows more sharply defined by selection and is less plas-
> tic to civilization than any other race in America. . . .
>   To the occupants as a class, moral distinctions are unknown, the
> limits of *meum et tuum* undefined. Whole families huddle together
> irrespective of sex or relationship. They have land but no gardens,

A RACE PROBLEM.

FIGURE 3.1. "A Race Problem." From Clare De Graffenried's quasi-
ethnographic essay, "The Georgia Cracker in the Cotton Mills," *The Century*,
February 1891, 484. According to De Graffenried and others, these descen-
dents of early Scotch and Irish immigrant farmers had "only the most primitive comprehension of Christianity" and were "less plastic to civilization
than any other race in America."

pasturage but no stock. Wasting their earnings on gewgaws, drink,
and indigestible foods, they are unhealthy and inefficient.[32]

Like Indians, crackers were thought to avoid any kind of work. The men,
women, and children were all addicted to chewing tobacco.

As a race, crackers were purported to be devoutly superstitious and have
only the most primitive comprehension of Christianity—a Christianity laced
with magic and faith in "witches and hobgoblins." Hundley pronounced that
crackers are "mostly of the Hardshell persuasion and their parsons are in the
main of the Order of the Whang Doodle."[33] De Graffenried concluded that
cracker Christians were hopelessly guided by uneducated, itinerant preachers
who roamed the countryside spreading spiritual ignorance. Angelene Price
described the way middle-class whites stereotyped the religious life of crackers:

in the early years of America, poor whites had a very low literacy
rate. The majority of the class existed as sharecroppers and tenant

farmers with little opportunity or inclination for formal education or organized religion. Lacking the ability to read the Bible, and receiving no formal explanations of Christianity, their religious experience was based on trips to tent revivals and outdoor camp meetings.

As far back as the 1830's, we see parodies of such lowerclass religious revivals in Southwestern humor sketches. Sweaty Protestant ministers leading congregations in unruly and spirit filled altar calls are the normal image, typically coupled with shady ushers taking the offering. These depictions are demeaning to the congregation as well as to the ministers. This stereotype has clearly survived in modern day treatment of television evangelists and fundamentalist preachers, in general.[34]

White people in America typically believed that they had inherited a noble legacy from the Anglo-Saxons. As much as they could look forward to a great and powerful racial destiny, they must diligently guard themselves against the "racial pollution" of crackers, Blacks, Native Americans, and all other sources of "degenerate blood."

The Problem of the Freedmen

Perhaps more than anything else, it was through reference to Blacks that Whites constructed their racial identity. Blacks were the omnipresent other, providing the opposing side of White America's racial and religious distinctions. As the second largest racial group in the country, Black people were a source of tremendous anxiety for Whites. Even while the Blacks were enslaved, many White Americans, such as Thomas Jefferson and Abraham Lincoln, expressed a wish to send them all back to Africa. The anxiety of Whites only increased when the slaves were emancipated.

Most White people believed that they were inherently qualified to be free citizens. Blacks, however, were often considered to be natural slaves who would only suffer under the burden of liberty. Indeed, as the slaves of White people, the physical and mental health of Blacks was actually thought to improve. Hard work was the only thing that could possibly "give liberty" to the minds of Blacks. In 1851, this point was made clear in an article published in the *New Orleans Medical and Surgical Journal* by Dr. Samuel Cartwright:

> according to unalterable physiological laws, negroes, as a general rule, to which there are few exceptions, can only have their intellectual faculties awakened in a sufficient degree to receive moral culture, and to profit by religious or other instruction, when under the compulsory authority of the White man. . . .

The Black blood distributed to the brain chains the mind to ignorance, superstition and barbarism, and bolts the door against civilization, moral culture, and religious truth. The compulsory power
of the White man, by making the slothful negro take active exercise,
puts into active play the lungs, through whose agency the vitalized
blood is sent to the brain to give liberty to the mind, and to open the
door to intellectual improvement.[35]

Hundley reported of slaves: "always and every where they are singing and
happy, happy in being free from all mental cares or troubles, and singing
heartily and naturally as the birds sing."[36]

White Americans were convinced that free Blacks were dangerous and
hopelessly attracted to a life of criminal vice.[37] Free Blacks forfeited the happiness enjoyed by slaves. The sad fictional account of Free Joe, who became
free after his master lost a card game, communicates the alleged misery of the
emancipated slave.

Neither his name nor his presence provoked a smile. He was a
Black atom, drifting hither and thither without an owner, blown
about by all the winds of circumstance and given over to shiftless-
ness. . . . In 1850, Free Joe represented not only a problem of a large
concern, but in the watchful eyes of Hillsborough, he was the embodiment of that vague and mysterious danger that seemed to be
lurking on the outskirts of slavery, ready to sound a shrill and
ghostly signal in the impenetrable swamps and steal forth under the
midnight stars to murder, rapine, and pillage; a danger always
threatening, and yet never assuming shape; intangible, and yet real;
impossible, and yet not improbable. . . .
    Under all these circumstances it was natural that his peculiar
condition should reflect itself in his habits and manners. The slaves
laughed loudly day by day, but Free Joe rarely laughed. The slaves
sang at their work and danced at their frolics, but no one ever heard
Free Joe sing or saw him dance.[38]

Some Whites apparently believed that slaves viewed their bondage as a
means to becoming white, a means they would not want to forfeit. Hundley
remarked that "the superiority of the white man over the black seems to be
pretty generally entertained by all negro races whatever, and is not by any
means confined to our Southern slaves." According to Hundley, one thing that
slaves

always dwell on with particular delight, and in which there may be a
grain of truth—is that after death they are to be changed into white
folks. Their idea of hell is, that the Devil is a black man, with horns
and a forked tail. . . . Their idea of heaven is, that in the New Jerusa-

lem they will (be) blessed with straight hair and a fair complexion.
. . . Southern slaves are always carding their own wooly heads, twist-
ing the wool out by means of cotton strings six days in the week, all
for the glory of having it look straight like white folks' hair on Sunday![39]

In the minds of many White southerners, the emancipation of slaves
would not only make blacks sad and miserable but would fill the land with
unbridled rapists. According to W. J. Cash,

the Southern woman's place in the Southern mind proceeded primarily from the natural tendency of the great basic pattern of pride
in superiority of race to center upon her as the perpetuator of that
superiority in legitimate line, and attached itself precisely, and before everything else, to her enormous remoteness from the males of
the inferior group, to the absolute taboo on any sexual approach to
her by the Negro. For the abolition of slavery, in destroying the rigid
fixity of the black at the bottom of the scale, in throwing open to
him at least the legal opportunity to advance, had inevitably opened
up to the mind of every Southerner a vista at the end of which stood
the overthrow of this taboo. . . . What Southerners felt, therefore,
was that any assertion of any kind on the part of the Negro constituted in a perfectly real manner an attack on the Southern woman.
. . . In their concern for the white woman, there was a final concern
for the right of their sons in the legitimate line, through all the generations to come, to be born to the great heritage of white men; and
the record is complete. Such, I think, was the ultimate content of
the Southerner's rape complex.[40]

White people in both the South and the North generally agreed that the
"freedmen" posed a dangerous threat to White society. However, there was no
agreement about how "the greatest social problem before the American people
today" should be solved. In 1885, the *Century* featured three successive articles
debating this issue, the latter two of which turn to religious principles to solve
"the race problem." In the first piece, a former Confederate soldier, George W.
Cable, outlined the most liberal position. Writing "in the name of the Southern
people," he began his article by recalling the nature of the relationship between
Whites and Blacks before the Civil War.

The discipline of the plantation required that the difference between
master and slave be never lost sight of by either. It made our master
caste a solid mass, and fixed a common masterhood and subservi-
ency between the ruling and the serving race. Every one of us grew
up in the idea that he had, by birth and race, certain broad powers

of police over any and every person of color. . . . One relation and feeling the war destroyed [was] the patriarchal tie and its often really tender and benevolent sentiment of dependence and protection. When the slave became a freedman the sentiment of alienism became for the first time complete.[41]

After the war, Cable argued, Whites in the South continued to cling to "arbitrary and artificial social distinctions" that maintained their superiority over Blacks. Whites were irrationally terrified of the unbridled energy of the Black race: "our eyes are filled with absurd visions of all Shantytown pouring its hordes of unwashed imps into the company and companionship of our own sunny-headed darlings. What utter nonsense!"[42] According to Cable, while Blacks were no longer held in slavery, White society subjected them "to a system of oppression so rank that nothing could make it seem small except the fact that they had already been found under it for a century and a half." Blacks were still categorically denied social equality in the South. The young men were herded into jails and made to work in chain gangs where they died young. Whites could not, Cable warned, hold down the Black race indefinitely. The safety and the honor of southern White people depended on their acknowledging the equal rights of the colored race. Cable looked forward to the day when "the whole people of every once slave-holding state can stand up as one man, saying, 'Is the freedman a free man?' and the whole world shall answer, 'Yes.' " Almost a year later, in response to one of his numerous critics, Cable wrote a second piece reiterating his position.

I maintain, and have asserted from the first, that much of the injustice and cruelty practiced upon the colored race springs not from malicious intent, but from mistaken ideas at war with the fundamental principles of human right and American government; and the gentleman himself (the critic) illustrates this by lifting up, after all, the standard of class-rule, race-rule, status-rule, as against the right to *earn* domination without regard to race, class, or status, by intelligence, morality, and a justice that is no respecter of persons.[43]

Henry W. Grady wrote the first reply to Cable's article, entitled "In Plain Black and White." He began by asserting that Cable had no right to speak on behalf of the South, since his parents had moved there from the North. The true southerner, both White and Black, clearly understands the need to maintain "the assortment of the races":

far from the there being a growing sentiment in the South in favor of the indiscriminate mixing of the races, the intelligence of both races is moving farther from that proposition day by day. . . . Neither race wants it. . . . The assortment of the races is wise and proper, and stands on the platform of equal accommodation for each race, but separate. . . . It is the pledge of the integrity of each race, and of peace between the races. . . .

When they turn to social life they separate. Each race obeys its instinct and congregates about its own centers. . . . Each worships in his own church, and educates his children in his schools. Each has his place and fills it, and is satisfied. Each gets the same accommodations for the same money. There is no collision. There is no irritation or suspicion. Nowhere on earth is there a kindlier feeling, closer sympathy, or less friction between two classes of society than between the whites and the blacks of the South today.[44]

Eleven years prior to the Supreme Court's infamous landmark decision *Plessy v. Ferguson*, which legally validated racial segregation in 1896, Grady adamantly defended the right of the South to solve the problem of the freedmen in its own creative fashion, with the doctrine of separate and equal accommodations. He rejected Cable's claims about injustice and maintained that the public facilities used by Blacks and Whites were of equal quality.

A month later, T. U. Dudley, the Episcopal bishop of Kentucky, wrote a third article concerning the problem of race relations after emancipation. As a cleric, Dudley was primarily concerned about the spiritual consequences of possible solutions. Regarding the racial integration, as suggested by Cable, the bishop wrote:

what may come in the far-distant future, when by long contact with the superior race the negro shall have been developed to a higher stage, none can tell. For my own part, believing as I do that "God hath made of one blood all the nation of men," I look forward to the day when race-peculiarities shall be terminated, when the unity of the race shall be manifested. I can find no reason to believe that the great races into which humanity is divided shall forever remain distinct, with their race-marks of color and of form. Centuries hence the red man, the yellow, the white, and the black may all have ceased to exist as such, and in America be found the race combining the bloods of them all; but it must be centuries hence. Instinct and reason, history and philosophy, science and revelation, all cry out against the degradation of the race by the free commingling of the tribe which is greatest with that which is lowest in the scale of development. The process of selection which nature indicates as the method of most rapid progress indignantly refuses to be thus set at naught. Our temporary ills of to-day may not be remedied by the permanent wrong of the whole family in heaven and earth.[45]

Dudley clearly rejected the possibility of separate accommodations. By segregating themselves from Blacks, White people shirked their sacred duty to protect and spread Christianity. Prior to emancipation, Black congregations were under the proper care of White ministers. After the war, however, Dudley asserted that the Blacks usurped control of their churches:

> the white pastors who for so many years had ministered unto them were cast out without ceremony; the guidance of the experienced and trusty Christian white men was repudiated, and in each congregation the government was given exclusively to black men. . . . Utterly ignorant men, gifted with a fatal fluency of speech, unable often to read the Bible in English, much less in its original tongues, became the blind guides of blind followers. . . . The orgies of their socalled worship are such as to cause any Christian man to blush for the caricature of our holy religion therein portrayed.[46]

> Left to themselves, under leaders of their own race, they have in almost every case made grievous failure, have made loud boasting of an uplifting which was just high enough to display their grotesque ugliness. . . . Their religion is a superstition, their sacraments are fetiches [sic], their worship is a wild frenzy, and their morality is a shame.[47]

In Bishop Dudley's opinion, Whites cannot escape their sacred obligation to guide Blacks toward Christ. If they withheld their guiding hands, Whites would be forced to watch Christians of other races succumb to the atavistic powers of spiritual darkness and superstition. Abandoned in their own pseudo-churches, Blacks were thought to no longer benefit from "the enlightening instruction, the helpful guidance, the pastoral care of the White man." "Segregation," he suggested, "has taken away one of the chief agencies which the White man could employ to educate the Black man to a true conception of citizenship; and alas! As the years go by, it must be more and more difficult for us to gain control of again (279)."

According to Dudley, White Christians need to actively seek out regular relations with Blacks. In preparation for that glorious future day of racial amalgamation—which must, of course, be centuries hence—the Whites must steadfastly work toward the perfection of their Black brothers and sisters. Dudley asked his readers:

> How shall the lower race be lifted up to higher stages of human development, for only so can the rights of the superior race be made secure for the present and for the future . . . ? I answer, by the personal endeavors of the individuals of the higher race; by their personal contact with these, their ignorant and untaught neighbors, exhibiting before their wondering eyes in daily life the principles of truth and justice, purity and charity, honesty and courage. . . . The

separation of the negro race from the white means for the negro
continued and increasing degradation and decay. His hope, his salvation, must come from association with that people among whom
he dwells, but from whose natural guidance and care he has been
separated largely by the machinations of unscrupulous demagogues.[48]

These three articles published in the *Century,* all focusing on "the problem
of the freedmen," illustrate how much the racial and religious identity of White
Americans depended on the presence of a "dependent" population of Blacks.
As a set of discourses, they also convey that there was room for debate about
White identity and how Whites should interpret the end of slavery. Professor
Wilbur Fisk Tillett of Vanderbilt University submitted one of the most original
opinions on this matter in 1887. In his article "The White Man of the New
South," Tillett expressed his thankfulness that the South had lost the Civil War.
If any race had been in bondage before the war, it was not the Blacks but the
Whites. Professor Tillett maintained:

it is the white man of the South more than the black that has been
freed by the civil war; and the greatest blessing which has thus far
resulted to the South from the emancipation of the Southern slaves
is its effect upon the white man of that region in transforming him
from a dependent idler, or "gentleman of leisure," supported by the
slaves, into an independent, self-reliant worker. . . . In physical, intellectual, and moral manhood the white man of the South, having
shaken off the shackles of his bondage and rejoicing in his liberty,
has joined the other freemen of the earth in running a nobler and
better race in life.[49]

For Tillett, owning Black slaves was detrimental to the progress of the White
race. Thanks to emancipation, the free White man could make "the Anglo-
Saxon race in the Southern States a more robust, earnest, and manly type of
character than was ever possible under the old civilization."[50]

United Missionaries to Barbarians

Until the end of the Civil War, White people in America had a relatively easy
time thinking of themselves as God's chosen people. In this age of imperialist
expansion and Manifest Destiny, divine favor was often equated with political
power. Who could deny the power of the slave master or cavalry captain? In
1880, the editor of the monthly journal *National Repository* commented:

originally our race stock was exclusively Caucasian, for though both
the American Indian race and the African were found upon our ter-

ritory, yet neither of these entered into the body politic or was a real factor in the social structure. So, too, we were a specifically English-speaking people and a Protestant nation as to all our mental habits and ideas of personal liberty both of thought and action; yet full of religious reverence, Sabbath keeping, Bible reading, and law abiding.[51]

The second half of the nineteenth century brought profound social changes that threatened the way "decent" White Americans represented themselves as a race. Not only did Blacks gain freedom but also they were given the right to vote alongside Whites. Degenerate Whites were rallying to the calls of proletarian demagogues. Native Americans were "allowed to wander about" outside of their reservations. After the German and Irish immigrants who came to the United States between 1820 and 1880, a second wave of immigrants began to pour into the land. Many more "Romanists" arrived from southern Europe, Jews came from eastern Europe, and "idol-worshiping" Asians entered from China and Japan. White Americans were beginning to feel ill at ease.

In 1882, Henry Cabot Lodge expressed the concerns of White America in an article entitled "The Census and Immigration":

the question of foreign immigration has of late engaged the most serious attention of the country, and in a constantly increasing degree. The race changes which have begun during the last decade among the immigrants to this country, the growth of the total immigration, and the effects of it upon our rates of wages and the quality of our citizenship, have excited much apprehension and aroused a very deep interest."[52]

The "vast masses of alien elements in the social and political body" Lodge speaks of significantly altered the appearance of Ben Franklin's "lovely white" country. White Americans searched for ways to protect their civilization from the polyglot, polytheistic other. Surely God would not submit them to a test that they were not strong enough to pass—with his merciful assistance. In 1880, one writer urged his readers to put their faith in the transforming power of the gospel:

Can the ascendancy of our American republic and Christian thought be asserted, maintained, and perpetuated among such tremendous disadvantages? . . . The hope of the American republic, and of the civilization, in which above all else we glory, will be found to abide in the practical effectiveness of its Christian element. Only let these strangers be brought under the power of the Gospel, and we may safely trust them with our civilization.[53]

To maintain their identity as the master race, White Americans increasingly relied on their religious assumptions. In an article detailing the value of

Christianity as a social science, published in 1884, Henry C. Potter suggested that the White man's religion was a true panacea:

> How shall we deal with these social problems of the hour—whether they concern the reclaiming of our fallen brethren and sisters here at our very side, or our fellow-creature, the despised Chinaman, who has found his way to our far off Pacific coast, save as we look at each and every one of them in the light that streams from the cross of One who gave himself *to lift men up?*[54]

The God of Whites, it was presumed, was already the God of all other people—even if others did not yet know this fact. No matter how many people came into the country, God was animating each one. The primary goal, then, was to haul the masses out of their cave of spiritual ignorance. According to the editor of *Scribner's*, writing in 1880, the United States "equals in extent ten of Paul's Macedonias, while our Home Missionary Territory is larger than the Old Roman Empire."[55] Considering all of the many different people who must be converted to Christianity, the editor noted that "some races are bright and speculative, others dull and practical; some are in the caves of superstition, others on the heights of philosophy; all are in the childhood of religion." Lyman Abbott, writing in 1890, had no doubt that his race's religion could solve all of the nation's problems, including those posed by Native Americans and the Blacks. Abbott reasoned:

> the Indian and the Negro questions are both phases of one and the same question: what duties, if any, do[es] a superior race owe to an inferior and subject race, living in the same territory, under the same government, parts of the same nation? The question cannot be answered by individual philanthropy or by missionary societies; the question is asked of the nation, and only the nation can answer it. If the law "Thou shalt love thy neighbor as thyself" is a religious law, if the question "Who is my neighbor?" is a religious question, then the Indian and the Negro problems are religious problems.[56]

The United States cannot exist unless all of its children are imbued with "that religious spirit which is essential to national life." According to Frances Ellen Watkins Harper, a Black delegate to the First National Congress of Mothers, which convened in 1897, the profound social inequalities between Whites and Blacks made it difficult, but not impossible, for both races to make the necessary adjustment from "the old oligarchy of slavery into the new commonwealth of freedom":

> you of the Caucasian race were born to an inheritance of privileges; behind you are ages of civilization, education, and organized Christianity; behind us are ages of ignorance, poverty, and slavery; and now

FIGURE 3.2. "The Doctrine of Eternal Punishment; or the Seventh Com-
mandment," *Harpers New Monthly Review*, September 1885, 541. A black
grandfather teaches his grandson that God will punish the thief of an apple,
and thus demonstrates the fulfillment of the "Great Commission." This
etching typifies the illustrations that often accompanied articles about the
duty of white Christians to teach moral and religious principles to people of
other races.

into your hands, oh, my favored sisters, God has placed one of the
grandest opportunities that ever fell into the hands of a nation or a
people. . . . Trample, if you will, on our bodies, but do not crush out
self-respect from our souls. If you want us to act as women, treat us
as women. If you want us to become good Christians, teach us concerning our high origin, our relation to God, our possibilities of ris-
ing so high in the scale of moral and spiritual life that from being a
little lower than the angels we may become one with God, even as
Christ was one—one in spirit and one in harmony.[57]

In the struggle to Christianize America and the world, religious leaders
called for interdenominational cooperation. "Like the scattered bones which
Ezekiel saw coming together into a great army they would at once start into
new life and activity as the *United Churches of the United States*," one writer
hoped.[58] In 1882, the editor of the *Century* pleaded:

the sectarian divisions of the Christian church in city and country,
by which in so many places its power is destroyed and its glory

turned to shame, all rest on non-essential differences. . . . Suppose we stop talking of union and of unity, and begin working to consider the duty of cooperation in Christian work. This is the desideratum—cooperation. In town and city and mission field, Christians, the disciples of a common Master, ought to cooperate. Can they cooperate? Who will deny it?[59]

In 1884, a reader of the *Century* wrote an open letter to the magazine in which he praised a recently printed story about a fictional organization called the Christian League. The writer said: "the spirit of the new theology is the spirit of the Christian League. It will not permit the details of creed and ritual to bar the way to Christian unity, for in Christ all contradictions are reconciled."[60] George R. Crooks, a Methodist minister, argued: "if such opposites as Jews and Gentiles could in the Pauline period be one body, much more can the Christian opposites of the modern period enter, through the life-giving Spirit, into the composition of one body. . . . As the human race is one, being of one blood . . . so the church is one."[61]

United in a "noble" spiritual effort, Protestants of English descent easily joined with German and Scottish immigrants. Strategic reasons were even found to work together with Catholics, sectarians, and Black Christians. "An inferior type of Christianity." wrote one commentator, "may have adaptations to particular nations because of its inferiority and admixture with error. Yet upon the possibility of overcoming these objections depends the future success of missions."[62]

Many White Christians began to note signs of increasing assimilation, attributing this success to cooperation between denominations. In 1885, Charles Dudley Warner observed that Blacks in the South were holding "more rational and less emotional" religious services.[63] After visiting a small group of Christians in San Francisco's Chinatown in 1900, the Baptist pastor Robert Stuart MacArthur reported:

our Home Mission Chinese church is a veritable oasis in this fearful moral desert. . . . Such sights, such odors, such sins! . . . Never did the work of our Home Mission Society seem to be more needed; never did it appear to be so beneficent as in the contrasts seen in these vile purlieus.[64]

In the late nineteenth century, many White Americans accepted a great commission: evangelize the country and assimilate the foreigners. Whites rallied around the hope that if Blacks, crackers, Native Americans, and the masses of immigrants could only be converted to genuine Christianity, they would also become Anglo-Saxon. Reverend Josiah Strong, general secretary of the Evangelical Alliance for the United States, published a book in 1893 hailing the

"Coming Kingdom." Concerning the "great marvel" of the Anglo-Saxon race, he wrote:

> the Anglo-Saxon is the great colonizing race of the ages; and in ful-
> fillment of its mission this race is carrying its civilization, like a ring
> of Saturn—a girdle of light—around the globe.
>
> To prepare the world for the coming of Him who should inau-
> gurate among men the kingdom of God, three races wrought
> through many centuries until the necessary spiritual, intellectual,
> and physical conditions were made ready. . . .
>
> The great marvel of the Anglo-Saxon race is not that it has at-
> tained the highest religious development of any, or that it has
> achieved as great individualism and freedom as the Greeks, or that
> it has shown a mightier mastery of physical conditions, a pro-
> founder genius for organization and government as the Romans.
> The great miracle is that these three supreme characteristics are all
> united in one and the same race.[65]

In Strong's forecast of the future, Americans of all races would become unified in Christ, becoming one homogenous Anglo-Saxon civilization:

> when such religion and such culture are thus united in every mem-
> ber of the human family the race will have been perfected, and there
> will then be a perfect organization of society as well as perfect indi-
> viduality; for when men are brought into perfect harmony with God
> they will be in perfect harmony with each other.
>
> North America, the future home of this great race, is twice as
> large as all Europe and is capable of sustaining the present popula-
> tion of the globe. Such a country, with its resources fully developed;
> such numbers, homogenous in their civilization; such a race, thrice
> fitted to prepare the way for the full coming of the kingdom, must,
> under God, control the world's future.[66]

The year 1886 witnessed the completion of the great statue by Frédéric-Auguste Bartholdi of "Liberty Enlightening the World." For Strong and MacArthur, this statue, called the "Eighth Wonder of the World," might have symbolized the divine mission of White Americans.

Discussion

Until the American Revolution, colonial Americans apparently thought of themselves as a racially homogenous population of Anglo-Saxon Christians. The presence of other races was of too little social significance to threaten this identity. The war and subsequent decades of hostility toward Great Britain coincided with the birth of a new White race in America. Americans considered themselves to have inherited England's role in the world. The United States would carry into full fruition the "noble" values that could only have sprouted on the rugged British Isles. Social changes after the Civil War challenged this self-concept. Free Blacks, American Indians, and a second wave of culturally and racially diverse immigrants dramatically altered the demographic character of America. In response to the presence of "vast masses of alien elements," White Americans activated themselves in the name of their God. People of all races, no matter how barbaric and vile, had to be converted to Christianity. As Christians, members of other races would become assimilated to Anglo-Saxon civilization. When men and women are brought into perfect harmony with God, it was thought, they become authentic White Americans.

From the start, religious discourse played a pivotal role in the construction of the White race in America. In the original colonies, the English distinguished themselves from Native Americans with the help of religion. According to the historian of colonial America James Axtell, "the charters of Virginia, Massachusetts, and most of the other colonies founded in the seventeenth century made it perfectly clear that the conversion of America's 'infidell people from the worship of Devils to the service of God' was virtually a 'national design' of the highest priority."[67] White Christians believed that God was testing their faith, placing them in the midst of unholy savages for the improvement of their moral discipline.[68] After the Narrangansett Indians mauled a colonial militia in 1675, for example, Captain Wait Winthrop wrote the following poem explaining why God had allowed His people to be beaten:

O New-England, I understand, with thee God is offended:
And thereforth He doth humble thee, till thou thy ways hast mended.

Repent therefore, and do no more, advance thy self so High,
But humbled be, and thou shalt see these Indians soon will dy.

A Swarm of Flies, they may arise, a Nation to Annoy,
Yea Rats and Mice, or Swarms of Lice a Nation may destroy.

Do not thou boast, it is God's Host, and He before doth go,
To humble thee and make thee see, that He His Works will show.

And Now I shall my Neighbors all give one word of Advice,
in Love and Care do you prepare for War, if you be wise.

Get Ammunition with Expedition your Selves for to defend,
And Pray to God that He His Rod will please for to suspend.[69]

The colonialists considered themselves to be saints and men. In their eyes, the Native Americans did not have an independent identity—even as killers and natives, they were mere tools of the White man's God.

As political and economic conflicts intensified between Great Britain and her American colonies, a new racial distinction was made. The Americans became "new and improved" Anglo-Saxons, in contrast to the old and corrupt British. White Americans assumed that they had inherited the birthright of the divine race. This distinction functioned conveniently throughout the late eighteenth and early nineteenth centuries, when Britain and the United States were at war. After all, how can one fight against oneself?

At the end of the Civil War, White Americans found it necessary to distinguish themselves from non-White Americans. Initially, they took it for granted that non-Whites were also non-Christian. Most slaves, of course, had been converted. However, their form of worship, like that of the carroty-haired crackers, was considered by enlightened Whites to be childish, fetishistic, and irrational.[70] Thus, White people could safely divide America into two distinct populations: Christians and non-Christians. This binary code had great appeal because White people felt the urgent need to assimilate the "alien races." Since Whites could not quickly change the race of other Americans, it made sense to put their trust in evangelism. Conversion to Christianity was considered the only logical way to produce Anglo-Saxons out of the tired and huddled masses. As a distinction, religion was used to transcend race. By accepting Christ, it was asserted, even Blacks could be made white as snow.

As it appears in the family house magazines and other texts from the Victorian period, the self-identity of White Americans revolves around a central theme: White Americans develop, racially and religiously, beyond the levels of other people. At the point at which other races stagnate, White Americans rally their racial energies and continue to progress. Whereas Blacks were allegedly content to remain close to the "Swamp," Whites were thought to have evolved to perfect the human race. From the Jews, who supposedly killed God's son, White Americans inherited the status of a chosen people living in a New Israel. As Christians, they accepted a great commission to "enlighten the world." From the Anglo-Saxons, morally corrupted by the power of the British Empire, White Americans purportedly inherited the manifest destiny of civilizing the world and spreading the seeds of democracy.

To make sense of the changing world of race in the United States, Whites in Victorian America turned toward religion, engaging in a double fantasy. On the one hand, they were convinced that God had given them a common identity, history, and mission for the future. The "United Churches of the United States" would transcend or neutralize all social distinctions among White Americans. One nation under God, White America would act as the heroic defender of Christianity, democracy, and civilization on Earth. On the other hand, Whites were also convinced that they knew the identity, history, and future of all other races and religions. Every knee shall bow. White Americans had the desire and assumed that they possessed the power to form other races in their own image. The destiny of all races was to follow in the footsteps of the Anglo-Saxons.

The double fantasy of White Americans could not last forever. The identity of the master race failed to withstand the centrifugal forces of competing intraracial identities. At the turn of the century, Whites could no longer ignore their own conflicting political, class, gender, religious, and regional interests. Furthermore, many non-White Americans were demonstrating that they were not willing to conform to the fantasy of Anglo-Saxons. Not everybody was willing to hop into the melting pot. Even Blacks who embraced the concept of racial amalgamation did not see it as a bleaching operation—they expected that "the white must also lose his identity."[71]

Yet during the nineteenth century White Americans joined racial and religious discourse to construct an enduring image of themselves as a social group. Writers and public speakers combined and recombined religious and racial observations to make meaningful distinctions between themselves and other groups of people. With their political and economic power, White Americans had the means to effectively communicate about themselves as a race. In print, delivered to the home, read by the whole family, the inseparable racial and religious discourse disseminated by the family house magazines and other popular publications helped produce and replicate a society of White Americans.

NOTES

1. David W. Wills, "The Central Themes in American Religious History; Pluralism, Puritanism, and the Encounter of Black and White," in *African American Religion*, edited by Timothy E. Fulop and Albert J. Raboteau (New York: Routledge, 1997), 7–20.

2. Werner Sollors, *Beyond Ethnicity: Consent and Descent in American Culture* (New York: Oxford University Press, 1986), 62.

3. Matthew Schneirov, *The Dream of a New Social Order: Popular Magazines in America, 1893–1914* (New York: Columbia University Press, 1994), 27.

4. Niklas Luhmann, *Die Gesellschaft der Gesellschaft* (Frankfurt: Suhrkamp, 1997).

5. Michael Omi and Howard Winant, *Racial Formation in the United States: From the 1960s to the 1980s* (New York: Routledge and Kegan Paul, 1986), 61.

6. Sollors, *Beyond Ethnicity*, 259.

7. Luhmann, *Die Gesellschaft der Gesellschaft*, 61.

8. Sander L. Gilman, *Difference and Pathology: Stereotypes of Sexuality, Race, and Madness* (Ithaca, N.Y.: Cornell University Press, 1985), 241–242.

9. Gilman, *Difference and Pathology*, 242.

10. John Lord, *Beacon Lights of History* (New York: James Clarke, 1885), 11:30; Israel Smith Clare, *Library of Universal History* (New York: Peale and Hill, 1897), 2654.

11. Edward Eggeleston, "The Beginning of a Nation," *Century* 3 (November 1882), 64.

12. Oliver Wendell Holmes, "The Americanized European," *Atlantic Monthly* 35 (January 1875), 79.

13. Thomas Paine, *Writings of Thomas Paine* (Washington, D.C.: National Home Library, 1935), 40.

14. Thomas Bailey, *The American Spirit* (Lexington, Mass.: Heath, 1974), 224.

15. Philip Gleason, *Speaking of Diversity: Language and Ethnicity in Twentieth-Century America* (Baltimore: Johns Hopkins University Press, 1992), 6; Sollors, *Beyond Ethnicity,* 95.

16. Charles Dudley Warner, "The Western Man," *Scribner's* 20 (August 1880), 551.

17. "What Is an American?" *Atlantic Monthly* 35 (May 1875), 562.

18. Holmes, "The Americanized European," 83.

19. Oakey A. Hall, "English and American Bar in Contrast," *Green Bag* 5 (May 1893), 242.

20. Charles Dudley Warner, "England," *Century* 3 (November 1882), 135.

21. Warner, "England," 137.

22. John Fiske, "Manifest Destiny," *Harper's* 70 (March 1885), 588.

23. T. U. Dudley, "How Shall We Help the Negro?" *Century* 30 (June 1885), 274.

24. Gilman, *Difference and Pathology,* 89.

25. Gilman, *Difference and Pathology,* 99.

26. Sallie S. Cotton, "A National Training School for Women," in *The Work and Words of the National Congress of Mothers, First Annual Session,* National Congress of Mothers (New York: Appleton, 1897), 210.

27. John W. Johnston, "The True South," *Century* 32 (May 1886), 166.

28. Ernest Lee Tuveson, *Redeemer Nation* (Chicago: University of Chicago Press, 1968), 168.

29. W. J. Cash, *The Mind of the South* (New York: Vintage, 1941), 24.

30. D. R. Hundley, *Social Relations in Our Southern States* (New York: Arno Press, 1973), 263–264.

31. Hundley, *Social Relations in Our Southern States,* 29.

32. Clare De Graffenried, "The Georgia Cracker in the Cotton Mills," *Century* 41 (February 1891), 484–486.

33. Hundley, *Social Relations in Our Southern States,* 266.

34. Angelene Price, "White Trash: The Construction of an American Scapegoat," revised February–March, 1996, available online at: http://xroads.virginia.edu/MA97/price/religion.htm (January 21, 2002).

35. Gilman, *Difference and Pathology,* 138.

36. Hundley, *Social Relations in Our Southern States,* 345.

37. Johnston, "The True South," 165.

38. Joel Chandler Harris, "Free Joe and the Rest of the World," *Century* 29 (November 1884), 117.

39. Hundley, *Social Relations in Our Southern States,* 350.

40. Cash, *The Mind of the South,* 118–119.

41. George W. Cable, "The Freedman's Case in Equity," *Century* 29 (January 1885), 411–412.

42. Cable, "The Freedman's Case in Equity," 417.

43. George W. Cable, "The Silent South," *Century* 32 (May 1886), 170.

44. Henry W. Grady, "In Plain Black and White," *Century* 29 (April 1885), 910–916.

45. T. U. Dudley, "How Shall We Help the Negro?" *Century* 30 (June 1885), 274–275.

46. Dudley, "How Shall We Help the Negro?" 272.

47. Dudley, "How Shall We Help the Negro?" 277–279.

48. Dudley, "How Shall We Help the Negro?" 275–278.

49. Wilbur Fisk Tillett, "The White Man of the New South," *Century* 33 (March 1887), 769–770.

50. Tillett, "The White Man of the New South," 775.

51. "The American Nation of the Future," *National Repository* 8 (August 1880), 190.

52. Henry Cabot Lodge, "The Census and Immigration," *Century* 46 (September 1893), 737.

53. "The American Nation of the Future," 191.

54. Henry C. Potter, "A Phase of Social Science," *Century* 29 (November 1884), 116.

55. "Economic Defects in Christian Missions," *Scribner's* 20 (May 1880), 103.

56. Lyman Abbott, "Can a Nation Have a Religion?" *Century* 41 (December 1890), 276.

57. Frances Ellen Watkins Harper, "The Afro-American Mother," in *The Work and Words of the National Congress of Mothers, First Annual Session,* 69–70.

58. Charles W. Shields, "The United Churches of the United States," *Century* 31 (November 1885), 78.

59. "Cooperation in Christian Work," *Century* 3 (November 1882), 142.

60. "The Christian League's Practicality," *Century* 29 (November 1884), 151.

61. George R. Crooks, "The Union of the American Churches," *Century* 33 (December 1886), 322.

62. "Economic Defects in Christian Missions," 106.

63. Charles Dudley Warner, "Impressions of the South," *Harpers* 71 (September 1885), 551.

64. Robert Stuart MacArthur, *Around the World* (Philadelphia: Griffith and Rowland, 1900), 24–26.

65. Josiah Strong, *The New Era* (New York: Baker and Taylor, 1893), 69.

66. Strong, *The New Era,* 71–75.

67. James Axtell, *The Invasion Within* (New York: Oxford University Press, 1986), 218.

68. Ronald Takaki, *A Different Mirror* (Boston: Little, Brown, 1993); Eggeleston, "The Beginning of a Nation," 63.

69. Richard Drinnon, *Facing West: The Metaphysics of Indian-Hating and Empire Building* (New York: Meridian, 1980); 54.

70. "Economic Defects in Christian Missions," 103.

71. Timothy E. Fulop, "The Future Golden Day of the Race: Millennialism and Black Americans in the Nadir, 1877–1901," in Fulop and Raboteau, *African American Religion* (New York: Routledge, 1997), 235.

4

The Catholic Afro Mass and the Dance of Eurocentrism in Brazil

John Burdick

It is early December 1996, and we are seated in one of the back pews of the cavernous Our Lady of the Conception Church, in Duque de Caxias, the great sprawling working-class city that sits on the northern rim of Rio de Janeiro. The church is standing room only, which means that nearly six hundred souls are here, mainly poor, some in sandals, all in their best ironed T-shirts and blue jeans and long cotton pants. Babies are crying, but you can hardly hear them. The warm summer air of early evening pulsates with the raucous beating of palms on cowskins, stretched tightly over the mouths of waist-high wood cylinders the color of ginger. Four men, dressed in brilliant green, red, and white, hammer at the drums on the raised dais of the altar. These are *atabaques*, the drums made famous in Brazil as the constant companion to all music with an "afro" beat, whether samba, reggae, or reggae-samba, and as the instrument of choice in *candomblé*, the mysterious, powerful afro-brazilian[1] religion inherited by the slaves and their descendants. While the four drummers make an ocean of sound, the voices of thirty young men and women produce a steady rain as they sing "Negra Mariana." On the stage too, a sinuous, sensual dance is performed by a troupe of ten women, whose spectacularly colorful dresses reveal as much as hide their bodies. Many in the audience stand, clapping and swaying to the beat.

One could be forgiven for mistaking this for a musical show, similar to those performed in outdoor squares by the troupe Olodum, were it not for the fact that behind the row of dancing women rises an enormous gold crucifix, on either side stand larger-than-life statues of Saint Francis and Mary, and above them towers a stained-glass clerestory window, rattling from the drumbeat. The incongruity is lost on no one. Excited whispers, raised eyebrows, and astonished gazes ripple through the crowd. The presiding priest steps to the altar clad in a glistening multicolored shawl and round, flat headdress. Several people seated near us exhale small gasps. All around us the air is dense with spoken or chanted words rarely heard in the Church: *axé* (African: life-force or energy), *orixás* (afro-brazilian: gods), "A negra é bonita" ("the black woman is beautiful"). As the crowd prepares to take the Eucharist, two vividly garbed youths arrange on the floor near the altar a tray of corn bread and fruit, of which everyone is invited to partake.[2] We are witnessing a "inculturated" or "afro" celebration of the Eucharist, organized by the parish's ten-person team of pastoral agents who call themselves "agents of the black pastoral" (*agentes do pastoral negro*, or "APNs").

Over the past twenty years, hundreds of such teams across Brazil have struggled, with great passion and purpose, to dismantle the equation between white Europeanness and Christianity. Their goal has been nothing less than to break the hold on the popular Christian imagination of the belief that all things African are demonic, and of the idea that the only form Christianity can take is the one laid down by white Europeans in Rome. Fired by the mission to undo the racism and Eurocentrism of their church and to build self-esteem among black Catholics,[3] the catechists, priests, and nuns of this movement have since the late 1970s sought to introduce elements of afro-brazilian expressive culture into the Catholic liturgy and to organize workshops to teach respect for afro-brazilian religions. While at first encountering little support from their bishops, since the late 1980s they have enjoyed official Church endorsement, as the ecclesiastical hierarchy have looked with growing favor on a set of directives coming from Rome to develop an "inculturationist" project, in which the message of Christian redemption is expressed though local cultural beliefs and practices.[4]

It is hard to overstate the social importance of the APNs' project. While the overall numbers of churchgoing Catholics in Brazil has declined in recent years, 75 percent of Brazil's 170 million people continue to identify themselves as Catholics, and on any Sunday, millions of Brazilians of all social classes may be found in Catholic chapels, churches, and cathedrals across the nation. It may thus be argued that the APNs' strategy of unwhitening and de-Europeanizing the liturgy has more potential than does the work of the non-Catholic black consciousness movement to change widespread negative images of afro culture and religion. Non-Catholic black activists' denunciation of Christianity is hard to swallow for the millions of Brazilians who consider themselves Christian, and their belittlement of the widespread popular fear of afro religion does little to counteract popular images of afro religion as demon-worship.[5] It is therefore extremely important that APNs have devoted themselves to legitimizing afro culture and religion by working directly with the faithful to address their stereotypes and biases against afro religiosity, and by associating afro religion and culture with the Mass, a set of symbols that has deep positive resonances with millions of Brazilians. The APNs' afro liturgy thus has the potential of dedemonizing afro culture and religion and of subverting, for a large segment of Brazil's population, the equation between Christianity and white Europeanness. As one of the visionaries who conceived of the afro Mass proclaimed, "once we have inculturated the Mass, Brazil will no longer be the same."

Given its noble goals and potential cultural impact, it may surprise readers to learn that the afro liturgy in Brazil has come under critical fire from academic intellectuals, segments of the secular black movement, and practitioners of afro religions. These critics contend that while the intentions of APNs may be honorable, their celebration of afro-brazilian culture is at bottom racist and Eurocentric. First, they say, the image of the black embraced by the afro liturgy embraces essentialist stereotypes of blackness inherited from a colonial past. "The *negro* is about more than just dancing and drums," complained Rosália, a leading figure in the Unified Black Movement. "And unfortunately, the Catholic Church has chosen to project the *negro* as that happy dancing body." At the tenth national meeting of the progressive wing of the Brazilian Catholic Church in July 2000, the "afro delegation" declared from the stage: "Enough of exhibitionism! We are not just dancing bodies!" Second, these critics disapprove of what they argue is the black pastoral's insistence that only those features of non-Christian religion have true value that resemble Christianity. "They only accept the pieces they want to accept," said Marianinha, a *mãe de santo* (ritual specialist) in one of Rio de Janeiro's main candomblé houses. "They say they respect us, but that is just for show; beneath it all it is the same old European Church."

How fair is this assessment? To what extent have the efforts of the progressive Catholic Church in Brazil to dismantle the ideological legacies of slavery and colonialism simply perpetuated these legacies in user-friendly format? To what extent has "Eurocentrism with a whip" been replaced by "Eurocentrism with a smile"? I address these questions in what follows by applying a dialectical approach to the analysis of ideology. Rather than presume a movement's ideology to be monolithic and unchanging, I assume that it often faces significant internal dissent and that this dissent pushes the ideology to change. Ideologies, including religious ideologies, often create their own internal opposition by making grandiose claims that contradict sympathizers' everyday experience. To the extent that dissent is able to find footholds in popular constituencies, the prevailing movement ideology must respond by adjusting and evolving.[6]

Applying this perspective, I argue in what follows that while it is important to acknowledge the creeping racist and Eurocentric tendencies within the ideology of the Catholic black pastoral, it is equally important to realize that in everyday practice, Eurocentric insinuations about the *negro* and afro religion must at some point confront the multiform experience of people at the grass-roots. As people compare both the implicit and explicit messages of the black pastoral with their own experiences, contradictions emerge. I focus on those parts of the black pastoral that have come under fire—its use of the drums and black body in the afro liturgy, and its stance toward afro religion. The contradictions, in turn, beget new modes of thinking at odds with the black pastoral's latent Eurocentrism. I will suggest that to the extent that such modes of thought find an institutional niche, and draw sustenance from a sympathetic audience, they present a challenge to the black pastoral's Eurocentric inclinations that may in fact already be reshaping those inclinations.[7]

The Black Body, Drums, and the Contradiction of Experience

The Dominant View of Blacks' Nature in the Catholic Black Pastoral

Like many segments of the black identity movement in Brazil (and, more generally, like identity movements of historically oppressed and enslaved peoples worldwide), the black pastoral has embraced the essentialist views of *negros* inherited from the era of colonialism and slavery, while reversing their evaluative signs. The pastoral thus takes categories and images that were construed as negative under colonialism and slavery as sources of positive identity and self-esteem. Such ideological tricks are notoriously difficult to pull off. For in the end, categories and images conceived as part of a European struggle to impose its authority are irrevocably marked, perhaps even imprisoned, by that history.

To begin with, most APNs say that *negros* are inherently "emotional," "warm-blooded," and "lively" and that whites are inherently "cool," "rigid," and "rational." "The black race is happier, looser," said Rosenil, an APN in his twenties. "Whites are cold and stiff." The white is drawn to the abstract, intellectual world, the *negro* to all things corporeal and sensuous. "The white is that rational, cerebral being," explained Francisco, an APN in his thirties.

> "He is the opposite of the *negro*! We appreciate the world of the senses more, we are more at home in our bodies, we experience our bodies more intensely, it seems, than whites do. When we feel the wind, or the sea, we feel that in our bodies; the white doesn't, he wants to do a science experiment."

Entangled in this view is the belief that *negros* respond instinctively to the beating of drums. "When the negro hears the drum," Francisco insisted, "he must drop everything and dance." "He may try to repress it," commented Sebastiao, another APN in his twenties, "but it can't be helped. Even when he does not move to the drumbeat, a voice is within him, crying out from Africa: dance, dance!"

The contrast between the natures of blacks and whites is presumed to result in opposing spiritual temperaments, manifested in the races' opposite reactions to the Roman High Mass. One of main theoreticians on the afro liturgy made the point clearly to me: "the *negro's* way of being [*jeito de ser*] is full of movement, dance, and celebration," he said. "He has a happiness that overflows. So he feels uncomfortable in a Mass that is cold, stark, and still." "When we *negros* witness the Roman Mass," remarked Jorginho, an APN in his twenties, "we are looking at a ceremony of white people, of Europeans. No question about it. You can tell it belongs to the whites, because it is slow, it is deliberate, it is dry. So boring!" "The white, when he worships, likes quiet, likes silence, he wants to concentrate," asserted Rosenil, but

> "the black, no. What is the moment of greatest communion with God in the white mass? The silence at the moment of the consecration of the host. What is the moment of greatest communion with the gods during a *terreiro de candomblé* [the ritual of the major afro religion]? The moment of the loudest drumming, the loudest dancing, the loudest singing. It's totally different. That is the way it is all through Africa. It is our culture, it is our race."

The afro liturgy is thus designed to accommodate *negros'* nature by renouncing the coolness and rationalism of the white European Mass, exalting instead the drumming and dancing connected to *negros'* subterranean African natures. According to the logic of this view, the influence of Africa within the black body may be obstructed for a time but ultimately bubbles up, like hot underground water, until it surges like a spring. When this happens, people of mixed descent, for example, find their white blood no match for the rushing geyser. "We must abandon the Mass that belongs to whites, to Europeans," proclaimed Rosenil,

> because we are not at home in that Mass. There we feel like we are repressing our race, our blood. When we hear the sound of a drum, that blood starts to move, we want to move. Me, though I have white blood, from my father's side, it is my black blood I feel, it's almost like it warms up, it is warm, it rushes from my heart to all my fingers and toes. I can't describe it! When I hear the drum, I look at the whites near me, and they are uncomfortable. But not us. Those of us with black blood respond. The drums warm that black blood, it rises up, it's hard to stop it. But for centuries the Church has told us we have to get a grip on ourselves and say no to what is natural in

us. . . . Now, finally, in the afro Mass, we can let loose and let our blood boil!

In this conception, *negros* abhor a percussive vacuum. When I asked an APN what he might make of a *negro* who preferred quiet to active drumming, he replied without hesitation: "If she does not like drumming at all, then I would be concerned about her *negritude*." Another APN echoed this sentiment exactly.

> What we need is a liturgy that is filled with music we can really move to, that touches our race. Look at what the *negro* is naturally drawn to. Look at who our musical artists are in Brazil. I mean the great ones. They all are either black or they have black blood. Milton Nascimento, Gilberto Gil, Paulinho de Viola, Martinho da Vila—all black. Who are all the great sambistas? All negros, every one. And if you have a good artist who is not Negro—say Caetano or Daniela Mercury—it's because they have black blood. Black blood! It's in the blood. So if we want the black to feel at home in the church, we must fill it with music.

While these images of black essence originated as Eurocentric stereotypes, the black pastoral seeks to turn them on their head, proclaiming them no longer sources of shame but rather of pride and self-esteem. As I will suggest, such a reversal of signs may indeed have the desired positive effect. Yet insisting on the essentially musical, rhythmic, drum-happy *negro* has negative effects as well. Not only does it contradict, as I will suggest, how many blacks experience themselves but it may also encourage the association of intellect, and the right to rule that goes along with it, with whites, while the "emotional" black is left out in the cold. When I asked a *negro* participant in the afro liturgy what he would think of electing a black to the presidency of the Republic, he replied:

> "Look, I don't know. I suppose so, but it would be hard. They would really have to work at it. A white can listen quietly to everyone, without yelling out. The black, no. They are expressive, they are playful, they want to dance. . . . You have gone to one of these *celebrações* [Eucharistic celebrations] right? Well, you can see there what is most important to the *negro*: it's to shake their booties."

The Contradictions of Experience

If the evidence presented so far suggests that the black pastoral does indeed perpetuate Eurocentric images of race, it is important to realize that so far I have focused primarily on the discourse of the leaders and architects of the pastoral. It is now time to look at how the afro liturgy is experienced on an

everyday basis. When we do, we discover that alongside participants who resonate positively to the images of themselves conveyed by the liturgy, there are
those who cannot find themselves in these images. These contradictions, I will
suggest, have led these persons to articulate an interpretation of racial identity
that differs in interesting ways from that espoused by the leading APNs, with
consequences for the dominant interpretation that are not yet altogether clear.

A sizable proportion of the *negros* we interviewed about the afro liturgy felt
it expressed something true and deep about themselves. Over a third of our
sample of forty *negros* said, in one way or another, that the drums and dancing
of the afro Mass[8] set in motion a mysterious substance hidden deep in their
bodies. "The first time I witnessed an afro Mass," insisted Benta, a school-
teacher in her forties, "the body movements were contagious. It touched my
whole body—and still does! Not just the voice and the head, not just the mind.
Here we move our legs and arms as well." The afro Mass allowed her, she said,
to satisfy bodily needs long "repressed by the traditional Mass." She described
these needs as a desire to be "whole." "In the regular Mass," she said, "I cannot
be whole, something is missing. It is cold, the body is not permitted to move
and express that joy we *negros* feel. Because we *negros* are a happy people, we
have that joy within us, we are more in tune with the rhythms of nature." Her
voice grew husky.

> And so too with the drums: that touches our natures. In the Euro-
> pean Mass, you are still: the more still you are, the more you are in
> . . . plenitude. But in the afro Mass, it is the opposite. In the afro
> Mass I can finally worship God in my way; it is the place I have to
> worship God while dancing.

Many blacks also respond to the afro liturgy in other ways desired by the APNs.
Thus, for instance, seeing black beauty celebrated in the Mass filled several of
the black women we interviewed with unprecedented pride in themselves. "I
look much more at *negra* [black] beauty now," said Carolina with much feeling.
"The inculturated Mass really taught me to think about this in a new way. To
believe that I am beautiful. That my color is a beautiful color." We found that
the afro liturgy contributed to several women's decision to shed the "mixed"
label and to identify themselves instead unequivocally as "negra." "The Mass
was very important to me assuming my negritude," said Oneide, a woman in
her forties who had always called herself "morena." (This term, translated
roughly, means "brown" and historically has been used as a euphemism to
minimize its subject's African ancestry). "Before that, before all these things
in the Church, I rejected my black blood, that was the last thing I admitted to
having. Even though it was obvious! Look at my hair! So I was living a lie." So,
I asked her, "What difference did the Afro Mass make to you?" "Oh, it was
central!" she declared. "I saw there that everyone wanted to be black, that it

was not something to be afraid of. I saw that. That you could be 'negra' and proud. So I decided that I wouldn't keep lying to myself, I had to assume my blackness."

So far, the architects of the afro liturgy might say, so good. But alongside these positive, affirming experiences, we also discovered a fascinating nonaffirming pattern of response to the afro liturgy. Put simply: for five of our informants, the experience of the afro liturgy was one of dissonance. What they carried away from their exposure to it was, above all, disquiet produced by the embarrassing fact that for them, the afro liturgy's drums and dancing *produced little or no bodily response.* For these women, breathless claims about drums and dancing drawing up their *axé* like water from the depths of their beings quite simply did not coincide with their experience. Indeed, by insisting so strenuously on the affinity between blackness, rhythm, and drumming, the afro liturgy created for these women the conditions for its own disproof. For these five women, we discovered, drew from their dissonant experiences the radical conclusion that *being negro does not necessarily entail the desire to dance to the beat of a drum.* Opposed to this image they posed another: the *negro* had no essential rhythmic dispositions at all but was rather capable of resonating with any and all types of music, including not only the drums of Africa but also the tranquil rhythms of European classical music, and even *with no music at all.*

Yvonne was one of the five informants who expressed this emergent view. An educated, unmarried woman in her twenties who worked as a clerk in a clothing store, Yvonne was proud to call herself *negra* (and, she claimed, had always done so) and asserted that she had suffered personally from racial discrimination. She wore her hair in the natural style, had no interest in straightening it, and declared herself in sympathy with the black movement's agenda of combating racism and building black self-esteem. She was exactly the kind of person one might expect to welcome the afro liturgy as an affirmation of negritude, and indeed she did, up to a point. "It is very good," she remarked, "to have a Mass that shows us that we must valorize ourselves, our culture."

Yet contrary to what she knew the APNs expected of her, as well as what she had at first expected of herself, Yvonne had discovered by attending the afro Mass that she did *not* feel moved at the deepest level of her being by the rhythms of the atabaque. "Look," she said,

> "It just doesn't speak to me. I don't feel any more at ease, any more 'myself' there in the afro Mass than in the traditional one. How many times have I gone to a traditional Mass and felt moved, so moved? And if I go to an afro Mass, sometimes I feel moved, sometimes I don't, depending on how I am with Christ. It is Christ that moves me, not because there is an atabaque there, or dancing. I could see that I was not having that rush that the others were having. I felt different."

Rather than relinquish identifying as a *negra*, Yvonne concluded that the ideologues of *negritude* had presumed that *negros'* spectrum of aesthetic response was narrower than in fact it was. A *negro* might like drumming, or not; might like quiet, or not; might like European instruments, or not. He or she had the right to like, or dislike, any of these things, Yvonne thought, and should not be confined by dogmatic ideas about his or her nature. She, for instance, though able to acknowledge the aesthetic value of the atabaques, rejected the idea that she possessed, by virtue of her *negritude*, an inherent point of contact with them. "Does it [the drum] speak to some hidden part of me?" she asked. "I just don't feel it. I also like classical music. And piano. Does that make me any less *negra*? Does this mean I am trying to escape my race? Don't I have a right to like classical music? Should I not like classical music just because it is European?" She found it especially hard to swallow the idea that as a *negra* she was unconcerned with peace and quiet. "I like having a few quiet moments during a mass," she insisted, "to reflect and concentrate. I like to be able to hear myself think. But with those drums constantly beating, it is hard to do that. Does that mean I am denying my race? Does being *negra* mean not wanting to hear your thoughts?"

We found similar processes at work among the other four rebels against the "*negritude-axe*-drum-dance" complex. A personal experience of feeling unmoved by drums led these women to reject the idea that blackness was bound to one kind of physical response and instead to imagine a broader, more inclusive concept of blackness. The case of Carolina, a woman in her forties who has always called herself *negra*, illustrates the pattern. "When I started participating in the afro celebration," she said,

"I was very excited, because the priest was saying that this was very different from what we were used to. And I think that at the start I thought . . . Well, I don't know. I have black blood, I am *negra*, but I had never had any opportunity to hear these other things, all my life in the Catholic Church. So I was very curious, very curious. I thought: if there is something in me this can touch, let it be touched. Because I feel it is important to have a root, you know? To be *negra*, I am *negra*, this is important, you know? So, anyway, you can imagine how disappointed I was when none of this happened. Nothing. I heard the drums, and I saw the girls dancing up there— and that is pretty, but nothing. Or, well, I liked it, but it wasn't so great!" There weren't any of those fireworks. And I was worried, because I saw everyone else jumping [*pulando*], but not me, not me. I wondered: Could it be that I'm not really *negra*? But no, that was nonsense. I am as *negra* as anyone else. So you know what I realized? All this stuff about how we have to feel this or that, that is *bobagem* [silliness]! I feel what I feel, OK? So that is what I thought."

These questions and doubts, stimulated by exposure to the practice and ide-ology of the black pastoral, led Yvonne and Carolina (and the three others) to imagine *negritude* in ways different from those set forth by the APNs. For Yvonne, *negritude* should be uncoupled from the idea of a *jeito de ser* (way of being). "I think," she said, "that this is discrimination, to say that the *negro* is more this or that. I feel what I feel: I don't want to be locked into a single jeito de ser. I like and enjoy various things." Consequently, she concluded that "we need a Mass which encourages the *negro* to be any way he wants, not take him out of one box and put him into another." Carolina, meanwhile, found herself questioning the notion that black blood carried a natural antipathy to quiet and silence. For though she appreciated the music and dance of the afro liturgy, she ardently loved the peace and quiet of the traditional High Mass.

> "I don't know. If this thing of being still is just a European thing, no. I don't know that. . . . In the traditional mass, there are many strong moments. Like when the Bible is read; and the consecration of the host. I experience this moment in my heart, with love and all my energy."

"But," I pointed out, "this [i.e., the consecration of the Host] is a quiet moment, a moment of silence."

"Yes! That is lovely, the European mass has that, it offers that. Because you realize yourself in the quiet too."

"What do you mean, 'you realize yourself in the quiet too' "?

"I mean, the *negro* can. Many say no, that is not possible, if you do you are 'whitening.' But I don't believe it. I don't know that much about Africa, the priests say that all they do there is jump and dance. But I wonder if that is true? I mean, there must be Africans too who value quiet sometimes." Later, in another conversation, one of the other five "rebels," Dona Ana, returned to this theme, when we were speaking of candomblé. "Now, I have gone to those places, and it is not all dancing and drumming! There are moments of quiet, even silence. So I don't think that these things just belong to the white, no."

We can detect, then, the outlines of an emergent, alternative vision of black racial identity here. Contrary to a vision that insists that African ancestry au-tomatically inclines the individual toward drumming, in this alternative vision people of African descent may feel unmoved by drums, and deeply touched by silence. The point is not to presume automatic affinity between *negros* and any particular piece of expressive culture but to destigmatize responses to all ex-pressive culture, wherever it comes from, so that blacks can feel free to respond as they will. "The way I see it," explained Yvonne, "if there are people—white, moreno, black—who like the drumming, then it was a good thing to bring it in [to the afro liturgy], because it wasn't there before, you see? You've made the celebração richer for everyone." The kind of liturgy she wanted to see would include "both fast and slow. Not that the fast are for the blacks, and the slow is for the whites. But that they are both there, they come from different cultures, everyone can benefit."

Consequences for Practice

Though small and still just emerging, the perspective I have described here appears to be exercising a minor influence on the everyday practice of the afro liturgy, at the level of the base communities.

Carolina, it turns out, is a member of her community's liturgy team, and for some time the parish priest has been urging her to help introduce "afro" elements into the celebração. She felt it was important to respond positively to the priest's call, for she believed in the need to teach the value of afro-brazilian culture. At the same time, Carolina let it be known in her liturgy team that she wanted to avoid the heavy drumming and exaggerated sensual dancing of the liturgical spectacles organized at the diocesan level—such as that described at the beginning of this article. As the team worked to refine how they would add the "afro" to the liturgy, everyone agreed that they would admit the use of the atabaques. But Carolina sounded a note of caution. "About these dances we see in the cathedral," she noted, "I have to say I'm not happy about that." There were appreciative murmurs, and another woman chimed in, "Yeah. . . . All that young flesh bouncing on the altar is shocking. Dona Ana said, 'This is indecent!'"

But Carolina's caution was not just about trying not to offend local prudishness. After the laughter had died down, she clarified her point. "No, no, Dona Giza. That's not the only thing. I agree with you that it is indecent. But I'm not worried about Dona Ana or the others being shocked. I'm worried about the image projected by this of Africans. It is the wrong image, the wrong image! It makes it look like all we do well is to shake our booties, dance the samba!" General hilarity, followed by reassurances: "No, no, of course not, Carolina!" But then, a joking "You mean you do something else too?" Guffaws.

Carolina: "No, people, listen to me, you can laugh, but that is the point I'm making! You see with those girls up there shaking like that, that is the message we are sending about African girls, that they are good for dancing, for shaking their bodies to those drums. It's no longer culture, that is folklore."

A chorus of "Yes, yes." "I am," Carolina continued, "all for us having some dancing, and valorizing the culture, but with respect, I don't want everyone going away and thinking that African girls are just about that."

The laughter had died down, and there were nods of assent. It was agreed that the comunidade's afro liturgy would look different from that run by the APNs at the parish level. In the big parish performance there was extensive rehearsal and numerous, elaborate "afro moments"; at the community level they would include only one or two understated "afro moments." At the central parish level, the priests had recruited a dazzling afro dance troupe to lead the celebration, replete with loud drumming and spectacular choreography reminiscent of stage shows. In the community, the appearance of afro dance would occur only twice, the beat of drums would be slower, the dancing would be less sensual, the bodies of youth more modestly covered and adorned. "This way," Carolina explained, "we move away from that idea of the black in the jungle. Here, the dance is more respectful, it is quieter. It shows seriousness and maturity." The celebração went ahead as Carolina and the liturgy team planned. Whether or not the scaled-back version of the afro liturgy had the desired effect is hard to know. Still, Carolina had succeeded in establishing a kind of practical compromise between the sensationalism she worried about at the parish level and her desire to destigmatize "afro culture." Other people in the liturgy team did not necessarily see the toned-down version as a blow for an antiexoticizing vision of the *negro*. The few participants I interviewed understood the "quieter" version simply as a concession to the prudishness of the more traditional Church ladies and continued to believe in *negros*' natural eroticism.

Yet even if the scaling back and toning down effected a subtle shift in perspective among a few people, that was already 100 percent more than nothing. In this spirit, it may be noteworthy that a churchgoer, a *negra* in her forties, commented: "The moment of the *negras* dancing was a surprise to me. Because I am used to seeing them dance like *mulatas* [i.e., in a sensual way], but here, no. That was different." It is hard to know how far such a rethinking of "difference" may go. Still, such testimony suggests that Carolina's mistrust of racial essentialism, born of her dissonant experience with the afro liturgy, may have generated a practice that at the very least makes possible a new, if small, set of ideas that challenge ideas about blacks' "natural" sensuality.

The Dance of Non-European Spirituality

It has been suggested that one of the ironies of the Catholic inculturationist project, of which the afro liturgy is an example, is that it perpetuates, in a new form, the very Eurocentrism it seeks to dismantle.[9] Inculturationism's call for respect for non-Christian spirituality is certainly positive: by registering doubt about the uniqueness and incomparability of Europe's religious tradition, this call strikes a salutary blow against the doctrine of European supremacy. But what inculturationism offers with one hand it takes away with the other. For when it is inspected more closely, it becomes clear that inculturation's call for respect is confined to features of the non-Christian tradition that can be readily interpreted as resembling Christianity. Where these features are lacking, the Church discovers them in its own reflection—a reflection found, as it were, in a pool beneath the debris of the Other's superstition. In the acerbic phrase of the theologian Ivone Gebara, "all the talk about grasping 'seeds of the Word' in the various cultures really cloaks a form of superiority of some above others."[10]

This process is by no means unique to Brazil or to the afro arena. Wherever the Catholic Church has sought to instill respect for non-Christian religions, the stance has generally served as a cloak for demonstrating the superiority of Christian ideas and values. Living among the O'odhma people of Arizona, Catholic catechists declared that I'itoi—one of the O'odhma's creator spirits—was "just another name for the God of the Bible." But the O'odhama actually believe that I'toi created only the O'odhama people, not the whole universe, a detail not easily reconciled with the Church's desire to represent all peoples as venerating the same God.[11] Or consider the catechists who insisted the deities worshiped by Q'ekchi in mountain caves in the highlands of Guatemala were the same as Catholic guardian angels: the main inconvenience was that Q'ekchi regarded these deities as having created the landscape they inhabited. No matter: Catholic inculturationists plowed ahead, declaring that Q'ekchi believed in a God that had "created the mountains and left them down here to watch over everything while He is in the sky."[12]

The willingness to squeeze the Other's religion into the Procrustean bed of Christianity is quite visible in the black pastoral. The APNs are eager to reassure Catholics that afro religions are really just Christianity dressed up in colorful garb. I recently heard an APN urge a community liturgy team in Maranhao to adopt a more open view of the afro religion *tambor de mina*. He sought to assure the group that rather than gods, *orixás* were really deceased African kings and warriors and that therefore veneration of them was similar to Catholic reverence for saints. "You see," he explained, "it is said that tambor de mina is polytheistic. But we can see that this is really reverence for the great people who have passed on." With a similar spin, Yemeja, the Yoruba sea goddess, became "a real-life African queen"; spirit possession became a "dance" in celebration of God and the ancestors; and offerings to the orixás became "a meal that brings together the people into a strong community."

The resulting portrait of candomblé was unrecognizable to its own practitioners. "The problem," Marinete, a *mãe de santo* ["mother of the saint," candomblé ritual leader], observed, "is that you cannot dance that way without knowing it as a dance of the orixás [gods] who take over our bodies! . . . You cannot just eat those foods, for they are the food of the orixas. They are being offered to the gods to eat." Another spirit medium in candomblé complained about the inaccurate translations of *orixás* into Christian terms. "When they say that Oxalá is like Jesus," she grumbled, "that is wrong. It isn't true. Oxalá is not Jesus. [And] Olorum is not the Christian God. Olorum did not give Moses anything. These are totally different ideas, different entities." Another *filha de santo* ["daughter of the saint," a female medium] in candomblé protested:

"I don't understand how the afro mass takes symbols from candomblé, and places them in Christianity. For example, he takes a bunch
of dirt—as we do in candomblé, because in candomblé this is the
material from which we came, and to which we will return—when
they use that dirt in Catholicism, and talk about the ancestors. But
they have a view of the dead that is totally incompatible with ours!
We don't have the theology of salvation. Totally different. So they are
negating the original meaning of the dirt!"

"The problem," Marinete explained, "is that they only want to respect those
things that already suit them. So they talk about how pretty the music is, but
they criticize us for sacrificing chickens. Is that respect?" "It is not really about
respecting our worldview," said Rosalia, *a filha de santo*.

"It is about taking from us to confirm theirs. So this is what I see:
the church wants to paint a picture of the happy negro, the one who
only knows how to sing and dance. Afro culture is much more than
happiness, *festa*, singing and dancing. All that is most sacred, most
solemn and serious, they don't want that part, because it doesn't go
along with the picture they want of Africans."

One might suppose that the afro liturgical movement would be acutely
conscious of such mistranslations, led as it is by progressive Catholics, presumably solicitous of the feelings of the marginalized and oppressed. Yet it is
often the politically progressive agenda of afro liturgy itself that is at the root
of such distortions. Liberationist clergy, it turns out, give themselves license to
select elements of the non-Christian tradition and shape them into a liberationist model. In his book on inculturation, Leonardo Boff expresses confidence in the ability of holders of liberationist values to pass judgment on the
cultural values of others. "The alienated cultures," he writes, "of the dominating and mimetistic groups, are evangelized only if they cease to be what they
are—that is, if their dominating character is destroyed."[13]

In this vein, APNs identify some features of Afro religion as signs of domination and inequality, and so reject them; while other features they take as
liberatory and democratic, and so endorse (and misconstrue) them. An APN
in Rio declared:

"Some things about Afro spirituality are, candidly, a product of domination and we don't want that in our Church; we are seeking liberation. Anything that symbolizes initiation, like the white clothing, is
about hierarchy, and we can have none of that; the part of candomblé we valorize is that they are strong communities, and so we adopt
the form of the circle, with everyone forming a circle around the altar."

(Presumably this APN would have "none" of the hierarchy of his own Church, either.) Knowledge of this interpretation of their circular ritual caused exasperation for a *mãe de santo*: "They can think that the circle in a *terreiro* [candomblé temple] symbolizes equality," she observed. "It doesn't. It symbolizes the submission of the *filhas* to the power of the orixás. Everyone in that circle is in a place defined by where they sit in the hierarchy." While these examples indicate the tendency of the afro liturgy to perpetuate a vision in which Christianity as defined by Rome defines standards of truth and value, it is important to recognize forces at the grassroots that are working both in and outside the afro liturgy and black pastoral to challenge and complicate their Eurocentrism. The very claim of the black pastoral, that it wishes to show "respect" for non-Christian traditions, has created the conditions for resistance against it, and its own consequent evolution.

In the mid-1980s, during the early phase of the development of the black pastoral, clerical leaders, enveloped in Eurocentric consciousness, undertook to create an afro liturgy with little input from non-Christian practitioners. A leader of the black pastoral explained that "we just didn't consult with them. We thought we didn't need to. We were sure we knew what 'afro' meant, so there was no need." This arrogant stance endured for several years, while leaders of candomblé remained silent, some from resentment, others from indifference. In the early 1990s, however, the silence was broken, as APNs "started to hear the concerns and challenges from candomblé." The proverbial straw was a dispute over drums. In a parish in Maranhão, afro liturgies had until then placed within the same rite the secular drum and the sacred drum used in the religion of *tambor* de mina. "We really weren't thinking of this as a problem," an APN told me, because "they were both expressions of afro culture, we thought, and the fact that one was sacred and one secular just didn't occur to us."

But in 1993 something happened. Some Franciscan [member of the Order of Saint Francis of Assisi] APNs were trying to initiate a dialogue with the leaders of a *terreiro de tambor*, without success. While they puzzled over the lack of responsiveness from the terreiro, one of the Franciscans discovered that the leaders of the *tambor* were angry. "We learned that the mães were infuriated with us. They felt we had offended their religion by bringing the tambor into a Catholic Church without their permission, and by playing it alongside an atabaque. That was the worst!"

This challenge pried open a space for APNs to think twice about what had until then been taken for granted: the right of Christians to manipulate afro religion as they saw fit. "Well, I tell you that day was very important for me," the Franciscan said. "That changed our behavior a lot, I'll tell you." The APNs felt duty bound by the norm of "respect" to respond to the criticism by instituting three changes. First, they promised that henceforth no *tambor* would be played in church without the express permission of a local *mãe de santo*. Second, they removed the *tambor* from the sacred sphere of the Catholic ritual and reserved it for "an appreciation of Afro culture" after the ritual was over. And third, they guaranteed that no one would play the *tambor* except for ritually qualified members of the *terreiro*. "We realized," said the APN, "that only they had the right to play these drums. Only they understood their powers. None of us was prepared for that."

This was a remarkable, path-breaking admission on the part of the guardians of Christian truth, which opened a new chapter in the relationship between APNs and the *terreiros*. Local *mães de santo* welcomed visits from the Franciscans, who began to consult them about the afro liturgy. The *mães* were delighted to see shows of respect toward their religion from the Church. When, for example, a *mãe de santo* pointed out that the lyrics to a Catholic hymn inappropriately invoked the name of a specific god, the APNs excised the chant. "We found this very gratifying," observed a local *mãe de santo*.

Similar episodes began to occur elsewhere in Brazil in the early and mid-1990s. In Rio de Janeiro, several *terreiros* de candomblé threatened to bring a lawsuit against the Church for having allowed the presence of shirtless *capoeiristas* [practitioners of the afro-brazilian dance known as capoeira] alongside the sacred drums of candomblé. Although in the end no lawsuit was filed, the event served as another wake-up call to APNs involved in the afro liturgy. "After that," one of them recalls,

> "I paid more attention to this. And the critique I heard was an important one. I heard from the terreiros that they felt that if we were going to bring the sacred drum of candomblé into our Mass, then they should have the equivalent right to perform the rite of communion in their *terreiros*. Let me tell you, that was a very powerful argument, and it changed the discussion. That has created a strong doubt in my mind about our liturgies, and makes me more careful about what we include in them."

If one source of pressure for dismantling the Eurocentric tendencies of the black pastoral came from the afro-religious community, a second originated within the Catholic community itself. After all, the Church, in its decades-long project of building grassroots communities, had been insisting for some time that Catholics should be confident in their opinions. And many churchgoing Catholics had an opinion about afro religion to be confident about, based on their own firsthand experience of it. It is rare to meet a practicing Catholic who has no friend or relative who has sought spiritual succor from a non-Christian source.[14] Yet here the Church was suddenly claiming that in many of its details, afro religion was entirely different from what many lay Catholics knew from their own experience. No wonder a growing number of lay Catholics were openly skeptical about what they saw as APNs' mischaracterizations of afro religion.

Consider the case of Lucilene. A thoughtful woman in her thirties, Lucilene had participated for much of her life in her Catholic community in Icatu, a small fishing village in Maranhão. Though she had no schooling beyond the sixth grade, she was a lay leader and regularly attended training sessions on liturgy, led by college-educated pastoral agents. At a meeting of the black pastoral that I attended, Lucilene listened patiently as the APN expounded on *candomblé*. When however he called Yemeja an "African queen," she gently but firmly protested. She raised her hand. She had, she said, been "visiting these places for a long time." Furthermore, "I have friends, and neighbors, even one of my godchildren, who are involved in this." She took a breath. Based on this familiarity, she had serious doubts about the propriety of saying that Yemeja had once been a real-life, human queen. "The way I understand it," she said, "Yemeja came out of the salt waters and created the oceans of the world. I don't think a queen does that." The pastoral agent backpedaled. "Of course, absolutely! Yemeja is a great, powerful goddess. I'm just talking about her origins in myth."

Lucilene knitted her brow. "Sure," she said,

> "but we're talking about whether these *orixás* are the same as [Catholic] saints. And what I see is that there is a difference! It isn't the same thing! These *orixás*, they are rivers, and snakes, and oceans, and fire, and all that. The ones that are people, I don't think you can say that they are like saints at all. Saints don't come down and enter into people! But those *orixás*, they believe that these spirits possess them."

The pastoral agent looked sheepish, and was forced to say simply, "Yes, Lucilene, you certainly are right."

Lucilene's role as catechist meant her view would have an impact. In the days following her intervention, I heard it referred to several times by locals. It will be difficult for the APN to push a simplistic version of Yemeja, at least in this community, anytime in the near future. As I left Brazil in July 2001, Lucilene informed me that the APN was planning to drop references to the *orixás* as saints. Through a slow accumulation of hundreds of just such micro struggles, the afro liturgy, and the inculturationist project more generally, will continue to evolve.

Conclusion

I have in this article developed two arguments. First, I have argued that the afro liturgy in Brazil, though designed by the black pastoral to dismantle white

European supremacy, remains, quite ironically, caught in the logic of white racism and Eurocentrism. By portraying blacks as inherently rhythmic and sensual, the afro liturgy perpetuates images encumbered by the history of white supremacy; and by seeking to legitimize afro religion through affinities with Christianity, the liturgy misrepresents afro religion and reinforces the notion that afro religion (or any non-Christian religion) cannot be respected on its own terms. While this racism and Eurocentrism are sadly ironic, given the afro liturgy's antiracist and decolonizing ambitions, they are not, in the end, entirely surprising. For after all, the black pastoral occurs within the Catholic Church, an institution still dominated by white European modes of thought.

At the same time, neither the black pastoral nor the Church within which it has found its home are fixed, static entities. This has been my second argument. For while the Eurocentric forms of the afro liturgy are durable, they continue to be difficult to sustain in pure, permanent form. By making unequivocal claims on matters about which their audiences have independent knowledge, these forms find themselves sooner or later contradicting that knowledge. In this process religious faith plays a key role. In the cases I have examined here, the key resource that mobilized individuals' willingness to think, speak, or act at variance with the way prescribed by pastoral agents and clergy was belief that sacred things were at stake. In the case of the five women who rejected the image of themselves purveyed by the APNs, their backbone came from the preaching of the progressive Church that God had endowed them with consciences and minds and they should trust these gifts from God. In the case of those who questioned the APNs' representation of non-Christian religion, both the Catholics and the *candomblécistas* who criticized the Church did so emboldened by the conviction that one must not trifle with beliefs in the sacred.

The antiracist struggle in Brazil has been going on a long time. While the role of the Catholic Church in the struggle has been important, its ideological contribution has been criticized in the ways suggested earlier, as being unwittingly but inescapably racist and Eurocentric. While these criticisms are valid, I hope to have shown in this article that there may also be good reasons to pause before giving up on the Church. Through a slow, incremental process of responding to challenges from below, it seems quite possible that the Church may develop over the long run a nonracist, non-Eurocentric vision. Indeed, might it be possible that some time this century we will see the emergence of a truly catholic—that is, "universal"—Church?

NOTES

    1. Throughout this article, I have kept the terms "afro-brazilian" and "afro" uncapitalized to echo Brazilian usage.
    2. John Burdick, *Blessed Anastacia* (New York: Routledge, 1998), 54.

3. Ana Lucia Valente, *O negro e a igreja catolica: O espaco concedido, um espaco reinvidicado* (Campo Grande, Miss.: CECITEC, 1994); Caetana Damaceno, "Cantando para subir: Orixa no altar, santo no peji" (M.A. thesis, Universidade Federal de Rio de Janeiro, 1990); John Burdick, "What Is the Color of the Holy Spirit?" *Latin American Research Review* 34, 2 (1999), 109–131; John Burdick, "The Evolution of a Progressive Catholic Project: The Case of the Black Pastoral in Rio de Janeiro, Brazil," in *The Church at the Grassroots in Latin America: Perspectives on Thirty Years of Activism*, edited by John Burdick and W. E. Hewitt (Westport, Conn.: Praeger, 2000), 71–84.

4. The inculturationist project has become increasingly important to the Vatican in the past fifteen years as it seeks to retain influence in a world where the majority of Catholics is fast becoming non-European. Analyses of the inculturationist project include Michael Angrosino, "The Culture Concept and the Mission of the Roman Catholic Church," *American Anthropologist* 96, 4 (1994), 824–832; Diego Irarrazavel, *Inculturation: New Dawn of the Church in Latin America* (Maryknoll, N.Y.: Orbis, 2000); Barry J. Lyons, "Religion, Authority, and Identity: Intergenerational Politics, Ethnic Resurgence, and Respect in Chimborazo, Ecuador," *Latin American Research Review* 36, 1 (2001), 7–48; Thomas Bamat and Jean-Paul Wiest, eds., *Popular Catholicism in a World Church: Seven Case Studies in Inculturation* (Maryknoll, N.Y.: Orbis, 1999); Leonardo Boff, *New Evangelization: Good News to the Poor* (Maryknoll, N.Y.: Orbis Books, 1992); Paula Elizabeth Holmes, " 'We Are Native Catholics': Inculturation and the Tekakwitha Conference," *Studies in Religion* 28, 2 (1999), 153–174; Andrew Orta, "Converting Difference: Metaculture, Missionaries, and the Politics of Locality," *Ethnology* 37, 2 (1998), 165–185.

5. For a fuller discussion of these issues, see Burdick, *Blessed Anastacia*, chap. 3.

6. This is a perspective associated with Raymond Williams, *Marxism and Literature* (Oxford: Oxford University Press, 1977), Anthony Giddens, *Central Problems in Social Theory: Action, Structure, and Contradiction in Social Analysis* (Berkeley: University of California Press, 1979), and Antonio Gramsci, *Prison Notebooks*, edited by Quintin Hoare and Geoffrey Newell Smith (New York: International, 1971).

7. The field material I rely on for this article derives from several research stints in Brazil: in 1988, when I interviewed fifty Catholics in Rio de Janeiro with some level of involvement in the black pastoral; in 1993, 1994 and 1996, when I, along with a research team of two Brazilians, interviewed forty women in the greater Rio de Janeiro region, of varying levels of involvement in the black pastoral; and in 2001, when I interviewed a dozen lay activists in Maranhao.

8. Following my informants, I use the terms "afro Mass," "afro liturgy," "inculturated Mass," and "inculturated liturgy" synonymously.

9. David Kozak, "Ecumenical Indianism: the Tekakwitha Movement as a Discursive Field of Faith and Power," in *The Message in the Missionary: Local Interpretations of Religious Ideology and Missionary Personality*, edited by Elizabeth Brusco and Laura Klein (Williamsburg, VA: *Studies in Third World Societies*, 1994), 91–114.

10. Ivone Gebara, "A Feminist Perspective on Enigmas and Ambiguities in Religious Interpretation," in Bamat and Wiest, *Popular Catholicism in a World Church*. For a similar critique applied to projects elsewhere in Latin America, see Pop Cal, "The Old Face of the New Evangelization," in *Crosscurrents in Indigenous Spirituality: Interface of Maya, Catholic and Protestant Worldviews*, edited by Guillermo Cook (Leiden:

Brill, 1997), 217–224; and Andrew Orta, "From Theologies of Liberation to Theologies of Inculturation," in *Organized Religion in the Political Transformation of Latin America,* edited by S. R. Pattnayak (Lanham, MD.: University Press of America, 1995), 97–124.

11. David Kozak, "Ecumenical Indianism," 100.

12. Richard Wilson, *Maya Resurgence in Guatemala: Q'eqchi Experiences* (Norman: University of Oklahoma Press, 1995), 305; see also by Wilson, "Anchored Communities: Identity and History of the Maya Q'eqchi," in *Crosscurrents in Indigenous Spirituality,* edited by Guillermo Cook (Leiden: Brill, 1997), 113–136.

13. Leonardo Boff, *New Evangelization,* 52.

14. José Guitherme Cantor Magnani, *Myptica Urbe* (São Paolo: Studio Nobel, 1999; Rowan Ireland, *Kingdom Come: Religion and Politics in Brazil* (Pittsburgh: University of Pittsburgh Press, 1991; Cecilia Mariz, *Coping with Poverty: Pentecostal and Christian Base Communities in Brazil* (Philadelphia: Temple University Press, 1993).

Race and Nation in the Mission Field

In the Americas and elsewhere, perceptions of racial, national, and religious identity are often defined through charged encounters with difference. In philosophical or psychoanalytic terms, there can be no "self"—individual or collective—without the contrastive experience of an "other." More concretely, and politically, a host of questions surround encounters with difference: Are these "others" enough like "us" to share a common social world? Are our differences innate, or might we somehow overcome them? Should we even try to overcome them, or work instead to shore up the lines between us? The answers to such fundamental questions define the contours of racial, national, and religious boundaries.

Throughout the history of the Americas, these questions have often been asked and answered in the distinctive context of Christian missionary work. Christianity is, arguably, unique among world religions in its foundational insistence on the assimilation of religious difference. Inspired in part by Jesus' Great Commission—the biblical injunction to spread the gospel—Christians around the world have worked to "make disciples of all peoples, baptizing them in the name of the Father and of the Son and of the Holy Spirit" (Matthew 28:19). And when the religious differences between Christians and others intersect—as they so often do—with differences of race and nation, the process of religious conversion becomes an arena for defining, and contesting, racial hierarchies and national boundaries. The production of new Christians may be linked to the production of new citizens. And though racial identities are not typically considered amenable to personal choice or transformation,

Christianization may nevertheless be linked to a cultural process of Whitening, and thus to the maintenance of a hierarchical racial order. Yet at the same time, by introducing an element of flux into ostensibly stable identity formations—by allowing the possibility of movement across the boundaries of difference—the process of conversion may destabilize racial, national, and religious essentialisms.

The essays in this section examine these double-edged politics of religious conversion, exploring how Christian missionary work in the Americas has simultaneously reinforced and undercut racial and national identities. In " 'Marked in Body, Mind and Spirit': Home Missionaries and the Re-Making of Race and Nation," Derek Chang discusses the work of the American Baptist Home Mission Society with African Americans and Chinese immigrants in the late nineteenth century. Chang explores the tensions between hierarchy and inclusion in the efforts of White evangelists to incorporate racialized minorities into the Baptist Church and the body politic, as well as the tensions that ultimately arose between White missionary discourses and the proselytes' own alternative visions of race, nation, and religion. Somewhat similarly, Julia Cummings O'Hara examines the unintended consequences of Jesuit mission work with the Tarahumara Indians of northern Mexico. In " 'In Search of Souls, in Search of Indians': Religion and the 'Indian Problem' in Northern Mexico," O'Hara shows how twentieth century Jesuit efforts to "civilize" the Tarahumara initially reinforced the racialized distinction between Indians and Whites but ultimately called into question the symbolic equation of Catholicism with Whiteness and Mexican national identity that lay at the heart of their evangelical project.

These essays chart the intersections of race, nation, and religion in substantially different contexts, but taken together they demonstrate the role of religion in a shared project of nation building in the late nineteenth and early twentieth centuries. Moreover, they reveal the complex tensions that inevitably plague the effort to define racial and national boundaries in the mission field.

5

"Marked in Body, Mind, and Spirit": Home Missionaries and the Remaking of Race and Nation

Derek Chang

In the three decades following the Civil War, the United States threatened to explode in a frenzy of racial violence. White reactions to African-American freedom and citizenship and to Chinese immigration and settlement approached a sustained level of ferocity. Black claims to equality and Chinese desires to live in the United States directly challenged the historic link between whiteness and American national identity, and European Americans reasserted their perceived privilege with a vengeance. In the South, whites responded to the promise of emancipation and Reconstruction with the Ku Klux Klan and Black Codes. After Reconstruction gave way to white reaction, violence and intimidation—most notably but not limited to lynching—fortified restrictive remedies to "the Negro Problem," including the legal segregation and disfranchisement of Jim Crow.[1] White responses to Chinese immigration proved equally brutal, and periodic race riots in cities and towns punctuated everyday acts of force and terror aimed at discouraging settlement.[2] As in the South, quotidian practices sustained limiting and punitive solutions to "the Chinese Question." In 1875, the U.S. Congress passed initial legislation restricting Chinese women from entering the country, and in 1882 a more sweeping Chinese Exclusion Act became law.[3] During this period, white Americans achieved a continental command over the nation, reuniting North and South and fulfilling America's "manifest destiny" through the linking of the

Atlantic and Pacific coasts by rail. Yet even as they celebrated this achievement of geographic breadth, they sought to narrowly restrict the nation's polity by reinforcing the racial bounds of citizenship.

It was within this racially and politically charged context that Reverend E. G. Robinson, former president of the Rochester Theological Seminary run by the American Baptist Home Mission Society (ABHMS), stood before the Baptist Autumnal Conference in Brooklyn, New York, on a fall evening in 1882 and delivered an address entitled "Race and Religion on the American Continent."[4] Robinson's words struck at the heart of European-American racial anxieties. Focusing his attention on blacks and Chinese immigrants, he spoke with frank concern about the current condition and future role of the "despoiled" and "half Christianized African of the South" and the "despised" and heathen "Mongol" settling on the Pacific Coast.[5]

Yet rather than joining the ever-increasing chorus of voices decrying the addition of these groups to the American polity, Robinson argued for a more inclusive definition of the nation. He boldly asserted that blacks deserved equal rights and that the Chinese should be welcomed.[6] The Baptist minister felt compelled to comment on the "Negro Problem" and the "Chinese Question" because he connected the acceptance of both groups to America's future as a Christian nation. Robinson believed that it was critical to proselytize to African Americans and Chinese immigrants if the United States hoped to fulfill its destiny as the divinely chosen vehicle for bringing about the reign of God's kingdom.[7] Indeed, he saw in those two much-reviled populations not only an opportunity but an obligation to further the cause of evangelical Christianity. Echoing the "divine injunction" of Christ to "Go Ye into all the world, and preach the Gospel to every creature" (Mark 16:15), Robinson reminded his audience of ministers, missionaries, and lay supporters of the ABHMS's fundamental commitment to the propagation of Christianity to *all*. "Christianity," he said, "knows no distinction among the races."[8]

Robinson's speech, later reprinted by the ABHMS in its official publication, neatly encapsulated the racial, religious, and national ideology of the Baptist denomination's principle organization for domestic proselytizing.[9] Funded and managed by native-born, European-American residents of the Northeast, primarily from New York, the ABHMS, at the time of Robinson's speech, directed missionaries in forty-eight states and territories, stretching from the eastern seaboard to the Pacific Coast and from the upper Midwest to the deep South. Its missionaries worked among ex-slaves in the nine states of the former Confederacy, as well as in Tennessee, Kentucky, and Washington, D.C., and among the Chinese in northern California and Oregon.[10]

Even as movements toward segregation, disfranchisement, and exclusion called on a somatic, or biological, definition of race to demarcate the boundaries of citizenship, Robinson and the ABHMS articulated an alternative vision of the nation in which Christianity stood as the primary standard for inclusion. Whereas advocates and practitioners of Jim Crow and immigration restriction responded to the perceived racial fracturing of the American polity with exclusionary measures, the evangelicals of the ABHMS found a remedy in the conversion of all non-Christians—white, black, and Chinese alike. As the ABHMS created missions for African Americans and Chinese immigrants, its ideology represented a vital—if often overlooked—part of the late nineteenth-century American racial and national discourse.

However, the inclusionary impulses of evangelical Christianity only tell part of the story. Although missionaries rejected the growing movement toward restriction and exclusion, they often found themselves caught in a process that required the delineation of social and religious hierarchies. Conversion was predicated on the "inevitably pejorative nature of missionary constructions of heathenism" at the core of evangelical calls for social and religious uplift and transformation.[11] This emphasis on *difference* threatened ultimately to undermine missionaries' more egalitarian aims.

Indeed, the aspirations and actions of black and Chinese mission participants cast the undemocratic aspects of evangelical work in a particularly harsh light. Finding themselves limited by the hierarchical assumptions of the ABHMS and its missionaries, African Americans and immigrants possessed the resolve to push the ABHMS toward meeting its inclusive ideals and used mission resources to create their own models of Christian community. In an often implicit but sometimes explicit rebuke of missionary discourse and practice, they created autonomous and semiautonomous networks of religious and educational organizations that did not rely solely on ABHMS patronage and that operated at least partially shielded from the gaze of white missionaries. American Baptist programs, then, both developed into and helped to launch critical institutions in which alternative meanings of race were forged not only by ABHMS missionaries but by African-American and Chinese proselytes as well.[12]

This essay will first discuss the inclusive—perhaps even egalitarian—trajectory of ABHMS ideology and labors. The next section will describe the countervailing and hierarchical aspects inherent in the process of proselytizing that limited the democratic possibility of American Baptist missions. Finally, the third section will underscore the agency of African Americans and Chinese immigrants, examining their uses of ABHMS resources and analyzing their desire for autonomous institutions. The actions and aspirations of blacks and immigrants are crucial to understanding the significance of American Baptist missions, constituted by white missionaries and non-white proselytes, in the history of American racial, religious, and national identity.

"Egalitarian Promise of Inclusion": A Democratic Trajectory

Rooted in the democratic traditions of the Second Great Awakening and the Great Revival, the ABHMS approached its work among African Americans and Chinese immigrants during the late nineteenth century from a perspective influenced by what the British historian Susan Thorne has called the "egalitarian promise of inclusion" at the heart of evangelical Christianity—a perspective that placed individual agency above predestination and held the possibility that all were equal in sin and salvation.[13] Although this belief in the equality of souls all too infrequently found its expression in worldly matters, it provided a basis for some of the ABHMS's most significant public stands on race. During the antebellum period, for instance, several prominent members established an organization to oppose slavery—a position that led to the schism between northern and southern Baptists in the 1840s.[14] Bonded labor, according to these antislavery activists, undermined the evangelical belief in all people as "free moral agents."[15]

During the late nineteenth century, American Baptists' ambitious policy goals concerning freedpeople and Chinese immigrants continued this egalitarian trajectory. In 1865, for example, the organization dramatically appealed for the "elevation of the liberated bondmen" through the extension of "the *elective franchise* . . . with all the privileges of whatever kind belong to American citizenship."[16] To support this bold aim, the ABHMS employed dozens of measures, none more significant than helping to establish schools for the education of freedpeople. Again, in this endeavor for which the group would become most well known, American Baptists insisted on the recognition of the "full, absolute, equal humanity" of African Americans as the prerequisite for any effective educational program.[17]

Meanwhile, as growing numbers of Chinese men—and a much smaller population of Chinese women—entered the Pacific Coast seeking to improve their lives, members of the ABHMS announced that they had "no hesitancy in affirming it as their judgment that the Chinese are destined to become before long a large and worthy portion of our adopted American citizenship; and that special missionary labor among them . . . is one of the most imperative duties of the hour."[18] This position went beyond mere words as the ABHMS established mission schools, prayer meetings, and, in some cases, congregations along the Pacific Coast to impart the gospel to Chinese populations and convert them to Christianity—practices designed "to make of these populations American citizens."[19]

In an era during which emancipation and Reconstruction gave way to the reaction of Jim Crow and Chinese immigration was halted by a fit of legal and extralegal white supremacist action, the democratic trajectory of the ABHMS's evangelical nationalist project dared to suggest a nation in which blacks and

Chinese would enjoy full and equal citizenship rights. This was indeed a radical notion, for after centuries of bonded African-American labor, "black"—or "colored" or "Negro"—had come to be equated with "slave." In a society envisioned by its European-American citizens as free, blacks embodied the very opposite of republican freedom and the nadir of the social and racial hierarchy.[20] Chinese immigrants were similarly affected by the white supremacist tradition that defined the American polity. Most notably, the Naturalization Law of 1790 had established the principle that the right to become a citizen of the United States was to be reserved only for "free white persons."[21] Moreover, representations of immigrants as "cheap labor" and "coolies" invited comparisons to slavery that fueled allegations of a Chinese threat to free white labor and thus to American republican democracy itself.[22] Within this context of racialized citizenship—in which "whiteness" equaled "citizenship"—the Society's position had revolutionary implications.

Significantly, American Baptists linked religion to the historical nexus of race and nation. For them, evangelical Christianity was to be the bedrock of American national identity. Six months after Robinson's address, Lemuel Moss, a Baptist minister and home mission advocate from Indiana, described the national role of evangelical Christianity: "a free people will never be constituted or held together by any iron band. They must be held together by something that is powerful enough to assimilate and purify and elevate and unify all those discordant elements that may come within its range."[23]

Missionary Discourse and Remaking Race

As Moss's statement suggests, evangelical nationalism was far from a formula for neutral inclusiveness. Rather, it hinged on two crucial factors that held enormous consequence for the meaning of race. First, missions were predicated on essential differences between proselytizers and proselytes. The goal of "elevating" target communities assumed their lesser condition and implied a sense of hierarchy. Second, inclusion could only come after conversion—a change manifested not only by a profession of faith but by its attendant social transformations as well. For American Baptists, this meant a thorough inculcation in the beliefs of evangelical Christianity *and* middle-class values. Significantly, the acceptance of class-bound gender prescriptions, such as the role of women as the central purveyors of piety and purity within the home, represented a central marker of the success of this transformation.[24]

These basic characteristics of home missionary work meant that evangelicals would have to determine and define the hierarchical difference that lay between themselves and their potential proselytes. The process of proselytizing begged the question: What was to account for the great disparity between ex-slaves or Chinese immigrants and white missionaries? Evangelicals answered by linking social and cultural practice to spiritual transformation, thus blurring the lines between "secular" and "religious" remedies. Home mission labors required concrete programs targeted at the temporal—as well as spiritual— lives of proselytes. As a result, home missionary discourse on the crucial racial questions of the day defined difference in comprehensive terms that emphasized alterable social, cultural, and environmental factors.

A statement by Samuel Haskell, chairman of the Society's Committee on Work Among the Freedmen, provides a vivid example of the sweeping interpretation at the heart of ABHMS understandings of racial difference. Freed-people, Haskell lamented, were "[a] people marked in body, mind, and spirit with their long and sorrowful affliction."[25] His comments at once registered the ABHMS's longstanding condemnation of slavery, established an interpretation of the effects of servitude, and intimated the enormity of the work that lay ahead. Haskell's summary precisely tied together the economic, social, and cultural forces that embodied the racialization of African Americans; they had, indeed, been "marked" by the imprint of 350 years of systematic bonded labor. The only way to efface the markings of servitude was through an exhaustive program of social and economic aid, education, and, in particular, religious conversion. In fact, conversion would be revealed in more than the profession of faith. It would manifest itself in social, cultural, and religious practice.

The attribution of difference to past experience ran counter to theories of racial biology that, even as Haskell spoke, were gaining ascendancy. Although ideas about the separate origins of "races"—such as African, European, or Mongol—had long been available to white supremacists, the advent of scientific inquiry into racial difference launched a powerful, aggressive, and enduring new phase of racial theory. The historian Hamilton Cravens notes that scientific racism in the late nineteenth and early twentieth centuries rested on the "assumption . . . that mental traits had a basis in physical structure, a notion borrowed from evolutionary science in general and Darwinian biology in particular," and that the resulting "evolutionary point of view" claimed that "each race had to pass through the stages of barbarism and savagery to civilization (the white man's perch)."[26] Thus, Joseph Le Conte, a professor of natural history and geology and a president of the American Association for the Advancement of Science, argued that blacks had little biological capacity for development outside the control of whites and were suited only for slavery.[27] By this standard, the ABHMS's culturally based conception of difference stood in stark contrast.

Nevertheless, this alternate vision rested on a complicated foundation of racial reformulation. Even as American Baptists posited a broader notion of citizenship, they worked to narrow the spectrum of religious and cultural difference by remaking African Americans and Chinese immigrants in their own image, and their project held hierarchical assumptions that undercut the egalitarian promise of its labors. As Matthew Frye Jacobson observes, the exclusions and inclusions governing who could become an American represented racialized determinations of what was required of a citizen.[28] In this sense, the Society's goal of admitting both groups as citizens turned not on reimagining a multicultural nation but on equipping them with what white evangelicals believed to be the necessary tools and traits of citizenship.[29]

In fact, the prejudice that assumed the necessity of transforming proselyte populations in the first place belied the inclusive promise of evangelical Christianity. The initial missionary belief that proselytes required "uplift" presupposed inequality. To be sure, missionaries attributed most of the inequality to alterable environmental, cultural, and religious factors. Yet even as this alternate notion held the promise of deemphasizing physiological distinctions, American Baptists reinscribed race through culture and religion.

Evangelicals' claims on America's specifically Christian national identity was crucial in this symbiosis of culture, religion, and race. As Ann Laura Stoler has observed, racism is not merely a "visual ideology in which somatic features are thought to provide the crucial criteria of membership."[30] Rather, she writes, "Cultural attributions . . . provide the observable conduits, the indexes of psychological propensities and moral susceptibilities seen to shape which individuals are suitable for inclusion in the national community."[31] Similarly, Paul Gilroy has noted the uses of nationalism and culture in redefining race. In his analysis of "ethnic absolutism," he examines the view that nations are "culturally homogeneous 'communities of sentiment' in which a sense of patriotic belonging can and should grow to become an important source of moral and political ideas."[32] In the United States, as Jacobson has demonstrated, cultural determinations of the "fitness for self-government" were crucial to the nexus of racial and national identity.[33] The supposed "laziness" of Native Americans, whose agricultural practices, land use, and gender conventions struck Europeans as immoral; the alleged dependency of African and African-American slaves on their masters; the tyranny of the Chinese political and social system—America's founders viewed all of these political and economic relationships in cultural terms that defined each group outside the bounds of both "American" and "white." Europeans were white and, therefore, could become Americans; Africans, Indians, and Asians were not white and, therefore, would remain aliens. Indeed, the net effect of slavery and the 1790 Naturalization Law (and its antecedents) was more than just to define who could *not* be Americans. It also necessarily determined who Americans were, and it characterized them racially as white.

American Baptists considered the moral order of Christianity and the appropriate style of worship and more general comportment of converted individuals to be germane to this assessment of racial identity. In 1880, Granville S. Abbott advocated the expansion of mission schools to educate immigrants because "the Chinese are here in the United States to stay," and it was necessary to teach them English and respect for and belief in Christianity.[34] Similarly, the ABHMS official H. L. Wayland maintained that blacks were "to be educated as American citizens" as well as Christians. According to Wayland, with the benefits and responsibilities of citizenship "there is the most urgent need of the elevating, guiding, inspiring influence of Christian knowledge and Christian principle."[35] Yet, as they extended this standard to embrace African Americans and Chinese immigrants, American Baptists threatened to transgress the historical barrier that equated whiteness and citizenship. This matrix of racial and national identity trapped the ABHMS's inclusive discourse within a web of meaning with contradictory consequences.

The process of missionary work—especially the phase that required the identification and characterization of religious deficiencies in target populations—served to buttress rather than to nullify racial distinctions. In fact, in the ABHMS's nationalist evangelical discourse, missionaries and officials articulated racial identity through religious difference. Ironically, the literature that sought to garner support for, justify, and explain evangelical work among African Americans and Chinese immigrants reinforced the distance between these groups and the missionaries. This distancing occurred in many stages of proselytizing but nowhere was more evident than in the literature produced by white evangelicals and missionary officials about the subjects of their labors.

As part of proselytizing, American Baptist officials and missionaries set about ascertaining the needs of African-American and Chinese immigrant communities by trying to establish the essential character of both populations. They carefully catalogued religious practices, social relations, familial customs, material conditions, and behavior, circulating their findings in the religious press, sermons, and speeches. This assessment phase of missionary work sought to determine a baseline for both groups so the Society could devise effective programs and attract supporters through a widely disseminated descriptive literature. Missionaries and officials thus produced a far-reaching ethnographic discourse that purported to reveal key characteristics of proselyte communities and cultures. Containing rich descriptions of Chinese society and ex-slaves' lives while positing explanations and interpretations for the effects of "heathenism" and slavery, ABHMS literature is best characterized by Joan Jacobs Brumberg's term "missionary ethnology."[36]

This reportage effectively reduced Chinese and African-American religious life and social relations to a set of descriptions expressed in a vocabulary of uplift and progress. Such "manners-and-customs portraits," according to Mary Louise Pratt, "work to normalize another society, to codify its difference from one's own, to fix its members in a timeless present where all 'his' actions and reactions are repetitions of 'his' normal habits."[37] Moreover, as the missionaries themselves were men and women who had extensive personal experience with African-American and Chinese communities, their reports offered the imprimatur of expertise.[38]

Not surprisingly, the missionary literature on ex-slaves and the Chinese dwelled in large part on religious practice.[39] American Baptist missionaries' observations of African-American services featured descriptions of strange rituals and confessions of frank bafflement, such as the one provided by a Northern teacher, Ellen Adlington, who witnessed a black Baptist gathering in Georgia. She related being "screamed at in a wild ignorant half rhapsody" and bemoaned that "not a word [was] said of the commandments."[40] The Christianity that missionaries witnessed was suffused with expressive emotion and seemed not at all like the orthodox practice they were accustomed to. The American Baptist missionary Jonathan W. Horton, stationed in Port Royal, South Carolina, professed to being "very much puzzled what to do about the religious feeling of these people."[41]

Whereas Horton experienced exasperation, Joseph T. Robert, head of the ABHMS school in Georgia, regarded the "utterances and . . . tears" during African-American worship as evidence of blacks' "intense interest in [the] study of the Holy Scriptures" and part of their "eminently emotional and imaginative" racial character.[42] In fact, Robert's perspective focused on what missionaries believed to be the sole redemptive quality to the strange behavior they witnessed: devotion. Although ex-slaves were thought to lack orthodox religious belief and practice—a situation to be remedied by ABHMS schools and formally trained ministers—they were nonetheless believed to possess an emotive devotion to Christianity on which few missionary observers cast doubt. American Baptist evangelicals repeatedly noted not only the enthusiasm of worship but the sacrifice made by congregants as they helped to build mission institutions. One missionary in Tennessee reported: "for every thing they eat or wear they have to pay enormous prices, and their opportunities for obtaining money with which to pay are very limited, the sufferings in consequence of their poverty are very great, and yet at their meetings last Sabbath they contributed four dollars."[43]

In observations of the Chinese, "heathenism" was an all-encompassing distinguishing trait. The term became code for a comprehensive set of ills that beset both the Chinese population in the United States and in Asia, for the lack of Christianity had left China and its people in the darkness of a backward civilization. Accounts led readers on tours of "heathen temples" and opium dens in Chinatown and explored the proliferation of prostitution and gambling.[44] In one colorful account of a temple "for the worship of heathen deities" in San Francisco, a missionary related what might be referred to as the "desacralization," or "heathenization," of the cityscape represented by the "external appearance" of a building that used Chinese architecture and design styles—a tangible reminder of the non-Christian nature of the Chinese population in the United States and, for many, an affront to the Christian roots of American culture.[45] Within this "miniature" version of a "house of gods," "darkness" reigned, and congregants worshiped not Christ but idols.[46] The missionary ethnology about the Chinese depicted a world to which most European-

American readers had no access and described a culture mired in a superstition and immorality not yet redeemed by Christianity.

Whereas efforts among African Americans aimed at altering nominally Christian practice, the missionary endeavor among immigrants hoped to completely replace non-Christian religions, and evangelical assessments of these religions remained central to descriptions of the "Chinese character." In an analysis of Western writings on Confucianism, for instance, Carl T. Jackson observes that missionaries credited it with both negative and ostensibly positive attributes.[47] Confucianism, according to missionaries, was the source "of the Chinese people's haughty attitude toward outsiders and mindless adherence to tradition" and of their "rational" mind.[48] Henrietta Hall Shuck, the first American Baptist woman in China, echoed the negative assessment, claiming that "pride" and "self-righteousness" were two of "the prominent characteristics of the great Confucius."[49]

Even the supposed positive aspects of Confucianism—its rational influence over the Chinese—became a critical barrier for conversion and stood as a fundamental difference. As missionary discourse generalized more broadly from its religious evaluations of the Chinese, for instance, Chinese rationality, combined with the arrogance so many evangelicals claimed to observe, became code for a decorous yet unfeeling and perhaps even unbelieving practice of Christianity. This contrasted directly with missionary depictions of the freedpeople, whom evangelicals considered to be enthusiastic but overly emotional and completely unorthodox. The Baptist minister and official E. G. Robinson noted: "the Mongol, with his Confucian ethics, will make, of the gospel religion rather than piety, while the African, with his emotional nature, will make, of the same gospel, piety rather than religion."[50] It is left unspoken yet obvious that European-American missionaries and, more generally, white Christians held the perfect balance between religion and piety. The representations of missionary ethnographers served as counterpoints to each other and were both viewed in contrast to the normative practices and beliefs of white evangelicals.

Significantly, this discourse, despite the inclusive aims espoused in its rhetoric and despite its focus on culture and environment, possessed a remarkable consonance with the dominant biological racism of the late nineteenth century. For instance, in explaining the hierarchy of races, Joseph Le Conte asserted that

> inferior races may be divided into two groups—viz., those which are inferior because undeveloped, and those which are so because developed, perhaps highly developed, in a limited way or in a wrong direction. . . . The Negro is the best type of the first group, and perhaps the Chinese of the second group.[51]

Through missionary ethnology the biological description of blacks and Chinese acquired cultural markers to create representations of the pious yet backward freedpeople and the coldly intelligent and formalistic immigrants. Ironically, then, evangelicals added a culturally and religiously shaded layer to late nineteenth-century efforts to solidify the racialization of African Americans and immigrants.

Alternative Visions

Even as missionary ethnology produced fixed representations of African Americans and Chinese immigrants, the potential proselytes themselves offered a significantly different view of their lives. Official missionary discourse overwhelmingly privileges missionary voices over those of their proselytes, and accounts produced by evangelicals provide only occluded views of African-American and Chinese spirituality and religious belief. Although often based on observations of material circumstances or events, missionary literature obscures the extent to which the proselyte practices it critiques might be viewed as alternative, counterhegemonic visions of racial, religious, and national identity.

The Afro-Christian practice observed by missionaries did, in fact, possess a remarkable emotional tenor, and its theological underpinnings may have seemed unorthodox to northern observers. Under slavery, African Americans had developed a religion that fused African traditions with the Christianity propagated by evangelical plantation missions.[52] The "shout" and "frenzy" that characterized the expressive crux of black Christian worship and conversion have been linked to African antecedents.[53] Shaped by the punishing oppression of servitude, the emancipatory faith and egalitarian spirit of African and Old Testament theology, and the relentless zeal for freedom of the slaves themselves, this religion developed beyond the gaze of watchful masters who hoped to use conversion for social control.[54] Ideologically, it was characterized by a typological relationship among the past, the present, and the future. For black Christians, the experience of moving from slavery to freedom held a direct link to the people and stories in the book of Exodus, and this connection confirmed a sense of "chosenness" or peoplehood among African Americans.[55] This sense was verified and reinforced by the numerous ex-slaves who fled biracial yet unequal churches in the aftermath of the war. Black Christianity, from its emotional expression to its theological content, evolved from a significantly different tradition and held an idea of the nation that was notably distinct from the evangelical nationalism of American Baptist missionaries.

The empirical foundation for missionary representations of the Chinese is harder to determine. Certainly, the brothels, opium dens, and temples described by evangelical discourse were not entirely fabrications of the missionary imagination. Although cast in an ominous light by Christian writings, these institutions were fundamental elements of ethnic enclaves whose inhabitants

had both limited economic opportunity and the need to escape the harsh realities of immigrant life.[56] Moreover, the existence of Buddhist temples attests
to the cultural resilience of the immigrant community, while the charge of
"formalism" and inauthentic belief probably referred to missionaries' bewil-
derment at the idea that immigrants might follow the works of Confucius *and*
Buddha or Confucius *and* Lao Tze. For men and women who believed that
Christ was the savior and son of the one true God, this ability to hold more
than one belief system sacrosanct was cause for suspicion. Each of these examples reflects the agency and resistance of Chinese immigrants to missionary
attempts at conversion. Although perhaps not as institutionally and ideologically cohesive as the creation of black churches in the South, these establish-
ments and religious articulations represented attempts to create social space
from which community institutions might develop and in which various cultural expression would be permissible. In this sense, immigrants attempted to
forge a distinctly Chinese-American culture in the United States.

Within mission institutions themselves, the activities of evangelicals were
underwritten by proselyte participation. Despite their absence as actors in most
examples of missionary ethnology, ex-slaves and immigrants played critical
roles in the creation of missionary institutions; in the simplest materialist
terms, ex-slaves and immigrants contributed from their modest incomes for
the establishment of missions. Moreover, a close reading of proselyte actions
and participation as ideological, religious, and political articulations provides
a glimpse into the ways both blacks and the Chinese sought to transform
missionary institutions. Although circumscribed by the discourse of uplift at
the center of missionary endeavors, African-American and Chinese immigrant
proselytes nonetheless used ABHMS-sponsored programs and the status they
acquired through mission education to advance visions of religious and racial
identity that were well beyond those imagined by white evangelicals.

The actions of mission participants rarely directly repudiated ABHMS assumptions about the hierarchical distance between proselytizers and proselytes. Rather, black and Chinese Baptists involved with ABHMS missions
found themselves hamstrung between a desire for access to American Baptist
resources to build institutions that would eventually be autonomous and the
acceptance of the religious, class, and gender norms embedded in the discourse of racial uplift. The top-down social theory of the ABHMS held that the
best way to reach proselyte populations was through the education of leaders,
especially ministers and teachers. Thus in 1866 the organization described the
blueprint for its project in the South: "in the colored preachers . . . are the
leaders of all social movements among the freedmen. If we can lead and elevate
them, we may through them hope to elevate the mass of the people."[57] By the
end of the 1860s, ABHMS institutions began training black women to be
teachers and missionary assistants—the female equivalent of the male reli-

gious leader. On the Pacific Coast, although seemingly more humble in its aims, the Baptist project nonetheless focused on training Chinese ministers, missionaries, and missionary assistants who would be able to establish self-sustaining missions and, eventually, congregations for the bulk of the immigrant population.

Many of the beneficiaries of missions could not help but absorb white evangelical understandings of religion, culture, and society. In Tennessee, for example, a black student of the ABHMS school in Nashville, like so many of his fellow ministerial candidates, spent his summer vacation teaching and preaching throughout more rural parts of the state. During the course of his travels, he witnessed a revival:

> such awful disgusting, and unchristian and heathenish practices are carried on that the strongest words in the language are perfectly tame and meaningless when one would attempt to describe the scene. . . . This is true not only of the locality where I was. My fellow students from all parts of the Southwestern states say that the same practices prevail wherever they have been. Some places are not as bad, but some are even worse than I have witnessed.[58]

This account echoes the same themes as white missionary-produced depictions of black worship during the same period. Clearly, the student had absorbed ABHMS norms for the practice of Christianity.

Dong Gong, a Chinese missionary who labored in San Francisco and Guandong (Canton) before establishing and then directing the Chinese Mission School in Portland, Oregon, had a similarly dim view of his unconverted compatriots. Addressing a crowd of mostly European-American supporters at the school's first anniversary concert, Dong commented disapprovingly on the "idol worship," superstition, and insularity of the Chinese.[59] Significantly, he reiterated a theme of missionary ethnology by alluding to the lack of emotional enthusiasm intrinsic to Chinese religion, noting that Christianity had altered that quality in him:

> I may tell you a little of the Chinese religion. The Chinese have different kinds of worship and different ways of forgiving sins. I have read many of their books, and have inquired the way of doing it, but none of them can stir my heart nor satisfy my conscience like the New Testament.[60]

As participants became inculcated with normative missionary-defined values and practices, they exemplified the transcendence of difference at the heart of ABHMS standards of inclusion and were able to establish themselves as leaders. Indeed, advancement within mission institutions provided ABHMS-educated individuals with a level of credibility in certain sectors of the local white populations as well as in their respective communities. Yet, while individuals might ascend the hierarchy defined by missionary ethnographic discourse, in the view of missionaries and proselyte leaders, the rest of the African-American or Chinese immigrant community remained unaffected.

Nonetheless, despite the limits of the hegemonic discourse of race and religion, these educated few sought to transform ABHMS institutions—and society in general—through their example of aspiration and advancement. Their inclusion, first as students and then as teachers and administrators, would set the stage for the eventual appropriation of mission projects. This, in fact, was the stated goal of the ABHMS's endeavors. In 1874, for example, the organization's Executive Board said: "we have no desire to retain permanently either the possession or the control of these schools. They must ultimately swing loose from us. And the sooner the better."[61] Although less explicit in the case of the Chinese, missionaries and sponsors expressed enthusiasm for greater proselyte financial support and participation, and one of the goals of converting and educating immigrants was to develop a transnational network of Chinese Christians to proselytize and organize self-governing churches in the United States and China.

Yet the ABHMS's standards for proselyte self-governance often clashed with the eagerness of the proselytes themselves to run mission-originated institutions. In fact, the determination of just when African Americans and Chinese immigrants were deemed ready for autonomy became the focal point of numerous battles. As the historian Paul Harvey has demonstrated, when a group of black Baptist organizations came together in the Consolidated American Baptist Missionary Convention (CABMC) and attempted to wrest control over the expenditure of missionary funds from the ABHMS, the northern white missionary organization refused.[62] Members of the CABMC astutely believed the paternalism of the ABHMS perspective prevented the northern benefactors from fulfilling its stated goal of turning its institutions over to black management.[63] A more subtle interaction with many of the same inflections occurred in the Baptist effort among Chinese immigrants. Despite being an ordained minister, a member of the sponsoring church, and the founding missionary, the Chinese Christian who conducted services and taught classes at the Chinese Mission School in Portland was never elected the institution's superintendent.[64] That role of authority was reserved for white patrons.

Nonetheless, individuals exemplified the aspiration for advancement and demonstrated the possibility of progress for the larger group. In Oregon, for example, Song Sam Bo not only converted to Christianity and became a member of the church as a result of the Chinese Mission School's catechism; he also navigated his way through the school's secular curriculum to earn white

Baptist support to attend McMinnville College and study for the ministry. Although Baptists on the Pacific Coast did not participate in formal "rescue missions" for Chinese women, as did Presbyterians, Methodists, and Congregationalists, persons seeking to escape the exploitation of prostitution sought the protection and resources of local churches and mission schools.[65]

In the South, men and women born in slavery or to slave parents eagerly attended ABHMS institutions to improve their lot. Examples abound: A. W. Pegues was born a slave in 1859, but by 1879, with the opportunities of provided by emancipation and Reconstruction, he had obtained some education and had saved enough money to attend the ABHMS's Benedict College in South Carolina.[66] He went on to earn a master's degree at Bucknell University and to become an educational leader and minister in North Carolina.[67] Reverend Thomas O. Fuller, the son of former slaves in Franklinton, North Carolina, graduated from Shaw University with honors in 1890, became a minister and leading educator, and, in 1898, was elected to the state senate as the body's only black member.[68]

These individuals, using American Baptist resources, carved out vital social, cultural, and political space not only for themselves but for their fellow blacks and immigrants as well—providing vital institutions rather than mere inspiration. In fact, while disputes continued within the ABHMS over when proselytes would be ready to control mission projects, black and Chinese students and former students set about creating their own institutions and networks. This process took many forms and artfully subverted missionary characterizations of African Americans and immigrants as underdeveloped. Black ministerial students and some Chinese missionary assistants and ministers took to the countryside to preach the gospel and organize educational and religious meetings for more isolated populations. The lack of constant missionary presence in these areas meant that the meetings—and in some case churches—that resulted would be run entirely by blacks or Chinese. In addition to providing space for religious and cultural expression away from the gaze of the dominant society, these assemblies and congregations were valuable community resources.

Students in ABHMS institutions were also instrumental in creating black and Chinese immigrant organizations that ran parallel to those run by missionaries. Many graduates of ABHMS schools in the South, for example, were called to the pulpit in black churches where Christian worship occurred away from the gaze of disapproving white missionaries. Moreover, these and other black ministers began to organize larger regional and state Baptist associations that lay outside the control of the ABHMS. Ceasar Johnson, Ezekiel E. Smith, and Nicholas F. Roberts, all members of the first official graduating class from the ABHMS's Shaw University in Raleigh, North Carolina, were early leaders of the African-American Baptist State Convention.[69] Finally, educators who trained at ABHMS institutions established schools throughout the South. The Waters Normal Institute in Winston, North Carolina, for example, was run by a Shaw graduate named C. S. Brown, and its staff included three female graduates of the Raleigh school, Miss Addie L. Hall, Miss Mamie S. Roberts, and Mrs. Meander S. Sessons.[70] These schools became a central training ground for African Americans as public resources for black education diminished during the age of Jim Crow.

Chinese immigrants were no less active. As Wesley Woo has discovered, Chinese Christians in San Francisco organized the interdenominational Youxue Zhengdaohui in 1871 as a tribute to the Baptist convert and preacher Fung Seung Nam, who had recently died.[71] Although the first meeting occurred at the Chinese Presbyterian Church, it seems that the chief organizers were Baptist followers of Fung.[72] This organization eventually fragmented into separate denominational societies, but each had similar rules and goals. They conducted their own worship services and study groups, and members were required to "love one another."[73] Moreover, in less formal ways, immigrant converts of ABHMS missions created a transnational network of Chinese Christians. Thus, after Dong Gong left his post at the Portland, Oregon, Chinese Mission School to return to China, he not only continued his labors as an evangelical but successfully encouraged his former students to contribute "several hundred dollars" for a mission and chapel there.[74]

The formal and informal networks established by aspiring participants of ABHMS missions repudiated white evangelical notions of black and Chinese inferiority and subverted the condescension of missionary discourse and practice. In these spaces for religious expression and social congregation, African-American and Chinese immigrant proselytes dismissed the deferential attitude of missionaries while accepting their resources. They pushed the ABHMS to fulfill its rhetorical promise of inclusion and equality without waiting for white missionaries and officials to validate this goal. In their churches, religious meetings, autonomous organizations, and schools, they demonstrated a broader version of Christian fellowship than that espoused by the missionaries who had converted them.

The activities of black Baptists and Chinese Christians thus amounted to alternative renderings of the ABHMS's racial and national vision for America. While the organization spoke of eventual inclusion, self-reliance, and autonomy for its proselytes, African Americans and Chinese immigrants actively and successfully carried out these ideals. However, their actions articulated more than mere inclusion. In each local institution, with each link in a given network, and in each expression of religious heterodoxy, blacks and immigrants asserted a form of Christian community that rested not on assimilation but on acceptance. Unlike that of ABHMS missionaries, their vision of the nation was both multicultural and inclusive.

Conclusion

The nineteenth century closed in a flurry of white supremacist legislation. Throughout the South, the 1890s witnessed the passage of Jim Crow laws to reinforce de facto segregation and second-class black citizenship that had been widespread since the end of Reconstruction in 1877. In 1892, Congress renewed the Chinese Exclusion Act and extended it for another ten years in 1902. For both African Americans and Chinese immigrants, the restrictive legislation rested on a foundation of terror.

In this context of white reaction, black and Chinese proselytes sought shelter within American Baptist home missions. They had helped to build these institutions by drawing on the resources provided by the ABHMS and by pushing the evangelical organization to fulfill its promise of Christian inclusion. But by the end of the nineteenth century, the Society's vision of evangelical nationalism had been eclipsed by a narrower conception. As participants were inculcated with normative missionary-defined values and practices, they exemplified the transcendence of difference at the heart of ABHMS standards of inclusion and were able to establish themselves as leaders. Indeed, advancement within mission institutions provided ABHMS-educated individuals with a level of credibility in certain sectors of the local white populations as well as in their respective communities. Yet, while individuals might ascend the hierarchy defined by missionary ethnographic discourse, in the view of missionaries and proselyte leaders, the rest of the African-American or Chinese immigrant community remained unchanged by America and its polity. Jim Crow and immigration exclusion had reinforced the historic connection between whiteness and national identity.

While no ABHMS-run mission schools and universities achieved autonomy during the nineteenth century, black and Chinese participants and former participants cobbled together autonomous organizations and informal networks that extended beyond individual missions. These institutions, in conjunction with mission churches and schools, provided a strong foundation for black and Chinese communities and even supplied a platform from which to advocate for inclusion in the nation through formal citizenship or legal residency. As the virulence of late nineteenth-century racialism grew, these sites became critical for sustaining black and Chinese dignity in an oppressive environment. Thus as disciplinary violence and intimidation, as well as restrictive legislation, reasserted white supremacy, the institutions that resulted from ABHMS missions offered a level of protection for African Americans and immigrants. Masked by a rhetoric of accommodation, black Baptists and Chinese Christians persevered. Indeed, they quietly went about expanding their institutions and, in the case of African Americans, would ultimately use these schools, churches, and other organizations to help launch and sustain the civil rights movement.

The ABHMS's work among blacks in the South and Chinese on the Pacific Coast exposed both the promise and the limits of its evangelical, nation-building, and racializing project. The desire to create a Christian America had led white evangelicals within the ABHMS to a conclusion full of radical possibility. Despite the recent model of black slavery and the longstanding 1790 Naturalization Act, which restricted citizenship rights only to those immigrants who were "free whites," the ABHMS believed that its evangelical nationalist project should be expanded to include freedpeople and the Chinese in America not just as coreligionists but as fellow citizens. Yet internal ideological contradictions and, especially, external opposition limited the application of this belief. Nevertheless, through its vigorous labors, the ABHMS provided important tools to African Americans and Chinese immigrants as *they* sought to dismantle the hierarchy of race.

In 1882, the ABHMS corresponding secretary and official historian Henry Lyman Morehouse declared: "the Gospel breaks the shackles of hierarchy."[75] Morehouse's words evoked the promise and possibility of an evangelical Christianity that ministered to Chinese immigrants in the aftermath of the Chinese Exclusion Act and to African Americans in the post-Reconstruction South. He believed that the acceptance of Christianity by men and women of diverse backgrounds would reduce social differences through assimilation. Yet Morehouse's simple statement of faith concealed a more complex process in which the hierarchy of race, rather than being eradicated, was rearticulated through religion. And while adhering to the Baptist faith in divine providence and the power of scripture, Morehouse neglected to credit the most influential earthbound opponents of racial hierarchy—African Americans and Chinese immigrants themselves.

NOTES

I thank Ian Lekus, Noeleen McIlvenna, Charles McKinney, Vince Brown, and Paul Ortiz for their thoughtful comments on drafts of this essay. Much of this essay was written while I held a fellowship for the study of Immigration and Religion from the Social Science Research Council.

1. The historian Raymond Gavins has written of Jim Crow in the South: "discrimination was grounded in everyday practice, including brute force, more than it was in law." The same was true of similarly segregationist practices aimed at the Chinese in the West. Raymond Gavins, "Fear, Hope, and Struggle: Recasting Black North Carolina in the Age of Jim Crow," in *Democracy Betrayed: The Wilmington Race Riot of 1898 and Its Legacy*, edited by David S. Cecelski and Timothy B. Tyson (Chapel Hill: University of North Carolina Press, 1998), 187.

2. Major race riots directed at the Chinese included those in Los Angeles (1871);

Chico, California (1877); Rock Springs, Wyoming (1885); and Seattle and Tacoma, Washington Territory (1886).

3. The historian Sucheng Chan has persuasively argued that the earliest federal exclusion efforts focused on restricting the immigration of women from China who worked as prostitutes in the United States. Sucheng Chan, "The Exclusion of Chinese Women, 1870–1943," in *Entry Denied: Exclusion and the Chinese Community in America, 1882–1943*, edited by Chan (Philadelphia: Temple University Press, 1991), 95.

4. E. G. Robinson, "Race and Religion on the American Continent," *Baptist Home Mission Monthly* 5, 3 (March 1883), 49–53.

5. Robinson, "Race and Religion on the American Continent," 52–53.

6. Robinson, "Race and Religion on the American Continent," 49, 52.

7. Robinson, "Race and Religion on the American Continent," 51.

8. Robinson, "Race and Religion on the American Continent," 52, 49.

9. For more on the roots, composition, and structure of the ABHMS, see Derek Chang, *"Breaking the Shackles of Hierarchy": Race, Religion, and Evangelical Nationalism in American Baptist Home Missions, 1865–1900* (Ph.D. diss., Duke University, 2002).

10. Executive Board of the ABHMS, *Fiftieth Annual Report of the ABHMS* (New York: American Baptist Mission Rooms, 1882), 115–158.

11. Susan Thorne, *Congregational Missions and the Making of an Imperial Culture in Nineteenth-Century England* (Stanford: Stanford University Press, 1999), 147.

12. I use "American Baptist" to refer specifically to Baptists with links to the ABHMS, not to denote the nationality of the Baptists in question. When referring to Baptists associated with the Southern Baptist Convention, I will use "Southern Baptists."

13. Thorne, *Congregational Missions*, 147. Thorne also discusses the resonance of a missionary movement that "conceded the humanity and dignity of all its supporters, offering a fleeting moment in the moral sun, in which the last sat alongside the first." Ibid., 161. The ideas that fueled the home mission movement in America during the 1830s derived from the "voluntary principle" of the Second Great Awakening. This reversal of the Calvinist concept of the elect held that anyone could "come to Christ" through prayer (and contact with those who already had experienced "new birth") and be saved. Home missionary associations developed as mechanisms to disseminate the Great Revival's religious, cultural, and social ideas over time and space, thus institutionalizing the era's spiritual passion. See Perry Miller, *The Life of the Mind in America: From the Revolution to the Civil War* (New York: Harcourt, Brace and World, 1965), 36–72.

14. For more on the American Baptist Antislavery Convention, see Chang, *Breaking the Shackles of Hierarchy*, 57–71.

15. Elon Galusha, "Address to Southern Baptists, Delivered 30 April 1840," reproduced in A. F. Foss and E. Mathews, *Facts for Baptist Churches* (Utica, N.Y.: American Baptist Free Mission Society, 1850), 46.

16. "Report of the Committee on the State of Country," in Executive Board of the ABHMS, *Thirty-Third Annual Report of the ABHMS* (New York: American Baptist Home Mission Rooms, 1865), 44.

17. H. L. Wayland, "Report of the Committee on Work Among the Colored Peo-

ple," in Executive Committee of the ABHMS, *Fiftieth Annual Report of the ABHMS* (New York: American Baptist Home Mission Rooms, 1882), 12.

18. G. S. Abbott, "Report of the Committee on the Chinese," in Executive Board of the ABHMS, "Minutes of the Forty-First Annual Meeting," *Forty-First Annual Report of the ABHMS* (New York: American Baptist Home Mission Rooms, 1873), 12. In 1860, the male to female ratio of the Chinese immigrant population was 18.6:1. In 1870, the ratio was 12.8:1. In 1880, after passage of the Page Act, which restricted Chinese female immigration, the ratio increased to 21.1:1. At the century's end, it stood at 26.8:1. Between 1860 and 1870, the total Chinese population in the United States grew some 81 percent; between 1870 and 1880, it increased another 67 percent. See Roger Daniels, "Table 3.1: Chinese American Population, Sex, Citizenship, and Sex Ratio, 1860–1940," in *Asian America: Chinese and Japanese in the United States since 1850*, 3rd printing (1988; reprint, Seattle: University of Washington Press, 1995), 69.

19. Editorial, *Baptist Home Mission Monthly* 1, 7 (January 1879), 102.

20. David Roediger, *The Wages of Whiteness: Race and the Making of the American Working Class* (London: Verso, 1991), 36.

21. Congress of the United States, House of Representatives, "An Act to Establish an Uniform Rule of Naturalization," in *The Public Statute at Large of the United States of America*, vol. 1 (Boston: Charles C. Little and James Brown, 1848), 103.

22. Stuart Creighton Miller, *The Unwelcome Immigrant: The American Image of the Chinese, 1875–1882* (Berkeley: University of California Press, 1969); Dan Caldwell, "The Negroization of the Chinese Stereotype in California," *Southern California Quarterly* 53 (June 1971), 123–131; Tomás Almaguer, *Racial Fault Lines: The Historical Origins of White Supremacy in California* (Berkeley: University of California Press, 1994), 153–182. Significantly, the racialization of the Chinese, like that of African Americans, began well before their arrival in the United States. See especially Gary Y. Okihiro, *Margins and Mainstreams: Asians in American History and Culture* (Seattle: University of Washington Press, 1994), 3–30.

23. Lemuel Moss, "Results of Home Mission Work," *Baptist Home Mission Monthly* 5, 5 (May 1883), 101.

24. For an excellent example of the ways the acceptance of class- and race-bound gender prescriptions marked spiritual and social transformation, see Evelyn Brooks Higginbotham, *Righteous Discontent: The Women's Movement in the Black Baptist Church, 1880–1920* (Cambridge: Harvard University Press, 1993). See also Peggy Pascoe, *Relations of Rescue: The Search for Female Moral Authority in the American West, 1874–1939* (New York: Oxford University Press, 1990); Susan M. Yohn, *A Contest of Faiths: Missionary Women and Pluralism in the American Southwest* (Ithaca, N.Y.: Cornell University Press, 1995).

25. Samuel Haskell, "Report on Work for Freedmen," in Executive Board of the ABHMS, *Thirty-Second Annual Report of the ABHMS* (New York: American Baptist Home Mission Rooms, 1864), 33.

26. Hamilton Cravens, "Scientific Racism in Modern America, 1870s–1990s," *Prospects* 21 (1996), 475.

27. Joseph Le Conte, *The Race Problem in the South* (1892; reprint, Miami, Fla.: Mnemosyne, 1969), 359–367.

28. Matthew Frye Jacobson, *Whiteness of a Different Color: European Immigrants and the Alchemy of Race* (Cambridge: Harvard University Press, 1998), 22–23.

29. The process of providing what the ABHMS deemed to be the essential traits of citizenship led the organization to aid in the establishment of missionary schools and universities. In the South, it funded and staffed seminaries and institutions to train black ministers and teachers, including Shaw University in Raleigh, North Carolina, Spelman and Morehouse Colleges in Atlanta, Georgia, and Benedict College in Columbia, South Carolina. Among the Chinese, American Baptist missionaries created Bible and Sunday schools, taught English classes, and helped to constitute congregations as foundations of Christian worship in cities and towns along the Pacific Coast from Los Angeles to Seattle. For a detailed examination, see Chang, *Breaking the Shackles of Hierarchy.*

30. Ann Laura Stoler, "Sexual Affronts and Racial Frontiers: European Identities and the Cultural Politics of Exclusion in Colonial Southeast Asia," in *Tensions of Empire: Colonial Cultures in a Bourgeois World*, edited by Frederick Cooper and Ann Laura Stoler (Berkeley: University of California Press, 1997), 116.

31. Stoler, "Sexual Affronts," 116.

32. Paul Gilroy, *"There Ain't No Black in the Union Jack": The Cultural Politics of Race and Nation* (1987; reprint, Chicago: University of Chicago Press, 1991), 59–60. It is important to note that while Stoler's later formulation echoes Gilroy's, she vehemently disputes the "newness" of the "new racism" at the center of Gilroy's examination of race, culture, and nationalism. As Stoler notes and as this essay argues, "cultural racism" of the type analyzed by Gilroy is not unique to the mid- to late twentieth century. See Stoler, "Sexual Affronts," 214.

33. Jacobson, *Whiteness of a Different Color,* 25–31.

34. Granville S. Abbott, "The Chinese in the United States," *Baptist Home Mission Monthly* 2, 4 (April 1880), 59, 62.

35. H. L. Wayland, "Report on the Committee on Work Among the Colored People," in Executive Board of the ABHMS, *Fiftieth Annual Report of the ABHMS* (New York: American Baptist Home Mission Rooms, 1882), 12–13.

36. Joan Jacobs Brumberg refers to letters and reports of American women foreign missionaries during the late nineteenth and early twentieth century as "missionary ethnology." Her study focuses specifically on the distinctions drawn by American missionary women between proselyte women and themselves and their complicity with imperialism. Brumberg, "The Ethnological Mirror: American Evangelical Women and Their Heathen Sisters, 1870–1910," in *Women and the Structure of Society: Selected Research from the Fifth Berkshire Conference on the History of Women*, edited by Jo Ann K. McNamara and Barbara J. Harris (Durham, N.C.: Duke University Press, 1984), 108–128.

37. Mary Louise Pratt, *Imperial Eyes: Travel Writing and Transculturation* (London: Routledge, 1992), 64.

38. According to James C. Thomas, Jr., Peter W. Stanley, and John Curtis Perry, missionaries were "the largest group of Americans who experienced China directly between 1842 and 1942," and they "became prime communicators of the one civilization back to the other." *Sentimental Imperialists: The American Experience in East Asia* (New York: Harper and Row, 1981), 45. For more on this theme, see John K. Fairbank,

ed., *The Missionary Enterprise in China and America* (Cambridge: Harvard University Press, 1974); Miller, *The Unwelcome Immigrant,* 57.

39. These accounts by religious observers worked hand-in-glove with secular accounts, such as journalistic and travel accounts by Northerners in the immediate post–Civil War South. See, for example, Whitelaw Reid, *After the War: A Southern Tour* (New York: Moore, Wilstach, and Baldwin, 1866); J. T. Trowbridge, *The South: A Tour of Its Battlefields and Ruined Cities* (Hartford, Conn.: L. Stebbins, 1866); Sidney Andrews, *The South Since the War: As Shown by Fourteen Weeks of Travel and Observation in Georgia and the Carolinas* (1868; reprint, Boston: Houghton Mifflin, 1971); and Linda Warfel Slaughter, *The Freedmen of the South* (Cincinnati: Elm Street Printing, 1869).

40. Quoted in Jacqueline Jones, *Soldiers of Light and Love: Northern Teachers and Georgia Blacks, 1865–1875* (1980; reprint, Athens: University of Georgia Press, 1992), 154.

41. Elizabeth Ware Pearson, ed., *Letters from Port Royal Written at the Time of the Civil War* (Boston: W. B. Clarke, 1906), 36.

42. Joseph T. Robert, "The Seven Freedmen Schools," in Executive Board of the ABHMS, *Forty-Fourth Annual Report of the ABHMS* (New York: American Baptist Home Mission Rooms, 1876), 29–30.

43. E. G. Trask, "Quarterly Report," reproduced in Executive Board of the ABHMS, *Thirty-Third Annual Report of the ABHMS* (New York: American Baptist Home Mission Rooms, 1865), 24.

44. A. W. Loomis, "Our Heathen Temples," *Overland Monthly* 1, 5 (November 1868), 453–461; A. W. Loomis, "Medical Art in the Chinese Quarter," *Overland Monthly* 2, 6 (June 1869), 496–506. A. W. Loomis was a Presbyterian missionary in San Francisco.

45. Loomis, "Our Heathen Temples," 453. I use "desacralization" and "heathenization" of the landscape in much the same way that Jon Butler demonstrates that the building of Christian churches as prominent parts of the landscape signified the increasing sacralization of England's American mainland colonies in the late seventeenth and early eighteenth centuries. See Jon Butler, *Awash in a Sea of Faith: Christianizing the American People* (Cambridge: Harvard University Press, 1990), 106–116.

46. Loomis, "Our Heathen Temples," 453, 461.

47. Carl T. Jackson, *The Oriental Religions and American Thought: Nineteenth-Century Explorations* (Westport, Conn.: Greenwood Press, 1981), 97.

48. Jackson, *The Oriental Religions,* 97.

49. Henrietta Shuck, *Sketches in China: Or, Sketches of the Country, Religion, and Customs of the Chinese* (Philadelphia: American Baptist Publication Society, 1852), 30.

50. Robinson, "Race and Religion on the American Continent," 53.

51. Le Conte, *The Race Problem in the South,* 362.

52. See especially Albert J. Raboteau, *Slave Religion: The "Invisible Institution" in the Antebellum South* (New York: Oxford University Press, 1978).

53. For more on the links between African traditional religious practice and theology—and particularly the "shout" and the conversion "frenzy"—see, especially, Raboteau, *Slave Religion,* 68–75, 243–45; Sterling Stuckey, *Slave Culture: Nationalist Theory and the Foundations of Black America* (New York: Oxford University Press, 1987),

10–17, 25–37, 84–97; Mechal Sobel, *Trabelin' On: The Slave Journey to an Afro-Baptist Faith*, 2nd ed. (Princeton: Princeton University Press, 1987); Paul Harvey, *Redeeming the South: Religious Cultures and Racial Identities among Southern Baptists, 1865–1925* (Chapel Hill: University of North Carolina Press, 1997), 114–123.

54. See James C. Scott, *Domination and the Arts of Resistance: Hidden Transcripts* (New Haven: Yale University Press, 1990), 115–117; Raboteau, *Slave Religion*, 212–213.

55. In this tradition of biblical interpretation, one scriptural story, phase, or figure is a "type" of the one coming after it and an "antitype" of the one coming before it. Thus the people of Israel in the story of Exodus prefigured African Americans' movement from slavery to freedom. They saw a direct connection between their plight and the ordeal of the Israelites coming out of bondage in Egypt. Theophus H. Smith, *Conjuring Culture: Biblical Formations of Black America* (New York: Oxford University Press, 1994), 7.

56. Robin D. G. Kelley has demonstrated the fundamental role of black working-class places of leisure as spaces for the building of community. The same was true within Chinese enclaves. Robin D. G. Kelley, *Race Rebels: Culture, Politics, and the Black Working Class* (New York: Free Press, 1994), 44.

57. Executive Board, "Minutes," *Thirty-Fourth Annual Report*, 17.

58. "My Summer Vacation" [no author], manuscript letter, 1879, Henry L. Morehouse Correspondence Files, box 9, folder 16, Archival Collection, Board of National Ministries, American Baptist Historical Society (BNM, ABHS), Valley Forge, Pa.

59. "Chinese Concert," clipping, Chinese Mission School, Portland, Oregon, 1873–85, Baptist Church Records, Oregon Historical Society (OHS), MSS 1560.

60. Ibid.

61. Executive Board of the ABHMS, *Forty-Second Annual Report of the ABHMS* (New York: American Baptist Home Mission Rooms, 1874), 39.

62. Harvey, *Redeeming the South*, 62–65.

63. Harvey, *Redeeming the South*, 63.

64. See Chinese Mission School, Portland, Oregon, 1873–85,Baptist Church Records, OHS, MSS 1560; First Baptist Church, Portland, Oregon, 1854–1906, Baptist Church Records, OHS, MSS 1560.

65. For more on Protestant rescue missions to Chinese immigrant women, see Pascoe, *Relations of Rescue*.

66. "A. W. Pegues, Ph.D., D.D., Raleigh, N.C.," in *An Era of Progress and Promise, 1863–1910: The Religious, Moral, and Educational Development of the American Negro Since His Emancipation*, edited by W. N. Hartshorn (Boston: Priscilla, 1910), 464.

67. "A. W. Pegues," in Hartshorn, *An Era of Progress and Promise*, 464.

68. See Thomas O. Fuller, *Twenty Years in Public Life, 1890–1910, North Carolina–Tennessee* (Nashville, Tenn.: National Baptist Publishing Board, 1910).

69. *Proceedings of the Eleventh Annual Session of the Baptist State Convention of North Carolina, 1877* (Raleigh, N.C.: Edwards, Broughton, 1878), 1; Calubert A. Jones, "A Brief Sketch of the History of Shaw University," *Shaw Bulletin* (1940), 13.

70. "Waters Normal Institute, Winton, N.C.," n.d., typescript, Henry L. Morehouse Files, box 9, folder 14, Archival Collection, BNM, ABHS, Valley Forge, Pa.; "Rev. C. S. Brown, D. D., Principal of the Waters Normal Institute, Winton, N.C.," in Hartshorn, *An Era of Progress and Promise*, 488.

71. Youxue Zhengdaohui was a translation of "YMCA" provided by the Protestant Pastor Ira Condit. Wesley Woo notes: "in English the organization was commonly called the 'YMCA,' although it was not related in any way to the American organization of that name." Wesley Woo, "Chinese Protestants in the San Francisco Bay Area," in Chan, *Entry Denied*, 226.

72. Woo, "Chinese Protestants in the San Francisco Bay Area," 226

73. Woo, "Chinese Protestants in the San Francisco Bay Area," 227.

74. Executive Board of the ABHMS, *Forty-Ninth Annual Report of the ABHMS* (New York: American Baptist Home Mission Rooms, 1881), 46.

75. H. L. Morehouse, "Historical Sketch of the American Baptist Home Mission Society for Fifty Years," in *Baptist Home Missions in North America; Including a Full Report of the Proceedings & Addresses of the Jubilee Meeting, and a Historical Sketch of the American Baptist Home Mission Society, Historical Tables, Etc., 1832–1883* (New York: Baptist Home Mission Rooms, 1883), 46.

6

"In Search of Souls, in Search of Indians": Religion and the "Indian Problem" in Northern Mexico

Julia Cummings O'Hara

We have undertaken the march toward our new destiny, in search of souls, in search of Indians, to live *among* them and, in so many words, to live *like* them.
                              —Father Pedro Maina, Sierra Tarahumara, 1924

As colonial powers, Spain, Portugal, and England devised starkly different systems for organizing the relationships between the Crown, colonists, and peoples of indigenous, African, and Asian descent in the Americas. From British colonialism, the United States inherited a conception of Indians as "uncivilized" beings who could never truly be integrated into "civilized society"—a conception that has contributed to a stark dichotomy between whites and other racialized populations. Spanish and Portuguese colonialism, on the other hand, seems to have produced societies characterized by relatively fluid racial identities and significant social mobility. Accompanying this distinction between the former colonies of the Americas has been the resilient assumption that the Latin American and Caribbean willingness to accept intermediate racial categories has resulted in a sort of "racial democracy" that has been absent in the binary racial systems of the United States and Canada.

Historians of Latin America have long argued that this characterization is particularly true of central and southern Mexico, where ideas about race and the colonial social order rested on the *sistema de castas*, or caste system. The caste system established a hierarchical continuum of races with Spaniards or whites at the top, people with varying degrees of racial mixture in the middle, and "pure" Indians and blacks at the bottom. Whiteness presumed "clean" blood (*limpieza de sangre*) and the possession of "reason" (*razón*). Although mixed-race people, called *castas*, or castes, were seen as "without reason" (*sin razón*), their social status and opportunities in life increased as they and their offspring approached the white ideal.[1]

In recent years, however, new scholarship has challenged the assumption of a Latin American racial democracy. The historian Jeffrey L. Gould, for instance, has shown that although the term *ladino* has typically been used in Central America to describe either people of mixed (Indian and white) parentage or acculturated Indians, in heavily indigenous areas of Nicaragua it has functioned as a synonym for "non-Indian."[2] Similarly, Mary Weismantel argues that "in actual practice within specific social contexts, there is no intermediate, or 'mixed' racial category: race operates as a vicious binary that discriminates superiors from inferiors."[3] In the Andes, Weismantel shows, the term *mestizo*, or "racially mixed," also functions as a synonym for "white."

Northern Mexico, too, has often been regarded as a region with a "peculiar" racial history that distinguishes it from central and southern Mexico and the rest of Latin America.[4] Until the late nineteenth century, the northern frontier was a chaotic and unruly region. Plagued by chronic warfare between white settlers, the Apache Indians, and other nomadic groups, the region remained well beyond the centralizing grasp of the Spanish colonial administration and (after independence in 1821) the Mexican federal government. Recent scholarship has demonstrated that ideas about race in the north, forged largely during the Apache wars, shared more with North American binary racial ideologies than with the fluid hierarchy of castes that central and southern Mexico inherited from Spain. Nearly three centuries of frontier warfare between "barbarous" Indians and "white" agents of civilization led to a distinctly northern Mexican, or *norteño*, pattern of racial formation in which racial difference was imagined not as a continuum but as a stark dichotomy, with "Indians" on the bottom and "non-Indians" on the top. This dichotomy did not accept racial ambiguity; one was either Indian or non-Indian. Over time, the lines of distinction between castes and whites were blurred, and "whiteness" became an accepted feature of those in the non-Indian category, regardless of a person's physical appearance or cultural background.[5] The northern Mexican case, then, supports Weismantel's assertion that "race . . . is fundamentally binary: white and nonwhite, superior and inferior."[6] Indeed, this essay draws inspiration from the work of Gould, Weismantel, and others who have helped to "expose the dialectic of Indian and white" and reveal the existence in Latin America of "a racist system that, like capitalist modernity itself, is divided into two halves that do not make a whole."[7]

The essay, however, takes the stark Indian-white dichotomy of northern

Mexico as a starting point from which to explore the more complex landscape of difference and inequality in the rugged, remote, and heavily indigenous Sierra Tarahumara region of the state of Chihuahua. Though the broad category of "race" has posited an unambiguous Indian-white binary in the Sierra Tarahumara, the concrete—and at times unexpectedly ambiguous—effects of this racial ideology cannot be fully understood without examining its multiple coarticulations with the (equally broad) categories of "religion" and "nation." Toward that end, this essay examines the efforts of Jesuit missionaries over the first half of the twentieth century to evangelize, assimilate, civilize, and otherwise "redeem" the Tarahumara Indians of Chihuahua.

With the virtual extermination of the "barbarous" Apache by the mid-1880s, the Mexican government, along with the Catholic Church and white Chihuahuan society, faced a new "Indian problem," reminiscent of the colonial encounter between missionaries and native peoples: how to assimilate the "tame" Tarahumara Indians into local white society and the national body politic. The Jesuits who settled in the Sierra in 1900 were confident that their presence would bring a "new light [to] erase from [the Tarahumaras'] souls the nebulousness of superstition and [the] mental inertia of their grandparents."[8] The missionaries' fierce dedication to the "redemption" of the Indians was initially predicated on the same fundamental assumption that propelled missionary Christianity in many other contexts the world over: that the Tarahumaras' "backwardness" was a characteristic of their race that could be separated from their subordinate social status and corrected through conversion and "civilization." In addition to bringing the Indians closer to God, "redemption" thus meant bringing them closer to whiteness and integrating them into modern Mexican society, through far-reaching changes in language, literacy, gender roles, family life, and other aspects of indigenous culture.

What is most significant about the Jesuit experience in the Sierra Tarahumara, however, is how quickly and thoroughly this assumption disintegrated. The Jesuits' letters, records, journals, and publications reveal that their efforts among the Tarahumara did not ultimately reinforce a dichotomous concept of racial difference or a unified vision of national identity. Throughout most of the twentieth century, the roles assigned to the multitude of actors in the Jesuits' evangelical project were ill defined and often contested. For example, the Jesuits' disappointment with the Tarahumaras' slow progress toward a "civilized," Catholic way of life was surpassed by their disillusionment with the progress of the Indians' white neighbors toward the same end. And as the missionaries themselves became allied with the Tarahumara, many came to question their roles in the process of evangelization and the stability of their own racial identities. In these and other ways, the Jesuits' civilizing mission in the Sierra Tarahumara tended to fracture the ostensibly rigid categories that undergirded their own efforts: "civilization" and "barbarism," "Indianness" and "whiteness," "Catholicism" and "Mexicanness."

Evangelization and Civilization: The Jesuit Mission
as a Racializing Project

In 1893 the bishop of Chihuahua invited Father José Alzola, the superior of
the Jesuits' Mexican province, to reestablish a mission in the Sierra Tarahumara.[9] The bishop expressed great concern for the neglected Sierra and, convinced that the Jesuits would find a suitable challenge among the Tarahumara,
urged Alzola to send a delegation to the region. The Jesuits officially reestablished their mission to the Tarahumara Indians on October 12, 1900. Among
the missionaries' first steps after reestablishing the mission was to visit the
remotest reaches of the Sierra and to bring children, both Tarahumara and
white, to the mission centers of Sisoguichi, Norogachi, and Tónachi for su-
pervised training. Bringing the Tarahumaras often required a combination of
persuasion and force. On their *visitas* (pastoral visits) in the dispersed villages
of the Sierra, the Jesuits went house to house to locate potential students. Some,
it seems, came willingly, while others were taken against their will.[10]

When the missionaries did successfully bring children to the mission,
their first tasks were to effect corporal, rather than spiritual, changes in the
Indians—corporal changes that were intimately linked to local imaginations
of racial identity and difference. Though the Tarahumara were generally un-
accustomed to wearing trousers, button-down shirts, shoes, and undergar-
ments, the first thing most native children encountered in mission residences
was the demand that they discard their own clothing in favor of Western gar-
ments. Similarly, although the Tarahumara seldom, if ever, cut their hair, the
missionaries immediately gave newly arrived students short haircuts, which
they considered necessary to the maintenance of proper hygiene. Moreover,
the missionaries' preoccupation with the reform of Tarahumara bodies extended beyond a concern with "Western" standards of hygiene. They also
sought to impose other physical manifestations of "civilization" and Catholic
Christianity. Eating with utensils instead of hands, eating at a table rather than
on the ground, behaving with solemnity in church, and performing the prescribed actions of Catholicism—such as kneeling, folding hands to pray, light-
ing candles, receiving communion, and making the sign of the cross—were
all markers of a civilized, Catholic lifestyle and, for the missionaries, outward
signs of success in their endeavors (see figure 6.1).[11]

Although mission priests continued to make frequent visits to outlying
villages, a centralized system of boarding schools, or *internados*, came to constitute the backbone of the missionaries' educational and evangelical project.
Ideally, Tarahumara boys and girls would enter single-sex internados at a young
age. After receiving "prudent, constant, but maternal vigilance" in the internados, male graduates were to be matched "with a Tarahumara girl of similar
education and training."[12] Thus joined in Catholic marriages—marriages that

FIGURE 6.1. The civilizing mission as the Jesuits imagined it. A Jesuit missionary and a Tarahumara Indian in Sisoguichi in the early twentieth century. From Filiberto Gómez, Rarámuri, Mi Diario Tarahumara. Mexico City: Tallares Tipográficos de Excelsior, Cía. Editorial, 1948.

linked changing gender roles and sexual mores to changing religious and racial identities just as surely as they linked young Tarahumara men and women— the pairs had their own plots of land and homes that they themselves constructed, where they were to raise their children with Catholic values. They lived and worked communally in *colonias* (colonies) "under the constant vigilance of whichever missionary [held] that responsibility."[13] After several generations, the missionaries hoped, their segregated Tarahumara Catholic colonies would produce the first Tarahumara priests and nuns. As the Jesuit publication *Nuestra Vida* editorialized in 1941, the colonies were "a giant step toward the flowering of religious vocations among the Indians."[14]

While the internados stressed the education and redemption of the individual, the colonies reflected the missionaries' need to save the community by addressing what they saw as the Tarahumaras' underdeveloped sense of family, domesticity, and society. The colonies were imagined as the cornerstone of their endeavor to transform Tarahumara culture by instilling gender, family, community, work, and religious relationships and practices that were recognizably white and Mexican and therefore civilized. For the missionaries, the education of girls and young women "[was] the only way to correct the bad habits of the family."[15] The task of girls' education and the formation of suitable Christian wives for male internado graduates fell to the Sisters of the Sacred Heart of Jesus and the Poor, an order of Mexican nuns who joined the Jesuits' Sierra mission in 1904. Observing the fruits of the internados and colonies in 1948, Father Ortiz wrote that the first generation of children born in the colonies "would be the men of tomorrow, and, educated in this way from an early age, in such healthy beginnings, they will no longer wander like lost sheep through the canyons and the forests, exposed to great dangers; they will be on the chosen path of the Divine Shepherd."[16]

Yet even while the missionaries expressed such great hopes for the minority of Tarahumaras who were educated in the internados and colonies, they just as frequently expressed frustration with the Tarahumaras' broader prospects for "redemption." The missionaries saw themselves as "the most important point of contact between the culture of the *blancos* [whites] and Tarahumara culture."[17] Yet they clearly did not see themselves as mediating between two fully realized cultures. Rather, they explicitly hoped to effect cultural change, and they tended to describe this change in racial and religious terms. Father Edmundo Galván, for instance, who wrote often to Mexico City describing the missionaries' doubts, raised the question of whether the Tarahumara *as Indians* could ever be successfully converted to Christianity. In a 1925 letter, he called Tarahumara adults "repugnant" and criticized their "superstitions" and "vices." Because of their "uncivilized" way of life, Galván concluded, it would be "impossible for a Tarahumara to be even half Christian." He argued that the missionaries would therefore "need to make [the Tarahumara] pass to some other state in order for them to think, believe, and work as Christians."[18]

Moreover, Galván continued,

> if we are to realize the conversion of these people, I have believed for some time that it will occur through the very special exercise of our mission as civilizers and not only as priests; but our work as civilizers is so complicated here! For this reason, one of the goals of our *visitas* to the *pueblos* is to study ways of changing these poor Indians from the savage state to the civilized state.[19]

Other Jesuits elaborated on the consequences of this transformation in more explicitly racialized terms. Father David Brambila affirmed that the colonies had transformed the Indian colonists into a new "type," unrecognizable to themselves and others. They were not quite Tarahumaras but definitely not whites. Brambila described one encounter during which "an outsider who visited the Mission observed: 'one looks at the colonists and at the other Tarahumaras, and concludes that they are two different races.'"[20]

Jesuits and Chabochis: Fractured Whiteness
in the Sierra Tarahumara

Jesuit conceptions of whiteness and Indianness were hardly as clear, however, as Father Galván's reflections on Tarahumara savagery might suggest. Although their efforts to remake native society tended to rest on an implicit equation of whiteness, Catholicism, and civilization, this equation was complicated by the missionaries' negative views of—and frequently hostile relations with—local whites. From the beginning, the missionaries considered nonindigenous residents of the Sierra Tarahumara, or *serranos,* to be as ignorant as the Tarahumara of the beliefs and practices of Catholicism. Moreover, they held whites responsible for the "exploitation" of the Indians and for the multiple, ongoing conflicts over land, language, resources, religion, and culture that tended to break down along racialized lines.[21] Father Manuel Piñan's letters from early 1900 reveal an unfavorable opinion of serrano whites and display little sense of racial solidarity with them. He described them as "ignorant people who harm the faith and morality of the Indians . . . and exploit them miserably."[22] Piñan even expressed a measure of doubt about the priests' ability to minister to the whites, demonstrating the missionaries' clear sympathy for the indigenous side of the local racial divide. His reports warned that

> those who cause more concern for the missionaries . . . will not be
> the Indians, but the whites and *mestizos.* . . . Many whites do not
> want missionaries, because they see, and not without reason, that
> their arrival will hinder their taking power over the lands of the In-
> dians. . . . Poor whites! If they do not change their ways, the Indians
> will not tarry in realizing all of this, judging by the discontent that
> reigns in the Sierra.[23]

The missionaries who succeeded Piñan also frequently expressed indignation at the state of relations between whites and Indians. Father Narciso Ortiz, a missionary in the Sierra from 1908 until 1949, presented an image of innocent, if uncivilized, Indians on the one hand and immoral whites on the other. In one letter he wrote that in the Sierra, "the worst plague are those who call themselves people of reason [*gente de razón*] and who ought to be called people without reason [*gente sin razón*]; the white men either live in a shameful condition or they are the first ones to get drunk."[24] By contrast, Ortiz described the Tarahumara in another letter, writing that "in these Indians there is something akin to a seed of natural goodness, and if they are prone to certain excesses, it is more out of ignorance than out of malice."[25] Father Manuel Ocampo, recounting the history of the mission's first fifty years, asserted that "many whites live for the mere pleasure of exploiting the downtrodden Tarahumara." Even more bluntly, he affirmed that "the penetration of *los blancos* in the Sierra is almost an uninterrupted series of crimes carried out by high-status personalities, in favor of their own interests."[26]

The Jesuits often demonstrated where their loyalties lay by adopting the Indians' disparaging term *chabochi* to describe non-Indians[27] and by mocking the tendency of Sierra whites to refer to themselves as *gente de razón*. Ocampo explained how humorous the missionaries found this, writing that the "*chavoche* [sic], as whites here are called, participate to a great extent in the coarseness of the Indian, although they do not want to be convinced of this. . . . They have baptized themselves with the pompous name here in the Sierra of '*gente de razón*.'"[28] Like Manuel Piñan, Father Manuel Cordero pondered the question of which groups should be included in the mission's purview. Cordero was also blunt about the relationship between the missionaries and white serranos. He described, in considerable detail, the missionaries' "open rupture with *los elementos chaboches* [sic]," and he echoed Father Piñan's reservations about including whites at all within the embrace of the mission, lamenting that "to give to *chaboches* [sic] what we receive for distribution among the Tarahumaras seems to me to totally lack a healthy morality."[29] Similar sentiments continue to be expressed to the present day. In 1994, Father Ricardo Robles, a Jesuit who currently works in the village of Sisoguichi, wrote that "while even today the missionaries continue to be accepted and adored allies [of the Tarahumara], *los 'chabochis' (no-indígenas)* continue to be their adversaries, feared and avoided even though they live together peacefully."[30] In a sense, then, serrano whites were (and continue to be) as much an "other" in the eyes of the missionaries as the Tarahumara themselves.

However, although the missionaries saw white serrano culture as coarse and, at times, immoral, they nevertheless tended to believe it was superior to the local alternative. Rather than attempt to overturn the hierarchical relationship between whites and Indians in the Sierra, they worked to place this racial hierarchy in the service of their evangelical agenda—hoping to turn an oppressive and abusive relationship into a benign and paternalistic one, while rarely questioning the inherently unequal distribution of power. And despite their troubled relations with white serranos, the missionaries did carve out a role for non-Indians in their plans for the resolution of the "Tarahumara problem."

Ideally, the whites would *participate* in the redemption of the Indians. Several priests found that the best way to contact the Indians was to have local whites act as intermediaries. On a 1921 visit to Aboreachi, for instance, Father Galván considered how to turn the historic domination of the Tarahumara by their white neighbors to the advantage of the mission. He wrote that "this village of Tarahumaras is completely dominated by a white man, whom we can easily make one of ours so that he can help us make good Christians of the Indians."[31] Toward that end, the missionaries devised plans for the formal education of serrano whites so that they would stop abusing the Indians. Father Galván insisted in 1924 that another mission station at Tónachi was necessary to these goals:

> The cultivation of the whites is very important, above all the cultivation of the generation that is being educated right now. I have never taken [this] as the main goal of my labors, but seeing its necessity, I have attended to their cultivation as much as possible. In order to win them over, or at least so that they do not hamper our work with the Indians, experience has taught me that medicines and schools help considerably: they are benefits that they appreciate and they provide us with the means to exercise influence over them.[32]

In addition to medicines and schools, missionary efforts to reframe relations between Indians and whites also relied, to a large extent, on gendered assumptions about local white women. The missionaries expected to find a more receptive audience for their evangelizing efforts among white women than white men, and, in fact, they initiated several organizations of lay women and girls to that end. The Hijas de María, an international Catholic association for young women, was composed in the Sierra of young white serranas who assisted the missionaries in their work among the Indians. Their Nonoava school in particular helped train white girls to become, themselves, future teachers and missionaries to their Tarahumara neighbors.

The 1923 letter of an eleven-year-old girl to Father José Mier y Terán illustrates the kind of tutorial role that the missionaries hoped local whites—and especially white women—would accept. The girl was a student of the nuns and a member of the Madres Reparadoras and Niños Apóstoles, two Catholic organizations whose membership was mostly white women and young girls. She wrote Mier y Terán with a lengthy description of her activities and sacrifices on behalf of the "Taramauritos" (sic), informing him that she had "decided to do everything in [her] power for those poor souls because [she] really wanted to save them."[33] Along with her letter she included a donation of twenty-eight pesos and fifteen centavos and a detailed description of how she had earned the money. Noting that her mother was a "catequista" and thus gave many prizes to the children whom she taught, the girl explained that she had sold her toys, books, and other personal items to her mother, as well as to the Tarahumara girls who worked as maids in her home. She ended the letter with an affirmation of affection for "saving" the Tarahumara, along with the promise of additional letters and donations to the mission.

Yet despite the sentiments of this young correspondent and others, the missionaries' success at involving local whites in the evangelization of the Indians was uneven. And to further complicate the imagined unity of whiteness in the Sierra, Jesuit advocacy for an autonomous ethnic space for the Tarahumara often met with bitter white resistance. The experiences of Father

Leonardo Gassó in 1905 provided sobering evidence of this resistance. Like Father Piñan before him, Gassó viewed the exploitation of the Indians as an obstacle to the missionary enterprise. Gassó, however, was far more uncompromising in his approach to the "Indian problem." Seeking not only the religious and cultural isolation of the Tarahumara, Gassó appealed to both President Porfirio Díaz and Chihuahua Governor Enrique C. Creel for the implementation of partial political autonomy for the Tarahumara. In his letters to Creel, Gassó called for Tarahumara self-government at the municipal level and the expulsion of abusive white serranos from the Sierra. He insisted on the necessity of

> making the Indians independent of the municipal presidents and commissions that use their authority to squeeze the juice out of the Indians. We must take back the Indians' land from the whites, which they possess without title or by tricks punishable by law, return it to the Indians and expel the troublemakers, as the law demands.[34]

Within the space of a few short months, Gassó founded several villages exclusively for Tarahumaras. Furthermore, the Indians came in large numbers to Sisoguichi during Father Gassó's tenure in the mission, and, "full of courage, they organized their processions outside of the churches; they presented their grievances, just or unjust, against the whites and even against certain indigenous criminals who had been hiding out until then. They felt supported by their Father Gassó."[35]

But whites in the Sierra, and especially those in the municipal government, were not nearly as accepting of Father Gassó. They argued that the priest's activities among the Indians were "nothing less than a great conspiracy" and demanded the expulsion of the "seditious" Father Gassó from the Sierra.[36] They accused Gassó of upsetting the fragile balance of peaceful ethnic relations in the Sierra, claiming that he was "trying to augment the hatred between *gente de razón* and the Tarahumara" and should be removed from the Sierra by the authorities of the state government.[37] Gassó's attempts to circumvent local authority led to fierce backlash against the Jesuits. As Piñan wrote in his notes for the history of the mission,

> the whites of the Sierra began to openly oppose all of the Father's plans. . . . They declared war on him, and with him on all the Jesuits, to the point that it was not unusual to hear that it was necessary to burn Father Gassó alive, not with dry firewood, but with damp.[38]

While on a visita to Cuiteco in 1905, Gassó was arrested by local authorities and falsely accused of inciting the Indians to riot. Upon his release, he returned to the mission in Sisoguichi and shortly thereafter was permanently transferred out of the Sierra Tarahumara by his Jesuit superiors.

Such hostilities outlasted Father Gassó, however. In January 1926, for instance, municipal authorities in the Bocoyna area forced Father Eduardo Iglesias to report for questioning. He was accused of being a fanatic, violating federal law, obstructing progress, being affiliated with foreign sects, impugning Mexico's greatest leaders and historical figures, and (last but not least) being a thief. He was threatened with fines and detention but was ultimately released.[39] Fathers Galván, Peña, Pichardo, and Ortiz were not as fortunate, as each spent time in jail between 1926 and 1929.

Indeed, resistance to Jesuit mission work has remained a vital current in the vernacular discourse of serrano whites to this day. In the 1990s, while carrying out archival research and collecting oral history testimony in the Sierra, I too detected a sometimes subtle, sometimes overt distrust and resentment of the Jesuits and other religious workers. My white informants and more casual acquaintances frequently insinuated that many priests were carrying on secret affairs with Tarahumara women, neglecting their religious duties in favor of drinking and dancing with the Indians and (the old standby) trying to incite the Indians to rebellion.[40] These accusations mark the complex tensions *within* the white society to which Jesuit missionaries have worked to assimilate the Tarahumara, and cast doubt on the Jesuits' own identities and affiliations— a topic I explore in the following section.

Blurring the Lines: Indian Catholicism, Jesuit Indigenism

As a result of these fraught relationships between Jesuit missionaries and local whites—and the conscious decision of many missionaries to make the Tarahumara the primary subjects of their mission work—missionary Catholicism in the Sierra Tarahumara came to be associated, almost exclusively, with Indians. And ultimately the Catholicism of the Tarahumara became, in itself, a marker of racial difference. Most local whites also identify as Catholic (despite the success of some Protestant missionaries among white serranos over the past 120 years)[41] but serranos nevertheless tend to link Catholicism with Indianness. This popular equation sometimes serves to reinforce the racial line between Indians and whites, by mapping a religious distinction onto a rigid system of racialized difference. Yet, at the same time, it sometimes blurs this racial line, and undercuts the broader system of racial and religious difference, by reversing the association of whiteness and Christianity that initially lay at the heart of the missionary enterprise.

To this day, many Tarahumaras see their own practice of Catholicism as distinct from—and superior to—that of their nonindigenous neighbors, and link this religious distinction to distinctions based on race.[42] One man told Father Francisco Pichardo, for example, that the Indians "are not like the '*chabochis*' (the whites), who sit down to eat without acknowledging God, who has given them food."[43] Some Tarahumara go so far as to condemn their white Catholic neighbors to eternal damnation for such sins—or for their whiteness alone—believing that "the souls of the Tarahumara and other Indians go to heaven [in the afterlife] while those of the non-Indians go to the underworld to spend eternity with the Devil."[44] Given these charged religious distinctions between Indians and whites, it is hardly surprising that when Tarahumaras burn Judas in effigy on Good Friday—a ritual widely practiced throughout Mexico but practiced more by Tarahumaras than by whites in the Sierra—the notorious betrayer of Christ is nearly always depicted as a non-Indian.[45]

The Jesuits often noted these distinctions with disdain and, at least at first, viewed them as part of the body of indigenous belief that had to be overcome. While traveling on visita to Papajichi, Pajuichique, and surrounding areas, Father Galván noted that in a number of pueblos in the Sierra "the people believe that Tarahumaras do not go to Hell because they do not bury their dead very deeply; in contrast, *los de razón* do go to Hell, because they do not take the same precaution," and concluded that "this superstition strikes me as one of the most harmful that there can be."[46] Father Galván also noted that during a mission-wide fiesta in 1921 "many of the Tarahumaras who received communion did so for the first time in their life, which constitutes a great stride forward, because there were no few Indians who had the belief that confession and communion were not for them, but rather only for the whites."[47]

Yet at the same time, the strict identification of the missionaries with the Indians opened a breach between "missionary" (read: Indian) Catholicism and "civilized" (read: white) Catholicism that most missionaries did little to discourage. When Father Pedro Maina described his work in 1924 he equated "mission style" celebrations with "Indian style" cultural practices, largely, it seems, because he had held mass outdoors, with the indigenous congregants seated on the ground. Describing a July fiesta for the mission, Maina wrote "as is natural, it was to be Mission style, which is to say, Indian style, conditioned, as it was, by the peoples' ignorance and their empty pockets, which contain more confidence in God than *pesetas*."[48]

The missionaries distinguished between their obligatory ministry to whites and what they felt was a specific calling to work with the Indians. Father Manuel Cordero and others made it clear that they did not want to be "just" a *cura*, or priest serving white serrano parishes. Cordero described his "calling" in the following terms:

upon hearing the voice of God calling me to these cliffs and canyons, I imagined settling into a purely indigenous environment, as the idea of only being a *cura* in some village caused me great repugnance. I dreamt of building my little church and shelter in the heart of the Sierra and turning myself over completely to the evangelization of the Indians.

He further suggested (with little result) that the Jesuits entirely "give up the *parroquias de blancos* [white parishes] so that, instead of *párrocos* [parish priests], we remain missionaries."[49] By 1924 there was far less talk of the priests' need to work with whites, who were increasingly seen as a disturbance, and more talk of living with and like the Indians. Since 1900, a new generation of priests (Fathers Cordero, Ocampo, Maina, and others) had been educated, and (having read the letters and other literature of the mission) had an eager calling to work *specifically* with the Tarahumara. As Father Maina wrote in 1924: "we have undertaken the march toward our new destiny, in search of souls, in search of Indians, to live *among* them and, in so many words, to live *like* them."[50]

White serranos as well as Indians appear to have noticed this strong identification between priests and Indians, and emphasized the gulf between the Jesuits as *missionaries* to the Indians and the parish priests *(curitas de aldea)* who might be found working in "civilized" white pueblos. If the colonial Jesuits had been allies of the Spanish soldiers, miners, and settlers who came to the Sierra Tarahumara in that era, in the modern period their alliances had shifted toward the Indians, a fact that no few white serranos resented. In 1924, Father Cordero recorded a number of interactions that indicated a measure of hostility, including one in which a white serrano slyly commented to Cordero: "I understand that you Jesuits live in caves and canyons in the middle of the Indians, but not in circumscribed villages like this one. You must prefer being missionaries to real parish priests."[51] And in fact, the Jesuits often did seem eager to blur the lines of their own identities, in a movement toward Tarahumara identity—or identification—that stood in tension with their role as agents of white "civilization." More so than any priest who preceded him, Cordero seems to have identified with the Indians, and rallied his missionary brethren to follow suit. He was concerned, for instance, with the image that the Indians had of the priests' racial identity, meaning that he intended for the Indians to view the priests *not* as chabochis but rather as *indios güeros* (white Indians). He proudly narrated his visita to Panalachi, which "had drawn a good number of Tarahumara boys, who, seeing that I did not have the face of a *chavoche* [*sic*], instead of running away, gathered around me."[52] He also described an encounter with a Tarahumara man who insisted that a second priest (possibly Father Brambila) was "a genuine Tarahumara, in no way a *chabochi*."[53] Brambila apparently spoke Tarahumara so well that "cases have occurred in which the Indians insist that 'Bramba' (Father Brambila) has to be the child of Tarahumaras."[54]

Moreover, Brambila, Cordero, and other Jesuits seemed far more concerned with the well-being of the Indians and their understanding of Catholicism than they were with that of the whites. Many went so far as to reverse the standard practice (used by parish clergy, local officials, and the federal government's "cultural missionaries") of speaking to mixed groups of whites and Indians in Spanish and then summarizing their speech in the Tarahumara language. Cordero patronizingly described his tendency to give brief Spanish summaries, noting:

> so that my kindness and condescension toward the *chabochi* can be seen, upon finishing each Tarahumara sermon I would give a summary in Spanish, just a short one so as not to bore the Indians, as a little gift to those who are ignorant of the language of the region where they live. I was satisfied to discover that my Tarahumara audience increased yet the group of *chabochis* did not diminish.

Cordero also reported scoffing at white serranos who questioned the missionaries' relationship with the Indians. In one of his letters he quoted a conversation with a group of white men, who told the Jesuit

> we know that your preference is for the Tarahumaras, but we are not sorry. We used to celebrate the fact that someone was even interested in those poor souls. . . . But no matter how much you want to, you cannot do without us. It is impossible for you to live in a Tarahumara environment without counting on the *chabochi*."[55]

Father Eduardo Iglesias shared Cordero's affinity for the Tarahumara at the expense of the Sierra's nonindigenous population. In his first letter back to Mexico City after arriving in the Sierra, he proudly recounted a nightmare that he had had in which he dreamed of disembodied voices taunting him: " 'you've come to be the *cura* of the *chavoches* [sic].' " He awoke at that moment, according to his account, to the pleasant thought that he would be, "in reality, 'missionary to Tarahumaras.' "[56] As I have shown, this evangelical project entailed a complex mixture of identification with and repudiation of Tarahumara culture and identity.

"Double Redemption": Mission and Nation in the Sierra Tarahumara

From the day they reestablished their mission in the Sierra Tarahumara, the Jesuits confronted numerous barriers to their ambitious project: rugged terrain and a harsh climate; an indigenous system of beliefs and practices they considered incompatible with a "civilized" Christian lifestyle; and a pattern of relations between Indians and whites that they regarded as tremendously exploitative and unjust. Beyond these local realities, moreover, the Jesuits found themselves in fierce competition with the liberal, anticlerical Mexican state for the loyalty of the region's indigenous and nonindigenous inhabitants alike. As this final section demonstrates, the complex ties of the Tarahumara, the serrano whites, and the Jesuit missionaries themselves to the Mexican nation and state were an integral component in the construction of—and relationships among—Indianness, whiteness, Catholicism, and Mexican identity in the Sierra.

Throughout the twentieth century, the Jesuits in the Sierra, like members of the clergy elsewhere in Mexico, frequently came into direct conflict with the government, which sought to instill a sense of secular citizenship in the Mexican populace, and to disabuse the masses of the notion that to be Mexican was also to be Catholic. The Jesuit missionaries in the Sierra actively worked to conflate these two identities, struggling vigorously against the state's efforts to disassociate "Mexicanness" from "Catholicism." Much as the Jesuits' evangelical mission ultimately blurred the supposedly clear distinction between "Indianness" and "whiteness" in the Sierra, so too did it subvert the state's secularist conception of the relationships among race, religion, and national identity.

And yet, despite this tension with the nation-building project of the Mexican state, the Jesuits in the Sierra Tarahumara consistently and aggressively claimed a patriotic foundation for their mission, arguing that their efforts to rehabilitate the "backward" culture of the Sierra Tarahumara held great significance for the future of Mexico. Father Pichardo summed up the role that the mission's educational ideals played within a national context, writing that the goal was

> to establish schools where a generation of truly Christian Indians
> will be educated and where white children will learn not to be like
> their parents, those unjust exploiters and inicuous corruptors of the
> Indians. We ask God . . . that [many people] might contribute to this
> work, which gives such glory to God and such great benefit to our
> Fatherland.[57]

The missionaries thus insisted that their work with both indigenous and non-indigenous serranos would contribute to the broader goal of nation-building, and especially to the resolution of the "Indian problem" nationwide. As Father Brambila wrote in his personal diary, published in 1950, "the internados . . . bring double redemption. . . . They rescue for the Fatherland and they rescue for God."[58]

The symbolic structure of mission rituals often worked to support this vision of evangelical patriotism and to link it explicitly to questions of race. A 1921 religious festival provides a telling example. For the festival, Father Ortiz composed a bilingual "hymn of coronation" to be sung "in the form of a dialogue between whites and Tarahumaras"—and moreover to be sung to the tune of the Mexican national anthem.[59] "I have composed the Misa Tarahumara for the coronation," he wrote,

and the Coronation and Consecration hymn that will be sung alter-
nately in Spanish and Tarahumara. Perhaps they will be the first
such verses in the Tarahumara language. The idea is for the whites
to invite the Tarahumaras to come to Christ, to consecrate themselves in Him, to express to Him their miseries and ignorance; and
the Tarahumaras will respond as the whites suggest, conversing
with Christ.[60]

This festival, and others celebrated in the Sierra, symbolically positioned Indians and whites by age and gender, according to the Jesuits' ideal of an ordered, hierarchical society, in which "civilized" white Catholic fathers, mothers,
and children constituted the model Mexican family. The Jesuits' depiction of a
religious procession to Sisoguichi in 1924 reveals this ideal. The procession
consisted of

women with their children, Indians on foot, some whites on
horseback, three *burros* and two goats . . . as well as a tiny, poor boy,
completely naked with no more to cover him than a bit of cloth,
who made the entire trip on foot . . . each person taking his place according to his or her dignity and his or her category.[61]

Arriving in Sisoguichi, the pilgrims discovered the image of the Sacred Heart
flanked by two majestic Mexican flags, and "the pontifical and the national
flags [flying] together" above the girls' *internado*.[62] Seeing these symbols, or
singing a new hymn to the tune of the national anthem, effectively blended
mission and nation: to be Mexican was to be Catholic, and to be both meant
playing a circumscribed role based on race and gender.

However, such symbolic renditions of religious patriotism belie the often
fierce competition between the church and state with regard to the "Indian
problem." The Jesuit experience established a paradigm for addressing the
"Indian problem" that the state (at local, regional, and national levels) alter-
nately contested and adapted for its own programs. The Chihuahua governor
Enrique C. Creel borrowed heavily from the Jesuits' methodology, and after the
revolution of 1910 the new federal government made the transformation of the
nation's Indians a priority. With José Vasconcelos serving as the first secretary
of public education, the revolutionary state aimed to assimilate the Indians
through a program of intensive education and training. Vasconcelos imagined
sending an army of secular "missionaries" into the countryside to deliver the
spirit of nationalism, progress, and rational, modern behavior to the masses.[63]
This conflict between religious and secular projects for the "redemption" of
the Tarahumara intensified in the 1930s. Under the anticlerical regime of President Lázaro Cárdenas, the federal government attempted to appropriate the
Jesuit project in the Sierra Tarahumara, commandeering the mission's buildings, educational materials, and often even the students themselves. In towns

throughout the Sierra, priests and nuns were ejected from their schools and living quarters while new state-sponsored missionaries replaced them. The creation of "colonies" for the Tarahumara topped the educational agenda, as the state aimed to replace the missionary church in its role as a "civilizing" influence and a bridge between whites and Indians.

Yet the missionaries contested the state's efforts in several key ways. First of all, though they emphasized the overlapping goals of mission and state, they also nurtured the conception that their own work was superior to that of the government. As Father Rufino Escamilla wrote in 1948,

> if the missionaries, practicing such self-denial, so lacking in self-interest, and working only for the love of God, can harvest such poor fruit, what can the Government, using employees interested only in their salaries and civilizing the Indian through legal coercion, hope to harvest? . . . The missionary is the only light that shines in the Tarahumara's impenetrable darkness. The missionary, that unknown hero whose superhuman struggle to save an entire race for God, for civilization, and for the Fatherland, will constitute the final act of the drama.[64]

Second, the Jesuits created a space within the missionary enterprise for Mexicans beyond the Sierra Tarahumara, so that they too could contribute to the resolution of the "Tarahumara problem"—and ideally create a nationwide constituency for the Jesuit evangelical project. Tarahumara children in the internados were encouraged to correspond with the governor and even the president, sending letters and gifts, such as cloth weavings and hand-stitched samplers, to demonstrate their progress in the mission schools. Similarly, visitors from other parts of Mexico—and even from abroad—were invited to the Sierra, where they could marvel at the missionaries' work.[65] In 1950, Father Manuel Ocampo was optimistic enough about the Jesuits' work to write that "in Chihuahua and in many other parts of Mexico, the Mission is known and, what is more, what we have now seen most clearly: the Tarahumara Mission is loved."[66]

In addition to bringing visitors into the Sierra and disseminating information about the mission's work, on occasion the missionaries took exemplary Tarahumaras, both students and adults, on trips outside of the Sierra. Father Ortiz described the glowing approval of Chihuahua's newspaper El Heraldo of the participation of Tarahumara boys from the internado in a local Cinco de Mayo parade. The article wrote, Ortiz reports, that "the group of Tarahumara Indians merits special mention, for they provided a palpable demonstration that, yes, these aborigines can be incorporated into civilization, as the Jesuit mission in the Upper Sierra Tarahumara is doing. This group was enthusiastically applauded throughout their whole route, as their excellent education was obvious."[67]

Beyond these small tokens demonstrating the mission's accomplishments, the Jesuits actively sought, and maintained close relations with, a broad network of benefactors and supporters of the mission in general, and the internados and colonies in particular. They equated the mission's well-being with that of the nation and used the widespread interest in the mission—and donations in support of its work—as proof of this fact. Father Ocampo wrote that

> this Mission [is] the source of innumerable benefits, not only for our Mexican Jesuit Province, but for the Republic itself, which is so far from God. Because as long as there are people who so dutifully dedicate themselves to the cultivation of those poor abandoned souls . . . I do not doubt that the good Lord will look upon us with love and grace both the Province and the Fatherland with many blessings.[68]

And finally, the missionaries often attempted to mediate between the Tarahumara and the government, intervening in their interactions and translating "official" persons or terms into religious or indigenous concepts. Father Cordero, for instance, noted that the priests often referred to agents of the state government as "Huarú Gubierno," or "Big Father Government."[69] The priests made little effort to respect—let alone reinforce—lines of demarcation between the church and state when ministering to the people of the Sierra. One priest reported saying mass and giving instruction in Christian doctrine to children at a boarding school in Yoquivo, claiming he had done so before realizing that it was, in fact, a government school.[70]

Consequently, many Tarahumaras drew heavily on their experiences with Catholic missionaries in interpreting their relationship with the state. No matter how profound the philosophical discrepancy between religious and secular approaches to the "Indian problem," the Tarahumaras' expectations of the government did not differ greatly from their expectations of religious missionaries. As a former federal rural teacher in the Sierra recently recalled, more than one Tarahumara student mistakenly called him "Father." And more than one rural teacher, he recounted, allowed this kind of error to pass without remark.[71] The Tarahumara have thus learned to conflate the religious and secular missionary projects, and government officials have allowed them to do so, hoping to ease the transition from religious to secular supremacy in the Sierra.

Indeed, Tarahumara legends have even come to equate the icons of Christianity with those of the nation-state—above all linking Jesus Christ himself to former president Benito Juárez. Unlike the many indigenous groups in Mexico that believe that their land has belonged to them since "time immemorial," Tarahumara legend assigns a specific historical origin to their landholdings: many claim that Benito Juárez, together with "el niño Jesús" (the Baby Jesus), gave the Tarahumara their rights to the land. Other legends hold that "Benito Juárez and Christ were sent by God to improve the luck of the Tarahumara."[72] As the anthropologist Claudio Lomnitz-Adler has suggestively noted, "anthropologists and historians are fascinated by the task of relating pre-Hispanic religion to Catholicism, where, in fact, the sociologically most important syncretism is between government (including official history) and religion (including cosmology.)"[73]

This complex syncretism between the myths of state and the legends of an indigenous community is the result of the longstanding competition between church and state for the hearts, minds, and souls of the Tarahumara Indians. Rather than heightening their sense of a secular national identity, the overlapping efforts of Jesuit and government missionaries have ultimately fused the racial, religious, and national identities of the Tarahumara.

Conclusion

This examination of Jesuit missionary work in the twentieth-century Sierra Tarahumara has, I hope, contributed to our ongoing effort to understand how the categories of "race," "nation," and "religion" are constructed and maintained at the contested margins of the nation-state.

During much of the twentieth century, and especially following the revolution of 1910, the Mexican state has struggled to generate new national narratives of race, culture, ethnicity, and religion—narratives aimed at incorporating both indigenous and nonindigenous peoples into a shared project of nation-building. The Jesuit missionaries in the Sierra Tarahumara played a crucial role in linking local understandings of race and religion to these national-level debates over the "Indian problem" and national identity. Their goal of incorporating the Tarahumara Indians into local white society and the national body politic helped to produce distinct regional understandings of difference that simultaneously upheld and complicated the stark racialized dichotomy between "Indians" and "whites" and, somewhat similarly, upheld and complicated the very idea of a unified Mexican nation.

The ambiguous status of the Tarahumara as subjects of the Jesuit missionary enterprise has perpetuated a complexly racialized discourse that permeates serrano society—embracing not only religion but also politics, economics, land tenure, cultural traditions, and everyday life. This discourse of difference has presented a challenge to the state's efforts at "missionary" work with the Indians and, perhaps above all, to the "mestizo" national identity that the state has tried to implant in Mexico throughout the twentieth century.

NOTES

1. For an excellent discussion of the *sistema de castas* in colonial Mexico City, see R. Douglas Cope, *The Limits of Racial Domination: Plebeian Society in Colonial Mexico City, 1660–1720* (Madison: University of Wisconsin Press, 1994). Jaime E. Rodríguez

O. provides a succinct synthesis of the distinctions among Spanish, Portuguese, English, and French colonialism in the Americas in "The Emancipation of America," *American Historical Review* 105, 1 (February 2000), 131–152.

2. Jeffrey L. Gould, *To Die in This Way: Nicaraguan Indians and the Myth of Mestizaje, 1880–1965* (Durham, N.C.: Duke University Press, 1998).

3. Mary Weismantel, *Cholas and Pishtacos: Stories of Race and Sex in the Andes* (Chicago: University of Chicago Press, 2001), xxxi.

4. Barry Carr, "Los peculiaridades del norte mexicana: Ensayo de interpretación," *Historia Mexicana* 22, 3 (1973), 321–46.

5. See especially Ana María Alonso, *Thread of Blood: Colonialism, Revolution, and Gender on Mexico's Northern Frontier* (Tucson: University of Arizona Press, 1995), and Oakah Jones, *Los Paisanos: Spanish Settlers on the Northern Frontier of New Spain* (Norman: University of Oklahoma Press, 1979). Jones asserts that "conditions on the frontier tended to erase differences between whites and mixed bloods . . . and it became common to classify people according to two generic categories: *indios* [Indians] and *no indios* [non-Indians]"; 95. Alonso sees this frontier society as more "egalitarian" than that of central and southern Mexico, arguing that "the subaltern groups that distinguished themselves in warfare [against the Apache Indians] and led a 'civilized' existence could achieve prestige and status despite 'impurities of blood.' . . . Since reason, or the capacity for civilization, was identified with Spanish blood, many Hispanicized mestizos and mulattos were able to 'bleach' themselves (*blanquearse*) and, as 'civilized people,' become de facto whites"; 54. See also Ricardo León García and Carlos González Herrera, *Civilizar o exterminar: Tarahumaras y Apaches en Chihuahua, Siglo XIX* (Mexico City: Centro de Investigaciones y Estudios Superiores en Antropología Social, 2000).

6. Weismantel, *Cholas and Pishtacos*, xxxii.

7. Weismantel, *Cholas and Pishtacos*, xxxiii.

8. Manuel Ocampo, *Historia de la misión de la Tarahumara, 1900–1950* (Mexico City: Editorial Buena Prensa, 1950) 9. The first four missionaries, Fathers Antonio Arocena, José Vargas, Pablo Louvet, and Brother Nicasio Gogorza, were joined in 1901 by Fathers Ignacio Borbolla, José Aguirregoicoa, and Brother Miguel Morera. Father Leonardo Gassó arrived in October of 1902, and by 1904 Fathers Rafael Vargas and Alberto Mir had also joined the mission.

9. The presence of Catholic missionaries in the Sierra Tarahumara originates in the colonial period, when the Jesuits first established missions among the Tepehuán Indians. Expelled from Spanish dominions in 1767, the Jesuits left behind more than twenty missions in the Sierra Tarahumara. There is little doubt that, with regard to churches and religious personnel, the Sierra was among Mexico's most neglected regions during the nineteenth century. Scholars estimate that by 1893 there was only one priest, resident in the pueblo of Norogachi, to minister to the entire Tarahumara region. See J. Ricardo Robles, "Los Rarámuri—Pagotuame," in *El Rostro Indio de Dios*, edited by Manuel Marzal (Mexico City: Centro de Reflexión Teológica, 1994), 30. See also Luis González Rodríguez, *Tarahumara: La Sierra y el Hombre*, 2nd ed. (Chihuahua, Mexico: Editorial Camino, 1994).

10. Archivo Histórico de la Provincia Mexicana, Mexico City (AHPM), *Carta del H. Bienvenido Gómez al P. Vicente Gómez, Norogachi, 20 de enero de 1909.*

11. For a detailed discussion of the concept of "bodily reform," see John and Jean Comaroff, "Bodily Reform as Historical Practice," in their collection of essays entitled *Ethnography and the Historical Imagination* (Boulder, Colo.: Westview Press, 1992).

12. AHPM, *Carta del P. Manuel Cordero* (n.d).

13. AHPM, *Carta del P. Manuel Cordero* (n.d).

14. AHPM, Anonymous, "El clero indígena," in *Nuestra Vida* (1941).

15. AHPM, "Residencia de Guadalupe y Calvo: 1940," in *Noticias de la Provincia Mexicana, 1945–1948.*

16. AHPM, *Carta del P. Narciso Ortiz al P. Romero, San Juanito, Chih.*, 14 de junio de 1948 in *Noticias.*

17. Pedro de Velasco Rivero uses this expression in his excellent study of Tarahumara popular religion. See *Danzar o morir: Religión y resistencia a la dominación en la cultura tarahumar* (Mexico City: Centro de Reflexión Teológica, 1987), 358.

18. AHPM, *Número 23 de la Misión de Tarahumara (July 1925)*, in *Noticias* de la Provincia Mexicana.

19. AHPM, *Número 23 de la Misión de Tarahumara.*

20. Quoted in Manuel Ocampo, *Album conmemorativo de la Misión de la Tarahumara en el Quincuagésimo aniversario de su fundación* (Mexico City: Editorial Buena Prensa, 1951), 10.

21. The racial classification of the nonindigenous inhabitants of the Sierra Tarahumara remains a difficult challenge for the historian. Nineteenth- and twentieth-century documents produced by observers from outside the Sierra, whether priests, anthropologists, government officials, or others, use the categories of *blanco* (white), *mestizo* (racially mixed), and *indígena* or *indio* (Indian) uncritically and provide little if any explanation of their use in a given situation. What is more, the documents produced by these sources tend to use the terms *blanco* and *mestizo* interchangeably to describe non-Indians. Nonindigenous serranos, however, have tended to identify themselves exclusively as *blanco* more consistently. Despite its instability as a racial category, in this essay I use the term *blanco*, translated to its English equivalent of "white," to describe the nonindigenous people of the Sierra Tarahumara. I admit that this invites comparisons to a U.S. ethnic identity that is unstable for entirely different reasons, but to distinguish between "Mexicans" and "Indians" is to deny the Tarahumara their citizenship.

22. AHPM, *Expedición apostólica del P. Manuel Piñan (agosto 1900).*

23. AHPM, *Expedición apostólica del P. Manuel Piñan.*

24. AHPM, *Carta del P. Narciso Ortiz, Cerocahue, diciembre 5 de 1909.*

25. AHPM., *Carta del P. Narciso Ortiz, Sisoguichi, diciembre 29 de 1909.*

26. Ocampo, *Historia*, 36, 46.

27. In the Tarahumara language, *chabochi* refers to any nonindigenous person. It can be translated as "whiskered one" or "hairy face" but refers to both male and female nonindigenous people. Although the term *gringo*, in reference to foreigners, especially Americans, is found in the Sierra, *chabochi* has become the more common term for non-Indians regardless of nationality.

28. AHPM, *Número 20 de la Misión de Tarahumara (November 1924)*, in *Noticias.*

29. AHPM, *Número 20 de la Misión de Tarahumara.*

30. Robles, "Los Rarámuri—Pagotuame," 29.

31. See AHPM, *Número 23 de la Misión de Tarahumara*. See also AHPM, *Número segundo de la Misión de la Tarahumara*, "Segunda excursión por Tónachic (*12–23 abril, 1921*)," in *Noticias*.

32. AHPM, *Número 24 de la Misión de Tarahumara (September 1925)*, in *Noticias*.

33. AHPM, *Número 14 de la Misión de Tarahumara (September 1923)*, in *Noticias*.

34. Archivo Particular Creel de Sisniego, Chihuahua, Mexico (APCS), Documents on the Sierra Tarahumara, document C-2. I gratefully thank Dizán Vásquez of Ciudad Chihuahua, Mexico, for his advice and for sharing these documents with me.

35. Ocampo, *Historia*, 90.

36. APCS,Documents on the Sierra Tarahumara, document A-4

37. APCS, Documents on the Sierra Tarahumara, document B-3

38. AHPM, "Apuntes inéditos sobre la historia de la Misión Tarahumara," October 1900–June 1914.

39. AHPM, *Número 26 de la Misión de Tarahumara (January 1926)*, in *Noticias*.

40. This last accusation, of course, may well stem from the pervasive nationwide fear during the late 1990s of "outside agitators" and "radical priests" in indigenous areas, a fear that emanated mostly from the 1994 Zapatista uprising in Chiapas, Mexico.

41. Friedrich Katz has pointed out that, in various parts of the Sierra Madre Occidental, "some of the most prominent families, such as the Orozcos, were receptive to the teachings of missionaries from the United States and converted to Protestantism." *The Life and Times of Pancho Villa* (Stanford: Stanford University Press, 1998), 23.

42. See, for example, William L. Merrill, "Conversion and Colonialism in Northern Mexico: The Tarahumara Response to the Jesuit Mission Program, 1601–1767," in *Conversion to Christianity: Historical and Anthropological Perspectives on a Great Transformation*, edited by Robert W. Hefner (Berkeley: University of California Press, 1993). See also William L. Merrill and Margot Heras Quezada, "Rarámari Personhood and Ethnicity: Another Perspective" *American Ethnologist* 24, 2 (1997): 302–310. Also Frances M. Slaney, "Double Baptism: Personhood and Ethnicity in the Sierra Tarahumara of Mexico," *American Ethnologist* 24, 2 (1997): 279–301. Much information on this theme can also be found in the manuscript and archival holdings of the AHPM.

43. AHPM, *Número 12 de la Misión de la Tarahumara (May 1923)*, in *Noticias*.

44. William L. Merrill, "Catolicismo y la creación de la religión moderna de los Rarámuris," in *Contacto entre Españoles e indígenas en el norte de la Nueva España: Colección Conmemorativa Quinto Centenario del Encuentro de dos Mundos*, compiled by Ysla Campbell (Ciudad Juárez: Universidad Autónoma de Ciudad Juárez, 1992), 158. See also Jerome Meyer Levi, "Pillars of the Sky: The Genealogy of Ethnic Identity Among the Rarámuri-Simaroni (Tarahumara-Gentiles) of Northwest Mexico" (Ph.D. diss., Harvard University, 1993), 265.

45. For further discussion of "Judas burnings" in Mexico, see William H. Beezley, *Judas at the Jockey Club and Other Episodes of Porfirian Mexico* (Lincoln: University of Nebraska Press, 1987).

46. AHPM, *Número Primero de la Tarahumara (January 1921)*, in *Noticias*.

47. AHPM, *Número Cuarto de la Misión de Tarahumara (1921)*, in *Noticias*.

48. AHPM, *Número 19 de la Misión de Tarahumara (September 1924)*, in *Noticias*. A letter from H. Salvador Martínez also described an outdoor mass as mass "a lo Tarahumara." See AHPM, *Número 24 de la Misión de Tarahumara*.

49. AHPM, *Número 24 de la Misión de Tarahumara*.

50. AHPM, *Número 24 de la Misión de Tarahumara*.

51. AHPM, *Número 20 de la Misión de Tarahumara*.

52. AHPM, *Número 22 de la Misión de Tarahumara (March 1925)*, in *Noticias*.

53. AHPM, *Número 23 de la Misión de Tarahumara*.

54. Ocampo, *Album*, 20.

55. Father Cordero responded: "I have lived in an exclusively Tarahumara environment for three months, doing without *chabochis* and their services, and the conclusion of my experiences is that I do not miss them at all, or their hindrance of my work with the indigenous element. Only good-for-nothings could defend the thesis that one cannot live without *chabochis*." AHPM, *Número 28 de la Misión de Tarahumara (May 1926)*, in *Noticias*.

56. AHPM, *Número 28 de la Misión de Tarahumara*.

57. AHPM, *Número 28 de la Misión de Tarahumara*.

58. David Brambila, *Hojas de un diario* (Mexico City: Editorial Jus, 1950), 31.

59. AHPM, *Número Cuarto de la Misión de Tarahumara*.

60. AHPM, *Número Tercero de la Misión de la Tarahumara (September 1921)*, in *Noticias*.

61. AHPM, *Número 19 de la Misión de Tarahumara*.

62. AHPM, *Número 20 de la Misión de Tarahumara*.

63. See Enrique C. Creel, *Exposición de motivos que presentó el Ejecutivo del Estado sobre la civilización y mejoramiento de la Raza Tarahumara y Ley expedida acerca del asunto por la Legislatura* (Chihuahua: Imprenta del Gobierno del Estado de Chihuahua, 1906). Of Mexican educators Alexander S. Dawson writes: "fancying themselves as the intellectual heirs of the earliest Catholic friars, they sent 'missionaries' into the countryside to preach the gospel of progress, developed rigid definitions of the appropriate forms of rural living, and even taught school chilren in Mexico City to paint according to pre-Colombian styles in order to build a harmonious nation." See Alexander Dawson, " 'Wild Indians,' 'Mexican Gentlemen,' and the Lessons Learned in the Casa del Estudiante Indígena, 1926–1932," *Americas* 57, 3 (January 2001), 329. See also Secretaría de Educación Pública, *Las misiones culturales en 1927: Las escuelas normales rurales* (Mexico City: Publicaciones de la Secretaría de Educación Pública, 1928). See also Enrique Corona, *Razón de ser de las misiones culturales de la Secretaría de Educación Pública* (Mexico City: Publicaciones de la Secretaría de Educación Pública, 1947).

64. Ocampo, *Album*, 19.

65. AHPM, *Número 23 de la Misión de Tarahumara*.

66. Ocampo, *Album*, 33.

67. AHPM (July–August 1951), in *Noticias*.

68. AHPM, *Número 19 de la Misión de Tarahumara*.

69. AHPM, *Número 24 de la Misión de Tarahumara*.

70. AHPM, *Número 13 de la Misión de la Tarahumara (July 1923)*, in *Noticias*.

71. Profesor Apolinar Frías Prieto, interview with author, May 11, 1999.

72. Filiberto Gómez, *Rarámuri, Mi Diario Tarahumara* (Mexico City: Talleres Tipográficos de Excelsior, Cía. Editorial, 1948), 84; in addition, my personal communication with Augusto Urteaga and oral history interviews carried out in the Sierra Tarahumara during the summer of 1999.

73. Claudio Lomnitz-Adler, *Exits from the Labyrinth: Culture and Ideology in the Mexican National Space* (Berkeley: University of California Press, 1992), 217–218.

Segregation, Congregation, and the North American Racial Binary

Since at least the late nineteenth century, racial formations in the Americas have been marked by a fundamental divide between North and South—between the starkly drawn Black-White racial binary of the United States and the more subtly drawn (and, some have argued, more fluid or flexible) racial distinctions typical of Latin America and the Caribbean. Though we in the United States must take care not to romanticize the fluidity of Latin American racial formations—which are founded, after all, on legacies of racial terror as harrowing as our own—it is important to bear in mind that most American societies recognize a broad range of racial categories and identities in between our "Black" and "White."

What, then, accounts for our distinctively binary thinking about race? How did the national borders of the United States come to coincide with a conceptual and political boundary in the hemispheric process of racialization? The answer lies, in large part, in the "one drop rule" that defined the children of masters and slaves in the United States—with as little as one drop of "Black blood"—as Black, and thus as property. But to explain the endurance of the North American racial binary we must look past its antebellum origins to the history of segregation that has kept "Black" and "White" in their place. And here we must look, perhaps above all, to the segregation of religious communities. As scholars of religion in the United States have often cynically joked, eleven o'clock on Sunday morning is the most segregated hour of the American week. The clichéd familiarity of this observation (and its implicit exclusion of non-

Christian religions) should not blind us to its fundamental insight. Religious communities have often been decisive battlegrounds in the contested effort to segregate—and thus, in a sense, to produce—"Blacks" and "Whites" in the United States.

The essays in this section explore how racial and national boundaries have been defined and contested through the segregation and integration of religious communities. In "Catholics, Creoles, and the Redefinition of Race in New Orleans," James Bennett examines the role of the Catholic Church in the Crescent City's shift, at the turn of the twentieth century, from the tripartite (Black-White-Creole) system of racial classification found throughout the Caribbean to the binary system of the United States. His analysis shows how Catholic officials worked to Americanize the local church by creating segregated Black and White parishes—at the expense of the city's historically Catholic Creole community. Danielle Brune Sigler, by contrast, examines the efforts of two charismatic religious leaders to create racially integrated communities in the mid-twentieth century. In "Beyond the Binary: Revisiting Father Divine, Daddy Grace, and Their Ministries," she contrasts Divine's wholesale rejection of racial thought and Grace's attempt to claim a Whiteness of his own. Each, in their own way, worked to build a religious community that transgressed the boundaries of Black and White, yet each had to contend with the pervasive racialization of the United States.

Taken together, these essays demonstrate the endurance, and resilience, of the North American Black-White binary. Yet they also document—and, in some sense, celebrate—aspects of religious life in and around the United States that cannot be contained by this reductive racial logic.

7

Catholics, Creoles, and the Redefinition of Race in New Orleans

James B. Bennett

In 1845, a Northern visitor to the St. Louis Cathedral in New Orleans was amazed at what he witnessed on a Sunday morning: "never had I seen such a mixture of conditions and colors. . . . White children and black, with every shade in between, knelt side by side. In the house of prayer they made no distinction of rank or colour. The most ardent abolitionist could not have desired more perfect equality."[1] Frederick Law Olmsted had a similar reaction during his 1854 sojourn in the Crescent City, when he observed "white and black women, bowed in equality before their common Father."[2] The unfamiliar degree of racial mixing emerged out of the tripartite racial organization of New Orleans. This three-caste racial order, which was typical of many predominantly Catholic Caribbean and South American societies, persisted in the Crescent City throughout the antebellum era. The city's third, or middle, caste consisted of free people of color—later known as Creoles of color—who were generally of racially mixed ancestry.[3] These free people occupied a distinct legal and social position that provided privileges unknown to persons of African descent living elsewhere in the United States. Nowhere was this distinctiveness more apparent than in the city's Catholic churches.

But racial identities in New Orleans underwent a fateful transition in the late nineteenth century. By 1920, the city's racially segregated Catholic churches presented a very different image from the mixed congregations that had so amazed earlier visitors. Twentieth-century travelers were more likely to encounter perspectives like those of the city's archbishop, who firmly denied that "the Good

Lord ever intended that the races should fraternize."[4] The archbishop's assertion revealed the extent to which the Crescent City had abandoned its triracial structure and capitulated to the biracialism and segregation that permeated the rest of the United States. Changes in religious institutions functioned as a crucial measure of the city's shifting racial landscape. Establishing separate parishes for black and white Catholics formed a pivotal event in the city's racial reorientation, as the city's white residents moved from a shaky racial fault line onto the seemingly firm ground of biracialism and segregation. Bolstered by these changes in the religious sphere, New Orleans emerged as one of the nation's most segregated cities in the early twentieth century.

Although the nineteenth-century Northern visitors had been most surprised by the racial mixing they observed, the uniqueness of New Orleans had derived less from its tripartite racial order than its geography. In the wider context of the Western Hemisphere, New Orleans marked the racial fault line that straddled the biracialism of British North America on one side and the complex, multiracial order of much of the Caribbean and South America on the other. New Orleans was caught between two types of racial structures: one multifaceted and fluid, the other binary and fixed. The city's shifting position between these options illumines the complex and varied constructions of race in postslavery societies throughout the Americas. While the march toward biracial segregation appears unstoppable in hindsight, the presence of these alternative social systems, combined with the widespread resistance to racial reconfiguration, indicates that the movement of New Orleans from one model to the other was far from inevitable.

This racial transformation affected Catholic Creoles of color more than any other group in New Orleans. In the second half of the nineteenth century, Creoles faced mounting isolation and a deteriorating racial climate that denied them the prerogatives available to their ancestors. As early as 1865, Creoles lamented that "from the social point of view, the rapprochement of the races seemed closer and more probable in 1815 than at the present."[5] Creoles' position only worsened in final decades of the nineteenth century. With the end of Reconstruction in 1877, federal troops withdrew from the South and left conservative Southern whites free to reassert the political power they lost during the Civil War and Reconstruction. Among their highest priorities were institutionalizing white supremacy and separating the races, which they defined solely in the binary categories of black and white. In New Orleans, the segregationist agenda included reconfiguring the city's unique racial order. White residents ignored previous distinctions and began classifying as "black" all whom they considered to be of African descent.[6] They lumped Creoles into a single race with former slaves and African Americans, subjecting them to the discrimination and oppression entailed in that racial identity.[7] Yet Creoles often had more in common with whites—culturally, educationally, and even in skin color—than with African Americans. Threatened by this racial ambiguity, white New Orleanians supported the newly imposed binary racial order they believed would eliminate any ambiguous middle ground and the racial interaction it had enabled. Throughout the shift in New Orleans from a tripartite to a bipartite racial organization, Creoles strove to retain a semblance of the unique identity and privileges once associated with their middle status.

In the struggle between Creoles of color and whites, Catholic churches formed an important locus for contests over racial identity. Between 1890 and 1920, both the white effort to impose a biracial society and the Creole defense of a distinct identity centered around parish organization in New Orleans. On one side, white Catholics tried to erase previous distinctions and impose a new Americanized racial identity that redefined Creole parishioners as black. Reconstructing racial categories along a black-white binary enabled white church leaders to create a system of segregated parishes that complemented the city's emerging biracial structure. On the other side, Creoles resisted segregation and the accompanying racial redefinition by emphasizing their tradition of racial distinctiveness and the intimate links between Catholic and Creole identity. The result was a long, highly contested battle over the racial composition of the city's Catholic parishes. In the end, Creoles emerged with a modified identity, albeit one in which Catholicism continued to play a central role.

The Origins of Creole Identity

Creoles were fighting to preserve a distinct identity they traced back to the free people of color, their ancestors in colonial and antebellum Louisiana. From the first colonial settlement, gender ratios favored the interracial liaisons that gave rise to the city's free population. Within the white population men outnumbered women, from the founding of New Orleans in 1718 until well into the nineteenth century. At the same time, women of African descent outnumbered men, especially among free people of color.[8] A community of free people arose from the tendency of French and later Spanish colonists, unlike their Anglo-American neighbors to the north, to free the offspring of their interracial liaisons.[9] Especially under Spanish rule (1763–1803), slave codes further encouraged the manumission of large numbers of slaves.[10] Louisiana colonists treated the growing class of free people of color as socially and racially distinct from the enslaved, often providing them with education, property, and income.[11] The gap between free and slave widened as free people gained socioeconomic status by learning skilled trades that made them vital to the growing economy of New Orleans. Militia service formed another means by which the city's free people earned special recognition and set themselves apart from both slaves and free people elsewhere in North America.[12] Between 1791 and 1809, an influx of refugees from the Haitian revolution bolstered the size, skill, and standing of the city's free population.[13] In 1803, New Orleans became part of the United States as a result of the Louisiana Purchase, which transferred Louisiana and most of the trans-Mississippi West from French to American governance. Only a few years after the American takeover, free people of color constituted a quarter of the population of New Orleans and had secured a distinct place in the city's emerging three-caste order.[14]

Legal codes also played an important role in constructing the tripartite racial organization of New Orleans. French colonial laws governing people of color, known as the Code Noir, outlined a wide range of rights that distinguished freed persons from the enslaved. Free people could inherit and own property, invoke the protection of the laws of the colony, sue in court, and even testify against whites. Under American rule, the Louisiana legislature placed greater restrictions on slaves. Because the slave legislation did not place comparable constraints on free people, it only strengthened their unique status. Instead, the protections the French and Spanish colonial governments had granted free people remained in force throughout most of the antebellum era. Louisiana state laws further institutionalized the triracial order in New Orleans by isolating free people as equally separate from both slaves and whites. Nineteenth-century marriage statutes, for example, placed as strong a prohibition on marriage between free persons and slaves as they did between free people of color and whites.[15] The state's judicial branch likewise upheld the city's tripartite structure. In an 1860 opinion concerning the African Methodist Episcopal congregation in New Orleans, the Louisiana Supreme Court outlined free people's unique legal status. While the Court ruled that "the African race [slaves] are strangers to our Constitutions," it also recognized free people of color as a distinct class: "as far as it concerns everything, except political rights, free people of color appear to possess all other rights of persons, whether absolute or relative."[16]

Still, free people's emergence as a unique caste would not have occurred without the approbation of the Catholic Church. Because French colonial policy dictated that all inhabitants must be Catholic, including slaves and their offspring, the church welcomed children of interracial liaisons into its midst. Priests baptized, confirmed, married, and buried persons of mixed parentage, reflecting the more racially liberal Latin Catholicism of the colonists and clergy of New Orleans.[17] While the Catholic Church in colonial New Orleans was including people of color in its worship and rituals, Anglo-Protestant colonists to the north were still debating whether churches and slave owners held any religious obligations to their slaves.[18] Catholic leaders also encouraged white fathers to acknowledge and support their mixed-race children. On rare occasions the Church even blessed unions across racial lines.[19] The acquiescence of the Catholic Church suggested a moral and religious assent to the interracial liaisons that resulted in the growing free population of New Orleans. The Church's acceptance also cultivated the centrality of a Catholic religious affiliation to a mixed-race, that is, Creole, identity.[20] Creoles of color thereby became crucial to the strength of Catholicism in New Orleans, forming the majority of attendees and financial supporters in several of the city's parishes. As late as 1875, a priest conceded that he did not want to offend Creoles in his congregation "because they are the chief support."[21]

As the Catholic Church welcomed free people, it also affirmed their distinctiveness from slaves, further institutionalizing the city's triracial order. Priests acknowledged Creoles' middle status as they refused to perform marriages not only between free and white but also between free and slave. Likewise, Catholic officials often utilized a tripartite classification in sacramental registers, categorizing people as either slave, free, or white.[22] The Archdiocese of New Orleans allowed the creation of separate societies set aside solely for free people of color, even as many church activities remained closed to slaves and white organizations likewise banned free persons. Catechetical schools, the Christian Doctrine Society at St. Louis Cathedral, and a separate women's religious order, the Sisters of the Holy Family, were the range of Catholic organizations serving the city's free population. Church seating also reflected the city's unique racial order. When congregations mandated separate seating, the most important distinction was between free people of color and slaves, not between black and white.[23] At St. Augustine Church, for example, Creoles rented nearly half the pews in the center of the sanctuary, while slaves sat on benches along the sides.[24]

One consequence of Catholicism's acceptance of the unique racial organization of New Orleans was a long tradition of racially mixed worship. The racial interaction and mobility typical of a tripartite racial order provided a stark contrast with the segregation that formed the hallmark of American biracialism. Antebellum visitors had frequently commented on the interracial worship within the city's Catholic churches. Post–Civil War visitors were surprised to discover that racially mixed worship continued. In 1874, Joseph Hartzell, a white Methodist Episcopal minister working in New Orleans, expressed his amazement that

> lips of every shade, by hundreds press with devout kisses the same
> crucifixes, and fingers of as great variety in color, are dipped in the
> "holy water" . . . in the renting of pews colored families have a
> chance, and we have seen them sitting as others in every part of the
> house.[25]

Priests continued to minister to black as well as white parishioners, forming the basis of the claim of the Catholic historian Roger Baudier that after the Civil War, "in most churches, the Negro was permitted and there was very generally no interference with his practice of his religion."[26] The Sisters of Mercy visited prisoners without regard to color, while nuns administering the House of the Good Shepherd for orphans likewise served both black and white children.[27] Throughout much of the nineteenth century, ongoing examples of

Catholic interracialism slowed the imposition of an Americanized biracial system. In turn, free people of color preserved their status as the middle caste within a tripartite racial order.[28]

The Decline of Creole Distinctiveness and the Emergence of Separate Parishes

Yet the Catholic Church, which had helped create Creoles' unique standing, also played a crucial role in dismantling the city's triracial structure. Church support for redefining Creole identity proved especially important. Following Emancipation, descendants of antebellum free people of color adopted the category "Creoles of color" to distinguish themselves from recently freed slaves, and African Americans more generally. But even "Creole" had become a contested identity. Prior to 1870, the broadly used term "Creole" referred to anyone born in Louisiana, without regard to skin color, whose cultural leanings were French rather than American. It was an ethnic rather than a racial designation.[29] The inverse became true with the movement toward American biracialism in the 1870s. White Creoles began arguing that Creole identity depended more on blood than culture—even a drop of African blood excluded one from the category of Creole. This attempt at racial redefinition represented the need of an ethnic minority to ensure they ended up on the white side of the city's increasingly Americanized binary racial order. The Catholic Church in New Orleans supported this effort to redefine Creole in racial terms. The archdiocesan newspaper, for example, printed reassurances in 1894 that although "in the North the idea is prevalent that a Creole has negro blood . . . it is entirely wrong."[30]

By the turn of the century, Catholic churches in New Orleans became a prime locus for renegotiating Creole racial identity. Though the Catholic Church is often described in terms of its hierarchy and universal character, these racial struggles happened at the lowest levels: in particular parishes, with the laity often taking an active role in both resisting and implementing segregation. Only with an eye to the local do the experiences of Catholics of color in New Orleans come into focus. The parish was rooted in the neighborhoods where Creoles lived, forming the place where sacred and secular merged.[31] The Church's impact on the city's shifting racial boundaries is most apparent in developments within these specific congregations, where the give and take over contested racial identities occurred most frequently. Given the longstanding link between Creole and Catholic identity, changes in parish organizations, boundaries, and practices stood among the transformations that most directly shaped Creole identity. White Catholics suppressed formerly acknowledged cultural distinctions that were central to Creole identity and assigned the city's Catholics more typical American racial identities as either black or white. This reclassification enabled church leaders to end the Creole-American divide that had previously characterized congregations, replacing it with a system of racially segregated parishes. Suddenly race, rather than language, culture, or even place of residence, determined where the city's Catholics worshiped. At the same time, Creoles of color resisted the creation of "black" parishes that denied their unique status and forced them out of congregations that they had belonged to for generations. These often-overlooked struggles formed the final chapter in the transformation of New Orleans' racial structure from a tripartite to a bipartite system of classification.

The initial battle over separate parishes centered around the 1895 opening of St. Katherine's, the first church in New Orleans set aside for Catholics of color. The new congregation resulted from the forceful efforts of Francis Janssens, the archbishop of New Orleans from 1888 to 1897.[32] The Dutch-born Janssens was the first non-French archbishop to serve New Orleans, and with his arrival came a new approach toward the city's Catholics of African descent. Janssens spoke repeatedly of his burden in Louisiana to care for the nation's largest population of black Catholics. At the midpoint of his tenure in New Orleans, he confessed that "there is nothing in my administration of the Diocese that worries me more than our colored people."[33] Yet Janssens also believed that by 1890, any appearance of mixed worship resulted from neglecting the needs of black Catholics rather than any lingering ideological commitment to interracialism. He therefore advocated establishing separate religious institutions as the best strategy to win back lapsed Catholics of color and to gain new black converts. Pointing to the apparent exodus of black Catholics into separate Protestant organizations, Janssens argued that only in similarly segregated Catholic churches would black parishioners find the dignity and freedom from racial oppression that Catholicism proclaimed they were entitled to.

Janssens's push for separate churches illumines the complex relationship between segregation and racism. Janssens unquestionably harbored racist tendencies, but his constant turmoil over the condition of black Catholics, his determined effort to improve their condition, and his rhetoric of equality indicate that he was less racist than most southerners, including the archbishops who both preceded and followed him. The course of action Janssens followed demonstrates that segregation is not necessarily a measure of racism, although it is undoubtedly an expression of it. The absence of segregation does not signal a dearth of racism. Nor does the growth of racism always result in a proportional expansion of segregation, even in the American South. Janssens moved the Archdiocese of New Orleans in the direction of segregation, even though his efforts arose out of longstanding concerns for African Americans and a genuine desire to reduce the pervasive grip of racism. Archbishops blatantly more racist than Janssens remained more reluctant to institute segregation. In Janssens, Catholics of color in New Orleans had the most dangerous of potential allies: one who in the name of good could inflict much harm.

Janssens considered the opening of St. Katherine's the capstone of his career. He believed he had improved the condition of the city's black Catholics while simultaneously convincing his archdiocese of the advantages of separate parishes. The archbishop deemed the 1895 dedication an auspicious occasion that generated "great hopes for the future" of additional segregated parishes. Noting the overflowing congregation at the opening mass, Janssens boasted of black members "who seemed delighted" in one report and "overdelighted" in another.[34] Only a few months after its opening, Janssens pronounced St. Katherine's an unqualified success and stopped calling it an experiment he would halt at the first sign of disappointment.[35] The archbishop had invested too much time, energy, and money to admit anything but triumph. For the remaining two years of his life, he expounded the supposed success of St. Katherine's to potential benefactors, hoping to raise funds to erect additional separate parishes in the Creole-dominated downtown neighborhoods.[36]

Yet the opening of St. Katherine's constituted an episode of successful resistance more than it signaled the inevitable start of segregated parishes in New Orleans. The city's residents of African descent, and especially the predominately Catholic Creoles of color, rejected efforts at parish reconfiguration that would homogenize and redefine their racial identity through the simplistic and naive categories of black and white—categories that denied the city's complex racial history and the Church's role in fostering that history. A careful examination of the resistance to St. Katherine's and its long-term effects suggests that the real significance of St. Katherine's lies in its disruption of Janssens's plans and the effective opposition to church segregation that it engendered among Catholics of color in New Orleans.

The city's black elite, who were mostly Creoles of color, led the opposition to St. Katherine's. Among the many petitions and delegations that bombarded the determined prelate, the most numerous and persistent were those from the Citizens Committee (Comité des Citoyens), the Creole civil rights organization that coordinated legal challenges to segregation statutes. At the same time the Citizens Committee was protesting Janssens's plans for St. Katherine's, it was also advancing the *Plessy v. Ferguson* case, in which the U.S. Supreme Court would validate the premise of "separate but equal" that undergirded Jim Crow segregation.[37] The Citizens Committee also published the *Daily Crusader* to publicize its efforts and disseminate its message. Committee members were mostly descendants of free people and included some of the wealthiest and best educated citizens of color in New Orleans. Janssens often complained of this politically influential mulatto elite—by which he meant French-speaking Creoles of color—hindering his efforts to create separate churches. A year before the opening of St. Katherine's, he groused about the "light mulattoes & politicians, who abuse me in public print for attempting to begin a new church for the colored people." The archbishop described Creoles as being "in language, manners & every way of thinking quite different from the col. people elsewhere." Their tendency to "look with disfavor upon separate churches" remained the characteristic that most troubled Janssens.[38] The archbishop's complaints acknowledged the longstanding distinction between Creoles of color and African Americans, even as he advocated segregated parishes that ignored such differences.

Creole protests against St. Katherine's reflected the complex position in which Creoles found themselves in a city undergoing a racial transformation. On the one hand, protesting against segregation was consistent with efforts to preserve a distinct Creole identity. Retaining any claim to a unique social position or cultural identity would become difficult if Creoles were forced into the same parishes as everyone else the church deemed "black." Creoles invoked the long tradition of their acceptance into mixed congregations, which was also an acknowledgment of the difference between their ancestors and those of African Americans. Creole protests also revealed their cultural distinctiveness as they called on the French ideals of *liberté, égalité,* and *fraternité,* in contrast to the African-American emphasis on the Declaration of Independence. For Creole leaders such as Rodolphe Desdunes, the cultural, linguistic and residential differences between the Creole, or "Latin Negro," and the "Anglo-Saxon or American Negro" remained significant at the turn of the twentieth century.[39] White priests likewise acknowledged that Creoles retained "a feeling of superiority on their part, owing to a higher grade of moral and social life . . . and their French social customs."[40] The biracial segregation characteristic of separate parishes denied such differences by organizing parishioners solely by the presence or absence of African blood, rather than alternative categories such as culture, language, education, or even place of residence.

On the other hand, Creole protests against St. Katherine's revealed a self-conscious collapsing of differences with African Americans. The interests of these once distinct castes increasingly coincided as both suffered under the weight of a racial oppression that denied any differences among people of African descent. Whether seeking to preserve their own distinct identity and position or simply resisting the broader tendency to homogenize and discriminate broadly on the basis of an "impurity" of blood, Creoles found increasing reason to make common cause with their African-American neighbors. Most Creoles underscored St. Katherine's offensiveness to all black citizens and Catholics, rather than invoking the more elitist and self-interested arguments that had characterized earlier Creole protests. The *Crusader's* opposition to segregation, in churches as well as on railroad cars, sought to protect and defend "the plain and common people" who were "the poor, the defenseless, the toiler, whether in the field, on the levee, in the shop or factory."[41] African-American Protestants reciprocated by joining the protests against St. Katherine's, among them the Methodists, who pronounced Janssens's plan "a surrender to a most cruel prejudice."[42] Ironically, this movement toward common cause was itself a tacit recognition of the very biracialism that Creoles were protesting.

Creoles feared that a separate parish would unnecessarily draw the "color line" both within and beyond the church, accelerating the capitulation of New Orleans to an Americanized racial order. A church that endorsed an overly simplistic biracialism remained unwelcome in a city with a long tradition of minimizing rather than emphasizing racial differences. "Such distinctions are unnecessary and even harmful, and we must deplore and discourage them," explained Rodolphe Desdunes in his protest of St. Katherine's.[43] Creoles believed that Janssens, despite his concern for bringing black Catholics to the faith, wished "to separate the races & to widen the gap which exists between the white and col. population."[44] While Janssens responded that attendance at the new church would be voluntary, most remained skeptical. Alice Ruth Moore (later Dunbar-Nelson) warned that "it won't be long before such gentle means as a quiet discrimination all along the parishes will force the colored worshippers into the 'Jim Crow' church."[45] Protesters were especially concerned about the influence church actions would have on society at large. Desdunes argued that Catholics in New Orleans should reject the segregated church because "separation in one form may bring separation in another."[46] "If men are divided by, or in, the Church," Desdunes wondered, "where can they be united in the bonds of faith and love of truth and justice?"[47]

Led by Creole concerns, the city's Catholics of color organized a formidable "storm of opposition" to St. Katherine's. They kept the archbishop "deluged with petitions, some lengthy, some pithy, some with many signatures, some with a few signatures that meant something." Others formed delegations that repeatedly visited the archbishop to persuade him of the practical and theological dangers of his plan.[48] Janssens and his visitors agreed that the current "prejudices which obtained in the churches" caused many to leave Catholicism.[49] But they could not agree on a solution. Janssens believed separate churches would stem the exodus. His visitors argued just the opposite: "if the Catholic authorities desire to lose their communicants among the colored population of this city," they warned, "the surest and most direct way to it is the organization of separate church edifices."[50]

Protests against St. Katherine's plagued the new racial parish, contrary to Janssens's declarations of unequivocal success. Janssens boasted of a packed congregation at the dedicatory mass, but even then, many opted not to participate. Prior to its opening, the Citizens Committee passed a resolution calling on black Catholics to "show their disapproval of the same by abstaining from the dedication services and from any subsequent frequenting of said church."[51] The prominent Creole philanthropists Thomy Lafon and Aristide Mary had created their own boycott by refusing Janssens's requests for funds for the separate parish, even though both had generously supported other Catholic projects. The protests continued long after the church opened, and most Catholics of color continued to avoid St. Katherine's. Black Catholics continued to withhold financial support from St. Katherine's. Nor did the new church result in the onslaught of conversions Janssens envisioned: over its first five years, only thirteen adults were baptized.[52] Creoles preferred their current churches, despite increasing discrimination. Even those who lived near St. Katherine's remained a part of the older St. Joseph's parish across the street, as entries in the visitation register make clear.[53] Seven years after its opening, Katharine Drexel, St. Katherine's benefactor, lamented the small numbers at Sunday mass. In her journal she rightly concluded that "the Colored prefer to go to Church with the Whites."[54]

The Creole-led resistance to St. Katherine's dealt a serious blow to the growth of segregated parishes in New Orleans. The new church failed to accomplish Janssens's most immediate goal of increasing the number of Catholics of color in New Orleans. The widespread and very public opposition also prevented Janssens from securing funding or recruiting religious orders to create additional separate parishes in New Orleans. As a result, Janssens's plan for segregated churches in New Orleans came to an abrupt and lengthy halt. No new separate parishes opened in New Orleans for fourteen years. Nearly two decades passed before a separate church opened in the downtown, Creole-dominated district where Janssens had hoped to create a second black parish shortly after opening St. Katherine's.

In 1897, two years after St. Katherine's opened, Archbishop Janssens died en route to Europe. That same year, the Creole-led Citizens Committee disbanded following the *Plessy v. Ferguson* ruling in which the U.S. Supreme Court upheld the legality of segregation. The archbishop and the members of the Citizens Committee could each look with pride and concern at the developments in New Orleans Catholicism during the previous decade. Given the mixed meanings of the events surrounding the opening of St. Katherine's, none could be certain of the church's ultimate direction concerning segregation. On the one hand, the Catholic hierarchy had succeeded in extending racial segregation into the sanctuary, the last bastion of Catholic interracial activity. On the other hand, organized opposition halted the further spread of segregated churches, enabling Catholics of color to remain in mixed parishes. The contested opening of St. Katherine's formed an uncertain midpoint in the transformation of the racial order of New Orleans. The Church had opened its doors to a segregation and biracialism that exchanged Creole identity for a monolithic blackness. But the Creoles of New Orleans had resisted the new identity that advocates of the emerging racial tried to impose.

The "Triumph" of Segregated Parishes

After a lull of almost two decades, the course of religious segregation in New Orleans and the position of Creoles changed dramatically. As late as 1915, most Catholics of color attended mixed churches rather than one of the two parishes set aside for black Catholics (the second had opened in 1909). Five years later, the inverse was true. Those five years witnessed an onslaught of separate black parishes in New Orleans, bringing the total to eight. Most of the expansion took place in the city's downtown neighborhoods, which had been the center of opposition to St. Katherine's. By 1920, Catholics in the same districts swelled the rolls of segregated congregations, and most Creoles identified separate churches as their home parishes. As Creoles negotiated a new identity within the biracial realignment, membership in a Catholic parish, even a segregated one, remained a central part of that identity.

The Americanization of New Orleans constituted a crucial shift that enabled the widespread implementation of segregated parishes. In the secular arena, Americanization meant conformity with the linguistic, cultural, and racial practices in the rest of the United States. These racial views were steadfastly biracial, emphasizing the difference between black and white, the necessity of keeping the races separate, and the lack of any middle ground between them. The Americanization of the Catholic Church in New Orleans incorporated the same themes as local church leaders conformed to Catholic practices prevalent throughout the United States. Americans had long considered the Catholicism of New Orleans different. Its French and Spanish roots, as well as the city's large black Catholic population, distinguished New Orleans from most of American Catholicism, which traced its roots to English Catholics in colonial Maryland. The lack of racially segregated parishes also set New Orleans apart. After the turn of the century, the city's Catholic leadership hoped to demonstrate the archdiocese's "Americanness" through closely related efforts to consolidate episcopal authority, establish parochial schools, create regular territorial parishes, and implement racial segregation. Beginning with Janssens, and accelerated under James Blenk (1906–1917) and John Shaw (1918–1934), Crescent City archbishops maneuvered their church toward the mainstream of American Catholicism.[55] In church no less than society, these leaders envisioned an American national unity with white racial superiority as its linchpin.

Changes in archdiocesan leadership formed an important measure of the Church's Americanization in New Orleans. Unlike any of their predecessors, the two archbishops who oversaw the rapid expansion of separate parishes, James Blenk and John Shaw, were not just Americans but southerners. These prelates advocated a particularly southern perspective on matters of race, typified in Shaw's denial that "the Good Lord ever intended that the races should fraternize."[56] Clergy working in New Orleans were also increasingly American in birth and outlook, in contrast to the foreign-born clerics who predominated throughout the nineteenth century. The ranks of American and even southern-born clergy increased especially after 1915, when World War I divided the United States from the European continent and its supply of priests.[57] Whereas the previous generation hailing from Europe largely opposed Janssens's effort to establish separate parishes, their American successors in the early twentieth century were nearly unanimous in supporting racially segregated parishes. Racial prejudices and the declining economic status of Creoles of color meant that by 1915 few priests shared their predecessors' concerns about the financial impact of losing Creole parishioners.[58]

The triumph of English over French marked another form of Americanization that facilitated the rise of separate parishes. Shortly after the opening of St. Katherine's in 1895, an article in the archdiocesan newspaper noted the growing use of English.[59] By the turn of the century, most Catholic churches in New Orleans included at least one English service.[60] At St. Rose of Lima, which had been a strictly French-speaking congregation, the pastor began offering an English sermon series in 1911. By the end of World War I he was marking all parish entries in English.[61] The language shift took place among black as well as white residents. As late as 1909, Archbishop Blenk stressed that French "is very much necessary for work among Louisiana Colored Catholics."[62] Three years later, however, the pastor at the city's second black parish warned his superior that "the colored here want good english speaking priests."[63] Even at Corpus Christi, in the heart of the city's Creole neighborhoods, the parish priest reported in 1917 that "the french is almost obsolete and it is no use trying to revive it."[64] Diminishing cultural differences resulted in greater consideration of racial distinctions. For the city's white Creoles, the declining use of French provided one less reason why they should worship with Creoles of color and apart from the city's other English-speaking whites. As New Orleans became more uniform in language and culture, churches put greater emphasis on alternate forms of categorization and separation, and especially on that most typically American form of division: race.

The widespread use of English also ended national language (ethnic) parishes, which further encouraged the creation of racially segregated churches. The nearly universal use of English suggested that national language parishes were no longer necessary. The dissolution of these ethnic congregations also enabled Archbishop Blenk to create a system of regular territorial parishes, which was another mandate of the American hierarchy. Yet Blenk knew that white Catholics would oppose territorial parishes unless he could assure them they would not have to attend racially mixed churches. In recent decades, German, Irish, and Italian national churches had increasingly functioned as bulwarks to protect white congregations against the influx of African Americans into the surrounding neighborhoods. These long-established patterns of interracial settlement in New Orleans made it impossible to create territorial parishes that were not racially mixed. Blenk resolved the racial conflict by erecting a separate system of territorial parishes for Catholics of color.[65] All others, including Irish, Italians, and Sicilians, who were once labeled "colored," were now welcome to sit and worship where black Catholics could not.[66] As other ethnic groups' adoption of English marked their entry into "regular" Catholic churches, Creoles' use of English coincided with their exclusion from the same Catholic churches, some of which their families had belonged to for generations. The church maximized racial differences as it minimized ethnicity, ostracizing native-born people of color as "other" even as it embraced ethnic newcomers as both white and American.[67]

The creation of two separate territorial parish systems both reflected and reinforced the city's emerging biracial order. Both parish systems shared the same geography but claimed entirely different constituents. Suddenly there were two Catholic churches for each community, one for white parishioners and another for black.[68] Church leaders divided the city's once unified Catholicism, creating one Catholic world for whites and a parallel, unequal one for all whom the Church deemed "black." Creole and white neighbors who had once attended the same church now attended different churches based on racial identity, as Creoles and European immigrants alike were reduced to the seemingly simple categories of black and white. The unacknowledged irony was that in the name of creating territorial parishes, place of residence became secondary to race in determining congregational affiliation. Efforts to abandon national and ethnic parishes did not result in a true territorial parish system, as the Vatican had called for, but rather a system of racially organized parishes that were only secondarily ordered along a territorial scheme.[69] As they reconfigured Catholicism in New Orleans, archdiocesan officials contributed to the national project of stressing Americanized biracial identities over ethnic differences. Lacking recognition altogether were the city's once esteemed Creoles of color.

Changes within the Creole community facilitated the growth of black parishes between 1915 and 1920. Political developments after the opening of St. Katherine's—the 1896 *Plessy v. Ferguson* ruling, disfranchisement in 1898, and the ongoing spread of Jim Crow legislation—diminished Creoles' ability to respond to the opening of additional segregated churches. After both the Citizens Committee and the *Crusader*, which had been regular voices in the controversy surrounding St. Katherine's in 1895, disbanded following the *Plessy* ruling, no society or publication rose to fill the void. The lack of black newspapers and civil rights organizations hindered efforts to coordinate protests at the time the rapid expansion of separate parishes took place. Disfranchisement likewise eliminated the political arena as a means to enact change. Jim Crow also dealt a devastating economic blow to the city's black elite. While prosperous Creoles of color such as Thomy Lafon and Aristide Mary had funded organizations such as the Citizens Committee in the 1890s, pervasive discrimination dramatically reduced the overall wealth of the city's Creole community.[70] Gone were the means to sustain the costly litigation and journalistic advocacy necessary to challenge white supremacy in church and society alike.

Catholic leaders used these changes to their advantage as they imposed racially segregated parishes. The American archbishops, James Blenk and John

Shaw, proceeded with an unqualified confidence in their project. They rejected the ambiguity and openness that facilitated the protests against St. Katherine's. Rather than publicizing their intentions in advance, Catholic leaders made the necessary arrangements in secret and revealed their intent to divide a congregation along racial lines only at the last minute. Often, as was the case at St. Dominic's, the mixed congregation had just built a new sanctuary. When the time came to move into the new facility, the priest would announce that only the white members were moving. The black parishioners remained in the old, inevitably inferior, facility to form a new separate congregation. The abandoned parishioners at St. Dominic's reported that the departing priest "only told them the sunday before he moved!" The unknowing parishioners had contributed funds for the new building, and not the least of their disappointments was that they could not even keep "their money for their [own] church."[71] These stealth openings, combined with the lack of a viable newspaper, prevented Creoles from mounting a preemptive public protest as they had with St. Katherine's.

In erecting separate black parishes, Catholics traded Janssens's gentle coaxing for strong-armed bullying. Whereas Janssens opened St. Katherine's as an alternative, guaranteeing protesters that no one would be compelled to attend the new church or excluded from their old parish, Blenk and Shaw offered no such assurances. Lay leaders followed the prelates' example. White ushers routinely turned away black worshipers with the excuse that they now had their own churches. A missionary to the city's black Catholics conceded that "the white churches seem to be taking our coming as a good excuse to freeze the Colored out."[72] At the same time, priests coordinated their efforts toward black Catholics "with a view to wean them from other [white] churches" once a nearby black parish opened.[73] Archdiocesan officials required that the records of black parishioners be transferred to the new separate parishes, making the new parish their official church home. Often the Catholics of color pushed out of formerly mixed congregations had longer ties to the church than the white parishioners who remained.

Once black parishes were established, differences in their administration underscored their separation from white congregations. The New Orleans hierarchy was unwilling to provide either clerical or financial support to establish separate parishes, even as they advanced a program of racial segregation. Catholic leaders protected their own resources by requiring that only religious orders and outside contributions build the system of black parishes. The Baltimore-based St. Joseph's Society of the Sacred Heart, known as the Josephites, staffed all but two of the city's black parishes. The Josephite mission was to minister exclusively to black Catholics. As a result, Josephite priests, who were white, served only black parishes and had no ties to any of the city's white congregations. Similarly, two women's orders, one white and one Creole, and both dedicated to the service of Catholics of color, administered and staffed the parochial schools at each of the black parishes. Neither women's order taught in any of the city's white churches. Those who served in black parishes experienced a marginalization that paralleled the experiences of their parishioners. A Josephite priest conceded that "the whites around here don't care much for us," noting that "one white said I was doing injustice to myself and a priest told me he sympathized with me."[74] Diocesan priests expressed their relief at not having to work with Catholics of color, while white parishioners were equally relieved they no longer had to share facilities and resources with blacks. To reinforce the separation between black and white churches, black parishes were refused membership in Louisiana's State Federation of Catholic societies.[75]

Reliance on outside financial resources further accentuated the differences between black and white Catholics in New Orleans. Neither the Archdiocesan leadership nor the city's white parishioners provided financial support for the system of separate parishes they deemed so necessary. The religious orders who engaged in the "colored" work were responsible for funding the churches and schools. Prominent among the benefactors was the wealthy heiress Katharine Drexel, who founded of the Sisters of the Blessed Sacrament, which staffed many of the black parochial schools of New Orleans. Using only external sources of funding and staffing not only emphasized the growing distance between black and white Catholics but also represented the accompanying tendency to homogenize all Catholics of color. The new churches were simply characterized as "black," without any distinction between them. Archdiocesan officials used the same financial appeals and the same religious orders in working with both uptown African-American and downtown Creole parishes. Absent was any recognition of each community's particular history, cultural needs, or distinctiveness. Representative of this homogenization was the decision of the Sisters of the Blessed Sacrament to begin the city's first black Catholic high school, which served primarily Creoles, in an uptown neighborhood well removed from the downtown Creole districts.[76]

Creole Catholic Faithfulness

Nonetheless, Creoles remained loyal to the Catholic Church even as it denied their distinctive identity and pushed them into racially segregated parishes. Some did leave for Protestant churches or abandoned Christianity and organized religion altogether. Others protested by continuing to attend white parishes. According to canon law, no Catholic could be excluded from any church, even though many congregations did their best to make black worshipers feel unwelcome. Still, most chose to attend separate black parishes for reasons deeply connected to their Creole identity. Separate parishes enabled Creoles to assume every level of lay participation (the priesthood remained closed to American blacks) from altar boys and ushers to committee leaders, all of which had been closed even to antebellum free people of color. Creoles were thus able to assert the leadership of which they believed themselves both capable and worthy, doing so within the community and the religion that remained central to their identity. Even at the once-despised St. Katherine's, the pastor reported that by 1919 "pews that once went empty are now filled: people that never came here are coming now."[77]

Education provided another important reason for Creole participation in separate parishes. Parochial schools attached to the separate parishes afforded a highly desired opportunity for a community that had always placed a premium on education. The options for religious education for black Catholics had been steadily declining. Between 1906 and 1916, nine parishes in New Orleans closed their black parochial schools while continuing to operate their white schools. After 1916, only two mixed parishes operated parochial schools for black students, one of which enrolled an average of only twenty students.[78] Only Protestant schools provided an alternative, but they also carried the risk of conversion. Parents seeking a Catholic education for their children thus flocked to the schools associated with the new separate churches, and in many cases to the churches as well. This had been Catholic leaders' strategy. Recognizing the importance of education to the city's Creole residents, they attracted children and families first to the schools and then encouraged them to attend the separate church associated with the school.[79] The results were impressive. At Corpus Christi, the school enrolled nine hundred children in grades 1 through 6 only three years after its opening. Teachers still had to turn away over half of those who wanted to attend, even with "two children sitting in one single seat." Corpus Christi soon became the largest Catholic school in New Orleans, black or white.[80]

Most important, however, Creoles remained loyal to the Catholic church because Catholicism continued to function as a crucial aspect of Creole identity. For most, to reject Catholicism would have been to abandon their Creole heritage. Few were willing to forsake an identity that many could trace back almost two centuries, even in the face of a segregated biracial order. Despite dramatic transformations in the city's social and religious organization, religious and racial identity remained so inextricably wedded that to reject one was to reject the other. Catholicism had been central in recognizing and advocating the rights of free people of color. Their descendants, the Creoles of color, were unwilling to abandon Catholicism even when some its representatives failed to uphold the church's universal ideal. Creoles would remind the Church of its inclusive claims and hold it accountable to those standards through their ongoing participation. In order to retain and assert a Creole identity, Creoles would remain Catholic, even if that meant doing so within separate parishes.

Ironically, separate parishes preserved Creole distinctiveness within the city's black community, even though the new parishes emerged from a white rejection of such distinctions. Residential patterns dating to the early nineteenth century meant that most African Americans lived uptown, while Creoles lived and worshiped in downtown neighborhoods. Certain parishes thus became centers for nurturing Creole identity simply because of their geography. In particular, Corpus Christi, which opened in 1916 and quickly became the nation's largest black parish, became synonymous with Creole identity. Other downtown parishes, especially the six that grew out of Corpus Christi, functioned similarly. Creole children could learn and affirm their distinct identity, while adults used parish affiliation to mark the bounds of that community. Membership in particular parishes became an emblem for the Creole community, although white Catholic leaders ignored the significance of such distinctions.[81] Insulating Creoles in separate parishes strengthened their sense of their identity against a segregation that ignored the unique role they had played in the racial milieu of New Orleans.

Creoles and Catholic Identity

By 1920 New Orleans had become a biracialized society, characterized by a pervasive segregation that contrasted with the opportunities for mixing more typical of its earlier tripartite racial organization. To the city's white residents, and to the Catholic leadership as well, differences within the binary categories of white and black mattered little. Creoles found little reason to hope that their Catholic heritage might yet offer a means to transcend the city's confining racial dualisms. As late as the 1890s, priests and even Archbishop Janssens had acknowledged the existence and role of a distinct community known as Creoles of color. By 1920, however, white Catholics offered no such concession. New Orleans Catholicism had completed the transition from a tripartite to a bipartite racial order, which was nowhere more evident than in its system of separate black parishes.

Throughout the city's racial reconfiguration, the link between religious and racial identity remained crucial. For Catholics in New Orleans, race did not merely intersect with religion at crucial moments. Rather, it was a constant albeit constantly changing aspect of religious identity. Churches functioned as crucial sites for negotiating one's own racial identity and for manipulating that of others. Whites used racially segregated congregations to reconstruct racial identity as simply black or white, attempting to suppress the significance of Creole identity. Yet recreating racial identities was never so simple. Congregations also offered a space to preserve identities or construct new ones that resisted those being imposed from above. While ultimately acknowledging the color line that represented the triumph of biracialism, Creoles nonetheless inverted the meaning of separate parishes to maintain for themselves a distinct identity derived from their unique cultural history.

The history of Catholic Creoles in New Orleans reveals that a biracial society, and the segregation that undergirded it, was not the only model of racial organization. Through their resistance, Creoles preserved the place of New Orleans as a fault line between racial systems in the Western Hemisphere, even as the city's white majority shifted attention away from the triracial model to the more typically American biracial order. While they were "black" within the Americanized biracial system, Creoles' communal identities in several of the city's separate parishes enabled them to emphasize their uniqueness first and foremost. Religion remained, as it had been, central to that identity. Even in the face of widespread social, legal, and religious restrictions, the city's Creole community found ways to preserve and strengthen their identity. The segregated racial order that pervaded New Orleans proved insufficient to destroy the Creole sense of self that remained grounded in an equally powerful Catholic identity.

NOTES

1. Thomas Low Nichols, *Forty Years of American Life, 1821–1861* (New York: Stackpole, 1937), 127–128.

2. Cited in John W. Blassingame, *Black New Orleans, 1860–1880* (Chicago: University of Chicago Press, 1973), 20. On visitors' reactions to New Orleans as distinctive in the American context, see Timothy F. Reilly, "Heterodox New Orleans and the Protestant South, 1800–1861," *Louisiana Studies* 12 (fall 1973), 533–551.

3. Generally, mixed parentage signaled free status, and "pure" African heritage pointed to slavery in New Orleans, although there were many exceptions to the rule. See Arthé Agnes Anthony, "The Negro Creole Community in New Orleans, 1880–1920: An Oral History" (Ph.D. diss., University of California, Irvine, 1978), 34, 108; Anthony G. Barthelemy, "Light, Bright and Damn *Near* White," in *Creole: The History and Legacy of Louisiana's Free People of Color,* edited by Sybil Kein (Baton Rouge: Louisiana State University Press, 2000), 256–257; Caryn Cossé Bell, *Revolution, Romanticism, and the Afro-Creole Protest Tradition in Louisiana, 1718–1868* (Baton Rouge: Louisiana State University Press, 1997), 2; Blassingame, *Black New Orleans,* 21; Virginia Domínguez, *White by Definition: Social Classification in Creole Louisiana* (New Brunswick, N.J.: Rutgers University Press, 1986), 24–25; Gwendolyn Midlo Hall, *Africans in Colonial Louisiana: The Development of Afro-Creole Culture in the Eighteenth Century* (Baton Rouge: Louisiana State University Press, 1992), 130; and Charles B. Rousseve, *The Negro in Louisiana: Aspects of His History and His Literature* (New Orleans: Xavier University Press, 1937), 26. As a result, *mixed-race, free person of color,* and *Creole (of color)* became generally interchangeable terms. *Free people of color* was a more common antebellum reference, and *Creole of color* an increasingly common postbellum term. In this essay *Creole* refers to Creoles of color unless otherwise qualified.

4. John Shaw to Louis Pastorelli, April 12, 1920, 69-S-30, Josephite Fathers Archives (JFA), Baltimore.

5. *La Tribune,* January 8, 1865, quoted in David C. Rankin, "The Forgotten People: Free People of Color in New Orleans, 1850–1870" (Ph.D. diss., Johns Hopkins University, 1976), 224.

6. The question of racial identity is problematic, and the shifting identities of Creoles forms a clear example that race is socially constructed rather than biologically determined. The ability of some Creoles to pass as white points to the difficulty of making racial categorizations on the basis of appearance. Historically, individuals and institutions alike have relied heavily on physical appearance and genealogy for racial categorization, with dark skin or the rumor of an African or even mixed-blood ancestor enough to make one be categorized as black, according to the one drop rule. Yet skin color does not necessarily indicate place of origin, and the identity of ancestors is not easily determined or agreed on. And which ancestors are relevant and to how many generations removed? On the problem of racial identity in Louisiana in particular, see Domínguez, *White by Definition*, esp. 1–4, 21–89, and 183–261. For broader discussions of the social construction of race, see Barbara J. Fields, "Ideology and Race in American History," in *Region, Race, and Reconstruction: Essays in Honor of C. Vann Woodward* (New York: Oxford University Press), 143–177; and Martha Hodes, *White Women, Black Men: Illicit Sex in the Nineteenth-Century South* (New Haven: Yale University Press, 1997), 96–122. Subsequent references to *persons of African descent*, which was a phrase often invoked by people of color in the late nineteenth and early twentieth centuries, will refer collectively to those who either self-identified or where considered by others as falling under the one drop rule.

7. Anthony, "Negro Creole Community," 44; Rankin, "Forgotten People," 185.

8. Paul F. LaChance, "The Formation of a Three-Caste Society: Evidence from Wills in Antebellum New Orleans," *Social Science History* 18 (summer 1994), 226–227; Joan M. Martin, "*Plaçage* and the Louisiana *Gens de Couleur Libre*: How Race and Sex Defined the Lifestyles of Free Women of Color," in Kein, *Creole*, 63–64; Rankin, "Forgotten People," 46.

9. Domínguez, *White by Definition*, 23; James H. Dorman, "Louisiana's 'Creoles of Color': Ethnicity, Marginality, and Identity," *Social Science Quarterly* 73 (September 1992), 616; and Laura Foner, "The Free People of Color in Louisiana and St. Domingue," *Journal of Social History* 3 (summer 1970), 413–414.

10. Kimberly S. Hanger, *Bounded Lives, Bounded Places: Free Black Society in Colonial New Orleans, 1769–1803* (Durham, N.C.: Duke University Press, 1997), 17–54; Foner, "Free People," 410; Thomas N. Ingersoll, "Free Blacks in a Slave Society: New Orleans, 1718–1812," *William and Mary Quarterly* 48 (April 1991), 180–192; Bell, *Revolution*, 36.

11. On greater toleration of Latin colonists for interracial liaisons and mixed children, see: Anthony, "Negro Creole Community," 16; Bell, *Revolution*, 65; LaChance, "Formation," 231; Domínguez, *White by Definition*, 23; Dorman, "Louisiana's 'Creoles of Color,'" 616; Martin, "*Plaçage*," 60; and Foner, "Free People," 409, 413.

12. Bell, *Revolution*, 41–64; Hanger, *Bounded Lives*, 109–110, 125–126, 134.

13. Bell, *Revoluation*, 37–40; Alice Dunbar Nelson, "People of Color in Louisiana," in Kein, *Creole*, 18.

14. Domínguez, *White by Definition*, 25, 116, claims that 23.8 percent were free colored in 1803, while Hanger, *Bounded Lives*, 12, says free people of color constituted 33.5 percent of the city's population in 1805.

15. Rousseve, *Negro in Louisiana*, 21; Domínguez, *White by Definition*, 25.

16. *The African Methodist Episcopal Church v. City of New Orleans*, quoted in Paul

A. Kunkel, "Modifications in Louisiana Negro Status Under Louisiana Constitutions, 1812–1957," *Journal of Negro History* 44 (January 1959), 3–4.

17. On the relative liberalism of Latin Catholics, see Anthony, "Negro Creole Community," 16; Bell, *Revolution*, 11–12, 65, 70; LaChance, "Formation," 231; Joseph Logsdon and Caryn Cossé Bell, "The Americanization of Black New Orleans (1850–1900), in *Creole New Orleans: Race and Americanization*, edited by Arnold R. Hirsch and Joseph Logsdon (Baton Rouge: Louisiana State University Press, 1992), 201–261; and Rousseve, *Negro in Louisiana*, 39–40.

18. On debates about the religious treatment of slaves in Anglo-American colonies, see Sylvia Frey and Betty Wood, *Come Shouting to Zion: African American Protestantism in the American South and British Caribbean to 1830* (Chapel Hill: University of North Carolina Press, 1998), 1–34; and Albert J. Raboteau, *Slave Religion: The "Invisible Institution" in the Antebellum South* (New York: Oxford University Press, 1977), 96–146.

19. Rodolphe Desdunes, *Nos Hommes et Notre Historie*, cited in Rousseve, *Negro in Louisiana*, 25.

20. On centrality of Catholicism to Creole identity, see Anthony, "Negro Creole Community," 24, 26, 32, 48, 128; Bell, *Revolution*, 3; Desdunes, *Our People*, 109; Domínguez, *White by Definition*, 164, 205, 219–224; Dorman, "Louisiana's 'Creoles of Color,'" 616; Kein, *Creole*, xiv; Rankin, "Forgotten People," 125; Robert C. Reinders, "The Churches and the Negro in New Orleans, 1850–1860," *Phylon* 22 (fall 1961), 242; Rousseve, *Negro in Louisiana*, 24; and Loren Schweninger, "Socioeconomic Dynamics Among the Gulf Creole Populations: The Antebellum and Civil War Years," in *Creoles of Color of the Gulf South*, edited by James Dorman (Knoxville: University of Tennessee Press, 1996), 57.

21. Canon Benoit Diary, April 9, 1875, JFA. Similarly, at St. Augustine's, Creoles provided much of the funding and helped construct the church. See Roger Baudier, *The Catholic Church in Louisiana* (New Orleans, [A. W. Hyatt Stationery Mfg. Co., Ltd.] 1937), 365; C. M. Chambon, Pastor, "Saint Augustine Church Yearly Report" (1940), Archives of the Archdiocese of New Orleans (AANO), 6; Charles B. Rousseve, "The Negro in New Orleans," typescript in Amistad Research Center (ARC), New Orleans, 5; John B. Alberts, "Origins of Black Parishes in the Archdiocese of New Orleans, 1718–1920" (Ph.D. diss., Louisiana State University, 1998), 88; Reinders, "Churches and the Negro," 242–243; and Rousseve, *Negro in Louisiana*, 41.

22. The sacramental records during the French period are inconsistent, but during the Spanish era, which also coincides with the emergence of a free population as a distinct population, the pattern of tripartite classification becomes more clear in the sacramental records. See Earl C. Woods and Charles Nolan, eds., *Sacramental Records of the Roman Catholic Church of the Archdiocese of New Orleans,* 10 vols. (New Orleans: Archdiocese of New Orleans, 1987–95).

23. Reinders, "Churches and the Negro," 242; and Bell, *Revolution*, 243.

24. Baudier, *Catholic Church in Louisiana*, 365; Chambon, "Saint Augustine Church Yearly Report" (1940), 6; Rousseve, "The Negro in New Orleans," 5; and Reinders, "Churches and the Negro," 242–243.

25. Cited in Blassingame, *Black New Orleans*, 200.

26. Roger Baudier, "Memorandum for Rev. Robert Guste: On White and Negro

204 SEGREGATION AND CONGREGATION

Relationships After War Between the States," Baudier Collection—Manuscripts, White and Negro Relationships, AANO, 3; Henry C. Dethloff and Robert R. Jones, "Race Relations in Louisiana, 1877–98," *Louisiana History* 9 (fall 1968), 315.

27. Roger Baudier, "The Negro and Catholic Education," Baudier Collection—Manuscripts, Catholic Education in Louisiana, AANO, 3; "The House of the Good Shepherd," *Daily Picayune*, November 1, 1896; *Colored Harvest* 1(October 1892).

28. Bell, *Revolution*, 65, 70.

29. An 1880 census report on New Orleans, for example, noted that "while there are French, Spanish, and even, for convenience, 'colored' Creoles, there are no English, Scotch, Irish, Western, or 'Yankee' Creoles, these all being included under the distinctive term 'Americans.' " George E. Waring, *Social Statistics of Cities: History and Present Condition of New Orleans, Louisiana, and Report on the City of Austin, Texas* (Washington, D.C.: Department of Census, 1888), 10. The meaning of *Creole* was, and remains, a highly contested and polemicized terrain. George Washington Cable engendered the disgust of his hometown for his insistence that people with African blood were Creole. On the meaning and development of the definition of Creole, see Anthony, "Negro Creole Community," 24–25; *Colored Harvest* 9 (October 1920), 7; Domínguez, *White by Definition*, 100–101, 106, 110, 114–130; Hall, *Africans in Colonial Louisiana*, 157–159; Rousseve, *Negro in Louisiana*, 23; and Joseph G. Tregle Jr., "Creoles and Americans," in Hirsch and Logsdon, *Creole New Orleans*, 131–185.

30. "The Meaning of 'Creole,' " *Catholic Morning Star*, August 4, 1894.

31. On the importance of the parish in shaping neighborhood and religious understandings, and its centrality to Catholic life, especially with regards to issues of race, see John McGreevy, *Parish Boundaries: The Catholic Encounter with Race in the Twentieth-Century Urban North* (Chicago: University of Chicago Press, 1996). For a broader and early emphasis on the importance of parishes, see Jay P. Dolan, *The American Catholic Experience: A History from Colonial Times to the Present* (South Bend, Ind.: Notre Dame University Press, 1992), esp. 158–220.

32. The basic outlines of the founding of St. Katherine's are told in Dolores Egger Labbé, *Jim Crow Comes to Church: The Establishment of Segregated Catholic Parishes in South Louisiana* (Lafayette: University of Southwestern Louisiana, 1971); Annemarie Kasteel, *Francis Janssens 1843–1897: A Dutch-American Prelate* (Lafayette: Center for Louisiana Studies, 1992), 275–324; Douglas J. Slawson, "Segregated Catholicism: The Origins of St. Katherine's Parish, New Orleans," 121–T–4, JFA; and Alberts, "Origins," 192–272.

33. Janssens to Katherine Drexel, August 8, 1893, Janssens Letters, 1893, Archives of the Sisters of the Blessed Sacrament (SBS), Bensalem, Pa.

34. *Mission Work Among the Negroes* (Baltimore: Foley Brothers, 1896), 15; Janssens to Drexel, May 21, 1895, Janssens Letters, 1894–1896, SBS.

35. Janssens to Drexel, August 19, 1895, Janssens Letters, 1894–1896, SBS.

36. Janssens to Dyer, April 24, 1897, 52 DY 33, JFA; "Series of Questions to be Answered by Applicants for Aid from the Commission for the Catholic Missions Among the Colored People and the Indians" (1895) in Reports to Commission for the Catholic Missions Among the Colored People and the Indians, 161 DY8, JFA, Janssens to Drexel, January 26, 1897, Janssens Letters, 1894–1896, SBS.

37. Homer Plessy embodied the complicated facets of race and racial identity in

New Orleans. In 1892, Plessy, a Creole of color in New Orleans whose skin was probably light enough to pass for white, bought a first–class railroad ticket and boarded the first–class car, which was also designated "white only." When Plessy refused to leave, he was arrested for violating the state's railroad segregation laws, which prohibited any person from entering a railroad car "to which by race he does not belong." The arrest, which was planned by the Creole community to test segregation laws by appealing to the Thirteenth and Fourteenth amendments, was appealed up to the United States Supreme Court, which ruled eight to one against Plessy, on the basis that "separate but equal" accommodations were not unconstitutional. Of course, the diligence of the South in advancing the separate part of the ruling was never balanced by a commitment to the "equal" part. The ruling guided southern segregation until it was overturned by the 1954 *Brown v. Board of Education* decision, which ruled school segregation unconstitutional. For background and documents on the Plessy case, see C. Vann Woodward, "The National Decision Against Equality," in *American Counterpoint: Slavery and Racism in the North–South Dialogue* (Boston: Little, Brown, 1964), 212–233; Olsen Otto, ed., *The Thin Disguise: Turning Point in Negro History, Plessy v. Ferguson, A Documentary Presentation, 1864–1896* (New York: Humanities Press, 1967); and Brook Thomas, ed., *Plessy v. Ferguson: A Brief History with Documents* (Boston: Bedford Books, 1997).

38. Janssens, "Series of Questions" (1892); Janssens, "Series of Questions," (1891), in Reports to Commission for the Catholic Missions Among the Colored People and the Indians, 161 DY8, JFA. See also Janssens to Drexel, February 13, 1894, April 29, 1894, and November 11, 1894, Janssens Letters, 1894–1896, SBS.

39. Rodolphe L. Desdunes, *A Few Words to Dr. DuBois with Malice Toward None* (New Orleans, 1907), n.p.

40. "What Is a Colored Creole?" *Colored Harvest* 9 (October 1920), 7.

41. Desdunes, "Our Constituents," *Crusader*, September 2, 1895, cited in Lester Sullivan, "The Unknown Rodolphe Desdunes: Writings in the New Orleans *Crusader*," *Xavier Review* 10 (spring 1990), 13.

42. E.W.S. Hammond, "For Colored People," *Southwestern Christian Advocate*, June 6, 1895.

43. R. L. Desdunes, "Mother Katherine Drexel and the Color Lines," *Crusader*, February 28, 1895, 1/24/1, Desdunes Family Collection, Xavier University Archives (XUA), New Orleans.

44. Janssens, "Series of Questions" (1895); "Colored Catholics: Archbishop Janssens Discusses the Old St. Joseph's Church Project," newspaper clipping, Archdiocesan Scrapbook, 1893–1897, AANO, 68.

45. Alice Ruth Moore, "Louisiana," *Women's Era* 2 (June 1895); "Colored Catholics: Archbishop Janssers Discusses the Old St. Joseph's Church Project," newspaper clipping, Archdiocesan Scrapbook, 1897, AANO, 68.

46. R. L. Desdunes, "Mother Katherine Drexel and the Color Line," *Crusader*, February 28, 1895, 1/24/1, Desdunes Family Collection, XUA.

47. Janssens to Drexel, November 11, 1893, Janssens Letters, 1893, SBS; Alberts, "Origins," 239.

48. Alice Ruth Moore, "Louisiana"; "Jim Crow Catholic Church," *Crusader*, n.d., clipping in AANO; Rousseve, *Negro in Louisiana*, 139, 158–159; Alberts, "Origins,"

239, 248; Marcus Christian, "A Black History of Louisiana, 1904–1942," Marcus Christian Papers, Earl K. Long Library, University of New Orleans (UNO), 4; "St. Katherine's Church: The Old St. Joseph's Puts on a New Dress and Changes Its Name," Archdiocesan Scrapbook, 1893–1897, AANO, 80.

49. "Jim Crow Catholic Church," *Crusader*, n.d., clipping in AANO.

50. "A Separate Church," *Crusader*, n.d., Rousseve Collection, ARC.

51. Arthur Esteves, President, and N. E. Mansion, Acting Secretary, "Citizen's Committee," *Crusader*, February 4, 1895, Rousseve Collection, ARC; Slawson, "Segregated Catholicism," 31.

52. St. Katherine's Parish Reports, 1896–1900, AANO.

53. St. Joseph's Roman Catholic Church Records, Sick Calls Registers, June 6, 1902–July 28, 1911, UNO.

54. Journal of Mother Katharine Drexel, quoted in Consuela Marie Duffy, *Katharine Drexel: A Biography* (Philadelphia: Peter Reilly, 1965), 314. On the sparse attendance in its first decades, see St. Katherine's Annual Reports, 1896–1918, AANO. On attendance at white churches, especially St. Joseph's across the street, see also Pierre LeBeau to Justin McCarthy, May 13, 1909, 28–N–21, JFA.

55. Beginning in 1908, the United States was no longer a mission field, meaning that New Orleans Catholics could no longer appeal to Lyon, or even to the Vatican, but had to work through and with the American hierarchy, thereby providing additional impetus to Americanization.

The theme of Americanization of New Orleans and its race relations figures prominently in both Bell, *Revolution,* and Logsdon and Bell, "Americanization of Black New Orleans." See also John B. Alberts, "Black Catholic Schools: The Josephite Parishes of New Orleans During the Jim Crow Era," *U.S. Catholic Historian* 12 (1994), 81.

56. John Shaw to Louis Pastorelli, April 12, 1920, 69–S–30, JFA.

57. Alberts, "Origins," 371.

58. See, for example, St. Laurent to Louis Pastorelli, November 8, 1920, copy in St. Laurent Correspondence, JFA.

59. "French and English," *Catholic Morning Star,* September 28, 1895.

60. *Catholic Morning Star*, April 2, 1898; Alberts, "Origins," 344–345.

61. Roger Baudier, *Centennial St. Rose of Lima Parish* (New Orleans: Archdiocese of New Orleans, 1957), 17, 48.

62. James Blenk to Katharine Drexel, March 25, 1909, Blenk Letters, 1909, SBS.

63. Pierre Lebeau to Justin McCarthy, April 12, 1912, 29–D–40, JFA.

64. Samuel Kelly to Katharine Drexel, May 28, 1917, Fr. Samuel Kelly, S.S.J., Letters, SBS, 13.

65. Alberts "Origins," 332. Alberts's dissertation is primarily about this process of creating territorial parishes that conform to the 1918 Vatican decree on regular parishes. On the push for territorial parishes and is implication for race and separate churches, see especially 316–321.

66. Alberts, "Origins," 282–290; George E. Cunningham, "The Italian, a Hindrance to White Solidarity in Louisiana, 1890–1898," *Journal of Negro History* 10 (January 1965), 22–36; Humber S. Nelli, *From Immigrants to Ethnics: The Italian Americans* (New York: Oxford University Press, 1983); Lydio F. Tomasi, ed., *The Italian in*

America: the Progressive View, 1891–1914 (New York: Center for Migration Studies, 1972). On Irish immigrants, see Noel Ignatiev, *How the Irish Became White* (New York: Routledge, 1995). For wider considerations of the relation of ethnicity to race, see Richard D. Alba, *Ethnic Identity: The Transformation of White America* (New Haven: Yale University Press, 1990).

67. Lizabeth Cohen, *Making a New Deal: Industrial Workers in Chicago, 1919–1939* (Cambridge, England: Cambridge University Press, 1990), 83–94; McGreevy, *Parish Boundaries,* 9–13, 29–38. Logsdon and Bell, "Americanization of Black New Orleans," 202, note this process as well, arguing that distinctions within the white community blurred more quickly due to ongoing waves of immigration that the black community did not experience.

68. In reality, there were far fewer black than white Catholic churches. As a result, many black parishioners, unlike whites, had to travel great distances to reach their "territorial" parish, since black congregations were assigned existing buildings rather than new facilities appropriately centered within the territory and community they served. Josephite priests often complained of this problem of location. See, for example, Lebeau to McCarthy, May 13, 1909, 28–N–21, JFA; Joseph Waring to Pastorelli, May 19, 1921, 39–V–11, JFA; and *Colored Harvest* 7(June 1920), 5.

69. Maps for each new black parish reveal the emerging black territorial system; Correspondence File, AANO.

70. Loren Schweninger, "Antebellum Free Persons of Color in Postbellum New Orleans," Louisiana History 30(Fall 1989), 345-364.

71. Pierre Lebeau to Justin McCarthy, March 12, 1909, 28–N–19, JFA.

72. John Albert to Justin McCarthy, April 1909, 28–K–3, JFA.

73. St. Laurnet to Pastorelli, May 22, 1920, and October 21, 1920, St. Laurent Correspondence, JFA.

74. Pierre LeBeau to Katharine Drexel, November 21, 1911, and January 22, 1912, Rev. P. O. LeBeau Letters, SBS.

75. LeBeau to Drexel, February 2, 1914, Rev. P. O. LeBeau Letters, SBS.

76. The difficulties surrounding Xavier's opening reflect this tendency toward homogenization on several fronts. Many working with the city's Creoles, including some members of the Sisters of the Blessed Sacrament, would have preferred to locate the new school downtown. However, the confluence of an available building and white opposition elsewhere—which also reflected the homogenization of the city's diverse population—left the uptown location as the only feasible possibility. Even then, the Sisters of the Blessed Sacrament encountered fierce neighborhood opposition, even though the building had previously housed Southern University, the state–sponsored university for black residents. Nonetheless, the opening of Xavier was a boon for black Catholics in general, and Creoles in particular, despite its location. On the events surrounding Xavier's opening see: Katharine Drexel to James Blenk, May 16, 1915, Sisters of the Blessed Sacrament, Correspondence, 1898–1917 (a), AANO; James Blenk to Katharine Drexel, Blenk Letters, 1915–1917, folder 7, SBS; Clarke to Justin McCarthy, June 12, 1915, 32–H–5, JFA; Patricia Lynch, *Sharing the Bread for Service* (Bensalem, Pa.: Sisters of the Blessed Sacrament, 1998), 204–207; "Blessed Sacrament," New Orleans, Louisiana, III–009, Josephite Material, box 3, XUA; Roger Baudier, "Development of Catholic Education," Baudier Collection—Manuscripts, AANO,

16; Roger Baudier, "Golden Jubilee: The Sisters of the Blessed Sacrament," typescript, Baudier Collected Papers, St. Katharine, N.O., AANO, 10; and "Xavier University Goes Forward with Good Speed," n.d. [ca. 1925], clipping in Josephite Collection, box 4, XUA.

77. John J. McWilliams to John Shaw, May 22, 1919, Vincentian Fathers (Lazarists), Correspondence, 1897–1932, AANO; Lebeau to Justin McCarthy, May 13, 1909, 28–N–21, JFA; Annual Reports, New Orleans parishes, AANO.

78. Annual Reports, New Orleans parishes; Roger Baudier, "Catholic Education in Louisiana: Catholic Schools by Parish, 1888–1918," Baudier Collected Papers, AANO.

79. Leo Gassler to Justin McCarthy, September 10, 1914, Josephite Fathers, Correspondence, 1911–1919 (a), AANO; John B. Alberts, "Black Catholic Schools: The Josephite Parishes of New Orleans During the Jim Crow Era," *U.S. Catholic Historian* 12 (winter 1994), 81–2.

80. Lally to Pastorelli, December 12, 1919, 37–K–17, JFA; Kelly to Drexel, January 9, 1920, Fr. Samuel Kelly Letters, folder 14, SBS; M. M. Agatha Ryan, SBS, "Proposed Sketch for Catholic History," n.d., Xavier Prep—SFXCA, SBS, 2–3.

81. Anthony, "Negro Creole Community," 139–62; Domínguez, *White by Definition*, 224; Aline St. Julien, *Colored Creole: Color Conflict and Confusion in New Orleans* (New Orleans: Ahidiana-Habari, 1977).

8

Beyond the Binary: Revisiting Father Divine, Daddy Grace, and Their Ministries

Danielle Brune Sigler

Black gods of the metropolis, black messiahs, black cult leaders. Scholars, reporters, and critics have applied all of these labels to both Father Divine and Bishop Charles Manuel "Sweet Daddy" Grace—two religious leaders who never identified themselves as black men and who each attempted to create multiracial congregations. Both men had alternative visions of their own race and created a new framework to express that vision within their religious organizations. Though they took vastly different approaches, these men relied on the relative freedom afforded them as heads of their own religious organizations to assert a racial—or in Divine's case, nonracial— identity outside of the American norm.[1]

Father Divine, whose movement had grown and flourished in Harlem since the early 1920s, forwarded a theology based in New Thought and the power of positive thinking.[2] He taught his followers that he was God and that they were responsible for establishing the kingdom of heaven on earth. His services centered around lavish banquets. Members of Divine's Peace Mission became well known for righting past wrongs they had committed: returning stolen items, paying overdue bills, and compensating former employers for incomplete work.[3] In addition, Divine encouraged his followers to become politically active and hosted a Righteous Government Convention, to which he invited America's leading politicians.

Daddy Grace, formally known as Bishop Charles Manuel Grace, preached an apostolic faith with roots in the revival at Azusa Street.[4] Starting in 1919, Grace established his religious empire, the United House of Prayer for All People, in Massachusetts and headed south

FIGURE 8.1. Daddy Grace and Chauffeur. Bishop Charles M. Grace, "Sweet Daddy," is assisted into a car by his chauffeur. © CORBIS.

along the eastern seaboard before expanding into Harlem and other northern cities. Daddy Grace hosted mass baptisms in lakes, rivers, city pools, and even on city streets via firehose. His services relied heavily on music unique to the House of Prayer, including the trombone shout band. Daddy Grace did not advocate political activity but focused primarily on economic strategies to improve the lives of his followers. He turned his attention inward to building a solid denomination and rarely participated in or commented on national politics.

Given America's disestablished and ever-changing religious climate in the early 1900s, Daddy Grace and Father Divine each created their own denominations with relative ease. In doing so, these men incorporated their own racial identities into their ministries, shaped the racial and religious identities of their members, and attempted to maintain these identities in a society that regarded their ideology as odd and even potentially dangerous.[5] Yet as the Peace Mission and House of Prayer gained in popularity and power, race subsumed religion as the defining characteristic for outsiders looking at these organizations—in spite of the fact that Father Divine rejected race as a legitimate organizing principle and Daddy Grace asserted a white racial identity and created a ministry for "all people."

If we revisit Grace and Divine with this in mind, their lives and ministries reveal far more than previous scholars have seen. They demonstrate the challenges and limitations of creating and sustaining integrated ministries in a largely segregated society. Both the Peace Mission and the House of Prayer illustrate how religion can serve as a force for challenging and redefining the racial status quo, yet they also show how innovative religious identities may be subjugated to the very same status quo when members of religious communities interact with the broader society. Grace and Divine both challenged the racial binary through explicitly religious means and thus can not be distinguished simply as religious leaders *or* apparently "black men" *or* innovative racial thinkers but must be seen instead as men whose identities, religious beliefs, and racial philosophies worked together as an integrated whole.

Bishop Charles Manuel "Sweet Daddy" Grace and the United House of Prayer for All People of the Church on the Rock of Apostolic Faith

Daddy Grace arrived in the United States at the turn of the twentieth century from the Cape Verde Islands as Marcelino M. deGraca.[6] Like many other Cape Verdeans, deGraca identified himself as a white man from Portugal.[7] On the islands, race was a far more fluid category than it was in the United States. In Cape Verde, as in Brazil and the Caribbean, race varied according to hair type, nose shape, and hair texture, with wealth and education shaping a person's racial classification as well. Accordingly, Cape Verdean immigrants often struggled to find their place within America's racial dichotomy—being rejected by "white" society and rejecting association with "blacks."[8] As more Cape Verdeans entered the country, they faced increasing prejudice. A New Bedford, Massachusetts, newspaper reporter writing in 1905 observed of the Cape Verdeans that "[their] presence in communities which were hot beds of abolitionism 35 years ago, has stirred up among the white inhabitants a prejudice comparable to that which exists in the south against the southern negroes, with whom the Cape Verder has little in common except color and ancestry."[9] This prejudice led to limited social and economic options for Cape Verdeans.

DeGraca, who anglicized his name to Charles M. Grace years before beginning his ministry, worked as a salesman at a grocery store. He held a number of other jobs, including working on the cranberry bogs and as a peddler throughout southeastern Massachusetts. Dissatisfied with the options available to a Cape Verdean man, Grace turned to a new occupation. In 1919, in the midst of the Pentecostal and Holiness awakening going on throughout the country, Grace founded his own church. He built the United House of Prayer for All People of the Church on the Rock of Apostolic Faith, in Wareham, Massachusetts, which soon attracted a dedicated following. From its inception, Grace emphasized the inclusive nature of his religious organization. He chose a name derived from Isaiah 56:7: "Even them will I bring to my holy mountain, and make them joyful in my house of prayer . . . for mine house shall be called a house of prayer for all people." While several other upstart religious organizations had adopted the biblically inspired name "house of prayer," Grace's inclusion and consistent use of the phrase "for all people" in the church's full name was atypical. Beyond setting the name of his church apart, it guided his religious mission throughout his life.

During the early days of his ministry, other Cape Verdeans, including Grace's family members, joined his congregation. Grace also welcomed African Americans. This is particularly noteworthy because many Cape Verdeans avoided association with African Americans in hopes that they would not be similarly categorized. Grace, however, took the name of his church literally and invited people of all backgrounds to join his congregation. As he traveled south along the eastern seaboard, Grace primarily attracted African-American members, but also held mixed-race meetings. He often drew the ire of local officials and clergy for doing so. At a 1926 House of Prayer meeting in Rock Hill, South Carolina, the Ku Klux Klan made its presence and disapproval known in the form of "a procession of several hundred white [robed] men in automobiles" that slowed up ominously [as it] passed the tent in which Bishop Grace conducted his services."[10] In spite of such shows of intimidation, Grace continued touring the south and preaching to anyone who would listen.

In creating this church for *all people*, Grace had also created a space for himself. His role as founder and undisputed bishop of the House of Prayer gave him a powerful position from which to assert his unique identity. In the age of Billy Sunday and Aimee Semple McPherson,[11] Grace was aware of the power of personality in the pulpit. In the realm of religion, difference and originality attracted potential followers. Thus when Grace took to the road in support of his denomination, he sometimes billed himself as a "Portuguese faith healer." His status as "Portuguese" may have given him relative freedom during his earliest trips in southern United States, though his skin color still put him at risk of discrimination. His sometimes vague but definitively foreign origins were obvious to the people who attended his revival meetings. He had a very noticeable accent and a unique intonation when he preached. He spoke to his followers in all of the many languages he knew, including French, Portuguese, and Spanish. This skill was impressive in its own right but may have also complemented the Pentecostal belief in speaking in tongues as a sign of the baptism in the Holy Spirit.

In addition to his Portuguese heritage, Grace incorporated his experiences and souvenirs from a 1923 trip to the Holy Land into his ministry. He brought costumes back from his trip and wore them while telling stories of his travels.[12] This link to the Holy Land, combined with Grace's pronounced accent, let audiences know that Grace was different. This difference gave him a sense of mystery and led generations of his followers to understand that "God was never in America until Grace brought him here." Whereas his nationality and ethnicity had been a barrier to success in everyday life, they were valued within the context of his religious organization. In his followers' eyes, Grace was uniquely endowed to be a prophet of God by virtue of his foreign origins and mysterious past.

Grace held a powerful position within the church, and the by-laws he authored ensured that no one challenged his authority: "the chief executive officer and spiritual adviser of the organization shall be designated as bishop. . . . The general assembly and congregations of this organization shall have no power whatsoever to interfere with his visions, rights or powers."[13] Grace controlled all aspects of the House of Prayer, from the theology to financial management. From this position of power, Grace necessarily condescended to his followers. From the earliest days of his ministry, Grace referred to his followers as "children." They in turn bestowed on him the affectionate title "Daddy." He once explained, "My people call me Daddy because I treat them like a father. They are my children."[14]

Arthur Huff Fauset suggested that at least some of Grace's power and condescension stemmed from his white racial identity. Members of the House of Prayer often noted Grace's unique appearance but usually observed that he was different not only from themselves but from anyone else in the rest of the world as well—black or white. A poem from the September 1960 issue of *Grace Magazine* entitled "DADDY GRACE, A Peculiar Looking Man," memorialized Grace:

> Some 30 odd years or more ago
> A peculiar looking man
> Set foot in this land. . . .
> "Who is He?" "Who is He?", people asked one another
> "He's strange, He's strange . . . He looks like none other!"
> He was strange-looking, yet handsome
> This peculiar man,
> And He stirred up the people,
> As only God can.[15]

This poem is telling, not only because it comments directly on Grace's "peculiar" appearance but also because it shows the reverence—through capitalization and the direct reference to God—with which Grace's followers regarded him. The poem concludes with a fictional vignette of the author addressing her child, who did not know Grace in his lifetime, and who comments that Grace was a very "strange-looking man." While looking at a photograph of Grace, the author explains to the child:

> To the world, who looked only at his skin, He was
> Known as Bishop Grace;
> Thank God, I looked beyond the skin and found

a Greater Grace.
For the man in that picture is the sweetest Father
Any child on earth can face.[16]

This discussion of "skin" is open to interpretation. Given the author's focus on Grace's unique appearance, skin may merely by a metaphor for his entire look. However, given that the world "looked only at his skin," the connotation may in fact be that others could not see past a perceived *blackness*. If this was the author's intent, it may be indicative of a different perception of Grace's racial identity than that which Fauset observed over fifteen years earlier. The poem illustrates that regardless of his perceived racial identity, Daddy Grace's appearance was central to the House of Prayer, and that while Grace's superiority partially stemmed from this "strange" and "peculiar" look it was also a product of his status as the "sweetest Father any child on earth can face."

Under Grace's leadership, the House of Prayer grew and became known primarily as a "black cult" although it technically remained multiracial. In a 1949 study the sociologist Chancellor Williams documented the continued participation of whites in the House of Prayer. He noted: "the membership is predominantly colored, although several hundred white people are included."[17] Even thirty years after the founding of the church, Williams found the "mixed membership of white and colored people under a colored leader" a "radical departure from American traditions."[18] In the same year, a church elder confirmed the House of Prayer's continuing commitment to all people via its official mission statement: to "erect, establish, and maintain Houses of Prayer where all people may congregate to Worship God in Spirit and Truth and receive, regardless of nationality, race or creed, the Truth: that all men know the truth of God and the fullness of Christ."[19] Thus the philosophy that had shaped the creation of the House of Prayer, its appeal to "all people," remained a fundamental tenet of the church as it entered its fourth decade.

In conjunction with the House of Prayer, Grace created a number of auxiliaries for his members, including Grace Majorettes, Grace Girl Scouts, Grace Boy Scouts, and Grace Guards. These auxiliaries, which sometimes had counterparts in the secular world, gave his followers an additional outlet within the organization and an alternative to mainstream organizations. Each auxiliary had its own uniform and purpose. Members could rise to leadership positions within these organizations. When Albert Whiting studied the House of Prayer in Augusta, Georgia, in 1952, he noted a "rather deep sense of individual worth and 'belongingness'" among members and suggested that the "paraphernalia . . . uniforms, badges," helped contribute to this feeling.[20] The Houses of Prayer, which hosted nightly meetings, did indeed create a community for followers. With apartment houses, restaurants, and stores, the House of Prayer took care of some of the most basic needs of its members. Through the auxiliaries, they differentiated themselves from each other, as well as members of other churches. Elder Mitchell, of the House of Prayer headquarters in Washington, D.C., preached in 1945: "there is not salvation outside the House of Prayer. Nobody can be saved outside of the House of Prayer. For Daddy is the very last of the prophets. He, and he alone, holds all the keys to Heaven. There is no getting in except through Daddy!"[21]

Though Grace could comfortably assert his racial and religious identities at the many House of Prayer functions, he struggled to gain respect and acknowledgement from American society. When Grace asserted his white, Portuguese identity to an American press that labeled him, among other things, the "Black Christ," they often scoffed. In the same story in which Grace explained that he was "not a Negro," *Ebony* magazine hailed him as "America's Richest Negro Minister." Critics who failed to understand the source of his identity leveled charges of race rejection. When Daddy Grace died in 1960, the verdict was still out. The *Pittsburgh Courier* said of Grace: "the question of his race, as a Negro or a white man, was never settled. A Howard University [study] held him 'colored.' He, himself, stuck to 'Portuguese.' "[22] Yet the American public's perception of Grace as a black man and the predominance of African-American followers led observers to consider the House of Prayer a denomination within the black church tradition. Grace, however, did not conceive of his ministry as falling into this category. Accordingly, the church failed to fulfill many of the roles expected of the "black church."[23] While he helped provide reasonable housing and dining options for his members, his initiative stemmed not from a race-based ideology but rather a religious and economic one. He rallied to the aid of his followers because they were members of the House of Prayer.

When Daddy Grace did address the inequities of American society, he usually couched his critique in the language of class, not race. After being taken to court on what proved to be a false alimony suit, Grace explained the source of his tribulations: "they say I married all kinds of women, but that's not true . . . you can tell it's not true by the way they talk. . . . Not like you and me. They are college men and college men don't tell the truth."[24] To counter this class persecution, Grace put his followers' donations into sound real estate investments and thereby demonstrated their collective financial power.[25] While Grace may have sought equality through this display of his financial success, he and House of Prayer members also understood his persecution to be a necessary consequence of their religious beliefs, not their racial identities. Following an IRS investigation, paternity suit, and murder investigation, Grace told his followers:

fools will persecute me but the more that I am persecuted the
greater will I be . . . me and the Lord . . . we will overcome them. . . .
All the men of God went to jail. Why shouldn't I? Going to jail don't
make me less, but greater. . . . They spoke evil of Jesus and all of the

prophets and you know that they will speak evil of me . . . I am
standing for the people and you stand with me.[26]

Grace, who had always described his mission in the context of the great prophets, expected the same persecution his predecessors had suffered. He believed
this persecution stemmed from the fact that he, like the prophets before him,
was preaching the true gospel. He never publicly suggested the he was a victim
of racially motivated attacks.[27]

Grace was correct in his assertion that persecution would not "make him
less, but greater." External criticism from the press, the courts, and mainstream
churches only redoubled Grace and his followers' faith in the United House
of Prayer for All People. Attacks from "traditional" African-American religious
leaders and denominations effectively drove a wedge between his African-
American followers and African Americans not affiliated with the House of
Prayer. Reverend Adam Clayton Powell, Jr., pastor of Harlem's well-respected
Abyssinian Baptist Church, claimed that Grace was "just another of the long
line of imposters who have each only lasted for a brief season."[28] Other Harlem
clerics denounced the House of Prayer as a movement with "no fundamental
or lasting value," a "disgrace to all decent-minded communities," and "just
another novelty."[29] These ministers viewed Grace and "cultists" like him as
"exploiters of the ignorance of poor people."[30] Grace and his followers united
along class and religious lines against such criticism. They identified primarily
as members of the United House of Prayer for All People.[31] While the bulk of
his membership was African American, external criticism, the church's explicit
focus on "all people," and Grace's own assertion of a white racial identity
prevented an explicit, church-wide racial solidarity.[32]

Father Divine and the Peace Mission

Father Divine took a drastically different approach to race and religion that
probably stemmed from his childhood experience of race. Divine grew up as
George Baker, the son of a former slave, in an area of Rockville, Maryland, that
was derogatorily called "Monkey Run."[33] His earliest experiences were undoubtedly tainted by segregation and racism. Baker traveled the country seeking out a wide range of religious alternatives. While New Thought theology
came to dominate his Peace Mission, Baker also sought spiritual guidance from
Methodism, Catholicism, and Holiness-Pentecostalism.[34] Inspired by the New
Thought teaching that the divine dwells in everyone, George Baker took a new
name that reflected his new status: Major Jealous Divine. He derived "Jealous"
from Exodus 34:14, which explained: "For the Lord whose name is Jealous is
a jealous God." Baker, as God incarnate, necessarily took the Lord's name.

His followers gave him the more affectionate title "Father Divine." In 1919
Divine moved his followers to Sayville, Long Island. He lived in a predomi-

nantly white neighborhood and operated an employment agency in conjunction with his ministry. As his ministry grew and his congregation became increasingly multiracial, his neighbors began to grow uncomfortable. Divine was arrested for disturbing the peace, convicted, and given the harshest sentence possible. When the judge who had handed down the sentence died suddenly of a heart attack, Divine reportedly said, "I hated to do it." The publicity surrounding this incident spread the word of Divine's power across the country.

Divine had far more success spreading his message internationally and among whites in the United States than did Daddy Grace. This appears to be due, in part, to his incorporation of New Thought ideology into his ministry. In the United States, New Thought was particularly popular among middle- and upper-class white Americans. Their interest in this philosophy generally and Father Divine's interpretation of it in particular made them likely candidates for membership in the Peace Mission.[35] The presence of wealthy whites in the movement led critics to suggest that Divine was merely a puppet. Divine, however, was solidly in control of the Peace Mission from its inception. One of his secretaries announced to the Harlem Renaissance writer Claude McKay: "Father Divine does not accept money from his followers. Rich people interested in his work have offered large sums of money which Father Divine has refused, because he does not want to be limited in the conception of his work."[36]

Divine's prohibition of sexual relations, even among his married followers, brought him under fire from critics, including Marcus Garvey.[37] Garvey believed that Divine's abstinence policy was a white-masterminded plan for race suicide. To Garvey, the very presence of whites in the movement made the Peace Mission suspect. Garvey's Universal Negro Improvement Association (UNIA) passed a resolution condemning Father Divine in 1936:

> WHEREAS the said J. M. Divine is surrounded by a coterie of white men and women whose motives are questionable, it is to be suspected that this "colossal racket" has been originated for the purpose of destroying religiously, morally, socially, politically, and financially, the character and standing of the Negro race in the United States of America. . . .
>
> WHEREAS the said J. M. Divine make[s] it a condition that all members of his kingdoms must separate themselves sexually from the bond of matrimony and not to reproduce the species of the race by having children;
>
> BE IT RESOLVED: That this constitutes a gross attempt at race suicide, leading to the complete extermination of the Negro race in the United States in one generation, and that this unholy practice should be condemned.[38]

FIGURE 8.2. Father Divine Passes Food to Young Bride. © Bettmann/
CORBIS.

This UNIA resolution reflects concern not only about race suicide but also the presence of whites in Divine's movement. Garvey's assumption that whites were pulling the strings of the movement was one of the problems of organizing a multiracial congregation.[39]

Divine persevered, and in conjunction with New Thought philosophy he taught his followers the power of positive thinking. He did not give voice to negative words and negative thoughts. He rejected the greeting "Hello" because of the presence of the word "hell" and instead opted for the greeting "Peace." In support of this philosophy, Divine did not believe in the use of racial descriptors. He felt that race was a negative and illogical way to categorize people, that it was divisive and counterproductive. Accordingly, Divine refused to call himself a black man or Negro. He explained to his followers, "I am not poor because I do not belong to a poor downtrodden race. If I was attached to a poor downtrodden race like some of you think you are . . . then I would be like some of you."[40] His beliefs had a direct bearing on his ability to lead. Upon being asked by Claude McKay to comment on society as a "Negro leader," Divine replied: "I have no color conception of myself. If I were representing race or creed or color or nation, I would be limited in my conception of the universal. I would not be as I am omnipotent."[41] Statements like this led to Divine's classification as a "race rejector."

Many commentators have argued that Divine's ideology of racelessness could not have overcome his appearance. Hans A. Baer and Merrill Singer claim that "despite the fact that Father Divine taught that color is of no consequence, he also was a living testimony of the notion that 'black is beautiful.' After all, had not God decided to take on the body of not only a short, squat, bald man but also one who was Black?"[42] Divine's appearance did influence some converts, including a former UNIA member who explained in a letter to Garvey: "I have discovered that you had forgotten what you had told us on more than one occasion; that GOD is supposed to be looking like us."[43] This is a consideration worth noting, but this analysis oversimplifies and devalues the ideology behind Divine's movement. It suggests that Divine's apparent blackness was more dominant than his teaching of racelessness. While people outside of the movement undoubtedly viewed Divine as a "negro," followers regarded him as God almighty, and God himself taught that he was of no race or color.

While outsiders who observed the presence of whites in the movement described the Peace Mission as multiracial, Divine's teachings encouraged his followers to create a *nonracial* congregation. Divine objected to *any* type of racial classification whether applied to himself or his followers, regardless of color. He attempted to fulfill his vision by actively integrating his followers at meetings and in Peace Mission cars.[44] According to Divine, "That which has been termed a race is NOT a race. . . . IT is a curse, and a cursed, vulgar name that was given to low-rate you, in short, to DISGRACE you."[45] Divine forbade the use of racial descriptors in his publications and in the speech of his followers. The descriptor "colored" would appear in Peace Mission publications only as "c." He and his followers were dedicated to eliminating "race words" in other publications as well. During their Righteous Government Convention, they passed a plank advocating the passage of legislation "making it a crime for any newspaper, magazine or other publication to use segregated or slang words referring to race, creed or color of any individual or group or write abusively concerning any."[46]

In order to adhere to Peace Mission tenets, members had to eschew any explicit "race pride." His biographer Jill Watts explained that Father Divine "tore down the racial identification of his followers and refashioned their self-perceptions."[47] Members often broke their family ties and lived and worked with only fellow members, in order to dedicate themselves fully to the Peace Mission. Divine operated boarding houses for his followers, segregated by sex, but not race, and created a number of stores in which his followers worked. At one point, the Peace Mission even operated a communal farm. In conjunction with their new lives, followers often adopted "spiritual" names to reflect their rebirth. With new Peace Mission names like Sing Happy and Faithful Mary, they created entirely new identities, based squarely within the teachings of the church. These changes support the view that their primary identification was as a member of Peace Mission. Personal pride stemmed from association with God [Father Divine] and creating heaven on earth.

Ironically, these new identities sometimes prevented them from implementing the social changes they desired. Divine encouraged his followers to register to vote and to participate in local and national elections in order to elect righteous candidates to positions of power. However, in a number of cities, Peace Mission members were denied the right to register to vote under their new, spiritual names. Divine addressed the issue while presiding over the Holy Communion table on August 20, 1944:

> "If some of my followers are not granted the right of franchise because they have names that do not sound like the crooked politicians want them to sound, then let us all—I mean everyone of us— go on strike and refuse to cast a ballot until they recognize God's presence, for I am here to stay!"[48]

Arthur Huff Fauset, the author of *Black God of the Metropolis,* supported Divine and addressed his followers in Philadelphia the next day. Fauset assured Peace Mission members:

> we shall fight to the end that Members of FATHER DIVINE'S
> Group, as well as any other groups in America, shall have the right
> to register merely because we are men and women over twenty-one
> years of age and not merely believe the fake and flimsy reasons
> these politicians given when they think we are not going to vote in a
> way that pleases them.[49]

In spite of the difficulty that their spiritual identities caused, Divine and his followers refused to back down and continued to work to change the society that often regarded them as foolish, ignorant, and even potentially dangerous.

A number of anonymous "concerned Americans," who regarded Divine and his Peace Mission as a "black movement" accordingly found the strength of the Peace Mission's power and resources threatening to society. These citizens took it upon themselves to write letters to the Federal Bureau of Investigation (FBI) alerting it to this grave menace to society. In 1940, Senator Theodore Bilbo, the notoriously racist congressman from Mississippi, forwarded an anonymous letter exposing the dangers of the Peace Mission to J. Edgar Hoover. The anonymous letter explained that Divine was "the most collosial [sic] fifth column in the world" and that Divine was planning to overthrow the government if the Nazis gained power in the world.[50] Bilbo explained to Hoover that "the contents of this letter are a revelation of what I suspected for a long time."[51] The FBI remained passive in the case but continued to compile letters accusing Divine of a variety of offenses. One writer even suggested that Father Divine's Peace Missions seemed to be located at "very strategic positions along coastlines" and asked: "Could this be a source of signaling to enemy U-boats?"[52] Ultimately FBI agents attended meetings and sifted through the Peace Mission paper, the *New Day*, but concluded that Divine and his followers, though politically active, were not a threat to national security[53]

Ironically, just three years earlier the Peace Mission had turned to the FBI for protection. Divine's attorney forwarded copies of threatening letters that the Ku Klux Klan had sent to Father Divine at his Baltimore address. These letters were a direct result of Divine's policy of racially integrated living conditions. On printed Klan stationery, the anonymous Klansman expressed his concern over the presence of a "mother and three children . . . of a white race," living in an organization "opperated [sic] by a negro who represents himself as Father Devine [sic]."[54] He threatened: "we do not consider the surrounding a suitable place for them to be, and we hereby give you warning to render these conditions at once," adding: "further action will be taken at once if this condition is not corrected."[55] The Klan followed up with a letter four days later that informed Divine that this was his final warning and that he must take action in five days to remove the white woman and her children from his "possession."[56] Within a few days, however, in a memorandum to J. Edgar Hoover, the assistant attorney general in the Department of Justice replied that Divine's attorney "has been advised today that an examination of the facts contained in the threatening letters which he submitted for consideration fails to disclose a violation of any Federal law or laws upon which action by the Department must be predicated."[57]

In spite of these and other threats and a lack of support from law enforcement, Divine and his followers were not content to create an insular organization in which their spiritual identities and assertions of racelessness would be accepted. Instead they directed their energies outward, working to pass a variety of legislation. Members of the Peace Mission fought to abolish lynching, capital punishment, and weapons of war. Divine hoped to take his mission worldwide and sought to unite people not merely across racial lines but also national borders. The Peace Mission issued a stamp in 1939 documenting a telegram that Divine sent to President Roosevelt encouraging him to unite North, Central, and South America: "Peace One Nation One Language One Flag One Speech. . . . Why not unite the three Americas as a national and international defense for peace? Let there be The United Countries of America."[58] While Roosevelt did not act on Divine's advice, the Peace Mission itself did cross national borders, spreading into Australia, Canada, the West Indies, and western Europe.

Whereas Daddy Grace had sought financial power to overcome persecution, Father Divine turned to quite literal "Divine retribution." When those who criticized Divine came to untimely deaths, he took "credit" for them. He also caused difficulties for businesses that failed to integrate or discriminated against their clientele. In 1947 Divine wrote to Dr. Edward Warner, president of the International Civil Airlines Organization, warning him "to bring an end to all segregation and discrimination and prejudice."[59] Otherwise,

> the airplanes will not stay in the air and a good many of them will
> continue to refuse to leave the ground . . . for the mouth of the
> LORD has declared it! Trains will not stay on the track and ships
> will not stay on the ocean filled and controlled with and by prejudice
> . . . with all of those detestable tendencies of men that try to destroy
> and put some up and put some down, all because of the color of
> their skins and because of their racial or national origin.[60]

While he and his followers participated in more conventional forms of protest like boycotts, the threat of the wrath of God always hung over those who opposed Divine.

Robert Weisbrot's study of Father Divine documented Divine's political activism and accordingly placed Divine in the context of African-American civil rights leaders. Jill Watts, however, accurately surmised that Divine expressed his political philosophy in religious language.[61] He would not lend his name or support to activities that identified themselves as "black" and "negro." He identified with causes that operated on behalf of humanity, not one particular race. He advocated integration in philanthropy just as he did in every other aspect of his life. While he did address issues directly linked to racial prejudice and injustice, his political activism, whether in the form of the Righteous Government Convention or lobbying Congress, was always based in religious ideology. He offered his advice based on his status as God. As the almighty, he could see the injustices afflicting all men and give the guidance necessary for remedying them.

Moving Beyond the Binary

The ministries of these so-called black gods demonstrate the variations that can occur at the nexus of race and religion. Divine and Grace harnessed the power of religious belief to alter society's rules and regulations. These men found the divine within themselves and used that power to change the lives of their followers. Daddy Grace was a prophet who turned to an apostolic faith, one that valued his unique ethnic heritage and multilingual abilities. Father Divine built a ministry based on New Thought, a theology that acknowledged the power of the mind to transcend simple racial categories. As God incarnate, he assured his followers that they could create heaven in their everyday lives.

Yet the members of the Peace Mission and the House of Prayer had to interact with a world that did not always acknowledge the validity of their self-prescribed identities. Each organization created an extensive network of associated auxiliaries and industries and held frequent meetings. These were attempts not merely to shelter their congregants from the harsh realities of life but to sustain them as they made their way in a world that did not always understand their racial and religious identities.

Similarly, academic studies of the House of Prayer and Peace Mission that have prioritized race at the expense of religion have missed the complexity of these ministries. By failing to acknowledge the power of religious beliefs to deconstruct and reconstruct racial identity and by considering these religions only as "black cults," scholars have denied Divine, Grace, and their followers the right to define themselves and their organizations. In order to truly understand the gap between a religious organization's self-definition and the identity society has granted it, we must study these religious organizations both as the multiracial organizations Divine and Grace believed they were *and* as the "black cults" the rest of the country perceived them to be. Both approaches are productive, and both can contribute to the understanding of these organizations. The previous "black cult" scholarship remains valuable, precisely because it points out *how* these religious groups fit or do not fit into the "black church tradition," while studying these organizations as multiracial religious groups begins to answer the significant question of *why* they do or do not, can or cannot fulfill the mission of the black church.

The success of both the Peace Mission and the House of Prayer demonstrate that these religious organizations that redefined, rejected, or embraced alternative racial identities found a willing membership, particularly among African Americans. As they became successful, Divine and Grace exposed the contradictions inherent in an American society that tolerated religious innovation but possessed steadfast beliefs about race. While Divine and Grace had the freedom to create their own religious organizations, when they linked religious and racial identity, they hit the limits of American religious tolerance and racial understanding.[62] The controversy surrounding both of these organizations—the FBI investigations, the IRS investigations, and the Klan attacks—demonstrate the fact that race served as the primary organizing category for most Americans, superseding religious identity. Most Americans saw Divine and Grace as the *New York Times* had in 1938, as a "little Negro evangelist who calls himself God" and "a stocky Negro of middle age," respectively.[63] Even as their followers identified primarily as members of the Peace Mission or the House of Prayer, society labeled them as members of "black cults" run by black leaders.

NOTES

1. Scholars who have examined these men only in the context of African-American religious traditions have necessarily arrived at a conclusion similar to that

of Wilson Jeremiah Moses: that both leaders were race rejectors who showed no real desire in "ushering in a black messianic era." Wilson Jeremiah Moses, *Black Messiahs and Uncle Toms*, rev. ed. (Philadelphia: University of Pennsylvania Press, 1993), 12. This type of analysis has led to an oversimplified, inaccurate depiction of each. Even those scholars, like Robert Weisbrot, who have devoted significant attention to Father Divine seem to be struggling to legitimize him within the context of African American religious traditions: playing down his claims of divinity and racelessness and emphasizing his social and political activism. Robert Weisbrot, *Father Divine and the Struggle for Racial Equality* (Champaign: University of Illinois Press, 1983). Grace, meanwhile, has received little attention from scholars, who have characterized him as a Father Divine imitator with no real theology. The fact that Divine and Grace were famous contemporaries, had paternal names, created unconventional denominations, and were regarded as black by most Americans has persuaded historians to link them together, glossing over their major differences in doctrine and ritual. Current scholarship, grounded primarily in African-American religious studies, does not recognize the significant differences between Grace and Divine. This confirms the need for an approach to these men and their congregations that acknowledges the co-construction of racial and religious identities.

2. According to Jill Watts, there were many varieties of New Thought philosophy but they all advocated three common beliefs: "God existed in all people, that the channeling of God's spirit eradicated problems, and that unity with God guaranteed salvation." *God, Harlem U.S.A.* (Los Angeles: University of California Press, 1992), 22.

3. For instance, on October 29, 1938, the *New Amsterdam News* ran a story entitled "Divine Praised for Good Work in Jersey," detailing a follower who paid off a twelve-year-old debt.

4. In 1906 William J. Seymour led the Azusa Street Revival in Los Angeles, California, generally regarded as the birthplace of Pentecostalism. People at the revival spoke in tongues as evidence of baptism in the spirit, a practice that would become an essential part of Pentecostal worship. In conjunction with his ministry, Seymour and his followers published a newspaper known as the *Apostolic Faith*.

5. Both the Peace Mission and United House of Prayer for All People survive today. However, this essay focuses on the state of these organizations while their founders were still living. Grace died on January 12, 1960. Father Divine died on September 10, 1965.

6. The material on Daddy Grace stems from my dissertation, "Sweet Daddy Grace: The Life and Times of a Modern Day Prophet" (University of Texas at Austin, 2002). To date there is no comprehensive account of Grace's life; much of the information about Grace is a product of my research. In contrast, Father Divine's life has been fairly well documented, most thoroughly by Watts in *God, Harlem, U.S.A.* While I have supplemented this work with additional research, her basic accounting of Divine's life is the foundation for my analysis.

7. Marilyn Halter, *Between Race and Ethnicity* (Champaign: University of Illinois Press, 1993), 4-5.

8. Halter, *Between Race and Ethnicity*, 35, 151, 166–167, and John C. Reardon, "Black, White, or Portuguese," in *Spinner: People and Culture in Southeastern Massachusetts*, vol. 1 (New Bedford, Mass.: Spinner, 1981), 34.

9. Cooper Gaw, "The Cape Verde Islands and Cape Verde," *Evening Standard,* July 29, 1905, 12.

10. "Bishop's Disappearance Misses Being a Miracle," *New Bedford Standard Times,* October 31, 1926, sec. 4, 1.

11. Billy Sunday was a professional baseball player–turned–evangelist who traveled the United States. He began preaching in 1896 and was regarded as one of the greatest revivalists of all time by 1917. He was well known for his athletic delivery and straight talk from the pulpit. Aimee Semple McPherson founded the Angelus Temple in Los Angeles in 1918 after touring the United States as an itinerant preacher. Hailed as a beauty, McPherson staged elaborate performances in conjunction with her ministry. The fame and personalities of these evangelists themselves were the biggest draw.

12. The legendary Harlem photographer James Van Der Zee photographed Grace wearing "Holy Land" robes c. 1938.

13. *Constitution and By-Laws of the United House of Prayer for All People of the Church on the Rock of the Apostolic Faith* (Charlotte, N.C.: Huneycutt, 1929), 10.

14. Quoted in "Daddy Grace Had Premonition of Death," *Pittsburgh Courier,* January 23, 1960, magazine section, 6.

15. "DADDY GRACE, A Peculiar Looking Man," *Grace,* September 1960, 4.

16. "DADDY GRACE, A Peculiar Looking Man," 11.

17. Chancellor Williams, "The Socio-Economic Significance of the Store-Front Church Movement in the United States Since 1920" (Ph.D. diss., American University, 1949). Williams cites a *Life* article in a footnote, but he had conducted extensive research at a number of Houses of Prayer such that he would have been equipped to contradict this estimate if he found it inaccurate on the basis of his personal observation.

18. Williams, "Socio-Economic Significance," 131. While members inside the House of Prayer may have understood Grace to be "white," outside observers would, as Williams suggests, still regard him as "colored."

19. "Fabulous Daddy Grace," *Pittsburgh Courier,* September 17, 1949, sec. 2, 13.

20. Albert N. Whiting, *The United House of Prayer for All People, A Case Study of a Charismatic Sect* (Ph.D. diss., American University, 1952), 210.

21. As quoted in Williams, *Socio-Economic Significance,* 125.

22. "Daddy's Chair Will Always Be Vacant,'" *Pittsburgh Courier,* January 30, 1960, magazine section, 3.

23. In *Prophesy Deliverance! An Afro-American Revolutionary Christianity* (Philadelphia: Westminster Press, 1982), Cornel West argues that the primary mission of the black church is to offer its followers liberation in "this world as well as the next."

24. Kevin Cullinane, "Yes Sweet Daddy," *Washington Daily News,* January 16, 1958, 18.

25. The FBI investigated Daddy Grace in 1941 but concluded that he was not a threat, due largely to the fact that the House of Prayer was not particularly political.

26. Originally delivered April 16, 1934. Sermon reprinted in *Grace Magazine,* December 1960, 8.

27. Grace *did* believe that people were jealous of his success and threatened by his power.

28. "Preachers Rap Daddy Grace," *New Amsterdam News,* March 12, 1938, 1.

29. "Preachers Rap Daddy Grace," 1.

30. "Preachers Rap Daddy Grace," 1.

31. Whiting discusses the fact that "what is evaluatively significant to the external observer is relatively meaningless to the sectarian" (216). In other words, what the critical public saw as exploitation followers interpreted as support for Grace and the House of Prayer.

32. Since Grace's death the church has shifted more in the direction of the "black church." Nevertheless, church members continue to emphasize the appeal of the House of Prayer to "all people," as evidenced in a public performance outside of Washington, D.C., in 1995.

33. Neither Divine nor the Peace Mission acknowledged this prior identity; Jill Watts in *God, Harlem, U.S.A*, provided the most conclusive link of Divine to his past as George Baker.

34. Watts, *God, Harlem, U.S.A*, 24–27.

35. Watts discusses this; see *God, Harlem, U.S.A*, 85–86.

36. Claude McKay, "There Goes God," *Nation*, February 6, 1935, 153. In the same article, however, he discusses Father Divine's disciple Faithful Mary, who did accept gifts and donations.

37. The Jamaican-born Marcus Garvey founded the Universal Negro Improvement Association in 1914. The Association was dedicated to a philosophy of African nationalism and racial uplift. The United States government deported Garvey in 1927, after which both his movement and power faded.

38. *The Marcus Garvey and Universal Negro Improvement Association Papers*, vol. 7, edited by Robert A. Hill (Berkeley: University of California Press, 1990).

39. When the Philadelphia police investigated Daddy Grace in 1933, they also suspected that Daddy Grace was manipulated by "white men" and that he was merely a front.

40. As quoted in Watts, *God, Harlem, U.S.A.*, 89.

41. McKay, "There Goes God," 153.

42. Hans A. Baer and Merrill Singer, "Toward a Typology of Black Sectarianism as a Response to Racial Stratification," in *African-American Religion*, edited by Timothy E. Fulop and Albert J. Raboteau (New York: Routledge, 1997), 271.

43. As quoted in Watts, *God, Harlem, U.S.A.*, 115.

44. Watts, *God, Harlem, U.S.A.*, 89–90. While actively pursuing integration, this attention to creating a precisely integrated atmosphere may have actually emphasized color difference among his followers.

45. *New Day*, as quoted in Robert Weisbrot, *Father Divine and the Struggle for Racial Equality*, 101.

46. Kenneth E. Burnham, *God Comes to America* (Boston: Lambeth Press, 1979), 40.

47. Watts, *God, Harlem, U.S.A.*, 115.

48. *New Day*, August 26, 1944, Anno Domini Father Divine (ADFD), 2. Divine's speech appears all in caps in *New Day*.

49. *New Day*, August 26, 1944, ADFD, 16.

50. Devine [sic], FBI file 62-32932, sec. 1, A Real American (White Girl) to Bilbo, May 30, 1940.

51. Devine [sic] FBI file 62-32932, sec. 1, Bilbo to Hoover, June 2, 1940.

52. Devine [sic] FBI file 62-32932, sec. 1, [sender's name deleted] to Hoover, August 10, 1942.

53. Devine [sic] FBI file 62-32932, sec. 3, Report, Made at Philadelphia by [deletion], October 12, 1946.

54. Devine [sic] FBI file 9-2512, copy of letter to Father Devine [sic] signed KKK, February 1, 1937.

55. Devine [sic], FBI file 9-2512, copy of letter to Father Devine [sic] signed KKK, February 1, 1937.

56. Devine [sic], FBI file 9-2512, copy of letter to Father Devine [sic] signed KKK, February 5, 1937

57. Devine [sic], FBI file 9-2512, copy of Memorandum for J. Edgar Hoover from Brian McMahon, assistant attorney general, Department of Justice, February 16, 1937.

58. Stamp in the author's collection.

59. Mrs. M. J. Divine, *The Peace Mission Movement* (Philadelphia: Imperial Press, 1982), 122.

60. Divine, *The Peace Mission Movement*, 123.

61. Weisbrot, *Father Divine and the Struggle for Racial Equality*, spends relatively little time discussing Divine's efforts to eliminate race (99–102). He places Divine's rejection of the term *Negro* in the context of other "black" leaders who objected to the label, failing to fully appreciate Divine's reasoning. For Watts, *God, Harlem, U.S.A.*, see xi–xii.

62. In *Busting the Black Gods*, a speech delivered at the American Studies Association National Convention, Detroit, Michigan, October 14, 2000, I discussed the FBI's investigation into Fauset, Divine, Grace, and Noble Drew Ali and his Moorish Science Temple. The Bureau's interest in these people and organizations was directly proportional to the racial philosophies inherent in each religion. While the multiracial aspect of Divine's Peace Mission may have been troubling, the FBI found the outright black unity of the Moorish Science Temple more threatening.

63. "Rival Casts Eye on Divine's Flock," *New York Times*, February 22, 1938, 23.

Policing the Racial and Religious Boundaries of "Civilization"

Over the course of the nineteenth century, the developing field of racial biology was wedded, in many contexts, to the evolutionary thought then dominant in the social sciences and humanities. "Races" defined by spurious theories of biological difference were ranked on a unilineal scale of sociocultural evolution—from "savage" to "barbarous" to "civilized"—with the social norms of White Euro-American educated elites standing, of course, as the benchmark of civilization. "Nations," as well, were ranked in terms of their cultural accomplishments. Indeed, in this crucial period of state formation in Europe and the Americas, the legal and bureaucratic machinery of the modern nation-state was considered an essential sign, and guarantor, of civilization. Religion, as well, played a crucial role in scholarly and popular definitions of savagery and civilization. The "fetish worship" of Black Africans and the "totemism" of native Australians were considered signs of their primitive social and spiritual development—and, according to some, their incapacity for further development. The birth of Western monotheism was widely considered a quantum leap forward in the path of civilization, a path typically thought to culminate in a "rational" and "restrained" deistic Protestantism, rather than in, say, Pentecostalism, Catholicism, Judaism, or Islam.

Given this symbolically and politically charged nexus of race and religion, savagery and civilization, it is hardly surprising that nineteenth- and early twentieth-century nation-states, in the Americas and elsewhere, took an interest in the religious lives of their citizens. Even the United States, with its developing tradition of church-state separation, worked to regulate the religious practices of those within its borders, in order to cultivate a "civilized" citizenry. And of course these nationalist efforts to legislate civilization often drew distinctions based on race.

The essays in this section examine the ambivalent effects of these attempts to police the boundaries of savagery and civilization. In "Legislating 'Civilization' in Post-Revolutionary Haiti," Kate Ramsey traces the efforts of nineteenth-century Haitian elites to repudiate the savagery so often attributed the world's first Black republic by outlawing "spells" and other "superstitious practices" associated with the syncretic Afro-Caribbean religion of Vodou. Unfortunately for these Francophile Catholic elites, however, foreign observers generally took their "civilized" penal codes as further proof of the "savagery" of Vodou—and Haiti itself. The United States was somewhat more successful, however, in equating civilization and citizenship, as Jennifer Snow shows in "The Civilization of White Men: The Race of the Hindu in U.S. vs. Bhagat Singh Thind." Snow examines a landmark 1922 case in which the United States Supreme Court denied a Sikh immigrant's application for citizenship under the 1790 statute restricting naturalization to "free white men." Despite his undisputed "Aryan blood," the court decreed, Bhagat Singh Thind could not become an American citizen because his "Hindoo" religion was inconsistent with "the civilization of white men."

By focusing on the contested boundaries of civilization, these essays shed light on the broader semantic and discursive fields that have lent meaning to racial and religious differences. And by focusing on the contested boundaries of the nation-state, they shed light on the concrete social institutions that have worked to enforce these symbolic distinctions.

9

Legislating "Civilization" in Postrevolutionary Haiti

Kate Ramsey

In the long history of Western discourses denigrating African and African diasporic religions, the Caribbean nation of Haiti has occupied a particularly central place. Born of the world's only successful slave revolution in 1804, Haiti became internationally known thereafter as the home of the "vaudoux cult." Portrayed by nineteenth-century colonial apologists as a form of sorcery involving rites of child sacrifice and cannibalism, "vaudoux" was figured as proof of an endemic barbarism that warranted Haiti's exclusion and isolation from the ranks of "civilized" nations. Moreover, "vaudoux" (or, as this word was increasingly rendered by anglophone writers, "voodoo") became an exemplary trope in the service of broader claims about the unfitness of peoples of African descent for liberation from the slave and colonial regimes against which they were then struggling across the Americas.

The utility of the construct of "vaudoux" for such contentions was well understood by Haitian intellectuals writing in the mid– to late nineteenth century. Most notably, in his 1885 book *De l'égalité des races humaines (anthropologie positive)* the lawyer, anthropologist, and diplomat Anténor Firmin analyzed two principal grounds (among others) on which "defamers of the black race" defended their allegations of black intellectual and moral inferiority: first, that black people were incapable of administering justice, demonstrating "an habitual contempt for the law," and second that they were incapable of true religion, that is, "unable to rise above fetishism and totemism."[1] As Firmin's contemporary Louis-Joseph Janvier observed in his *La république d'Haïti et ses visiteurs (1840–1882)*, these two cornerstones of racist thought were frequently worked together in the writings of Haiti's detractors, so that the persistence of the "vaudoux cult" became evidence for the inability of Haitians, and thus that of blacks generally, to govern themselves.[2] In fact, these arguments had become so conflated in anti-Haitian rhetoric by the end of the nineteenth century that Monsignor François-Marie Kersuzan, a Catholic bishop posted in northern Haiti, attempted to rally elite Haitian support for a church campaign against the practice of "vaudoux" in 1896 by declaring: "it is a question, let us not forget any longer, of . . . knowing if a black people can civilize itself, govern itself, and, finally, form a nation worthy of this name."[3]

This article considers the links between race, religion, law, and "civilization" by focusing on the series of penal prohibitions promulgated by the Haitian state against "vaudoux" over the course of the nineteenth century. It examines how these statutes were pressured by colonial and ecclesiastical ideologies and also how they materialized the historical force of such ideologies. I will begin by studying how successive postrevolutionary governments relied on juridical law both as a sign of political modernityand as a space for the repudiation of the so-called primitive in Haiti. Indeed, the codification of Haitian law along French models between 1825 and 1835 might be understood as having served, in itself, as a counterargument against the claims of Haiti's detractors. I will argue that this was never more the case than in the penal laws issued against "les sortilèges," or "spells," in 1835 under the government of Jean-Pierre Boyer and revised and tightened in 1864 under that of Fabre Nicolas Geffrard.

I will then go on to examine the political force and frequently paradoxical effects of such statutes at times when they were strictly applied, and also when they were not. This article will focus on two significant episodes of enforcement of these laws following the return of the Roman Catholic Church to Haiti in 1860. At this point, popular ritual practice fell, in effect, under a second punitive regime, even as the newly arrived foreign clergy also pressed the Haitian state for stricter enforcement of the penal laws already in place. I will argue, however, that the application of what were frequently consolidated after 1860 as "les lois divines et humaines" against "vaudoux" proved, repeatedly, to be impossible for both state and Church. At the heart of this study lies the vexed question of what precisely the sign "vaudoux" (or, as it is generally written today, Vodou), referenced and encompassed.[4] Ironically, the word that came to signify the "whole" of Haitian sorcery among often hostile outsiders over the course of the nineteenth century has long been figured in popular Haitian usage as contrary to such practices. The disparity between how this word was constructed through penal and ecclesiastical laws versus how it was popularly understood thus became, I will argue, the key point on which both the state's and the Church's campaigns against popular ritual invariably foundered.

"Les Lois Divines et Humaines"

Upon taking office as president of the Haitian southern republic in 1818, General Jean-Pierre Boyer instituted a commission for the consolidation of Haitian laws into an ensemble of legal codes, modeled after those that had been recently adopted in France.[5] Haiti's Code d'Instruction Criminelle and Code Pénal were the final two codes to be framed, and for these Boyer instructed his commission to be sure to "consult the spirit and the particular character of the people; experience will prove what is the nature of the crimes to which they are most inclined, those calling for the most prompt repression and the most decisive measures."[6] If in the end, as legal historian Thalès Jean-Jacques notes, the Haitian Code Pénal published in 1835 hardly differed from its French counterpart (dating from 1810), it did nevertheless feature one anomalous set of articles.[7] The penultimate section of the final law, covering "Contraventions de Police" (misdemeanors), was entitled "Des sortilèges," or "Spells":

Art. 405
All makers of *ouangas, caprelatas, vaudoux, donpédre, macandals* and other spells, will be punished by one to six months of imprisonment, and a fine of 16 to 25 gourdes; not taking into consideration the stronger sentences that they might incur for offenses or crimes committed in preparing or carrying out their evil spells.

Art. 406
People who make a profession of fortune-telling, or of divination, of foretelling dreams or of reading cards, will be punished by six days to one month of imprisonment and a fine of 16 to 25 gourdes.

Art. 407
Furthermore, the instruments, utensils and costumes used or destined for use in the acts foreseen by the two preceding articles will be seized and confiscated.[8]

Léon Nau, an early twentieth-century annotator of the Codes Haïtiens, suggested that article 406 of the Code Pénal "proceed[ed] from the same feeling of reprobation as the act incriminated by Article 479, Number 7 of the French *Code Pénal*," which likewise prohibited divination, fortune-telling, and dream explication.[9] Otherwise, "Des Sortilèges" was a section of the Haitian criminal code that had no direct precedent in the French code on which it was modeled.

Rather, the antecedents of the law lay in the proliferation of ordinances promulgated in late colonial Saint-Domingue interdicting, in ever more specific and strenuous terms, the ritual practices of slaves, *marrons* (maroons), and *affranchis* (free people of color) that were believed to be politically and magically subversive of colonial order. Like those supplements to the blanket prohibition of slave gatherings in the 1685 French Code Noir, article 405 of Boyer's Code Pénal suggests an investment in precise nomination. "Spells" are not simply subject to a categorical prohibition but are rather first inventoried as a class of offense encompassing a range of specific practices. Article 405 does not preclude the possibility, and prohibition, of other forms of spells but rather through a strategic economy of specificity and generalization aspires to criminalize an entire field of popular practices.

However, the precision that seems to characterize the law against les sortilèges, and particularly its Article 405, belies an ambiguity that stemmed, paradoxically, from that same listing of popular names. Nowhere does the law define what constitutes "un sortilège" except through that list, and these names are defined only by their categorizaton as "sortilèges," a circularity that introduces another problem. Namely, "les sortilèges" was not a popular category, and the practices that the Haitian state sought to comprehensively subsume by this penal classification were in popular understanding neither objectified as such nor grouped together in such a way.[10]

One might object that, with one significant exception, all the names constructed and prohibited as "sortilèges" in article 405 bore some relation to popular conceptions of magic (in Haitian Kreyòl, *maji*). However ambiguous for not explicitly defining the practices it banned by name, the 1835 statute might thus have achieved a certain coherence were it not for the inclusion of the word "vaudoux" in this inventory. Again, without definition or description, this reference is a node of uncertainty: what acts were implicated by the state's banning of "vaudoux"? In fact, the assimilation of "vaudoux" as popularly understood to the register of "spells" confounded the law, given that "vaudoux" (or, rather, Vodou) has been traditionally figured by practitioners as antithetical, even constitutively opposed, to practices of criminal maji.

In an influential 1977 essay entitled "The Meaning of Africa in Haitian Vodu," Serge Larose examines how contemporary *sèvitè* ("servants") of the Vodou spirits "take much pain to point out the differences between them and other groups mainly pre-occupied with other sets of powers, all more or less related with the practices of sorcery." He notes that this is a moral distinction that is generally figured "in terms of fidelity to l'Afrique Guinee," standing for "tradition, unswerving loyalty to the ancestors and through them to the old ways and rituals they brought from overseas" and in opposition to "innovations" that are "assimilated to magic."[11] Larose acknowledges that, of course, the categorization of what qualifies as Guinea (or in standard Kreyòl orthography, "Ginen") versus maji is by no means stable from one generation to the next, or even from person to person. Moreover, as he writes, "everyone is Guinea in his own way and everyone denigrates his neighbour for having added to and thus diluted the inheritance."[12] Yet what interests me in thinking about the significance of such transformative processes historically, is Larose's suggestion that while the practices classified as "Ginen" or "maji" can in no sense be absolutely defined, the moral opposition of those categories in the service of particular kinds of social legitimation and authority seems to be longstanding.

I do not mean to suggest that contemporary analyses of the nature and scope of the particular practices referred to as "Vodou" among sèvitè in Haiti today can be unproblematically ascribed to their ancestors of generations ago.[13] However, I want to take seriously Larose's proposition that Ginen "needs and always needed magic as its ground-figure." That is, as I understand his implication, the Vodou rites associated with Ginen have been historically valued and shaped in constitutive relation to the figure and practices of criminal maji, however these, at any given point, were defined. It thus seems, as I will examine hereafter, that from the viewpoint of those dedicated to the service of ancestral spirits, the Ginen *lwa* (spirits), article 405's incongruous classification and prohibition of "vaudoux" as a form of sortilège lacked not only justice but also intelligibility. The law made a category mistake.

However, to whatever extent the authors of Boyer's 1835 Code Pénal were aware of such distinctions, they were clearly not their principal concern in framing articles 405–407. If the codification of Haitian law on French models was itself a benchmark of official national modernity, these codes also served as a site for official repudiation of practices constructed in the West as "primitive." In this light, "vaudoux" was a particularly important constituent of the list of prohibited "sortilèges" in article 405, as this word was already in the process of becoming a gloss for Haitian "sorcery" internationally and thus a primary sign of the barbarism attributed to Haiti by its detractors in western Europe and the United States. It is, however, notable that the 1835 law figured "vaudoux" as a single rather than encompassing term, within a greater field of prohibited "spells," along with other names that would not have been familiar to most foreign observers. This signals that as much as it is crucial to understand the way in which the prohibition against les sortilèges was pressured by unremitting white Western hostility toward and maligning of the postcolonial "Black Republic" in the mid-nineteenth century, it would be a mistake to read this law as simply an official disavowal directed at the West. To do so would be to disregard the local stakes and effects of the law, both at times when it was strictly applied and also when, as was more generally the case, it was not.[14] In fact, the inclusion of the word "vaudoux" among the other forms of "sortilèges" prohibited by article 405 criminalized the majority of the Haitian population before the law, subjecting practitioners to the arbitrary regulation of local authorities and at times to more serious persecution under its regime.

Yet, for the most part, the mid-nineteenth-century Haitian state was less focused on the strict or severe suppression of such practices than on their legal construction and negation as a mark of primitivism. The historian Hénock

Trouillot aptly characterizes the intermittent episodes of persecution to which sèvitè of the lwa were subject after the 1835 promulgation of articles 405–407 as "passing storms."[15] This was because, whatever public claims they made, each government depended on popular religious communities for political power, if not also, at times, spiritual and magical works and protection. While there was considerable popular pressure on authorities to apprehend those suspected of causing harm through magical means, any sustained assault on public and private rituals serving the Vodou spirits, or on the range of services that *oungan* and *manbo* (male and female priests) provided to individuals and families—such as divination, healing, the creation of charms—would jeopardize a government's longevity. There is today a considerable folklore in Haiti about presidents who fell because of their interference with popularly affirmed traditional practices, as well as about those who cultivated particularly close ties with popular spiritual and/or magical societies. Thus, as the sociologist Laënnec Hurbon writes, successive Haitian postrevolutionary governments were torn between "maintaining Vodou as an inadmissible support to their power, and appealing to the Catholic Church as [Haiti's] single official religion."[16]

Roman Catholicism had not always enjoyed this official status in independent Haiti. The 1805 Constitution promulgated by the imperial government of Jean-Jacques Dessalines forbade the establishment of any such "predominant religion" (article 50), and Haiti's so-called schism with Rome began just after the Revolution, during Dessalines's rule.[17] For over fifty years, the Roman Catholic church had no formal or official relationship with Haiti, even as "la religion catholique, apostolique et romaine" was identified as the state's own by every government after Dessalines's assassination in 1806. In the decades of diplomatic isolation that followed Haitian independence, the establishment of a concordat with the Vatican assumed a vital political and economic importance for its elite advocates. Such an agreement promised further international recognition, the establishment of an education system, and, perhaps most important, proof of the Republic's rightful place among the ranks of "civilized" nations.[18]

By the mid–nineteenth century, this status had been thrown repeatedly into question in the writings of "scientific" race theorists such as, most prominently, Joseph-Arthur, Comte de Gobineau, who in his book *De l'inégalité des races humaines* (1853–1855) deplored the "retrogression" of civilization in Haiti since the overthrow of French rule and slavery and figured this charge as evidence that peoples of African descent could not govern themselves. Gobineau was writing during the government of Faustin Soulouque (1847–1859), who installed himself as emperor of Haiti (Faustin I) in 1849 and became the object of great Western ridicule for, according to such accounts, combining delusions of imperial grandeur with close ties to "vaudoux" societies. Soulouque was overthrown in 1859 by General Fabre Nicolas Geffrard (1859–1867), a member of the light-skinned elite and strong Catholic who proclaimed Haiti's return to republicanism and, in practice, reproduced the oligarchic power base of his predecessors.

In March 1860, negotiations between Geffrard's government and the Vatican concluded with the document that became the Concordat. While the pursuit and eradication of "superstition" may not have been explicitly mentioned in this convention, it was understood by both parties to be a principal function of the Church's work in Haiti. Some eighty-two years later, upon the failure of the Church's severe campaign against "superstition" between 1939 and 1942, the archbishop of Port-au-Prince, Joseph Le Gouaze, wrote a confidential pastoral letter to clergy in Haiti saying: "our anti-superstitious Crusade continues and cannot not continue" because "it is the *raison d'être* of the Church."[19] This rather extraordinary admission suggests the extent to which the Catholic Church in Haiti historically defined itself in opposition to the popular practices it constructed as "superstition" and depended on that opposition for self-identity.[20]

With the Concordat, popular ritual practice in Haiti fell, in effect, under a second legal regime: henceforth the practice of "superstition" would be denounced by both Church and state authorities with reference to "les lois divines et humaines." Geffrard exhorted his compatriots to "hasten to remove from our land these last vestiges of barbarism and slavery, superstition and its scandalous practices."[21] The Church's periodic campaigns against "superstition" thereafter took Haitian penal laws against sortilèges as an authorizing basis but also became the occasion for the promulgation of new sets of disciplinary measures, emanating from the ecclesiastical power and exercised by the clergy. Classifying attendance at *sèvis* (ritual services) as a "crime of idolatry," such "statuts synodaux" and "ordinances épiscopales" established rigorous sanctions against those reputed to be "magiciens," including the denial of baptism, communion, the right to be godparents, and the right to a Catholic burial, with somewhat lesser penalties but still severe penitence prescribed for those who having once "given themselves over" to superstitious practices under the influence of such figures then decided to convert to Catholicism.[22]

That the blessing of penitential clothes (in Kreyòl, *rad penitans*) was itself banned by Church authorities in 1898, because priests suspected that this Catholic practice had been incorporated into the expansive repertory of what they called "superstition," draws attention to how problematic the concept of "conversion" was when laws of the Church were either already embodied in, or always potentially assimilated into, Haitian popular ritual practice.[23] As I will examine hereafter, this history points to the ways that sèvitè significantly altered the nature and application of penal and ecclesiastical regimes against "le vaudoux," in part through such subversive appropriations, and in part through direct political pressure.

"Nearly All Moan About the Reprehensible Tolerance . . ."

The first Catholic clergy authorized by the Concordat arrived in Haiti in 1864, the same year that what became known as the *affaire de Bizoton* took place. In his book *De la réhabilitation de la race noire par la république d'Haïti* (1900), Hannibal Price proposed that the arrival of the French priests in the midst of the public uproar surrounding this case predisposed them to "believe themselves transported into an absolutely savage milieu, among wild men whom they were called to civilize."[24] If, as Price suggests, this timing sheds light on the nature of the clergy's subsequent missions in Haiti, one might wonder how the arrival of the foreign priests may likewise have conditioned the Haitian government's response to the events that had allegedly taken place in Bizoton, on the outskirts of the capital city, early that year. As narrated in a circular sent by President Geffrard to arrondissement commanders concerning "vaudoux," these events were as follows: "a crime unheard of in our annals has been committed in Bizoton, in the arrondissement of Port-au-Prince. Cannibals, eight in number, four men and four women, strangled a poor child, cut her body into pieces and ate it while indulging in practices and spells of the vaudoux sect."[25] One of the women, Jeanne Pelé (also spelled Pellé), was reputedly a manbo, who, at the behest of her brother, allegedly killed the child, a girl named Claircine, identified as their niece. Tried and convicted, the eight alleged conspirators were publicly executed by firing squads in Port-au-Prince on February 13, 1864, a market day, in front of, reportedly, a crowd of cheering spectators.

Both the crime and the capital punishment that swiftly followed received great publicity in Haiti, not least of all through state organs. A week later, the government's official journal, *Le Moniteur Haïtien*, featured an account of the proceedings: "Can this be? One would refuse to believe it, but the criminals have been arrested, tried, convicted, executed."[26] However, even Sir Spenser St. John, British minister to Haiti at the time, whose infamous account of this trial in his *Hayti, or The Black Republic* (first edition 1884, second edition 1889) would for years thereafter associate "vaudoux worship" with cannibalism in the imperial imaginary, cast doubt at one point on its justice: "the prisoners were bullied, cajoled, cross-questioned in order to force avowals."[27] St. John, of course, intended such disclosures to throw into question Haitian official commitment to the "principles of justice" and, no doubt as well, capacity for justice. Certainly, he did not mean to question the guilt of the eight accused, of which he had no doubt. Here, my aim is not to establish what "actually" took place in the town of Bizoton, as if such a transcript were even recoverable. Rather, I am interested in examining the government's reconstruction and explanation of those events, and how the Haitian official response was interpreted by imperialists such as St. John as evidence for the regression of civilization in Haiti, rather than for its defense by the country's ruling classes.

The account published in *Le Moniteur* only a week after the executions had taken place already reflected state concern over how reports of the crime abroad would be misconstrued by those "having no knowledge of the country" and who, "reading from afar about what just happened, will see a fact from which to generalize."[28] The possibility of such a generalization may have seemed particularly threatening to the author of this report, given that, as it emphasized, the "abominable crime" was committed not in some remote section of the countryside but at the very "doors of the Capital": the perpetrators had mingled in society; they were even churchgoers. This prompted the author to ponder what could have induced them to commit such an atrocity. It is striking, as the literary scholar Léon-François Hoffmann has noted, that neither this account, nor those published in the government's subsequent circulars raise the possibility that "the assassins could have been a bad lot or mentally ill."[29] Rather, the official reports attribute the crime entirely to the persistence of "superstition" in Haiti, and specifically to "vaudoux," this "barbaric religion imported to us from some corner of Africa," as *Le Moniteur* puts it. It goes on: "their cannibalism is only the result of their idolatry; thus, destroy the cause, and you destroy the effect."[30]

In the wake of Bizoton, such official discourses figured "vaudoux" not as a symptom of peasant barbarism but rather as its unique source, as well as its encompassing term. This was a departure from the classificatory scheme of article 405 of the Code Pénal, in which "vaudoux" was only one of several crimes listed under the heading of "spells." In these writings, "it" now seemed to gloss all the practices subsumed under the generic expression "superstition." This usage was, notably, consonant with the way "vaudoux" (among its various cognates) was constructed and circulated in Western discourses—encapsulating all of the barbarous rites attributed to Haitians. In likewise consolidating "superstition" under the capacious sign of "vaudoux," the author of the *Moniteur* account effectively isolated "it" as the sole source of the barbarism imputed to Haiti by the hostile West. The extirpation of this "culte barbare" became, in this formulation, all that stood in the way of civilizing the Haitian masses and preventing future depravities on the order of Bizoton: "destroy the *culte*, we have said, and you destroy the cannibalism which is its consequence."[31]

However if, according to this writer, "the moral state of the masses undeniably leaves much to be desired," the popular response to the execution of the eight convicted anthropophagists in Port-au-Prince should prove to the world that a "notion of good and evil" is not entirely foreign to them. The author had walked among the crowds that day and was heartened by the cheers of "Vive le President d'Haïti! Vive la civilisation!" that greeted the spectacle, in spite of, as he notes, the highly unusual circumstance that four of those executed were women. If many of those gathered at the execution still lived under the baleful influence of "vaudoux," he reasoned, such expressions of popular outrage, and not the crimes against which they were directed, should be the point on which foreign observers generalized about Haiti.[32]

It is striking that the author of this official account does not attempt to reconcile the horror popularly expressed against the alleged crimes of ritual cannibalism in Bizoton with his proposal that these were propelled, in the first place, by the idolatrous "vaudoux" cult. In fact, they are irreconcilable points. In constructing "vaudoux" as the root of such barbaric criminality, he cannot acknowledge that the public furor that he finds so heartening might itself have been borne of popular religious belief and feeling itself—namely the afore-mentioned distinction drawn by Larose between fidelity to Ginen versus in-dulgence in practices of malicious maji. Might not the rejection of such crimes be closely related to the social affirmation of Vodou, as, in his words, "Guinea, absolutely"?[33] In that case, as Laënnec Hurbon has suggested, the expressions of outrage at the crime and acclamation of the punishment that so reassured the author about the morality of the Haitian masses would need to be under-stood as emerging, at least in part, *from* popular religious convictions, not in spite of them.[34] This was not, of course, a conclusion the Geffrard government entertained, at least publicly, what with the arrival of the Concordat clergy and hallucinatory reports of the Bizoton crime circulating internationally.[35] Three weeks after the executions had taken place, Geffrard issued a circular to arron-dissement commandants, warning them that it was not enough simply to have punished the crimes committed in Bizoton but rather was the "imperative duty" of authorities to prevent them from taking place at all, "because a crime so horrible, if it does not stay isolated, would be a disgrace for the Haitian nation."[36]

The president's circular then reviewed the relevant penal code articles, ordering the local authorities across the country to "pursue seriously all those who, in the reach of your command, indulge publicly or secretly in practices of vaudoux, to arrest them and deliver them to the judicial authority to be tried." The commandants were likewise instructed to conduct searches to seize "the objects and instruments used in such practices and spells" and deposit them as evidence at the office of the civil court of that jurisdiction. Interestingly, Geffrard exhorted the local commanders to show "the most rigorous severity in executing these orders," not simply because these practices were a sign of barbarism but also because they were one of the "last vestiges of slavery[,] . . . introduced and propagated under the colonial regime, in order to stupefy and better enslave the populations." If not many followed Geffrard in attributing the existence of the practices he objectified as "vaudoux" to a colonial strategy, the identification of such practices with slavery, both historically and ontolog-ically, became one of the great discourses of anti-"superstitious" rhetoric, par-ticularly, in later years, on the part of foreign clergy. Haiti might be free and independent, these appeals to national pride and patriotism went, but its masses were still enslaved to the oungan.[37] In Geffrard's text, the overthrow of superstition by "le vrai culte du vrai Dieu" was figured as fulfilling the promise of the Revolution, freeing the population from this remnant of colonialism that perpetuated its own regime of subjugation.

Hannibal Price describes the series of raids launched by Geffrard's circular as violent and arbitrary: "flags, drums, all the material of the societies" were seized and burned, and "all individuals reputed, wrongly or rightly, to be papaloi or maman-loi" were arrested and imprisoned "as cannibals, as anthropophagists."[38] Yet it seems that Geffrard's campaign soon crashed on the rocks of its own political impossibility. Just two months after Geffrard issued his circular to the arrondissement commanders, on May 2, 1864, his secretary of state for justice and worship (itself an intriguing conjunction of appointments in this context) sent another circular "concerning Vaudou" to the government commissioners to the civil courts. It reviewed the circumstances and motivations that had compelled Geffrard to issue his earlier orders, which had resulted in the "arrest of a throng of individuals prevented from indulging in spells, vaudou and other infamous practices derived from superstition." Significantly, "vaudou" is no longer figured here as the encompassing term of this index but rather is distinguished from "spells" and is inventoried as one manifestation of superstition among others. The reasons for this subtle yet significant reclassification, along with its implications, might be read between subsequent lines. Among the many imprisoned, whether convicted or still awaiting trial, the circular continued, "nearly all moan about the reprehensible tolerance which not long ago had represented to them as permissible what is formally forbidden by human and divine laws." They swore to the errors of their ways and sought repentance. Given that the chief of state subscribed to the "maxim that it is better to prevent errors than to have to punish them," he was ordering the local courts "to grant full and entire clemency . . . to all the individuals arrested for having practiced vaudou, and even those already tried and convicted for infractions of this nature."[39]

It seems to me that this reversal speaks to the political force of popular belief and will in the face of the state's disciplinary regime against Vodou. Read against its grain, the reference to prisoners "moaning" about the "reprehensible tolerance" that, until then, led them to believe in the permissibility of these prohibited practices might prove particularly suggestive. If there was "moaning" among those imprisoned on the subject of such "tolerated illegalities," is there not ample evidence, even in the action of the government's second circular itself, to suggest that this more probably took the form of protest rather than repentance?

In his book *Discipline and Punish*, Michel Foucault argues that in prerevolutionary France "the least favored strata of the population did not have, in principle, any privileges" but "benefited, within the margins of what was imposed on them by law and custom, from a space of tolerance, gained by force or obstinacy; and this space was for them so indispensable a condition of existence that they were often ready to rise up to defend it."[40] If Haitian peasants were subject to an arbitrary and inherently exploitative regime of local regulation on the part of some *chefs de section* (section chiefs), popularly sanctioned religious practices nonetheless attained a measure of protection from any *sustained* attack on the part of Haitian state authorities because their status was like what Foucault describes. With its abrupt decision to free all those who had been arrested and imprisoned for practicing "vaudou," even those already convicted and sentenced in the local courts, the Geffrard government seems to have conceded the political untenability of its campaign in the face of public pressure to end it.

Through his minister, Geffrard exhorted local magistrates not to "relax the active surveillance prescribed by the expired circular," as the government persisted "in its unshakable resolve to combat the errors which endangered the future of the country." However, in perhaps the most revealing instruction of all, the president requested that those authorities particularly focus their surveillance "on the individuals designated by public outcry as being the heads of the sect, and indulging in these practices towards a criminal or self-seeking end."[41] Thus it was not simply that this circular ordered the sudden release of all of the prisoners. Even more significant, local authorities were instructed to follow "la clameur publique" in enforcing the penal laws reprised by the earlier circular. Henceforth, in other words, the popular sense of justice was to be the arbiter of the application of these laws. This amounted to a hardly surreptitious official acknowledgment, and even endorsement, of the constitutive popular distinction between criminal maji and Ginen—on the one hand rituals employed for malicious ends, and thus properly subject to punishment, versus those on the other whose toleration by the authorities was, in Foucault's formulation, an "indispensable . . . condition of existence" for the majority of the population. If, as the second circular suggested, a conversion had taken place as a result of Geffrard's campaign, did it not seem more likely that it was the law that had been chastened by the force of popular will, rather than the people who had been chastened by the force of the law?

"The Law Always Has a Trap Inside of It"

Yet the concessions that Geffrard's instructions to local authorities in early May 1864 seemed to signal were not recognizable in the government's revisions to the Code Pénal several months later. In October 1864, Geffrard expanded and tightened articles 405–407, lengthening minimum prison stays and raising fines several-fold. Notably as well, a second paragraph was added to article 405 that seemed calculated to further expand its field of prohibition and make it that much more comprehensive and encompassing: "all dances and any other practices that are of a nature to maintain the spirit of fetishism and superstition in the populations will be considered spells and punished with the same penalties."[42] Of all the revisions to "Des Sortilèges," it is this extension that appears most contrary to the government's instructions to local magistrates six months earlier. Rather than bringing the law more in step with popular definitions and local regulatory customs, the addition of this paragraph seems to pull the continuum of popular spiritual practices further into the domain of "spells."[43]

"Des Sortilèges" was one of only three sections of the Code Pénal to be revised in 1864. That it was singled out for expansion and tightening in the wake of the alleged events at Bizoton, and in spite of the government's hasty abandonment of its subsequent campaign against "le vaudoux," again raises the question of how such laws were meant to function as systems of signification, no less than as prescriptions for punishment. Pierre Buteau has suggested that the trial of the alleged Bizoton anthropophagists, attended by "a good number of representatives from the diplomatic corps of the epoch," might itself be understood as "an effort to show the international community that the Haitian Government really wanted to insert itself in the 'civilized' world."[44] Likewise, the expansion of the category of sortilèges and its placement under a harsher penal regime needs to be understood, at least in part, as an effort on the part of Geffrard's government to repudiate the barbarism relentlessly attributed to Haiti by detractors abroad. As "vaudoux" was figured as the primary sign of that barbarism in such literatures, subsuming all of its other supposed manifestations, penal laws and criminal procedures against those identified as practitioners became an increasingly important space of defense and disavowal for the nineteenth-century Haitian state. Read in a certain way, such laws not only signaled the state's will to "civilize" and modernize rural Haiti but, as performatives, seemed to back this authorizing intention with force.

Yet prohibition has a dual and paradoxical nature: as much as it negates, it also seems to affirm.[45] In prohibiting "les sortilèges" the Haitian state sought, in part, to provide evidence of its own civilizing offensive and political modernity. However, in the late nineteenth and early twentieth century, these laws and the court proceedings through which they were sometimes enforced were, paradoxically, seized on by Haiti's denigrators as positive, even official "proof" of the reality and existence of the practices that the Haitian state, through interdiction, sought to disavow.

There is a Haitian proverb, "Lwa toujou genyen yon zatrap ladan"—law always has a trap inside of it. It is a saying borne of a history in which juridical law has often provided more grief than protection to poor Haitians, particularly around questions of property. Yet perhaps this saying also helps to illuminate how Haitian legal discourses and proceedings that placed "les sortilèges" in general and "le vaudoux" in particular under an ever-tightening regime of penalization wound up being deployed in the late nineteenth century by imperialists as evidence of a residual or regressive barbarism that ultimately sub-sumed the state itself.[46] Paul de Man has argued that laws, as performatives, never refer "to a situation that exists in the present" but rather point "toward a hypothetical future," much like promises. Thus there is a temporal delay between the law's descriptive (or "constative") moment, when it says what it prohibits, and its performative moment, when that ban is enforced. It seems to me that this temporal gap was precisely the "trap" that defamers of Haiti exploited in their perverse interpretations of the law against les sortilèges. The fact that the application of a law is not simultaneous with its promulgation enabled St. John and James Anthony Froude, among others, to read these prohibitions as descriptive statements of the existence of barbarism in Haiti rather than as performative texts signaling the state's will to abolish "supersti-tious practices" through the force of law.[47]

However, such writers often took their conclusions even further, proposing that the laws against les sortilèges were actually arrested in this descriptive state and almost never had a performative moment. The charge that these laws were rarely enacted could then be deployed as evidence of the state's own implication in the practices that it banned. In introducing the second edition of his book, St. John disclosed that he had "trustworthy testimony that in 1887 cannibalism was more rampant than ever," explaining: "a black Government dares not greatly interfere, as its power is founded on the goodwill of the masses, ignorant and deeply tainted with fetish-worship."[48] Writing in the late 1880s as well, James Anthony Froude attributed what he characterized as the Haitian state's recent disinclination to prosecute crimes of "vaudoux" to fear of negative exposure: "a few years ago persons guilty of these infamies were tried and punished, now they are left alone, because to prosecute and convict them would be to acknowledge the truth of the indictment." He suggested that the imperial reading of the 1864 trial as evidence for, rather than against, the image of Haiti as a "pays de barbares" convinced the Haitian government that such proceedings were more damaging than they were rehabilitating to the country's reputation.[49]

Whether interpreted as a politics of appeasing the masses or of amelio-rating the country's image abroad, the Haitian state's supposed nonenforce-ment of the laws against les sortilèges became one of the great themes of anti-Haitian propaganda in the late nineteenth and early twentieth century. It ought to come as no surprise that this trope was anticipated by Gobineau, who in arguing for the permanence and fixity of "racial" characteristics attributed a wide discrepancy between Haitian legal discourse and penal practice. After stressing the European derivation of Haiti's political institutions, and noting, for example, that "nothing African has remained in the statute law," he asserted that such pretensions of "civilization" were but a facade. While the constitution "sleeps harmlessly upon the paper on which it is written," he wrote, a hypo-thetical "high official" had "ultimately no serious preoccupation except chewing tobacco, drinking alcohol, disemboweling his enemies, and conciliating his sorcerers."[50] It was not a far cry from discourses of "conciliation" and "appeasement" to charges that the Haitian political class was itself thoroughly implicated in, even accomplice to, the "vaudoux" crimes that went, according to these accounts, so irregularly punished.[51]

La Ligue Contre le Vaudoux

Such accusations did not go unchallenged on the part of Haitian writers across the political spectrum in the later decades of the nineteenth century. Their published rebuttals addressed to specific defamers became the occasion for broader vindicationist statements about racial equality and the exemplary status of Haitians as, in J. Michael Dash's formulation, "the avant-garde that would rehabilitate the black race."[52] Writers such as Louis-Joseph Janvier, Hannibal Price, and Duverneau Trouillot emphasized the decline or demise of the popular practices that were constructed in western Europe and the United States as evidence of the regression of civilization in Haiti. In his 1885 *Esquisse ethnographique: Le Vaudoun: aperçu historique et évolutions*, Trouillot, for example, observed that "it is certain that if an old Guinéan passed by, he would no longer recognize himself in the midst of the dance and ceremonies of vaudoux today."[53]

Yet when the Catholic Church organized its first sustained campaign against "vaudoux" in the mid-1890s it was not a discourse of decline but rather one of resurgence that was mobilized to justify the missions. According to Church history, in July 1895 Monsignor François-Marie Kersuzan, bishop of Cap-Haïtien, circulated a query to his clergy requesting information on the prevalence of "superstition" in their parishes and asking to what extent Church faithful might themselves be implicated in such practices. Six months later, Kersuzan issued a pastoral letter reporting that

> superstitious and pagan ceremonies, degrading dances ravage our countrysides, and even our cities are far from being sheltered. These practices which formerly hid themselves in shadowy dens in the mountains and were only carried out under the cover of night, now flaunt themselves in broad daylight. . . . And what we can only say with tears in our eyes, the very people who claim themselves Christians and who frequent the sacraments, are not afraid to participate in them, as if they could serve Jesus Christ and the devil at once.[54]

Kersuzan never addresses the most intriguing implication of his narrative: namely that the resurgence he alleges would have taken place, according to this chronology, under the Church's watch. His report suggests that since the signing of the Concordat and the arrival of Catholic clergy, the practice of "vaudoux" had actually become more public, pervasive, and intrusive in Haiti. Marc Péan, who has written the most thorough account to date of the Church's "crusade" against superstition in the late nineteenth century, suggests that the bishop's call to action in early 1896 found fertile ground in the social milieu of elite Cap-Haïtien society, focused on the pursuit of "progress."[55] Two months after Kersuzan wrote this pastoral letter, he founded a new Catholic weekly based in Cap-Haïtien, entitled *La Croix*, which became the principal mouthpiece for the movement against both "vaudoux" and, significantly as well, the growing social and political influence of Protestants in Haiti.[56] Directed by a former member of the Haitian legislature, the newspaper announced its intention to lead "a vigorous campaign" not simply for the health of souls but also for the honor and development of the country. "The existence of Vodou is a dishonor for us all," an editorial of May 16, 1896, asserted, noting that hostile white foreigners, despising both the black race and the Haitian nationality, figured such practices as a sign that Haitians were undeserving of a place "in the concert of nations." Thus, the editorial went on, "the responsibility of the patriot is to erase this stain from the face of the homeland. Let us prove to the foreigner that we are a civilized people."[57]

While *La Croix* was distributed principally in the North, it soon established a national profile and readership, particularly in the capital where its polemical appeals came to the attention of the new president, Simon Sam (1896-1902). In late May 1896, his Minister of the Interior, General Buteau, issued what became a widely publicized circular to arrondissement commanders across the country, ordering stricter enforcement of laws against "la danse du vaudoux," which had re-emerged with an "unusual recrudescence in our cities."[58] Péan notes that Buteau's circular, which officially endorsed the call for a "crusade" first proclaimed by Kersuzan, marked "a new stage in the anti-superstitious struggle." A series of public lectures was thereafter convened, the first given by Kersuzan himself on August 2, 1896 at the Cap-Haïtien marketplace before an audience that *La Croix* estimated at 2,000. In the course of his address, the Bishop argued that the political and civil conflicts that had rocked the country over the past twenty-five years were divine retribution for the tolerance of paganism: "a death sentence presses on us because of our idolatries. . . . It is my conviction that the radical abolition of vaudoux would make one of the principal causes of our revolutions disappear."[59]

Kersuzan's choice of the term "abolition" in this context was, of course, a calculated one; his talk was laden with metaphors of slavery, revolution, and emancipation. Practitioners of "vaudoux" were oppressed "under the yoke of bocors" (or *bòkò*—those who "work with both hands," for both good and ill), who exploited their credulity with swindling ways; they were also enslaved to the "demons" they served as gods, unable, as individuals, "to break their chains."[60] But in joining the crusade the Bishop heralded, they would find the power to "achieve the conquest of [their] independence."[61] Kersuzan appealed yet more explicitly to Haitian patriotism in emphasizing the high stakes of establishing national honor: "it is a question of rehabilitating ourselves in the eyes of the civilized world, it is a question of saving our very existence gravely compromised by the vampires who suck our fortune," and, as quoted earlier, "it is a question . . . of knowing if a black people can civilize itself, govern itself, and, finally, form a nation worthy of this name."[62]

At the end of his *conférence*, the Bishop called for the adoption of several "principles of action": "1) To combat, by all the means in their power, all superstitious practice, all commerce with *bocors, chapiteurs, devineurs*, etc; 2) To never hesitate to bring justice against the *faiseurs de caprelatas;* 3) To denounce to the authorities and, when necessary, public opinion, by means of newspapers, all public practice of vaudoux, and the existence of all places consecrated to vaudoux meetings."[63] Thus *La Croix* began publishing lists of oungan and manbo who practiced in the northern department, along with locations of sanctuaries.[64] Meanwhile, pressure was exerted on authorities in Cap-Haïtien to prosecute individuals who had been accused of forms of criminal maji. These proceedings took place in early October 1896 and "brought no decisive proof as to the guilt of the accused" yet, according to the newspaper, were "[f]ollowed with passion by a large crowd."[65] However, when troupes of "danseurs champêtres" (country dancers) were also arrested in violation of article 405, the newspaper *Le courrier du Cap* reported widespread popular protest: "alas, what outbursts by all the city, what savagery, what shame. . . . We run towards our old African lairs while making desperate efforts to prove on paper that we are models of the civilized."[66]

The outrage over the latter arrests might have alerted the bishop and lay campaign promoters to the conflicts of interpretation on which their movement would eventually founder. However, if anything, the "crusade" gained momentum in the late months of 1896. On December 27, "La Ligue Contre le Vaudoux" (The League Against Vaudoux) was officially founded under the presidency of Kersuzan, with a "comité d'action" that included prominent members of elite Capois society. Soon after the news that President Sam had officially endorsed the campaign appeared in the Cap-Haïtien press, the two principal governmental representatives of the Northern Department, General Nord Alexis (who would serve as president from 1902 to 1908) and his deputy Albert Salnave, wrote to the comité d'action as well, offering their support.[67] Thereafter, Kersuzan reported, rural populations were "prepared" for his open-air popular *conférences* by local military commanders, who "reinforced our speech and added to our curses against fetishism."[68]

That division of labor draws attention, again, to the way, following the Concordat, practices of popular ritual fell under a double legal regime—"les lois divines et humaines," as the expression went. Shortly after the founding of the Ligue, the Church published an "ordinance épiscopale" that expanded and tightened the "statuts synodaux" that had been promulgated in 1872 against "magiciens" and those who participated in "superstitious rites." During his missions across Haiti's northern region in 1897, Bishop Kersuzan announced and publicized the new sanctions, which subjected those who took part in a "vaudoux ceremony or dance" to "severe penitence" and a "deprivation of communion." That such measures were indeed applied by clergy during the period of antisuperstitious proselytizing that followed their promulgation might be gathered by the fact that, a year later, Church authorities were compelled to revise these statutes. As noted earlier, clergy had discovered to their dismay that the wearing of "penitential clothes" had itself been incorporated into the repertory of so-called superstitious practices.[69] This instance of the Church being forced to turn the regime of prohibition back on its own punitive practices was symptomatic of the impossibility of this and every subsequent anti-Vodou or anti-"superstitious" mission it undertook in Haiti, which always seemed to culminate in acts of self-proscription and self-destruction.

As for the application of les lois humaines against the practices objectified in the penal code as sortilèges, Péan reports that it was common to find notices in the Cap-Haïtien press announcing arrests for contraventions of article 405.[70] However, even as a new chapter of the Ligue Contre le Vaudoux was being organized in Haiti's Southern Department, conflicts were developing in the North between the Ligue's comité d'action and the region's military authorities, precisely around the enforcement of these penal laws. Again the problem centered on different perceptions of what their proper object should be. Significantly, it was the government's representatives, General Nord Alexis and his adjunct, Albert Salnave, who emerged as the most prominent antagonists of the Ligue's interpretation of these laws, in defense of popular views of their legitimate application. Thus, for example, the generals balked when the Ligue's comité d'action called for a ban on the dances performed in the streets during Carnival on the grounds that they were manifestations of "vaudoux." The controversy finally had to be arbitrated by Haiti's minister of the interior, who decided in favor of the Ligue's position, outlawing such performances that year.[71]

This incident, among others with similar stakes, fueled resentment against the Ligue and its apparent determination to repress practices that, in the view of the vast majority, presented no justifiable cause for penalization. Polemics had been appearing in local and national newspapers against the tactics employed by the Church in its "crusade." Monsignor Jean Marie Jan recorded a litany of these in chronicling the religious history of the diocese of Cap-Haïtien:

[when] We went so far as to denounce magicians as criminals . . .
and We provoked all honest people to unite to defend themselves
against these public enemies and to force them to renounce their
odious practices: then, oh! then especially, what cries of indignation!

what scandal! the Minister of God of peace and of charity preached
hate, sowed division, armed one citizen against another![72]

Jan further regretted that "the instructions of the Buteau circular were not
everywhere observed. In the public, a certain indulgence manifested itself for
ancestral customs, too old not to be tolerated."[73]

Yet clergy continued to enlist the backing of local military and police, both
in conducting missions among rural populations and also, at times, in raiding
suspected "superstitious" sites. In 1899, Father Bertin, the curé of Déréal,
confronted an oungan named Valbrun with an armed guard drawn from local
civil and military authorities. Valbrun, according to Jan's recounting of the
incident, denied having anything to do with "vaudoux." However, others present "let out a stream of recriminations" against the curé, charging that "the
priest had overstepped his rights in wanting to take away from them the freedom of doing what to them seemed good." Jan reports that they even threatened
Bertin's life, declaring "that if the Father had been alone, he would have been
assassinated."[74]

If the Church considered the strict enforcement of "les lois divines et
humaines" against "vaudoux" to be the principal aim and means of its crusade,
it was precisely the application of such laws on which the campaign consistently foundered and ultimately self-destructed. The *coup de grâce* played out
in late 1899 and early 1900 in Plaine-du-Nord, a commune of the arrondissement of Cap-Haïtien, which Péan identifies as "at once a high place of Catholicism and of Vodou." Thus the patron saint of this parish, St. Jacques (in
Kreyòl, Sen Jak, and in English, St. James), whose images adorned the local
church, was popularly recognized as the senior member of the Ogou family of
military spirits. Clerical anxiety over such syncretic identifications frequently
fixated on what the Church viewed as excessive popular attachment to pieces
of religious statuary, representing the virgin or particular saints, which, it was
suspected, were worshiped as "pagan idols." There were two statues of St.
Jacques at the church of Plaine-du-Nord. One, called "le petit Saint-Jacques"
even though it was full sized, was a recent gift to the parish from the late
former president Florvil Hyppolite. The other, known as "le grand Saint-
Jacques," was a plaster tableau, sculpted in relief, that had hung above the high
altar of the church since colonial times and was, according to Péan, the object
of an "extraordinary veneration" on the part of local parishioners. One evening
in late December 1899, the cord from which "le grand Saint-Jacques" had long
hung snapped, and the sculpture fell to the ground, cracking into pieces. Given
his suspicions about popular feeling for the tableau, Kersuzan reportedly regarded the event as a welcome accident. However, he was soon visited by General Nord Alexis, the governmental representative to the department, who informed the bishop of his intention to have the statue repaired. Kersuzan
proposed sending the statue to France for restoration and wrote a letter to the

curé at Plaine-du-Nord instructing him to relinquish the fragments of statuary for this end.

These were collected by the communal magistrate of Plaine-du-Nord, who set out en route to Cap-Haïtien and soon became the center of a high-spirited procession, during which, according to Jan's history, stops were made at various *ounfò* [Vodou temples], where "there were songs, vaudoux drums, dances."[75] The fragments of the statue were, in fact, never sent to France but rather pieced back together in Cap-Haïtien by a local sculptor, and on July 19, 1900, the restored "grand Saint-Jacques" was returned to Plaine-du-Nord in a procession on the order of a political parade.[76] General Nord Alexis led the escort himself, accompanied by other notables from Cap-Haïtien, with banners flying, drumming, singing, dancing, and cheering onlookers along the way. According to Jan's history, once the statue was restored to its place of glory above the high altar, an "orgy" took place in the church of Plaine-du-Nord: "crying, singing, drinking, a veritable sabbath."[77]

When Kersuzan heard a report of these events he notified the government in Port-au-Prince. Two months later, still waiting for their intervention, he traveled to the church of Plaine-du-Nord himself, surrounded by an entourage of priests. There the bishop told the assembled parishioners that he had come to remove the tableau from above the high altar in order to place it at the back of the church. Kersuzan was in the midst of his explanation when the protests started. As the unrest grew, he warned the congregation that he was prepared to close the church if it continued. When the unpopular curé of the parish, Père Lacrampe, began removing sacred ornaments and vases for safekeeping in the presbytery, a "veritable riot" broke out, from which, according to Jan, the clergy narrowly managed to extricate themselves.[78] Two days later Kersuzan announced the excommunication of those who had been involved in the "sacrilegious scenes" of July 19 and September 30 and placed the church of Plaine-du-Nord under an order of interdiction. While the bishop was eventually able to arrange for the removal of the statue through the intervention of President Sam in April of the following year, the debacle forced the Church and what was left of the Ligue Contre le Vaudoux to abandon their foundering northern campaign altogether.

I have elaborated this episode at some length because I think it illuminates the ultimate impossibility of Kersuzan and his supporters' efforts to eliminate "vaudoux" through the application of les lois divines et humaines against "its" practice. Is it not striking that the Church's efforts to see these prohibitions enforced finally end in self-interdiction, with Kersuzan imposing a ban on the church at Plaine-du-Nord itself? Far from being an exceptional or extraordinary step, this action was of a piece with the kinds of self-destructive measures in which the Church's campaigns against "vaudoux" (or "superstition") inevitably seemed to culminate. As the lengths to which the bishop went to have the tableau of St. Jacques removed from above the high altar at Plaine-du-Nord reflect, the Church always suspected and feared its takeover for "superstitious" purposes. However, because Catholicism was syncretically internalized in and transfigured by popular belief and ritual in Haiti, any attempt to attack the "contaminating" belief, the "idolatrous" practice, or the "superstitious" site always put the Church in the paradoxical position of shutting itself down, banning its own rites, and destroying its own iconography.

The confrontations at the Plaine-du-Nord church also underscore, again, the ultimate *political* impossibility of a campaign that initially inspired expressions of governmental support and congratulation at every level. One need not cast doubt on the sincerity of Nord Alexis's earlier offer of assistance to the Ligue in order to understand his later forceful opposition to their efforts. The problem, again, was one of legal interpretation. As had been the case under Geffrard in 1864, any attempt to strictly enforce these laws that did not follow popular consensus on what their proper object should be was doomed in advance to failure. It was not that most people were opposed in principle to the application of laws against "les sortilèges"; indeed, given popular dread and condemnation of malicious maji, the announcement of a tightened regime of penalization against "spells" was usually met, as it seems to have been in this case, with acclamation. Yet the Church's insistence that this legal regime encompassed rural dances, carnival traditions, and, of course, devotional sèvis for the Vodou spirits was met with outrage and protest on the part of affected communities and recalcitrance and sabotage on the part of the local political/ military authorities who not only policed but also politically represented them.[79]

Conclusion

While mediated by multiple narrations and translations, including my own, there still seems to be a powerful clarity in the way in which those who confronted Father Bertin on his antisuperstitious raid in Déréal in 1899 formulated their protest. In charging, according to Church history, that he had "overstepped his rights in wanting to take away from them the freedom of doing what to them seemed good," they foretold the ultimate impossibility of any clerical or official campaign that made "vaudoux" the object of its repression. Such campaigns rallied Haitians to defend the honor of both nation and race against the barbarism attributed to them by imperial denigrators through the figure of "vaudoux"—this one word, as Hannibal Price wrote in 1900, from which sprung "all the misunderstandings, sincere or not, spread against the Haitians in the world."[80] Nineteenth-century apologists for slavery and colonialism constructed "vaudoux" as an all-encompassing sign of civilization's regression in the postcolonial "Black Republic." In Haiti itself, such representations underwrote and empowered Mgr. Kersuzan's claim that the stakes of the Church's "crusade" against "vaudoux" were no less than proving to the world that a black people could achieve "civilization" and national self-determination.

Yet both the Haitian state's and the Church's campaigns eventually foundered in the face of popular understandings of Vodou that were antithetical, even constitutively opposed, to the definitions of "sorcery" and "witchcraft" that had long circulated in colonial and ecclesiastical discourses and that, in 1835, had been defensively assimilated into article 405 of the Haitian Code Pénal. If, in part, foreign demonization of "vaudoux" pressured the promulgation of this penal law, the popular construction and affirmation of Vodou as Ginen arguably proved to be the more politically powerful discourse in Haiti. I proposed earlier that it is important to understand the way the nineteenth-century Haitian legal prohibition of "vaudoux" was forceful even when not strictly enforced, rendering the vast majority of the population delinquent before the law. However, what these histories also make clear is that if laws against "vaudoux" sometimes served as a pretext for the subjugation of popular communities, the religious practices that sèvitè identified by the same name (Vodou) became in such cases a key locus and instrument of political struggle, through which and in defense of which repressive state and Church regimes could be brought in line with popular conceptions of justice.

NOTES

For their generous support of my archival research in Port-au-Prince, I would like to thank Frère Ernest Even at the Bibliothèque Haïtienne des Frères de Saint Louis de Gonzague, and Ephèle Milce and Sabrina Réveil at the Bibliothèque Haïtienne des Pères du Saint Esprit. For their valuable input during the research and writing of this article I wish to thank Karen McCarthy Brown, Yanick Guiteau Dandin, Marvel Dandin, J. Michael Dash, Carolyn Fluehr-Lobban, Henry Goldschmidt, Steven Gregory, Laënnec Hurbon, Gérarde Magloire, Elizabeth McAlister, Rosalind Morris, John Szwed, Michael Taussig, Gina Ulysse, Tim Watson, and Kevin Yelvington. I am grateful to have received research and writing funding from Columbia University and the Institute for Collaborative Research and Public Humanities at The Ohio State University.

1. Anténor Firmin, *The Equality of The Human Races (Positivist Anthropology)*, translated by Asselin Charles with an introduction by Carolyn Fluehr-Lobban (New York: Garland, 2000), 313, 339.

2. Louis-Joseph Janvier, *La république d'Haïti et ses visiteurs (1840–1882)*, vol. 1 (1883; reprint, Port-au-Prince: Les Editions Fardin, 1979), 111.

3. Monsignor François-Marie Kersuzan, *Conférence populaire sur le vaudoux donnée par Monseigneur l'Évêque du Cap-Haïtien, le 2 août 1896* (Port-au-Prince: Imprimerie H. Amblard, 1896), 17. All translations are my own unless otherwise indicated.

4. The historical instability of this sign is reflected in the perennial uncertainty surrounding its orthography: nineteenth-century French and English spellings in-

cluded *vaudoux, vaudou, voudou, voodoo, vodoo, vodoun,* and *voodoo.* In the pages that follow I preserve these different spellings in the citations in which they appear, and likewise in the case of quotations from secondary sources that adapt earlier orthographies to contemporary usage (usually "Vodou").

5. The Haitian legal historian Thalès Jean-Jacques describes a sense of urgency as having propelled this project on the part of Boyer's government, stemming from the "incoherence" of the laws then in effect, which, he writes, threw "judicial decisions into confusion rather than clarifying them." This situation was exacerbated by the fact that since 1806, two years after independence, the country had been riven by civil war; by 1807 it was divided into a northern state (and eventual monarchy) ruled by Henry Christophe, and a southern and western republic governed by Alexandre Pétion. Upon Christophe's death by suicide in 1820, the two polities were reunited under Boyer, and the work of Haitian legal "unification," then already underway, became incorporated into the larger project of centralizing the state apparatus, which Boyer ensured took place in the political and economic interest of the southwestern *mulâtre* elite with whom he identified. See Thalès Jean-Jacques, *Histoire du droit haïtien* (Port-au-Prince: Imp. Nemours Telhomme, 1933), 269.

6. Quoted in Jean-Jacques, *Histoire du droit haïtien,* 789. See also Crawford M. Bishop and Anyda Marchant, *A Guide to the Law and Legal Literature of Cuba, the Dominican Republic, and Haiti* (Washington, D.C.: Library of Congress, 1944), 238.

7. First versions of these Codes were voted on by the Haitian Corps Législatif in 1826. According to Jean-Jacques, "some years after, the imperfection of all our Codes promulgated in 1826 was recognized; and on the observations of the courts, which demonstrated to the Grand-Juge the gaps that they contained, a commission of civil servants was named in 1834, united under the presidency of Secretary General Mr. B. Inginac, to the end of effecting in our legislation all the modifications that it would judge to be useful." *Histoire du droit haïtien,* 789.

8. Reprinted in *Code d'instruction criminelle et code pénal,* collected and annotated by Linstant Pradine (Paris: A. Durand et Pedone-Lauriel, 1883), 186.

9. *Les Codes Haïtiens: Code d'instruction criminelle et code pénal,* annotated with annexes by Léon Nau (Paris: Librairie Générale de Droit et de Jurisprudence, 1914), 324. Article 479, number 7 of the French Code Pénal (also classified under the title of "Contraventions de police et peines") criminalized "les gens qui font métier de deviner et pronostiquer, ou d'expliquer les songes." See H. F. Rivière, *Codes Français* (Paris: Librairie A. Marescq Aîné, 1882), 101.

10. Michel-Rolph Trouillot and Sidney Mintz note that "there is no generalized word for 'sorcery' in Haitian Creole," the closest formulation being *fè mal,* a construction "which literally means to do bad but is not restricted to the use of supernatural forces." Sidney Mintz and Michel-Rolph Trouillot, "The Social History of Haitian Vodou," in *Sacred Arts of Haitian Vodou,* edited by Donald J. Cosentino (Los Angeles: Fowler Museum of Cultural History, 1995), 131.

11. Serge Larose, "The Meaning of Africa in Haitian Vodu," in *Symbols and Sentiments: Cross-Cultural Studies in Symbolism,* edited by Ioan Lewis (London: Academic Press, 1977), 85, 89.

12. Larose, "The Meaning of Africa in Haitian Vodu," 86. He also writes: "the idea that a concrete group could embody a pure Guinea tradition has no foundation

and no such group should be looked for in Haiti. God is always 'on our side,' and Guinea is a similar concept, a complex figure through with power is legitimated"; 92.

13. Traditionally, the word "Vodou" has been used to refer to a particular set of rites within the Rada religious repertory and not as a gloss for all popular Haitian spiritual beliefs and ritual practices, which, until recently, have tended not to be so objectified among practitioners. See Karen McCarthy Brown's illuminating discussion of the question of terminology in her entry on Vodou in *The Encyclopedia of Religion,* vol. 15, edited by Mircea Eliade (New York: Macmillan, 1987), 296–297.

14. Criminal justice in the Haitian countryside was administered in the first instance by *chefs de section* (section chiefs), officers of the rural police who were appointed from the peasantry and endowed with a military commission to supervise each of the commune's *sections rurales*, or rural sections. The most intolerable features of Haitian rural and penal law were usually tempered in the face of popular will under the authority of the chef de section. Thus the penal article prohibiting "vaudoux," as a form of spell-making, was, for the most part, not strictly applied against socially sanctioned rites across rural Haiti. Yet the official prohibition of such practices meant that they were subject, at the very least, to "informal" regulation by rural authorities, who came to rely on this oversight as a source of revenue. A system developed whereby oungan and manbo (respectively, male and female priests) were obliged to purchase permits from chefs de section to hold particular sèvis (services or ceremonies), without which they would be subject to disciplinary measures.

15. Hénock Trouillot, *Introduction à une histoire du vodou* (1970; reprint, Port-au-Prince: Editions Fardin, 1983), 103.

16. Laënnec Hurbon, *Comprendre Haïti: Essai sur l'état, la nation, la culture* (Port-au-Prince: Editions Henri Deschamps, 1987), 145.

17. Furthermore, Dessalines's Constitution made marriage a "purely civil act, authorized by the government," legalized divorce, and granted the same rights to children born out of wedlock as to those born of married parents. The Vatican viewed those provisions as highly provocative and pernicious, particularly coming on the heels of attacks on Catholic clergy during the Revolution and the nationalization of Church property thereafter.

18. On this point, see Laënnec Hurbon's insightful analysis in his *Le barbare imaginaire* (Port-au-Prince: Editions Henri Deschamps, 1987), 117.

19. Joseph Le Gouaze, "Communication de Son Exc. Mgr l'Archevêque de Port-au-Prince," Port-au-Prince, March 20, 1942. Found at the Bibliothèque Haïtienne des Pères du Saint Esprit, Port-au-Prince, Haiti.

20. Making a similar point, Elizabeth McAlister argues: "institutional Catholicism depends on its opposition to Vodou, for it is its position against what is impure and illegitimate that strengthens Catholic virtue in Haiti." See Elizabeth A. McAlister, " 'The Jew' in the Haitian Imagination: Pre-Modern Anti-Judaism in the Postmodern Caribbean," in *Black Zion: African American Religious Encounters with Judaism,* edited by Yvonne Chireau and Nathaniel Deutsch (New York: Oxford University Press, 2000), 215.

21. Quoted in David Nicholls, *From Dessalines to Duvalier: Race, Colour and National Independence in Haiti* (1979; reprint, New Brunswick, N.J.: Rutgers University Press, 1996), 84, his translation.

22. See, for example, "Statuts Synodaux Promulgués le 22 février 1872 par Mgr Guilloux," reprinted in Carl Edward Peters, *La croix contre l'asson* (Port-au-Prince: Imprimerie la Phalange, 1960), 250–251.

23. See the ordonnance épiscopale promulgated by Church authorities in 1898, quoted in Peters, *La croix contre l'asson*, 250.

24. Hannibal Price, *De la réhabilitation de la race noire par la république d'Haïti* (Port-au-Prince: Imprimerie J. Jerrollot, 1900), 488.

25. Quoted in Léon-François Hoffmann, *Haïti: Couleurs, Croyances, Créole* (Montréal: CIDIHCA, 1990), 133. Also cited by Peters in *La croix contre l'asson*, 282.

26. "Le Vaudoux en Haïti—Jeanne Pelé," *Le moniteur haïtien*, February 20, 1864. Pamphlet in the collection of the Bibliothèque Haïtienne des Frères de Saint Louis de Gonzague, Port-au-Prince, Haiti.

27. Sir Spenser St. John, *Hayti, or The Black Republic* (1889; reprint, London: Frank Cass, 1971), 215.

28. "Le Vaudoux en Haïti—Jeanne Pelé." Hurbon suggests that the Geffrard government's concern for foreign perceptions of the crime was particularly high, given the ridicule to which Soulouque had been subject. Hurbon, *Le barbare imaginaire*, 117.

29. Hoffmann, *Haïti: Couleurs, Croyances, Créole*, 133.

30. *Le moniteur haïtien*, February 20, 1864, quoted in Hurbon, *Le barbare imaginaire*, 116.

31. *Le moniteur haïtien*, February 20, 1864, quoted in Hurbon, *Le barbare imaginaire*, 117.

32. "Le Vaudoux en Haïti—Jeanne Pelé."

33. Larose, "The Meaning of Africa in Haitian Vodu," 112.

34. See Hurbon's incisive analysis of the *Moniteur* text in *Le barbare imaginaire*, 117–118.

35. The historian Hénock Trouillot once observed that the degree to which popular religious practices were persecuted under nineteenth-century Haitian governments depended on the one hand on "the religious faith of the holders of power" and on the other on "what foreign writers were saying at the time." He thus makes the crucial point that if these laws were, at times, enforced against socially sanctioned ritual practices under the pressure of foreign powers operating in Haiti, they were also, at times, enforced in this way by Haitian authorities on account of the pressure of the *writings* of foreigners. Trouillot, *Introduction à une histoire du vaudou*, 99.

36. Fabre Nicholas Geffrard, "No. 4034—Circulaire du Président d'Haïti aux Commandants d'Arrondissement, concernant le Vaudou," reprinted in Peters, *La croix contre l'asson*, 282.

37. A more recent formulation of this argument, mobilized by the Church, Protestant missionaries, and various foreign relief agencies in Haiti is that Vodou has been, and continues to be, an obstacle to development in Haiti. See Laënnec Hurbon's critical analysis of this claim in his *Culture et dictature en Haïti: L'imaginaire sous contrôle* (Port-au-Prince: Editions Henri Deschamps, 1987), 20–21.

38. Price argues that such persecution drove the targeted practices underground in a way that was sometimes paradoxically preservative: "the rare *hounfors* which could escape the active surveillance of the police therefore came to be sacro-sanct

places where the proscribed fetishism would be conserved in all its primitive purity." Price, *De la réhabilitation de la race noire par la république d'Haïti*, 442.

39. V. Lizaire, "No. 4044—Circulaire du Secrétaire d'Etat de la Justice et des Cultes aux Commissaires du Gouvernement près les tribunaux civils de la République, relative au Vaudou," reprinted in Peters, *La croix contre l'asson*, 283.

40. Michel Foucault, *Discipline and Punish: The Birth of the Prison*, translated by Alan Sheridan (London: Penguin Books, 1977), 82.

41. Lizaire, "No. 4044—Circulaire," reprinted in Peters, *La croix contre l'asson*, 284.

42. *Les Codes Haïtiens: Code d'instruction criminelle et code pénal*, annotated with annexes by Léon Nau, 322.

43. In so doing, it reprised the late colonial prohibition against slave dances, especially the *calenda*, which were banned not only because they afforded slaves an opportunity to congregate but also because they were believed to camouflage interdicted ritual and magical practices under their cover.

44. Pierre Buteau, "Une Problématique de l'Identité," *Conjonction: Revue Franco-Haïtienne de l'Institut Français d'Haïti* 198 (April-May-June 1993), 21.

45. Or, as Jacques Derrida once enigmatically observed, "the essence of law is not prohibitive but affirmative"; "Force of Law: The 'Mystical Foundation of Authority,'" *Cardozo Law Review* 11, 5–6 (July–August 1990), 929.

46. Derrida theorizes that the signifying power of performatives (such as laws) derives not from an originating intention, but rather from the fact that they can be quoted: that is, from the very property that can potentially destabilize original intention. The "trap" of performative language, as he himself puts it at one point, then ought not be figured as "an abyss situated outside of or in front of itself" but rather as "its internal and positive condition of possibility"; "Signature Event Context," translated by Samuel Weber and Jeffrey Mehlman, in *Limited Inc.*, edited by Gerald Graff (Evanston, Ill.: Northwestern University Press, 1988), 17.

47. See Paul de Man, "Promises (*Social Contract*)," in *Allegories of Reading: Figural Language in Rousseau, Nietzsche, Rilke, and Proust* (New Haven: Yale University Press, 1979), 273. See also Christopher Bracken's discussion of de Man's essay with reference to Canadian laws banning "potlatches" among First Nations peoples in the late nineteenth century: *The Potlatch Papers: A Colonial Case History* (Chicago: University of Chicago Press, 1997), 121–127. My thanks to Jacqueline Shea Murphy for directing me to Bracken's study.

48. St. John, *Hayti*, xii.

49. The expression is attributed to Napoleon III and is featured as an epigraph on St. John's title page: "Haïti, Haïti, pays de barbares." James Anthony Froude, *The English in the West Indies, or, the Bow of Ulysses* (New York: Scribner's, 1892), 344.

50. Joseph-Arthur, comte de Gobineau, "Selections from *The Inequality of Human Races*," in *Contemporary Civilization Reader*, 6th ed. (New York: American Heritage, 1997), 175, their translation.

51. Thus, writes Stephen Bonsal, a New York–based journalist, "the real charge against Haytian civilisation is not that children are frequently stolen from their parents and are often put to death with torture, and subsequently eaten with pomp at a Voodoo ceremony, but that Haytian officials, often the highest in the land, not only

protect the kidnappers, but frequently take part in the cannibalistic rites which they make possible. This is the charge which I bring and which I am prepared to substantiate in every particular upon evidence which appears to me, and to many others to whom I have submitted it, to be absolutely unimpeachable"; *The American Mediterranean* (New York: Moffat, Yard, 1913), 90.

52. J. Michael Dash, *The Other America: Caribbean Literature in a New World Context* (Charlottesville, Va.: University Press of Virginia, 1998), 45. For a synthetic and illuminating analysis of nineteenth-century Haitian social thought, see Patrick Bellegarde-Smith, "Haitian Social Thought in the Nineteenth Century: Class Formation and Westernization," *Caribbean Studies* 20, 1 (March 1980), 5–33.

53. Duverneau Trouillot, *Esquisse ethnographique: Le Vaudoun: Aperçu historique et évolutions* (Port-au-Prince: Imprimerie R. Ethéart, 1885), 28.

54. Mgr. François-Marie Kersuzan, "Lettre Pastorale Pour le Carême, le 6 janvier 1896," reprinted in Peters, *La croix contre l'asson*, 241–242. See also Mgr. Jean Marie Jan, *Collecta III: Pour l'histoire religieuse du diocèse du Cap-Haïtien* (Port-au-Prince: Editions Henri Deschamps, 1958), 49–50.

55. Marc Péan, *L'illusion héroïque: 25 ans de vie capoise, 1890–1915*, vol. 1, *1890–1915* (Port-au-Prince: Imprimerie Henri Deschamps, 1977), 123.

56. *La Croix* figured "vaudoux" and Protestantism as "two enemies of religion and of the country." Mgr. Jean Marie Jan notes: "at the same time as its campaign against superstition, the newspaper led the struggle against Protestants. The sect, very few in number, came to hold important posts in all the administrations and schools. The journal . . . pointed out its combative spirit, its intolerance, and the pernicious influence that it exercised." *Collecta III*, 60.

57. Editorial, May 16, 1896, *La Croix*, quoted in Péan, *L'illusion héroïque*, 124.

58. Quoted in Peters, *La croix contre l'asson*, 246. Sam's predecessor, Florvil Hyppolite, who had died in office, was rumored to have been a frequent patron of the well-known sanctuary Nan-Campèche in Plaine-du-Nord, and, following his death, this affiliation became the subject of veiled denunciations by members of both Catholic and Protestant clergies. Perhaps Sam saw the campaign beginning to mobilize in the North as a means through which to distinguish himself, preemptively, from the stigma attached to his predecessor, and to holders of political power more generally. See Péan, *L'illusion héroïque*, 128.

59. Kersuzan, *Conférence populaire sur le vaudoux*, 13.

60. Kersuzan, *Conférence populaire sur le vaudoux*, 10. Note that the identities of *oungan* and *bòkò* were collapsed in the Church's anti-"vaudoux" campaigns and literature.

61. Kersuzan, *Conférence populaire sur le vaudoux*, 8.

62. Kersuzan, *Conférence populaire sur le vaudoux*, 17.

63. Kersuzan, *Conférence populaire sur le vaudoux*, 22.

64. Jan, *Collecta III*, 60.

65. Péan, *L'illusion héroïque*, 132.

66. *Le Courier du Cap*, June 3, 1896, quoted in Peters, *La croix contre l'asson*, 246.

67. Péan, *L'illusion héroïque*, 133.

68. Quoted in Jan, *Collecta III*, 55.

69. Quoted in Peters, *La croix contre l'asson*, 250.

70. Péan, *L'illusion héroïque*, 134.

71. Péan, *L'illusion héroïque*, 135.

72. Jan, *Collecta III*, 58.

73. Jan, *Collecta III*, 60.

74. Jan, *Collecta III*, 62.

75. Mgr. J. M. Jan, *Monographie religieuse des paroisses du Cap-Haïtien* (Port-au-Prince: Editions Henri Deschamps, 1950), 47.

76. Note that this would have been just prior to the annual feast of Saint-Jacques (Sen Jak), held at Plaine-du-Nord on July 25 and preceded by three days of popular ceremonies in honor of Ogou, drawing pilgrims from near and far. On the contemporary event of this festival, see Donald J. Cosentino, "It's All for You, Sen Jak!" in *Sacred Arts of Haitian Vodou*, edited by Donald J. Cosentino (Los Angeles: Fowler Museum of Cultural History, 1995), 243–246.

77. Jan, *Monographie religieuse des paroisses du Cap-Haïtien*, 49.

78. Jan, *Monographie religieuse des paroisses du Cap-Haïtien*, 53.

79. This case spotlights the extent to which many of these appointees, whether arrondissement commanders or section chiefs, were themselves invested in maintaining the customary status quo vis-à-vis these laws, and not only because they relied on the fees that informal regulation generated to supplement their meager salaries. As Geffrard's hasty reversal in 1864 made clear, the sustained enforcement of these laws against practices that were sanctioned by the vast majority of the population was politically untenable for those who wished to remain in their posts. What is more, most of the members of the local military/police apparatus would themselves have been implicated as practitioners in the continuum of practices that the Church sought to repress.

80. Price, *De la réhabilitation de la race noire par la république d'Haïti*, 163.

10

The Civilization of White Men: The Race of the Hindu in *United States v. Bhagat Singh Thind*

Jennifer Snow

In Portland, Oregon, in 1920, a man stood before the court bench of Judge Wolverton, federal judge of the Ninth Circuit. Portland bustled with the excitement of a new city, an American city, dedicated to progress, wealth, the conquest of nature, the re-creation of what most thought of as the finest civilization on earth. Very few of the good citizens of Portland noticed a dark-skinned foreigner, turban-bound and bearded, entering the courtroom. Probably none of them knew that he had already petitioned to be made an American citizen.

His name was Bhagat Singh Thind. In his petition to the court, his lawyers described him as a "high caste Hindu from the Punjab, of pure Indian blood." These were not his own words. He was not of the "Hindu" religion but a Sikh; he wore his turban as a sign of his religious loyalties. He did not mind, however, being identified as an Indian; born in 1892, in British-ruled, famine-struck, poverty-ridden Punjab, he was proud of his heritage and his homeland. When Indian immigrants to the United States began a revolution in exile to destroy the British rule of India, Thind supported their cause and visited the leaders in jail after they were arrested at the request of the British government.

He had worked in the lumber mills each summer since he had entered the country as a student in 1913, and he had enlisted in the American army during the war and been given an honorable discharge in 1918. His family, decades later, kept a picture of Thind in the army uniform of the World War I, with his long black beard and his white turban. In his brief time in America, he had encapsulated many aspects of the Indian immigrant experience: army service, hard work in the sawmills, railyards, forests, and fields, a university education.[1]

What was citizenship? What did it mean to Bhagat Singh Thind? His later life suggests that he had found a true home in America and had no desire to ever return to India; but citizenship was desirable in itself, and there were good reasons that an Indian immigrant would not want to remain, in the legal sense, an alien. A citizen could not be deported as an "undesirable alien," as had happened to the unfortunate members of the Ghadar Party, a group of Indian immigrants who had agitated and organized for Indian independence. A citizen could own land and real property. California in 1913 had already passed a law denying the right to own property to any "alien ineligible for citizenship"— a category that in practice was largely limited to the "Asiatic," as I will show. A citizen could bring over a wife with little concern for the immigration laws, in defiance of the local animus against "Orientals." He could vote, run for office, sit on juries. A citizen was not a stranger but, legally at least, a member in good standing of an egalitarian, democratic community. In practice, citizenship often meant community membership only in name, but that name meant enough to Bhagat Singh Thind to bring him into federal court.

Citizenship meant protection from other Americans, as well. His fellow laborers, not "Hindoos" but "whites," jealous of their precarious income, hated all "Asiatics." The Indian immigrants working in local sawmills had been attacked by mobs in Bellingham, Washington, in 1907; at Live Oak, California, in 1908; in St. John, Oregon, in 1910. As British nationals, the immigrants had to depend on the intercession of the British government to defend them and make good their claims; that aid was slow in coming, while England spent much energy encouraging the deportation of pro-independence Indians. Becoming an American citizen would give Thind a place to stand against such groups as the Asiatic Exclusion League, which had published pamphlets and harangued politicians on the topic of the dirty, wage-stealing, immoral "Hindoo." Newspaper editors and journalists, primarily from California, Washington, and Oregon, decried the "Hindoo" threat to America's wealth, morals, and civilization, but as an American citizen, Thind could afford to ignore them.[2]

But Thind, like other Asan immigrants, had a problem. According to naturalization statutes in place since 1790, only "free white persons" could become naturalized citizens of the United States. The statute, RS2169, had a long and curious history. Originally specifying only "free white persons" as citizens, Congress included people of "African nativity or descent" after the Civil War. A printing error in 1873 accidentally omitted "white," and some Congressional leaders thought the statute should be kept "white"-free. After rancorous Congressional debate, however, "white" was restored to the statute books, specifically in order to exclude Asian immigrants. At that time Asian immigrants were mostly Chinese, and the Chinese Exclusion Act of 1882 ensured that very few Chinese would apply for citizenship in any case. But in case after case involving Persians, Arabs, Armenians, and Indians, the federal courts had to wrestle with the surprisingly complex question: was a given candidate for citizenship "white?"[3]

Was Bhagat Singh Thind?

His lawyers argued that Thind was, indeed, "white." The best ethnological researchers of the time had declared that the common notion of a "white" race should be defined more scientifically as "Caucasian," a racial group that ethnologists generally agreed included two major subtypes: "Semitic" and "Aryan." "Aryan," in turn, was thought to include not only the peoples of Europe but also some of the peoples of India, and particularly northern India. Relying on such ethnological specialists, Bhagat Singh Thind's lawyers were able to argue that Thind, as a racially "Aryan" northern Indian, was by logical necessity "Caucasian" and therefore "white." Such an argument might be called "genealogical," as it depends on a concept of race as purity of descent, as heredity. And in the case for Bhagat Singh Thind, this purity of descent depended, in turn, on religion—on Thind's supposed "Hindooism" and above all on the caste system, which Thind's lawyers described as a system of marriage laws designed to keep "Aryans" from "mixing" with other races. Strange as this argument may sound today, it was at the time neither new nor unusual. Thind's lawyers did not have to be very creative, nor did Judge Wolverton need to shake his head in incredulity. The genealogical argument for the "whiteness" of "Hindus" had been used repeatedly in citizenship cases—and it had always been successful.[4]

Thind's opponents attacked the credibility of ethnology as "science" but not the syllogism of ethnological whiteness itself. The ethnological equivalency of Aryan, Caucasian, and "white" was well known, and few people argued that "Hindus" were not "Aryan." Instead of trying to undermine this syllogism, the lawyers moved the argument against Thind to another venue entirely. While retaining its racial connotations, the lawyers for the Bureau of Immigration and Naturalization removed "white" from the realm of ethnological inquiry and genealogical reckoning, arguing instead that it denoted a race or racial type that was naturally suited to—and had in fact created—a certain type of "civilization" that had reached its peak in America. "White" people thus became those who could "assimilate" or "amalgamate" with this "civilization"—such assimilability not being decided by empirical investigation but rather by the a priori assumptions of the investigator, whether a muckraking journalist or the chief justice of the Supreme Court.

Bhagat Singh Thind was an intelligent, educated man, and he knew that his chances for citizenship were good; many other Indian immigrants had received it, over the objections of the Bureau of Immigration and Naturalization. Nonetheless, when Judge Wolverton granted his petition and certified him as an American citizen, he surely must have been ecstatic. He left the Portland courtroom no longer an Indian but an American, surrounded by the congratulations of his lawyers, returning to the celebrations of his friends.

Unfortunately for Bhagat Singh Thind, his relief was short-lived. Though no different from the Indian Americans who had gone before, Thind was unlucky enough to become the subject of the test case, the turning point in a long battle over race, religion, and the nature of the American citizen. The Bureau of Immigration and Naturalization challenged the legality of his citizenship, claiming that, despite Judge Wolverton's decision and ethnological authorities, he was not "white." Caucasian or no, he was and would always remain a "Hindoo." And a "Hindoo," the Bureau's lawyers claimed, could never be "white," never a citizen. Thind's citizenship, they argued, was fraudulent and must be revoked.

A few months before his case went before the Supreme Court, another immigrant suing for his citizenship, a Japanese from Hawaii named Takao Ozawa, lost his appeal. His misfortune might have appeared as a good omen to Thind, for the Supreme Court justices wrote in the Ozawa decision that "white" was equivalent to "Caucasian," and since ethnologists agreed that Ozawa was not Caucasian, he could neither be white nor American.[5] The arguments of Thind's lawyers ran along such similar lines that a victory seemed within their grasp. They broke out the big ethnological guns for their brief in Thind's favor, arguing to the point of exhaustion that a "high-caste Hindu" must be of pure Aryan blood, and therefore Caucasian, and therefore "white," and therefore a citizen. Thind, however, was not so sanguine. Not relying solely on his lawyers' arguments, he wrote a petition in his own words to be appended to the brief; he was an educated man, he had bought Liberty bonds, he believed in the Constitution, and if anthropology could carry the day, why, his skin was fair and his skull shaped just as it should be.[6] It did not avail him.

The Supreme Court handed down its decision on February 19, 1923. The opinion, written by Chief Justice Sutherland, himself an English immigrant, was unanimously approved. Thind, as a "Hindoo," might well be Caucasian, noted Sutherland; however, he certainly was not "white," and therefore the Bureau of Immigration and Naturalization was upheld. Thind's citizenship was rescinded as fraudulent; not white, not American.

In this opinion, Sutherland reversed his own recent statement, in the Ozawa case, that white did indeed mean Caucasian. The Thind decision was brief, compressed, even contemptuous in its dismissal of Thind's claims. Sutherland snidely remarked that white people would surely be surprised to discover that their race included such "heterogenous elements," according to foolish ethnologists, as Indians and Arabs. He did insist, as a gesture of magnanimity, that the refusal of citizenship to such people was intended not as a mark of racial inferiority but "merely racial difference, and it is of such character and extent that the great body of our people instinctively recognize it and reject the thought of assimilation."[7]

Bhagat Singh Thind, and his lawyers, were no doubt shocked and dismayed, as well they might be. Why had arguments that had always previously proven themselves in court suddenly been rejected, without even the courtesy of a reasoned-out refutation? Sutherland's written decision simply dismissed the ethnological experts out of hand, refusing to meet the argument as such at all.

Bhagat Singh Thind stood at a turning point in America's history of race relations. Although the Bureau had argued against the granting of citizenship to Indians at least from 1894, when they protested the naturalization of a Parsee in New York City, never before had its lawyers actually followed through on their threats of appealing the decision of a federal judge. Only a few months after his final rejection, with the 1924 passage national quota restrictions of the Johnson-Reed Act, the United States effectively closed the doors to immigration from areas other than the "old" northwest European countries, primarily, and more or less openly, for "racial" reasons. But the arguments that fueled his opponents' rhetoric had a longer history. Thind's lost citizenship can only be comprehended by examining the deep layers of discourse that underlay the compressed illogic of Justice Sutherland's opinion, a discourse on the meaning of "white person" and "white civilization," the racial nature of "Hindoo," the racial connotations of religion, and the religious connotations of race.

We can begin to understand Thind and his history by, for a moment, taking literally the academic idea of "discourse," as a conversation a society has with itself, about itself. A conversation such as this takes place on a scale greater than a single author or speaker. The particular conversation relevant to the Bhagat Singh Thind decision, for instance, could be traced through time for almost a century, and through space covering all of the United States, Britain, Europe, and India. Thousands of individual contributors added their ideas to the great discussion, hanging their ideas on those that had come before, creating what the literary theorist Mikhail Bakhtin has called "dialogized heteroglossia," a discursive situation where any word spoken cannot avoid awakening the echoes of previous words, ideas, and statements in the delicate, complex, and immense web of social conversation, "brushing up against thousands of living dialogic threads woven by socio-ideological consciousness."[8] Thind's lawyers, and the lawyers for the United States, skillfully played on this echoing web, choosing deeply resonant words to support their claims about the race and religion of Bhagat Singh Thind—"Hindu," "civilization," "American," "white," "citizen."

All legal decisions are the historical residue of complex conversations. In fact, our legal system as such is nothing more than the record of opinions rendered by judges of the truth or falsity of other peoples' stories. Precedent, the recorded opinions of the judges of the past, sets the parameters for all future decisions; but precedents can be broken, or overturned, or ignored, and then the conversation takes a new turn. Bhagat Singh Thind and his lawyers relied on precedent in their petition for citizenship. Many courts had already heard stories very similar to Thind's and had rendered favorable decisions. The Supreme Court was not and is not bound to respect the precedents of lower courts, but what is striking about the Bhagat Singh Thind opinion is the lack even of citations for the precedents being overturned, the arguments that had been acceptable to the lower courts. The written decision of Justice Sutherland silenced the long and vigorous social conversation about race, religion, and citizenship by affirming, and endorsing, only one side of it; it is an attempt to muffle the echoes of the great web. Only by carefully listening to all the ringing overtones, however, can we truly unravel the misfortune of Bhagat Singh Thind.

Genealogical Whiteness

> Being a high caste Indian and having no intermixture of Dravidian, or other alien blood, and coming from the Punjab, one of the most northwestern provinces of India, the original home of the Aryan conquerors, unless all the historical, ethnological and philological authorities cited in this brief are disregarded it must be held that Bhagat Singh Thind belongs to the Caucasian or white race.[9]
>
> —*United States v. Bhagat Singh Thind,*
> Brief for Bhagat Singh Thind

The case for Bhagat Singh Thind's whiteness, as laid out by his lawyers, reflected both a venerable legal tradition and Euro-American scholarly conceptions of Hinduism. For the lawyers of Bhagat Singh Thind, and for the American legal practice at large, "white" had been roughly defined as "Caucasian" for over half a century.[10] This was largely set up as an exclusivist category, for "Mongolians" such as the Chinese, and later Japanese, Koreans, and Southeast Asians, were thus cut out from citizenship. Yet equating "white" with "Caucasian" had two unintended effects.

First, for legal purposes, "race" was removed from popular conceptions in favor of newly minted academic ethnological precision. Impressionistic or visual ideas of "whiteness" were disallowed by the courts, replaced by strict definitions of genealogical purity. Authority for pronouncing on this purity of race now lay in the hands of a new kind of academic: the ethnologist, anthropologist, or anthropometrist. Second, this system of genealogical race-identification allowed many individuals to become citizens whom popular opinion would never have acknowledged as white. Beginning with a Parsee in 1894, the federal courts, over the objections of the Bureau of Immigration, naturalized Armenians, Arabs, Syrians, Afghans, Persians, and "Hindus" or East Indians, on the basis of ethnological works that, via the claim of "Aryan" ancestry, placed all these in the "Caucasian" fold.[11]

In what is surely one of the great ironies of ideological history, the concept of an "Aryan race" had its origin in a perception of racial kinship and a desire for closer, more respectful relations between what today's racial categorizations would identify as "white" and "nonwhite" peoples. Friedrich Max Müller, the famous nineteenth-century linguist and Vedic scholar, wanted "Aryan," a term for the family to which most European and Indian languages belonged, to signify the kinship of the British rulers and the Indian ruled, between European and Indian civilizations. In a notorious and controversial statement, cited by Bhagat Singh Thind's lawyers, he dared to argue that the same blood ran in the veins of the "dark Bengalese" and the English soldier; that in fact "there is not an English jury nowadays, which, after examining the hoary documents of language, would reject the claim of common descent and legitimate relationship between Hindu, Greek, and Teuton."[12] Thomas Trautmann has demonstrated how, as the British Empire grew and metaphors of domination became more central to racial discourse, "Aryan," much to Max Müller's dismay, came to signify instead a very small and racially "pure" group of people who were responsible for civilizing most of the world and teaching their Aryan tongue to non-Aryans. Such a relational idiom was much more suitable to an imperial age.[13]

For Bhagat Singh Thind, Aryan-justified citizenship depended on American perceptions of his "Hindu" religion. As a "high-caste Hindu from the Punjab," his claim to Caucasian blood was fortified by longstanding academic and popular understanding of the racial and religious history of India. According to this theory, India had been shaped by the conflicts between two races, the superior, fair-skinned "Aryans" who had invaded India millennia before, and the indigenous "Dravidians," an inferior, dark-skinned race. As Bhagat Singh Thind's lawyers put it, quoting an eminent European authority, "the Aryans spread themselves over the Punjab (home of Bhagat Singh Thind) and the plain of the Ganges at the expense of a barbarian aboriginal population, which they excelled in mental endowments and physical beauty."[14]

Many American authors, both for and against the idea of kinship with the Indian, used the Aryan theory in terms indicating that it was a tidbit of knowledge slightly less than common—something identifying the writer as an "expert," something to be shown off—but nonetheless far from esoteric or obscure. Even a yellow journalist could display his knowledge in this fashion, acknowledging that the turbaned menace is of the same "ancient Aryan stock" as "that of the land it threatens," while a more sympathetic author of a missionary bent wrote: "some authorities hold that the Hindu and the American both belong to the Aryan race, and that whether we like it or not, these Hindus are bone of our bone. Our speech bewrayeth [sic] us, according to the philologists. . . . The Hindu is not a Mongolian, but our long-lost brother."[15]

These Aryans, again according to scholarly consensus, attempted to keep their race pure through the religious practice of caste distinctions, identified by the same experts as the very essence of Hinduism and India itself. In ethnological shorthand, if Bhagat Singh Thind was a "high-caste Hindu" from northern India, then he was an Aryan, whose blood had been kept pure by caste, therefore Caucasian, therefore "white," and therefore entitled to American citizenship. Bhagat Singh Thind's entire legal defense was predicated on this simple yet deeply problematic syllogism. While this argument rests on a definition of "whiteness" as genealogical racial purity, this purity itself is constituted as an effect of religion. The "white" blood of Bhagat Singh Thind and other Asian Indian immigrants could, in this view, be traced back to the Aryan invaders of ancient India, but only insofar as such race purity had been guarded by Hindu caste laws.

European and American observers were fascinated by India's "castes," which they saw as the eternal, unchanging heart of Indian society and which they simultaneously blamed for India's supposed supinity before conquest, "female" irrationality, political ineptitude, and economic impoverishment. Yet "caste" was more than an excuse for British administration of India, more even than a perverted social order that English administrators, over the generations, would somehow dismantle. "Caste" reflected darkly imperialist concerns about racial purity and racial destiny, for Europeans and Americans alike saw "caste" as the result of racial conflict.[16]

Thind's lawyers paraphrased the famous "Institutes of Manu," believed by Euro-American scholars to be among the oldest religious texts in the world, to explain Hinduism to the Supreme Court:

> The institutes of Manu declare that Brahma created the four great
> castes of India—the Brahman, the Kshatriya, the Vaieya [sic] and the
> Sudra. These were briefly the priests, the warriors and gentle folk,
> the traders and servile classes of human society. It was most repre-
> hensible for one of a higher caste to marry one of a lower caste. . . .
> It is obvious from this caste system prevailing in India that there
> was comparatively a small mixture of blood between the different
> castes. . . . This caste system has proven a most effective barrier to
> prevent a mixture of the Aryan with the dark races of India.[17]

Their logical slip from religious law to miscegenation law reflected the opinions of the greatest Orientalists of the age, many of whom had studied Hinduism and caste in India as officials of the British Raj. The "real" reason for caste, the colonial official H. H. Risley argued, was not religious; such explanations were mere "pious fictions" after the fact. Caste was the result of the "natural" desire of the Aryan invaders to protect their purity of blood, through sanctions on intermarriage with the "inferior" race they had conquered. In fact, Risley wrote,

> the principle upon which the system rests is the sense of the distinctions of race indicated by differences in color: a sense which, while too weak to preclude the men of the dominant race from intercourse with the women whom they have captured, is still strong enough to make it out of the question that they should admit the men whom they have conquered to equal rights in the question of marriage.[18]

Similarly, the 1911 *Encyclopedia Britannica* (in its article on "Hinduism") told readers that "when the fair-coloured Aryan immigrants first came into contact with, and drove back or subdued the dark-skinned race . . . the preservation of their racial type and traditionary order of things would naturally become to them a matter of serious concern."[19]

Thind's own lawyers identified him as a Sikh, "that being the religion of the inhabitants of the Punjab." Since one of the tenets of Sikhism—theoretically, at least—is the denial of caste strictures, it seems peculiar that his lawyers would voluntarily identify him as such alongside their claims that he was a "high-caste Hindu." Even more peculiar, both Thind's lawyers and the lawyers for the United States cited a 1913 citizenship case in which the Indian immigrant, Akhay Kumar Mozoomdar, told the court flatly, "The great bulk of the Hindus in this country are not high-caste Hindus, but are what are called sihks [*sic*], and are of mixed blood."[20] Though Sikhism might well have undermined Thind's claim to Aryan purity, no one seemed to notice.

In ignoring Thind's acknowledged religious affiliation, the lawyers on both sides of case simply replicated general American indifference to distinctions between Indian religions, despite efforts of Indian immigrants and the occasional American journalist to inform American readers about the variety of Indian life and cultures—Muslim, Hindu, Sikh, Jain, Christian, and the diverse groups within and between traditions. Indian immigrant journalist Sant Nihal Singh noted wryly that, to Americans, "everyone that hails from Hindostan is a 'Hindoo.' " In America, Indian meant Hindu, and Hindu meant caste.[21]

Scholars wrote of a "race instinct" or "caste instinct" as something inborn in humanity, which miscegenation laws, religious or secular, simply codified and made explicit. British scholars pointed to the situation of the American Negro after Emancipation as evidence for the "naturalness" of "race-feeling": though the African American was now a citizen, miscegenation laws continued to exist, and white Americans continued to try to keep themselves separate from black Americans. The only problem with the Indian attempt to channel this "natural" instinct, as Orientalists saw it, was that it hadn't been completely successful, and Aryan purity had declined with the ages.[22]

Yet, while vocal segments of American society were deeply concerned with "eugenics" and the preservation of the Anglo-Saxon race, Americans in general were less worried about purity of blood than the British scholars who informed them about India and the Aryans. The concept of "whiteness" as pure genealogy was less popular, in America, than another, more subtle form of "whiteness," which Thind's opponents called on to defeat his bid for citizenship.

Assimilative Whiteness

> If [the Founders] meant to include only men of the white races, does it follow that they intended to include all who could possibly be classed by ethnologists as white? We think not. The words "free white person" meant to them men representative of a composite type, a combination of color, race, and social institutions, with which they were familiar, men who collectively had developed and were maintaining a civilization of which they themselves were a part, the civilization of white men.[23]
>
> —*United States v. Bhagat Singh Thind,*
> Brief for the United States

The strategy of the United States in stripping Thind of his American citizenship along with his "whiteness" did not consist of a direct response to the traditionally successful claims of Aryan blood. As noted earlier, American writers both academic and nonacademic, both for and against "Hindu" naturalization, accepted as valid the "Aryan" status of "high-caste Hindus." The attack on the "whiteness" of Bhagat Singh Thind instead appealed to a different complex of scholarly and popular beliefs, still centered, as was the Aryan theory, on the meaning of caste and the racial nature of Hinduism as a religious system.

The case against Thind depended on a much more vaguely bounded concept of "whiteness," signaled by the term "assimilation." The lawyers for the United States attacked Thind's "assimilability" by defining caste, and Hinduism as a whole, as an alienating and barbaric social and religious system, one that rendered "Hindus" utterly unfit for membership in the "civilization of white men." The idea of the "caste mentality" was an important part of American anti-Indian racism. "Hinduism" itself appeared as an insinuating, degrading influence, as represented in travel writings, missionary works, and scholarly monographs.

The United States brief includes no citations from ethnological authorities but rather a single extended quotation from Edmund Burke, the British opponent of the East India Company in the 1790s, when the American Naturalization Statute was written. This long quotation, running to almost four pages of a twenty-two-page brief, defines caste as that which eternally separates the

English and the Indian. Burke describes details such as loss of caste, eating and marriage rules, and the "four orders" (as understood by eighteenth-century English scholars). Caste, according to Burke, is "his all" to the Indian, symbolizing "a great gulf fixed between you and them . . . that gulf which manners, opinions, and laws have radicated in the very nature of the people." The quotation, according to the lawyers for the United States, proved decisively that at the time that the Naturalization Statute was written even "friends of the Indian" did not consider them capable of joining with Europeans in social or political fellowship. The words of Edmund Burke "show that at the time the first naturalization law was passed the Hindus were regarded as a people utterly alien to Western civilization and utterly incapable of assimilation to Western habits and customs, mode of life, political and social institutions."[24] Though Burke had taken caste to demonstrate the self-sufficiency of Indian society and its natural antagonism toward English colonial administration, in the service of "white civilization" caste became a symbol of the impoverishment of the Hindu soul and the degeneration of the Hindu race, its complete lack of sympathy with the rest of humanity.

The eloquent rhetoric of the United States lawyers called on the nature of "whiteness" as symbolic of a form or type of civilization and morality deeply inimical to the Indian, or Hindu, mind. "Whiteness," they argued, is

> inclusive only of such men described by the adjective "white" as belonged to the civilization known as the white civilization . . . that which had been developed by the races of white men and differed from the civilization of Asia in almost every distinguishing peculiarity. The white races had put their brand upon organized social and political life, and the social and political life, in turn, had put its assimilating mark upon all who had come within its influence.[25]

In such statements, "race," "religion," and "civilization" become intertwined beyond any hope of disentanglement; each category is the basis and defining characteristic of the other. Nor was this categorical confusion—as it appears to us today—the result of unusually poor logic on the part of the United States lawyers, for a clear analytical separation between "race," "religion," and "civilization" is a relatively recent American development. Most Americans of the time would have heard such statements as perfectly sensible and well grounded in "fact." Longstanding links between race and religion in American thought were made explicit in 1875, with the publication of the first truly popular book on comparative religion in America. Extremely influential through the end of the century and beyond, James Freeman Clarke's *Ten Great Religions* oriented the reader with the statement that "each race, beside its special moral qualities, seems also to have special religious qualities, which, cause it to tend toward some one kind of religion more than to another kind. These religions are the flower of the race."[26] The connection between "Oriental" religion and the "Oriental mind" was taken for granted by almost all writers on Asian religions, regardless of how they conceived the connection. A popular series of books by Percival Lowell, for instance, used "Oriental religions" (generally referred to impressionistically) as evidence for his claim that "Orientals" lacked a sense of individuality.[27]

In tying Hindu to caste, more specifically, the lawyers for the United States made strategic use of the echoes set up by "caste" itself, negative ideas about caste practices that were well established in scholarship alongside the ideal of caste as preserver of race purity. Despite the "naturalness" of caste as an expression of the race-purity instinct, scholarly experts on India and Indians were unwilling to give Indians credit for creating an institution of which they themselves approved. Instead, European scholars argued that Indians, as was their wont, had taken a good idea too far. Risley, for instance, wrote that the "caste instinct must have been greatly promoted and stimulated by certain characteristics of the Indian intellect—its lax hold of facts, its indifference to action, its absorption in dreams, its exaggerated reverence for tradition, its passion for endless division."[28] Maurice Bloomfield, a premier American Orientalist, wrote of caste as a "black cloud" hovering over India, whose "grotesque inconsistencies and bitter tyranny have gone far to make the Hindu what he is."[29]

The missionary bishop J. M. Thoburn, after listing the many positive attributes of the Indian people, wrote sadly that nevertheless "they bear many of the marks which always accompany a religion which denies the immediate authority of God." Polygamy, child marriage, the abuse of widows, and the rest of the usual suspects exemplify the "spirit of Hinduism," and Thoburn added that "no man can be, in the best sense of the word, a man . . . unless he can be induced to trample on the system of caste."[30]

Many travelers, scholars, and missionaries argued that the poverty, disease, and immorality of Indian life were entirely the result of Hinduism—not the "philosophical" Hinduism beloved of American transcendentalists but the "popular" Hinduism of the great mass of the Indian people. Bloomfield told his American audience that

> the dreadful institution of Suttee . . . the car of Juggernaut; the sect
> of the Thugs; and the practice of self-hypnosis to the point of pro-
> longed trance or apparent death, are evidences of the frenzying qual-
> ity of Hindu religion, and the way it has of overshadowing individ-
> ual sanity and public interest.[31]

These words, written in 1908, reflect a fascination with the sensational aspects of Hinduism, as these were reported by missionaries and British colonial officials, rather than any fundamental reality of Indian religious life. That they could be written by a successful professor of Vedic studies at Johns Hopkins

University shows how deeply such ideas had become ingrained in American thought.

Not everyone agreed, of course. A minority tradition in American intellectual life celebrated the possibilities of "Hindu" philosophies and other "Eastern" or "Oriental" traditions. Swami Vivekananda, a speaker at the 1893 World Parliament of Religions in Chicago, taught American inquirers yoga and Vedanta. More creative religious work by Americans interested in India led to the foundation of the Theosophical Society. These developments, however, were very much the province of a sensational minority. Most Americans were far more familiar with the predominantly missionary-informed picture of Hinduism which historian Carl Jackson calls the "black legend." In this vision of Hinduism, Indians became almost inhuman–sensual, irrational beings who reveled in cruelty and sacrificed children and women to custom, caste, and deity. American readers thrilled to descriptions of Hindu "fakirs" entering trances where they would endure all sorts of pain and torture unflinchingly: the bed of nails, of course, but also "hook-swinging," where devotees inserted large hooks into their flesh and swung from poles to demonstrate their transcendence of pain. Such grotesqueries, readers were assured, were typical of India; similarities to extreme Christian ascetic practices were never mentioned. The "car of Juggernaut" was a sensationalist trope on the festival of Jagannath, where the deity was drawn through thick crowds in the street on an immense cart. It sometimes happened that observers were trampled or injured in the press of hundreds of thousands of pilgrims. From the early nineteenth century on, however, Americans read missionary accounts of devotees deliberately throwing themselves under the cart, to be crushed to death in their misguided fanaticism. Missionaries would flock to the annual festival in Orissa in the hopes of seeing this bloodthirsty pageant enacted. The most reviled practice, perhaps even more so than caste distinctions, was the immolation of widows, or sati. The image of the burning child-wife made excellent press and was probably the single most cited justification for British rule of India. The fact that sati had been illegal for over fifty years did not stop any American writer in the early twentieth century from describing it in lurid detail, as the summa of Hinduism's destruction of all natural human moral sense.[32]

Indeed, according to such writers, the morals of "heathens" were low in all areas of family life: polygamy, child and arranged marriage, abuse of widows, slavery, drunkenness, adultery and sensuality, even feeding one's children to the Ganges crocodiles were all laid at the door of Hinduism. As one longtime missionary put it, "the mere mention of [child marriage] is sufficient to show that a non-Christian country has a conscience that is neither quick nor tender."[33] Arley Munson, a missionary doctor relatively sympathetic to India and Indians, was called to her vocation by the sight, as a child, of a missionary book showing a Hindu mother throwing her baby to the crocodiles as a sacrifice, and despite her generally mild tone she manages to touch on nearly all the list of supposed Hindu inhumanities in her book, describing in gory detail animal sacrifices and the use of children as "demon priests" in horrible rituals.[34]

The same scholars who described caste as both the heart of Hinduism and the source of all India's woes simultaneously emphasized the inefficacy of caste as a preserver of race. Without explicitly saying that such and such a group was of "pure" or "mixed" blood, with the "precision" of the anthropometrist, Orientalists pointed to entire social and religious life of India as emblematic of the evils of "race mixing." Indian society, with Hinduism itself, was thus the result of the intermingling of the superior Aryans and the inferior Dravidians. Isaac Taylor, an English popularizer of Aryan theories, described the process with his usual fertile metaphors: "the purity of the race was soiled by marriage with native women, the language was infected with peculiar Dravidian sounds, and the creed with foul Dravidian worships of Siva and Kali, and the worship of the lingam and the snake."[35] The 1911 *Encyclopedia Britannica*, less florid but more authoritative, referred to the "religious practices of the lower race" as gradually affecting the upper strata of society, including "grossly idolatrous practices" that demonstrate the "racial characteristics of the people."[36]

Evangelical Christians rarely resorted to racial characterizations of the Indian people, for their missionary work depended on the notion that, while the Hindu religion was degraded and degrading, the Indian people were capable of living good "Christian" lives. Bishop Thoburn, for instance, wrote that while "inventive genius" is not notable in India, "it may be assumed that when India becomes a Christian country her people will no longer be found apparently destitute of this important gift."[37] Writers freed from the bonds of Christian charity were often more contemptuous and more ready to blame race, as well as religion, for Indian shortcomings. The travel writer Michael Shoemaker had no shortage of insulting remarks about Hinduism, often focused on the filth and superstition of the practitioners; "it is singular," he wrote, "that the temples and holy places of a religion which uses flowers so freely in its worship should smell and be so vile . . . this spot is the resort of pilgrims and stinketh accordingly." However, he did not believe that Christianity could rescue the Indian population from ignorance and unsanitary living, for he clearly considered the Indian people racially deficient, repeatedly describing them as "rats" and "snakes"; when faced with a "converted" Hindu, he noted that he was still naked and poor, and he agreed with the "boy's" English employer that "these boys can live on the smell of a greased rag."[38]

Thus the United States could write that Bhagat Singh Thind was completely inassimilable to American life, and hence neither white nor eligible for citizenship, by claiming that he represented, or rather embodied inescapably, the moral and racial life of a civilization antithetical to that of "white men."

They offered no proof of this relevant to Bhagat Singh Thind as an individual, but were able to awaken the echoes of the discursive web of race and religion with a few well-chosen sentences about "white civilization," the alien civilization of the Hindu, and "assimilation." The words written by a lawyer arguing before the Supreme Court were little different from and no more supported by fact than the sentiments of the Asiatic Exclusion League:

> the color of the Hindoo, as of the Chinaman, is in itself immaterial. As a mark, however, of a people who are wholly different, if not in origin at least in their political and moral ideals, their age-long training, and their form of government, social, religious, and political, it is conspicuous and shows them to be so diverse from white people or Occidentals as to make it no less a risk to admit them to citizenship than it would be to confessedly admit Chinese, Japanese, Malays, and others, as to whom it is by general consent believed that the doors to naturalization should be closed.[39]

Or, as a California paper put it in an editorial on Indian immigrants buying land, "the laws of their mind, the laws of their civilization, the laws of Nature and physiology, render the thought of amalgamation an impossible one."[40]

Conclusion

In the unanimous decision stripping Bhagat Singh Thind of his American citizenship, the Supreme Court declared that the words "free white persons" in RS 2169 connoted a racial test for citizenship but specified that

> the term "race" is one which, for the practical purposes of the statute, must be applied to a group of living persons now possessing in common the requisite characteristics, not to groups of persons who are supposed to be or really are descended from some remote, common ancestor, but who, whether they both resemble him to a greater or less extent, have, at any rate, ceased altogether to resemble one another.[41]

What were these "requisite characteristics?" Apparently, no more and no less than "resembling" white people—not in terms of skin color, for the Supreme Court noted that dark-skinned Europeans are "white," but in some other, poorly specified sense. Justice Sutherland decisively rejected the genealogical definition of "white" (though he couldn't resist simultaneously joining the chorus on race-mixing by saying that caste had not kept the Dravidians and Aryans apart effectively, anyway). The new criteria of "assimilability," however, remained vague and subjective.

Children of European immigrants, according to the opinion of the Court, "merge into the rest of our population and lose the distinctive hallmarks of their European origin." Such immigrants, and no others, qualified to the Founding Fathers as "bone of their bone and flesh of their flesh," and this was as much detail about assimilation as the Court was willing to venture.[42] More specific, though still less than concrete, is the effort of the Asiatic Exclusion League to discredit the assimilability of Hindus and their Asiatic kin, whose

> idea of life, liberty and pursuit of happiness is different from ours.
> Their habits and customs, their morals and domestic economy are
> different from ours. . . . If the surplus millions of the teeming
> hordes of India, China and Japan were permitted to immigrate to
> the United States, they would soon outnumber and dominate our
> present population, subvert our form of government, degrade our
> standard of living and substitute the semi-barbarous heathen civili-
> zation of Shintoism and Brahma, Buddha and Confucious, for our
> Christian civilization.[43]

Those who argued for the inclusion of Indian immigrants in the American polity, many of whom were missionaries, nevertheless agreed that the standard of citizenship must be assimilability. The sole difference between the anti-immigrant and the pro-immigrant stance on this point was that the inclusivists wanted to judge assimilability on an individual rather than group basis. The basic principle argued for in these more liberal formulations was that "America shall admit only so many immigrants from any particular people as she can genuinely Americanize."[44] For these pro-immigrant activists, "whiteness," in the form of "the civilization of white men," can (and should) be acquired by the diligent of all skin colors.

The widespread acceptance of such a poorly articulated standard of "white-ness" as "assimilability" explains the reference to the shadowy "common man" who appears as the arbiter of racial standards in the final decision of the Supreme Court. The decision, highly compressed and somewhat confusing on the first (and even second and third) reading, makes sense only when the background of American discourse on race and religion becomes clear. In brief: European immigrants who are nonetheless "swarthy" may be included in the category "white," for they are members of "white civilization" who will "readily amalgamate" with the "white population," while the dark skin of Indian immigrants acts as "physical evidence" of their nonwhiteness, for the Hindu is not assimilable with "white civilization."[45]

Yet even in this broader discursive context, the equation of whiteness with assimilablility rests on an oddly circular argument, for it makes "race" a property of the racializing society itself rather than a property of racialized individuals. In the genealogical concept of "whiteness," race inheres in an individual, whether symbolized by skin color or decreed by an ethnologist. In the assimilable concept of whiteness, race becomes a quality granted by an unknown observer. It is, in effect, alienated from the person being seen. Circularity ensues when assimilability is defined as not being noticed, not needing segregated schools, not being barred from marriage with white women—as becoming similar, even identical, to "white people," who themselves have been granted that status by others. Thus the *Dictionary of Races,* created for the Senate in 1910 by the Dillingham Commission on Immigration, begins its entry on "the Caucasian or white race" rather confusedly, as "all races which, although dark in color or aberrant in other directions, are, when considered from all points of view, felt to be more like the white race than like any of the four other races."[46]

The co-constitution of race and religion in the American concept of "Hinduism" played its part in such distinctions. The hostility of the Bureau of Immigration and "white" Americans toward "Hindus" was founded on popular ideas of the dangerous alien qualities, the unassimilability, of the "Hindu" race in particular and "Oriental" races in general, an alienness symbolized by and symbolizing their religions. As the lawyers for the United States put it to the Supreme Court,

> it could never have been contemplated . . . that naturalization should be thrown open to the teeming millions of Asia, subject only to the presentation of a certificate by some student of ethnology to the effect that the particular applicant, whatever might be his customs, religion, habits of thought, language, could probably trace his ancestry back through thousands of years to membership in the race.[47]

From the point of view of the exclusivists, the defeat of the ethnological experts meant that the dangers of a battle of civilizations had been averted, the unassimilable alien finally defeated.

One of the most striking aspects of the race-religion equation was the collapse, in the popular mind, of all Asian religions into one racial "civilization" that was "inherently inimical to ours," in the words of a California newspaper editor.[48] Bhagat Singh Thind, like almost all of the East Indian immigrants of his time, was a Sikh; indeed, the mark of Sikh religious commitment, the turban, was so universal among Indians that the derogatory term for them was "rag-head." Yet no one listened to Thind when he said that he was a Sikh or to other Indian immigrants who insisted on the uniqueness of their religions in the face of American indifference and ignorance. All Indians were "Hindoos," with all the accompanying ideological baggage of caste and heathenism, regardless of whether they were orthodox Hindus, Brahmo Samaj members, Parsees, Sikhs, Muslims, Christians, or, like many Indians prior to British census categories, unconvinced of the reality of such religious boundaries.[49] Recently, this American habit of thought has contributed to the tragedy of violence against Sikhs misidentified as Muslims in the wake of September 11, 2001—and, of course, against all Muslims or vaguely "Middle Eastern" people, popularly associated with violent fundamentalism.

Ironically, those missionary and travel writers who did acknowledge the existence of Sikhs and Sikhism created an alternative discourse emphasizing the similarities between Sikhism and Protestantism. Early missionaries considered Sikhism a great improvement upon both Islam and Hinduism and hoped that it would prove a conduit for civilization and Christianity in India. It was generally described approvingly as a "Protestant" movement, one that dispensed with idols and unnecessary pageantry, denied caste, and worshiped the One God. Even Indian writers in America went this route, linking Guru Nanak with Luther and using phrases such as "the Brotherhood of Man" to make his teachings more familiar. Had anyone taken Thind's Sikh identity to heart, a different argument could have been made on his behalf, emphasizing not the genealogical whiteness of Hindu caste but the "Protestant" nature of the Sikhism and the demonstrated amenability of Sikhs to "white civilization." No one ever attempted citizenship in this fashion—though, given the evident American animus against "Asiatics," it would have been unlikely to succeed.[50]

The trial and defeat of Bhagat Singh Thind had serious consequences for Indian immigrants in America. California newspapers were gleeful; along with the Alien Land Law, which denied noncitizens the right to own real estate, a Supreme Court ruling keeping "Asiatics" as permanent noncitizens would surely "save California for the white race."[51] Indeed, following the 1924 passage of the Johnson-Reed Act, which set restrictive quotas for southern and eastern European immigration and completely barred it from Asia and India, immigration from the Punjab slowed to an illegal trickle from Mexico.[52] The United States government, armed with the Supreme Court decision against Thind, began a crusade to rescind citizenship from "fraudulent" whites. Most of these cases, directed against Armenians, Arabs, Afghans, and "Hindus," succeeded. At least one East Indian immigrant, a successful California merchant, committed suicide on being stripped of his citizenship. Despite the efforts of himself and his family to "Americanize," Vaishno Das Bagai wrote in a suicide letter, published in the *San Francisco Examiner,* they now were adrift without a country, unable either to return to India or become Americans.[53]

Bhagat Singh Thind's ending was happier. Though he could not become a citizen, he was still a legal resident and could not be deported. He married an Anglo-American woman, received a doctorate in the biological sciences, and became what today might be called a "New Age" author, writing books on the essential unity of all religions and giving well-attended lectures on spiritual truth. His success in the religious field was aided by yet another aspect of the race-religion equation. His provenance as a Sikh, his "exoticism" and dark skin, would have, in the minds of some, symbolized his religious integrity, his spiritual wisdom. This aspect of American visions of "Hinduism" has not been investigated here, for it played no part in Bhagat Singh Thind's case before the Supreme Court, but it did have an important role in his later life and in the lives of other Indian immigrants. Indeed, despite the claims of the Asiatic Exclusion League, Bhagat Singh Thind was highly assimilable; a place had been prepared for him in American society, two generations at least in the making. The vision of "Hinduism" as wisdom from the mystic East, brought by the brown for the enlightenment of the spiritually empty white, had a long history of its own in America. Yet it, too, was a co-constitution of race and religion; it too essentialized differences between the brown and the white and placed the heart of these differences in religion.[54] The supposedly eternal and unequal opposition of the two types of humanity is made manifest by Arley Munson, the gentle missionary Doctor-Sahib, who wrote of her beloved charges that

> if you will imagine the exact opposite of a typical American of the United States, you will have the East Indian as he appeared to me. The more I saw of India, the more I was convinced that

> "East is East and West is West, and never the twain shall meet,
> Till Earth and Sky stand presently at God's great Judgment Seat."

> Fortunately for us and for them, we do not expect them to become like us in the unimportant details. We do, however, want them to be not beasts of the field, but men.[55]

These inseparable links between race and religion were inescapable in the America of Bhagat Singh Thind—tying "whiteness" to rationalist Christianity and "nonwhiteness" to heathen imagination and emotion, or else to spiritual wisdom transcending rationality. Thind, like everyone else, had to find his way around it, and use it to his advantage when he could, as he attempted to do before the Supreme Court and later succeeded in doing with his series of books on spiritual truth. These links are no less prevalent, though perhaps more subtle, in America today. The complex iteration of religion and race continues to shape the lives of immigrants and the ideals of American citizenship.

NOTES

1. "Roots in the Sand," www.pbs.org/rootsinthesand/I_bhagatı.html (April 2001). This website and the film on which it is based is an excellent resource on early Indian immigration and ethnicity.

2. "Mob Drives Out Hindus," *New York Times*, September 6, 1907, 1; Rajani Kanta Das, *Hindustani Workers on the Pacific Coast* (Berlin: de Gruyter, 1923), 11; Joan M. Jensen, *Passage from India: Asian Indian Immigrants in North America* (New Haven: Yale University Press, 1988).

3. Revised Statutes, Title XXX, "Naturalization," Sec. 2169: "the provisions of this Title shall apply to aliens being free white persons." For further discussion of RS 2169 in court cases, see Ian Haney-Lopez, *White By Law: The Legal Construction of*

Race (New York: New York University Press, 1996). Chinese immigrants actually challenged their exclusion frequently in the federal courts as well, as chronicled by Lucy Salyer, *Laws Harsh as Tigers: Chinese Immigrants and the Shaping of Modern Immigration Law* (Chapel Hill: University of North Carolina Press, 1995).

4. Some precedents include *In re Balsara*, 171 F. 294; *In re Mudarri*, 176 F. 465; *In re Akhay Kumar Mozumdar*, 207 F. 115; *Dow v. United States*, 226 F. 146; *In re Mohan Singh*, 257 F. 209; *In re Najour*, 174 F. 735. Legal cases are collected in volumes according to the court that heard them and identified by their volume, series, and first page number. Most naturalization cases were heard by federal circuit courts and thus are collected in the *Federal Reporter* (F in these citations); Supreme Court cases are collected in three reporter series; and frequently all three are cited at once. The *In re* specification defines the case as "nonadversarial," supposedly undertaken for the good of the person named; when such cases are appealed, they become "adversarial" in nature and gain a *versus* in the title.

5. *Ozawa v. United States*, 260 U.S. 178, 43 Sup. Ct. 65.

6. *United States v. Bhagat Singh Thind*, 261 U.S. 204, 43 Sup. Ct. 338, Appellee's Brief, Appendix to Appellee's Brief.

7. *United States v. Bhagat Singh Thind*, 261 U.S. 211, 215.

8. M. M. Bakhtin, *The Dialogic Imagination: Four Essays by M. M. Bakhtin*, edited by Michael Holquist, translated by Caryl Emerson and Michael Holquist (Austin: University of Texas Press, 1981), 276.

9. *United States v. Bhagat Singh Thind*, 261 U.S. 204 Appellee's Brief, 28.

10. *In re Ah Yup*, 5 Sawy 157, Fed Cas No. 104; *In re San C. Po*, 28 N.Y. Sup. 883; *In re Halladjian*, 174 F. 834.

11. *In re Balsara*, 171 F. 294; *In re Mudarri*, 176 F. 465; *In re Akhay Kumar Mozumdar*, 207 F. 115; *Dow v. United States*, 226 F. 146; *In re Mohan Singh*, 257 F. 209; *In re Najour*, 174 F. 735

12. Friedrich Max Müller, quoted in *U.S. v. Bhagat Singh Thind*, 261 U.S. 204 Appellee's Brief, 11.

13. Thomas R. Trautmann, *Aryans and British India* (Berkeley: University of California Press, 1997).

14. Peschel, *Races of Men* (Leipzig: 1874), quoted in *United States v. Bhagat Singh Thind*, 261 U.S. 204 Appellee's Brief, 14.

15. Herman Scheffauer, "The Tide of Turbans," *Forum* 43 (June 1910), 616; Mary Bamford, *Angel Island: The Ellis Island of the West* (Chicago: Women's American Baptist Home Mission Society), 1917, 20–21.

16. Ronald Inden, *Imagining India* (Oxford: Blackwell, 1990).

17. *United States v. Bhagat Singh Thind*, 261 U.S. 204 Appellee's Brief, 20–21.

18. H. H. Risley, *The People of India* (n.p., 1915), 275.

19. *Encyclopedia Britannica*, 11th ed. (New York, The Encyclopedia Britannica Company, 1911), "Hinduism," 502.

20. *In re Akhay Kumar Mozumdar*, 207 F. 116. *United States v. Bhagat Singh Thind*, 261 U.S. 204 Appellee's Brief, 15.

21. Sant Nihal Singh, "The Picturesque Immigrant from India's Coral Strand: Who He Is and Why He Comes to America," *Out West* 30 (January 1909), reprinted in *Asian Religions in America: A Documentary History*, edited by Thomas A. Tweed and

Stephen Prothero (Oxford: Oxford University Press, 1999), 82–86. There is also the point, currently debated, that Sikhism might not have been completely separated from Hinduism in this era; some argue that the creation of Sikhism as a separate "world religion" came about due partly to British insistence on discrete census categories and partly due to Sikh reformers in the late nineteenth and early twentieth century. On this ongoing debate, see Harjot Oberoi, *The Construction of Religious Boundaries: Culture, Identity and Diversity in the Sikh Tradition* (Chicago: University of Chicago Press, 1994). It is extremely unlikely that American audiences in the early twentieth century were sophisticated enough about Indian religions to appreciate this point, however. For an uncommon example of an American journalist differentiating between Sikh and Hindu, see Annette Thackwell Johnson, "Rag Heads—A Picture of America's East Indians," *The Independent*109, no. 3828:234-235 (1922), and by the same author, "Armageddon?" *The Independent* 109, no. 3830:296-298 (1922).

22. J. D. Anderson, *The Peoples of India* (Cambridge, England: Cambridge University Press, 1913), 33; Risley, *The People of India*, 273. Interestingly, no American writer on race and caste will make this comparison; at most, like Bishop Thoburn (408-409, see note 30 for full reference), they will compare the oppressive position of the lower Indian castes with that of American Negroes before Emancipation.

23. *United States v. Bhagat Singh Thind*, 261 U.S. 204 Appellant's Brief, 8.

24. Edmund Burke, quoted in *United States v. Bhagat Singh Thind*, 261 U.S. 204 Appellant's Brief, 11–14.

25. *United States v. Bhagat Singh Thind*, 261 U.S. 204 Appellant's Brief, 16.

26. James Freeman Clarke, *Ten Great Religions: An Essay in Comparative Theology* (Boston: James R. Osgood, 1875), 16–17.

27. Carl T. Jackson, *The Oriental Religions and American Thought: Nineteenth Century Explorations* (Westport, Conn.: Greenwood Press, 1981), 206–210.

28. Risley, *The People of India*, 275.

29. Maurice Bloomfield, *The Religion of the Veda: The Ancient Religion of India (From Rig-Veda to Upanishads)* (New York: Putnam, 1908), 5.

30. J. M. Thoburn, *India and Malaysia* (Cincinnati: Granston and Curts, Hunt and Eaton, 1882), 37,-40, 89, 94, 239, 365-402.

31. Bloomfield, *The Religion of the Veda*, 9.

32. For more detail on missionary depictions of India, see Jackson, *Oriental Religions*, 85–102, and Jennifer Snow, "A Border Made of Righteousness: Protestant Missionaries, Asian Immigration, and Ideologies of Race, 1850–1924," Ph.D. dissertation, Columbia University, 2003 (197–207). For discussions of more favorable American responses to "Eastern" religions, see Jackson, *Oriental Religions;* Thomas Tweed, *The American Encounter with Buddhism (1844–1912): Victorian Culture and the Limits of Dissent* (Bloomington: Indiana University Press, 1992); Stephen Prothero, *The White Buddhist: The Asian Odyssey of Henry Steel Olcott* (Bloomington: University of Indiana Press, 1996).

33. Thoburn, *India and Malaysia*, 39.

34. Arley Munson, *Jungle Days: Being the Experiences of an American Woman Doctor in India* (New York: Appleton, 1913).

35. Isaac Taylor, *Origin of the Aryans: An Account of the Prehistoric Ethnology and Civilisation of Europe*, 2nd ed. (London: Walter Scott, 1892), 212.

36. *Encyclopedia Britannica,* 1911 ed., 505.

37. Thoburn, *India and Malaysia,* 33.

38. Michael Myers Shoemaker, *Indian Pages and Pictures: Rajputana, Sikkim, the Punjab, and Kashmir* (New York: Putnam, 1912), 31–40, 191–194.

39. *Proceedings of the Asiatic Exclusion League, 1907–1913.* Anti-Movements in America (New York: Arno Press, 1977), November 1909, 6.

40. "The Hindu Question," *Marysville Appeal,* April 28, 1912, 4.

41. *United States v. Bhagat Singh Thind,* 261 U.S. 209.

42. *United States v. Bhagat Singh Thind,* 261 U.S. 209, 215, 213.

43. *Proceedings of the Asiatic Exclusion League, 1907–1913,* March 1910, 12.

44. Sidney L. Gulick, *American Democracy and Asiatic Citizenship* (New York: Scribner's, 1918), x.

45. *United States v. Bhagat Singh Thind,* 261 U.S. 213, 215.

46. Daniel Folkmar, *Dictionary of Races and Peoples: Senate Reports of the Immigration Commission* (Washington, D.C.: Government Printing Office), 1911, "Caucasian," 30.

47. *United States v. Bhagat Singh Thind,* 261 U.S. 204 Appellant's Brief, 16.

48. "The Hindu Question," 4.

49. Harjot Oberoi, *The Construction of Religious Boundaries.*

50. See Tweed and Prothero, *Asian Religions in America,* for examples of early constructions of Sikhism; Rajani Kanta Das, in *Hindustani Workers on the Pacific Coast* (Berlin: Walter de Gruyter, 1923) draws parallels between Luther and Guru Nanak and calls Sikhism the "Brotherhood of Man," as does Anderson, who describes the Sikh creed as "The Unity of God and the Brotherhood of Man," *The Peoples of India,* 93. Bishop Thoburn, on the other hand, names the three religions of India as "Hinduism, Mohammedanism, and devil-worship": *India and Malaysia,* 72.

51. "Hindus Too Brunette to Vote Here," *Literary Digest,* March 10, 1923, 13.

52. Jensen, *Passage from India.*

53. Letter from Vaishno Das Bagai, *San Francisco Examiner,* March 17, 1928.

54. On transcendentalism and theosophy, and the "wisdom of the East," see Jackson, *The Oriental Religions;* for the Ghadar Party and Vedanta Society, see Jensen, *Passage from India.*

55. Munson, *Jungle Days,* 45. Rudyard Kipling was an authoritative arbiter of race relations as much or more as any academic ethnologist. He is quoted frequently in American writings on India—even in Indian writings on East-West relations—and in his famous poem "White Man's Burden" was referred to in *United States v. Bhagat Singh Thind* by the lawyers for the United States.

Sense and Sensuality in Rituals and Representations of Race

Though "race" is, first and foremost, a structure of power defining hierarchical relationships within the *social* body, concepts of racial difference have nearly always been closely linked to perceptions of the *human* body. In addition to marking phenotypic features, like the color of one's skin, "race" has shaped perceptions of bodily practice and embodied experience. The way one walks, or dances, or eats, or sweats, or touches, or is touched—these and countless other elements of everyday human experience have been resignified by "race" and used to define racialized social orders. Perhaps above all, throughout the Americas differences between Black and White have been shaped by popular images of Black sensuality—images of excessive sensuality, symbolically linked to fears and fantasies of simple-minded emotionalism and transgressive sexuality, and opposed to ideals of White rationality and restraint.

These tropes of sensuality have often been used, by Blacks as well as Whites, to distinguish Black and White religious practices. Black folks, we are told, tend toward "hot" or "passionate" forms of ritual and "emotional" expressions of faith, while White folks tend toward "cold" or "cerebral" forms and "intellectual" expressions. Though these distinctions rest on racialized and sexualized fantasies of difference, these fantasies nevertheless draw upon—and resignify— real and enduring differences in the aesthetic and performative registers of African and European religious traditions. African and African-derived ritual practices often do, in fact, incorporate elements of kinesthetic experience—distinctive forms of music, movement, sexuality, and ecstasy—that have been considered profane (or far worse) by European and Euro-American religious authorities. The contrast between "Black" and "White" religious aesthetics thus presents us with an issue at the heart of any analysis of racialized difference: How may we do justice to the empirical cultural differences between racialized communities, while distinguishing these differences from fantasies of difference produced in the service of racialized hierarchies?

The essays in this section grapple with this fundamental question through analyses of ritual aesthetics and performance in rather different social contexts. In "The House of Saint Benedict, The House of Father John: Umbanda Aesthetics and a Politics of the Senses," Lindsay Hale examines the experiential differences between two sites of Umbanda worship in today's Rio de Janeiro, exploring the central roles of music, narrative, sacrifice, spirit possession, and other ritual forms in marking these sites—and their congregations— as "Black" and "White." Although he is critical of lurid popular images of Afro-Brazilian religion, Hale nevertheless stresses the social reality of embodied aesthetic differences. Judith Weisenfeld, however, shifts our attention toward the ways representations of such differences have been used to essentialize Black identities—and marginalize Black communities. In "Projecting Blackness: African-American Religion in the Hollywood Imagination," Weisenfeld focuses on the 1929 film *Hallelujah* to show how popular films from the 1920s through the 1940s used racially coded images of religious faith and ritual practice to reinforce racist perceptions of African-American moral simplicity and wanton sexuality.

Taken together, these essays show how embodied experiences and popular representations of religious practice have marked the boundaries of racialized communities throughout the Americas. More broadly, they offer a subtle analysis of the dialectical relationships between representation and experience, discourse and practice, ideology and everyday life, in the process of identity formation.

II

The House of Saint Benedict, the House of Father John: Umbanda Aesthetics and a Politics of the Senses

Lindsay Hale

When I think about my research with Afrobrazilian religion I often find myself not thinking, or at least not doing what I usually mean by that word. I catch myself instead immersed in a flood of remembered sensations, swept along by a current of sounds and smells and colors and movements. My mind's eye follows the swirl and float and gravity of costumed dancers; the smells of sweat and blood and decaying food offerings wafts to my remembering nostrils; a repertoire of drum rhythms pulses in my chest and puts me through a series of profound moods. Not the usual stuff of social science discourse; more like an aesthetic, or sensual, reverie. *Deixe passar*—let it pass, put it aside—and get back to work. Write like a social scientist, in the language of class and race and identity and history, the objective facts, please. And yet I cannot help but think that the flood of sensations that I remember and millions of Brazilians experience, in somewhat different ways perhaps, is as much a social fact as any other. Indeed I leave my reverie suspecting it to be a crucial fact, an aesthetic nexus that articulates the whole architecture of history, agency, and power that constitutes Afrobrazilian religion.

This article explores the relationship of Umbanda aesthetics to contested and ambivalent ideologies of race and identity. It deals with a problem familiar to anyone who has had much experience with Afrobrazilian religion. That is: one encounters enormous diversity within Afrobrazilian religion. In my research on the Umbanda religion, for example, just within Rio de Janeiro, I worked with groups whose practices ranged from the most ethereal congeries of New Age, Spiritualism, and medieval esoterica to the earthy aesthetics of Angolan Candomblé—styles represented here by the House of Saint Benedict[1] and the House of Father John, which I discuss in detail hereafter. The range of style is stunning; in comparison, a Sunday service at a Primitive Baptist church would look like a fraternal twin to an Anglican mass—both nominally Christian of course but strikingly different. What are we to make of this extraordinary diversity of religious practice among people who all call what they do Umbanda?

I will advance a rather conventional sociological explanation: that the differences are firmly imbedded in contested and ambivalent feelings about race and identity, and these feelings are in turn firmly grounded in the familiar drama of Brazilian history. Yet I will do this somewhat unconventionally by focusing on aesthetics. I will argue not only that Umbanda aesthetics is shaped by social forces—in fact a whole history of domination and struggle and hegemony is etched in a language of gesture, ritual, and sensual phenomena—but also that it is an ethically (and ethnically) saturated discourse on being, and being Brazilian. It is a discourse situated not only at the level of words but also in the depths of embodied experience. In short, what I present is a politics of the senses. Needless to say, I approach this task with a certain trepidation. One runs the risk, in writing a politics of the senses, of reinscribing racist, essentialist assumptions that locate people of color within the domain of the sensual, the bodied. That is not my intention; my claim rather is that through the sensual, through sound and smell and dance and touch, we can read a whole history of racism and struggle. I risk being misunderstood, and certainly I risk misunderstanding what I see. But if these historical struggles are fought at the level not only of ideas but at the level of the senses, then the risk, I think, must be taken.

A word first about my research, and about Umbanda. Umbanda is the most widely practiced of a number of popular Afrobrazilian religions that include Candomblé, Batuque, Xangô, and Casa das Minas.[2] There are no reliable figures, but there can be no doubt that millions of Brazilians are regular Umbanda participants and millions more have had occasion to attend rituals. It is most popular in Rio de Janeiro, but it is a national presence—Manaus, for example, deep in the Amazon, has a number of Umbanda centers.[3] While Umbanda is more prevalent among the urban poor and working class—of course, most workers in Brazil are poor, or at least economically stressed—Umbandistas can be found among all socioeconomic strata. Umbanda is ethnically diverse as well. For the most part, people initially come to Umbanda because they are suffering—from illness, bad luck, stress and emotional problems, marital strife or romantic disappointment, joblessness—in short, from a whole range of problems, chronic and acute. At Umbanda centers, sufferers can seek the healing and advice of spirits, incorporated by mediums—mediums who themselves came to Umbanda for healing, and stayed with it. There are a number of different types of spirits, but the most prominent categories are the old slaves *(pretos velhos)*; and the *caboclos,* who usually represent Brazilian Indians.[4] In addition, Umbanda pays homage to the African deities called Orixás.

I have carried out field research on Umbanda in Rio since 1986.[5] I have worked with several different Umbanda centers, encompassing a wide range of socioeconomic and religious diversity. As a social anthropologist, my abiding interest has been the processes through which persons and groups appropriate—and remake, and invent—the cultural resources available to them to actively construct viable identities, ideologies, and ethos as they deal with the contradictions, pains, and possibilities of their lives. This article explores one such process that revolves, in large part, around a central contradiction in Brazilian society and history.

That contradiction has to do with the conflicted ideology and practice of race. Brazil is known for its myth of racial democracy—the belief that racism is not a problem in Brazil, certainly not to the degree that it is in the United States. According to the myth, the Portuguese colonizers were not prone to the virulent racism of their American counterparts. Without a hint of irony, the fact that masters frequently engaged in sexual relations with their slaves is adduced as evidence of a lack of prejudice. It is also cited as an important mechanism mitigating racism, by supposedly blurring racial boundaries and at the same time transcending these divisions through ties of consanguinity and affinity. One often hears Brazilians describe themselves as a nation of "mixed blood" *(mistura de sangue)*—in every Brazilian, the story goes, there is at least a drop of African, a drop of Indigenous, and a drop of European blood. A paradoxical trope; at one level, it melts racial boundaries; but at another, it reifies them in essentialist equations of blood and identity. The myth of racial democracy is of course contradicted by the historical and contemporary realities of racial prejudice;[6] a statement more of how things ought to be, not how things really are. The myth valorizes the Afrobrazilian contribution to national identity, and it denies and implicitly condemns racism—while papering over the deep currents of stigmatization and racism that run through Brazilian history and contemporary society.

Umbandistas, like other Brazilians, struggle with these contradictions. In part they shape their religious practice around these contradictions. Indeed, Renato Ortiz convincingly argues that the kind of Umbanda I will describe for the House of Saint Benedict is the product of a self-conscious "whitening" or de-Africanization—strikingly evoked by the title of his book *A Morte Branca do Feiticeiro Negro* (The White Death of the Black Sorcerer).[7] But not all Umbanda is the product of whitening; there are numerous Umbanda centers that self-consciously identify their practices—and by extension, themselves—with Africa. The House of Father John is one such place that embraces the Afrobrazilian heritage.

The House of Father John

A sacred place is a space encrusted with stories and rituals and myths that saturate that particular location with ultimate meanings. One such story involves the origins of the House of Father John. I say one such story, but it is a story that different people involved with the house tell in different ways, with significant differences in important details. Here is my telling of it, incorporating the main events from several tellings and transposed to fit the narrative conventions and language of a North American reader.

> Some centuries ago an Angolan man, not young but in the prime of his life, waged a guerrilla campaign against the Portuguese slave traders in his land. His African name we don't now know, but he was a warrior and a sorcerer. He was eventually captured, clapped in chains, and shipped off to Brazil. [Note: for at least one of my informants the story never gets this far: Father John dies fighting, choosing death over captivity.] Somehow he was able to hide on his person certain objects, including a cutting from a root. [Some say it was the root of a *gamaleira branca,* the tree that is Tempo, the ancient and mysterious Orixá of Time. Others say it was the root of some powerful sorcery herb; others say "sei la"—who knows? And in some tellings, the root is not mentioned at all.] In any event, he managed to keep it with him through the passage. The slavers named him John, and sold him off [some say to a coffee plantation in the state of Rio de Janeiro.] Eventually John, now old from forced labor, beatings, and bad food, escaped. [Another variant: Father John leads a rebellion on the plantation and escapes with his followers.] Hunted down by *capitães do mato* ["captains of the forest": these were professional slave hunters, often themselves slaves or former slaves], moments before his capture, Father John, knowing his death was imminent, scratched a hole in the red clay with his bare hands and planted his root. And where he planted it, the House of Father John now stands.[8]

As one might surmise from any of the variants of this origin myth, high value is placed on Africa and on the Afrobrazilian heritage at the House of Father John. To some degree this can be attributed to the demographics of the congregation. While it is a commonplace of Brazil's myth of racial democracy that every Brazilian has some European, some African, and some Indigenous blood—I heard that numerous times, especially from my whitest friends—this is visibly true at the House of Father John. Comments such as "My ancestors were slaves and thanks to the Orixás they passed through those hard times, and we will too," underscore Afrobrazilian identity. But there is more to it than that. Being nominally placed in a given ethnic category does not guarantee that one embraces that identity—self-hatred and denial are all too common legacies of racism. (Perhaps that is why old slave spirits tell stories of black overseers and captains of the forest inflicting the worst cruelties of all. Tales of the past are so often parables about the present.) Brazilians of color embrace Afrobrazilian identity at Father John's while everyone there, white congregants included, celebrates Africa and Afrobrazil. These connections are constituted through stories, like the tale of Father John's martyrdom, and through explicit invocations of Afrobrazilian identity but also through congregants' senses.

The image of Father John's fingernails clawing the wet fetid clay to plant his African root captures striking aspects of the look and feel of the House that bears his name. The House of Father John is located in one of those patches of tropical forest that abut the urban space of Rio de Janeiro. One enters through a gate, walking down a packed clay dirt path that is wet and slick and fragrant with the musty smell of clay and rotting vegetation whenever it rains. Inside its three walls—the back opens on the forest and a collection of outbuildings housing various shrines—the floor is all packed clay, the benches for the attendees rough hewn, the built space all earthy, rugged, redolent of the primitive, the rural, the jungle and the village, the slave quarters. In fact, when the spirits of old slaves are present, the place is called a *senzala* (slave quarters), and one can easily imagine it as such, especially when it rains in the winter and the wet chill settles in, or when the summer sun turns it into a sweltering oven. It isn't always a senzala—when the Indian spirits are called down, it becomes *aldeia* (village), and the image is at times embellished by covering the floor with leaves, as in a forest clearing—but most of the time the aesthetics of the senzala rule.

Africa and Afrobrazil are palpably, visibly present at every turn. The Orixás are represented in various shrines. For example, there is a boulder with a triangular piece of iron somehow, miraculously—the man who first showed it to me swore it was not the work of human hands—embedded in it near the gate. That is for Xangô, the Orixá of thunder and justice, who is also patron of quarries and stoneworking; the iron is one of his thunderbolts, the boulder the material of his craft. Another shrine encloses what was once a spring. When they found this place and began building the House of Father John, the workers came across the spring. Around it, I was told, they discovered tools and other artifacts, and eventually established that the spring had fed a tank where the slaves had drawn water and washed. Back inside, the ritual space where the Orixás descend and the various spirits attend to the needing people is dominated by a suite of three drums and a central pole. The central pole connects the heavens with the earth, the earth ultimately the ancestral land of Africa. The drums are African, made in the Angola or Congo fashion and played, the drummers tell me, in the Angola style, that is, with the hands and not with sticks as in the West African style of Candomblé.

The rituals can be placed into two categories. Before the routine weekly sessions in which the old slave and Indian spirits are invoked and made available to those in need, a *gira* [a series of dances performed in a circle] is held for the Orixás. The drummers play a series of *toques* (drum songs)—typically three or seven—for each of several Orixás in turn, while the mediums sing the corresponding lyrics and dance in the fashion characteristic of the particular Orixá. Usually one or more mediums will be "mounted" by the Orixá whose rhythm is being played, embodying, in gesture, movement, *grito* (shout), expression, and attitude, the mythical personage. The second type of ritual takes place on the saint's day associated with each Orixá. These are all-night affairs. A medium or mediums, for whom that Orixá is the spiritual parent, emerges from a ritual seclusion of several days, elaborately costumed as, and deeply possessed by, the Orixá. These calendrical rituals, attended by very large audiences, dramatically present the deity, and with it a rich and powerful and multilayered symbolization of Africa and Afrobrazilian tradition, to the community of Father John. But both the dramatic annual celebrations and the routine weekly giras both invoke Africa through language (many of the songs are in Angolan or Yoruban dialect), music, dance, gesture, costume, and sacrifice.

Clay and rain and rotting leaves are not all that one smells at the House of Father John. There is also blood and decomposing flesh. Unlike many Umbanda centers, the House of Father John maintains elaborate traditions of blood sacrifice. Before the weekly sessions, the calendrical rituals, before initations, before anything, an offering is made to Exu, the mercurial trickster who mediates between humans and the Orixás—*Sem Exu, não faz nada* ("Without Exu, nothing is done"). The eternal go-between, Exu resides at the gate, by the door, at the crossroads—the liminal places of choice and transformation. At Father John's, the offering is a bowl of manioc flour and onions, doused in pungent, bright orange-yellow palm oil, and a chicken, sacrificed on the spot. The killing is essential. As the blood flows and life ebbs, the vital and spiritual force—the *axé*—of the bird is released, energizing the offering and charging the moment with axé. Blood and breath are the vehicles *par excellence* of axé, but axé resides also in the heart that pumps blood, the liver that makes it (in folk belief), the genitals that generate life, the brain, and in the organs of locomotion. Thus the wings, the feet, the head, the heart, and the liver go into the offering for Exu.

Beyond that, each Orixá has its menu of birds, mammals, and, for some, reptiles and even invertebrates and mollusks. From snails to bulls, there is a whole system of ritual, a semiotics of blood. I will not concern myself with that here. I will just say that the transformation of life to death—through acts of killing, attended by a release of axé, blood and flesh, fresh hides of goats and bulls and sheep nailed to the walls, bowls of the axé organs watered with blood, the eddying currents of smells and fragrances—brings spiritual life. The river of axé, the pounding, swirling flow of drums and dancing, the mythology written in architecture and objects—the aesthetics of Father John is an enveloping, sensual celebration of Africa and Afrobrazil.

The House of Saint Benedict

I was introduced to the House of Saint Benedict by a friend of a friend, a clinical psychologist I will call Elisa, who attended weekly healing sessions at an Umbanda center not far from the House of Father John. Elisa worked with the mediums and their spirits, contributing her insights from Jungian and mainstream behavioral and family therapy approaches within, as she called it, "holistic therapy," combining spiritualist and Western psychological models. The personnel there explicitly identified their center as a clinic, and indeed the center had the look and feel of a clinic—everything was whitewashed, spick-and-span, people made appointments, mediums and others dressed in white nurse-like uniforms and consulted about "patients" and other issues in staff meetings, and the recommendations that spirits made during their meetings with sufferers were written down on prescription pads with the center's name printed at the top—with a space for the spirit's name and the patient's, the date, and the time. While this would have been an interesting field site, I thought, on the basis my preliminary visit, Elisa regretfully informed me that the director was concerned that my role as an observer might conflict with their therapeutic mission. So Elisa introduced my to her friend Cici, who had frequented an Umbanda center, the House of Saint Benedict, for several years, and was learning to become a medium.

Cici prepared me for my introduction to the House of Saint Benedict by telling me about the mediums at the center—mostly middle-aged women, married like herself to men of the professional class—and by aesthetically characterizing the rituals there. At the House of Saint Benedict, she told me, our Umbanda is "clean" and "light." For example, she said, we never make food offerings to the Orixás—well, they are pure spirit, why would they want gross material food?—no, we give them offerings of colored ribbons, candles, perfume, and flowers. As for blood sacrifice—*nem pensar!* Out of the question!

Invisible from the street behind a high whitewashed wall secured by a metal gate, the House of Saint Benedict is located in a solid middle-class neighborhood on a quiet street among well cared for homes. In existence for over half a century, it was founded by the husband of the present leader, Dona Lisa, cheerful and energetic and appearing much younger than her actual eighty-plus years might suggest. Dona Lisa recalls that when her husband was alive, the house was always full for sessions. Full of people but full also of joy, positive energies, optimism, and mostly, a spirit of charity toward those troubled people who would come seeking help from the spirits. Many of these were poor, uneducated, and of color, in marked contrast to the founder, Dona Lisa, and the mediums I met there.[9] Without her husband, whose portrait is prominently displayed in the hall, that level of activity is no longer possible, but Dona Lisa maintains, with obvious satisfaction and pride, that then as now, the Umbanda you find here is very special—clean, light, pure, virtuous, a thing of beauty, so energizing! We are a family here!

Passing through the portals into the House of Saint Benedict for the first time leaves an indelible impression. Picture a door opening from the dark night into a twilit hall, quiet and still and tinged in blue. The blue radiates from a halo atop the wavy chestnut locks of a larger-than-life plaster Christ, arms outstretched and palms out, robed in white and beige and blue and scarlet. Large vases of lilies and roses are deployed around the lightly tanned savior. A soft white light shines on the statue, but it is the blue of the halo and the blue light of a neon tube framing the scene that colors the vision.

And it is a vision. As one's eyes adjust to the cool blue half-light, as one's ears are washed by swelling chords of strings and flutes from hidden speakers, as one takes in the polished wood of the pews, the soft gleam of polished floors, the open empty welcoming arms of the fair-skinned Christ, one is engulfed in a white Umbanda vision of what lies beyond and so far above—morally, spiritually, spatially—flesh and blood and breath: a cool, orderly, quiescent eternity.

The ritual begins with Dona Lisa, dressed all in white, walking in from stage left to lay prone and touch her head to the floor at the feet of the Christ statue and then kneel in whispered prayer before the image. She stands, turns, faces the audience, blesses and welcomes the handful or so seated in the pews, and stands off somewhat to the left. One by one, the mediums—there are usually four—approach her, touch their foreheads to the ground at her feet, receive her blessing, and rise. From a darkened hallway off to the right, the medium Paulo, dressed all in white, emerges, almost gliding in on his white cotton slippers. Round, cherubic, smiling, carrying a blue-tinged glass carafe in his hand, he approaches the railing in front of the pews. He offers each of us a sip of spring water, remarking on the lightness it imparts to spirit and body, before in his turn touching the ground at Dona Lisa's feet and receiving her blessing. The mediums line up side by side, with their backs to the audience, facing Dona Lisa, who recites a short prayer and intones the opening notes of what will be half an hour of soft, slow, mostly minor-key hymns to Jesus, the Orixás, and the spirits who will be summoned that night. There are no drums—clapping accompanies a few hymns; the dancing is done in place, never much more than a restrained shifting of the feet; and the moment of possession when it comes is marked by little more than a shiver. Finally the spirits arrive, the mediums take their seats on low stools if it is a session for the old slave spirits *(pretos velhos)* or remain standing if it is a night for the Indian spirits *(caboclos)*. People from the audience are beckoned in turn to come consult with the spirits; when they are through, they return to the pews and sit quietly, meditating perhaps or silently praying under the gaze of the plaster Redeemer. The spirits' work is done in about an hour. A hymn sends them on their way; another, upbeat, asks that the star that guided our Father guide his children (us), whatever roads we may take. A prayer is said, Paulo returns to offer us each a sip of water from the carafe, and it is over.

In broad outline, the structure of the ritual is quite similar to that at the House of Father John. (Indeed, the closing hymn is word for word the same.) But in look, feel, sound, smell, emotion, movement, it could not be more different. Ethereal, bloodless, passionless, restrained, disembodied: aesthetically, sensually, it would be difficult to imagine a more striking contrast with the sweat and blood and sacrifice and the acrid and sweet and fetid and fertile smells of Father John. My argument is that this aesthetic contrast mirrors, or perhaps better, *traces,* the historical (and continuing) struggles over race, identity, and legitimacy in Umbanda specifically and Brazil more generally.

The House of Saint Benedict, the House of Father John; both call themselves Umbanda, and there are many similarities in their theories of this world and the world beyond, and participants at both places would largely agree on questions of right and wrong. And yet they represent two radically different ethos, embodied in strikingly different aesthetics. To understand this divergence, a brief consideration of historical circumstances is in order.

Historical Context

It is generally accepted that Umbanda began in the early decades of the twentieth century in the Rio de Janeiro metropolitan area.[10] The religio-scape of Rio was then (and is now) diverse and complex; besides the Catholic Church, there were Spiritualists, Comtean Positivists, Protestants, Jews, immigrants from Europe, the Levant, and the Brazilian countryside with their varied folk traditions, and of course followers of Afrobrazilian religious traditions.[11] Umbanda represented a self-conscious fusion of Afrobrazilian and Spiritualist beliefs and practices by persons uncomfortably situated within the contradictory dynamics of race and class in a rapidly evolving political economy. These persons could be lumped into two broad groups. One would consist of persons from the middle classes, bourgeois in their aesthetics and ethics and yet drawn to the experiential spirituality, mystery, and healing reputation of Afrobrazilian religion. The other was drawn from the urban masses, people of color and marginally situated whites, familiar with bourgeois values yet steeped in Afrobrazilian traditions and working class culture—poor and marginalized but with middle-class, "modern" aspirations. One might say they were people clinging with one hand to that sturdy root planted in the fetid clay by Father John and the other hand grasping at the ladder of upward mobility. Pulled at once in two different directions, Umbanda emerged not as a point but as a continuum, a range of possibilities, represented in this article as the House of Father John at one end and the House of Saint Benedict at the other. Before exploring these dynamics from a sensual and aesthetic perspective, further historical contextualization is in order.

The Afrobrazilian religious traditions within which Umbanda began have a long history as a vibrant presence within Brazilian culture. Their strength and persistence is largely related to the specific features of Brazilian slavery, which ended in 1888. Unlike the United States, where the slave trade effectively ended rather early, Brazil continued to import large numbers of Africans—and with them their religious and cultural traditions—well into the middle of the nineteenth century. The continual influx of African culture-bearers was even more significant because of very low rates of natural reproduction of the slave population. At the same time, while the plantation and mining economy depended on slavery, the urban economy too was largely carried on by persons of African descent. Coastal cities such as Salvador and Rio were places were large numbers of Afrobrazilians were concentrated. The Latin American propensity toward manumission accentuated the potential of the large urban Afrobrazilian population for voluntary association, including association along religious lines. The fact that the Catholic Church provided an existing structure of devotional brotherhoods that offered valued roles and benefits for Afrobrazilians, as well as an institutional nucleus around which African religious traditions could be reframed, seems to have also been a crucial factor.[12] Far from withering, African traditions regenerated in these urban centers and emerged as thriving Afrobrazilian religions, dynamic centers of Afrobrazilian life and culture before and after abolition. In Salvador, for example, Candomblé *terreiros*[13] such as Engenho Velho (also known by its Yoruba name, Ilê Iyá Nassô) were well established in the mid-nineteenth century and continue today as powerful symbols of Afrobrazilian identity and paragons of religious tradition.

But they did so in the face of virulent, often violent, opposition. At various times the state vigorously repressed Afrobrazilian religion, branded as an affront to Catholicism, an outrage against public morality, a symbol and source of superstition, and a threat to public order. Police raids were common during the early decades of this century. The great Brazilian novelist Jorge Amado eloquently testifies—fictionally but nonetheless truthfully—to police terror against Candomblé terreiros in Salvador: beatings, destruction of altars, smashing of drums and images, profanations and violence. The Civil Police of Rio displayed as museum exhibits drums, costumes, statues, and other items seized in their campaigns against Afrobrazilian religions.[14] Besides police violence, the ideological organs of church, state, and press waged a vigorous campaign stigmatizing Afrobrazilian religion. The repression and stigmatization were articulated with genuine revulsion, and by a deep conviction that Afrobrazilian religion represented a diseased condition of ignorance, barbarism, degeneracy, a profound threat to elite visions of an orderly, progressive, modern Brazil. A nineteenth-century writer, Joaquim Manoel de Macedo, who opposed slavery in part out of concern for the cultural legacy its victims would leave (he titled his novel *The Torturing Victims*) captures the visceral depths of this revulsion in his lurid, sensual description of an Afrobrazilian ritual. I quote Macedo at some length because his language paints a vivid picture of the stigmatized Afrobrazilian other, a picture etched not only in his mind but more broadly in Brazilian society. It was against the background of such images that Umbanda would emerge:

witchcraft has its pagoda, its priests, its cult, its ceremonies, its mysteries: all of it, however, is grotesque, repugnant, scandalous.

The pagoda is usually a solitary house; the priest is an African slave, or some worthy descendant and disciple of same, though born free or manumitted, and there is never lacking a priestess of the same sort. The cult takes place at night by candlelight, or firelight. The ceremonies and the mysteries are of the most incalculable variety, depending on how unbridled the imagination of the liars.

Free persons and slaves come around at night, at the appointed hour, to the sinister house. Some come to cure themselves of sorcery, with which they suppose themselves infected; others to become initiates, or to seek enchanted means to do evil or to obtain favor.

The gross instruments [are] reminiscent of the savage festivals of the Brazilian Indian or the Negro from Africa are heard; one sees rustic talismans and ridiculous symbols. The priest and the priestess ornament themselves with feathers and emblems and living colors. There are prepared, by the fire, or at the old and filthy table, beverages: unknown infusions of nauseating roots, almost always or sometimes rotten . . . the priest breaks into a frenetic, terrible, convulsive dance. . . . The priestess goes around like a lunatic, coming and going, [and] returns just to turn around and leave; she throws leaves and roots on the fire that fill the disagreeable and infected hall with a suffocating smoke, and after an hour of the contortions, demonic dances, anxiety, and crazed activity of this partner of the liar, she returns at last from the backyard, from where she was out of sight, and announces the arrival of the genie, the spirit, the god of sorcery, for which there are twenty names, each one more brutal and burlesque.

The dance, now spreading, comes again to a boil; the obscene

Negress and her partner move lewdly. Interrupting their violent dance, they carry to each and all the vase or gourd containing the beverage, telling them to "drink *pemba*," and each one takes a swig of the dangerous and filthy pemba. Those who are sick from sorcery, the candidates for the office of sorcerer, [and] those who use sorcery for good or bad ends subject themselves to the most absurd, repulsive, and indecent ordeals and to the most squalid of practices.

The bacchanal is complete; with the cure of the bewitched, with the torments of the initiations, with the concession of remedies and the secrets of sorcery is mixed the firewater, and in the delirium of all, in the infernal flames of depraved imaginations, are evidenced, almost always shamelessly, an unchecked, ferocious, and torpid lewdness.

All this is hideous and horrible, but that is how it is.[15]

Stripped of its lurid language and thoroughly racist, sexist, and elitist perspective, Macedo's description resonates with scenes I have observed from Afrobrazilian Umbanda at the House of Father John: there are infusions, and dancing culminating in ecstatic possession, and costumes, and dramatic entries of mediums possessed by the Orixás. But how different they appear in Macedo's nightmare! What Macedo's words actually paint is the picture of his own (and not just his) terrifying racial fantasy. Its demons are black, sexualized—most pointedly, the women, the "lewd Negress"—intoxicated, intranced. It is a scene of noise, disorder, and lunacy, drenched with a sexualized sensuality, threatening in itself and, one suspects, even more threatening for its projection of repressed desires onto the racialized other. Macedo's account crystallizes the depth and shape of the stigma heaped on Afrobrazilian religion, a crucial part of the background against which Umbanda would take form.

Around the turn of the century, while Afrobrazilian religion was subjected to physical and verbal assault, another affront to Catholicism enjoyed a rather different reception. Spiritualism, also known as Kardecismo in Brazil, was systematized by Hippolyte Denizard Rivail (1803–1869), a Frenchman who styled himself a student of grammar, medicine, and science and wrote under the name of Allan Kardec. Concerned with psychic and otherworldly phenomena, Spiritualism posited a dichotomy of the spiritual and material orders of existence (the former elaborately detailed), reincarnation and spiritual/moral evolution, and the reality of communication with spiritual beings—that is, persons who had once lived an earthly existence. Couched in erudite, scientist language, Spiritualism resonated with the positivist values and progressive aspirations of substantial segments of the Brazilian elite. Far from being stigmatized as a form of superstition and degeneracy, like Afrobrazilian religion, Spiritualism was associated with the elite and educated (and, by implication, white) sectors of Brazilian society. João do Rio, for example, reported that Spiritualists could be found "among our most lucid minds"; he mentions generals, admirals, doctors, members of the bar and press.[16] Indeed, though Spiritualism was certainly not acceptable to the Church, it was nevertheless steeped in prestige.

It is from the fusion of these two currents—Afrobrazilian religion and Kardecite Spiritualism—that Umbanda emerged in the early decades of the twentieth century. It would be fascinating to explore the various ways that different Umbandistas relate and reconcile beliefs and practices from these two very different traditions, fashioning them into a coherent, satisfying code of thought and action. But for this article I must limit myself to the symbolic value of Spiritualist and Afrobrazilian currents, to their functions as ideological markers and emotionally laden signs that provide a telling clue to the strikingly different aesthetics represented of the House of Father John and the House of Saint Benedict.[17] It is time to turn from an objective historical sketch and return to stories Umbandistas tell about the origins of their religion. Especially important is the encounter with, and incorporation of, Spiritualism, at once a historical fact and a mythic event. The following passage, from the Umbandist writer Israel Cysneiros, recounts the birth of Umbanda.

> The mentors of the superior astral plane, however, were attentive to what was going on [the alleged proliferation of black magic, superstition, and, especially, the kind of scenes depicted by Macedo]. They organized a movement to combat the negative magic that was spreading with frightening speed. At first the movement was aimed at the humble classes, the ones most subject to the influence of the climate of superstition that reigned in that epoch.
>
> There were formed then, at this time, the phalanxes of spiritual workers in the form of caboclos and pretos velhos in order for [the message] to be more easily interpreted by the masses. In the Spiritualist sessions, however, these caboclos and pretos velhos were not accepted; seen in such guises, they were considered backward or low spirits. . . .
>
> The situation remained unaltered at the beginning of the year 1900. The orders of the Astral Plane, however, would be carried out.
>
> On the fifteenth of November, 1908, there appeared at a session of the Spiritualist Federation in Niteroi, then under the direction of José de Souza, a young man of seventeen years from a traditional *fluminense* [from the state of Rio de Janeiro] family by the name of Zélio Fernandes de Morais. He had just recovered, the day before, from an illness whose cause the doctors had vainly sought to discover. His unexpected recovery, thanks to a spirit, caused enormous surprise. Neither the doctors who attended him nor his uncles, who were Catholic priests, could offer a plausible explanation. The family

was receptive, therefore, to the suggestion of a friend that he accompany Zélio to a meeting of the Spiritualist Federation.

Zélio was invited to participate at the table [the ritual and the piece of furniture where mediums receive spirits]. When the proceedings began, spirits who identified themselves as slaves and Indians manifested themselves. The director warned them to leave. At that very moment, Zélio felt himself overcome by a strange force and heard his own voice demanding to know why the messages of Blacks and Indians were not accepted, and if they were considered backward simply because of their color or their social class. This nearly started a brawl. There followed a heated discussion in which the directors attempted to teach [i.e., dissuade] this spirit who argued with such self-assurance. Finally, one of the mediums asked the spirit to identify himself, in consideration of the fact that he appeared enveloped in an aura of light. . . .

"If you wish to know my name . . . then try this one: I am the Caboclo Seven Crossroads, because for me all roads are open!"

He continued to announce his mission: to establish the basis of a religion, in which the spirits of Indians and slaves would come to fulfill the will of the Astral. The next day . . . [he would] found a temple, symbolizing the true and total equality that must exist between men.[18]

Versions of this origin myth are well known to Umbandistas and researchers.[19] I heard variations from Umbandistas at various centers, especially at the House of Saint Benedict, where everyone seemed to be familiar with it. Like most myths, this one has some basis in actual events. There was indeed a Zélio de Morais, and sometime in the early decades of the century (Cysneiros makes it 1908, Diana Brown, who actually interviewed Zélio, places the events "around 1920") he began a ministry of curing and counseling at a place known as the Waterfall of the Macacu Tree. Known as the Spiritual Center of Our Lady of Piety, the center flourished, even after the founder's retirement in the 1960s. As Diana Brown tells us, Zélio and the "founders" came primarily from the "middle sectors"—bureaucrats, the military, commerce—and from the professions situated above them and the respectable occupations below—laborers, teachers, and so on.[20] Many of his followers came from those sectors, but many others came from the working classes and the marginalized, largely Afrobrazilian poor. The current of Umbanda that began flowing from the place near the Waterfall of the Macacu Tree (and that runs through the House of Saint Benedict) is often referred to as White Umbanda (also Pure Umbanda) by researchers[21] and participants alike. Participants apply the adjective because "White" is associated with good, purity, moral rectitude, innocence, but it also resonates eloquently, if unintentionally, with the racializing, de-Africanizing tendencies at places like the House of Saint Benedict.

While at one level the myth explicitly protests racism and elitism—the new Umbanda would welcome the spirits of the marginalized and minister to the masses they represent, while the haughty Spiritualists are bested by the true spiritual power and moral force of the plain-speaking, rustic Seven Crossroads—it also conveys an implicitly anti-Afrobrazilian message. The new religion is sent by the superior beings of the Astral realm to clean up the "negative magic"—what Macedo might have characterized as "scandalous," "savage," "grotesque" ritual—allegedly permeating Afrobrazilian religions. The myth in fact is a charter for rooting out the Afrobrazilian traditions from Umbanda. Another myth, this one from the House of Saint Benedict, makes the point explicitly and fleshes out the racism underlying it. The story was told to me by an old slave spirit called Father Mané,[22] who, unlike other old slave spirits I talked to, spoke with perfect grammar and clear diction, and displayed quite an acquaintance and fascination with Greek mythology, New Age spirituality, big band era jazz, popular science, and European history—especially Enlightenment France. Like most of these stories, this one varies from telling to telling; the version here, in my words, synthesizes Mané's full telling of the story one evening with several other conversations we had concerning details.

It seems that long, long ago the highest wise men of the planet Cabal took up the charitable mission of spreading truth and enlightenment outward to all the other inhabited planets in the universe. They selected their brightest, most educated, and spiritual young people and sent them forth in all directions on spaceships capable of light speed travel, so that they could search indefinitely for peopled planets; as Einstein demonstrated, time and therefore aging stops when one reaches those velocities.[23] One such ship happened upon Earth, a raw and savage place inhabited mainly by brutes lacking all but the rudiments of culture and language (the most "advanced" earthlings, living along the Nile, in Mesopotamia, and India, had the beginnings of writing and culture, but they were still little more than tribesmen). The Cabalan missionaries set to work, the fruits of which we see in the development of writing and mathematics, the Neolithic revolution, and the almost simultaneous invention of civilization in Syria and Egypt and China and a little later in the New World. The center of it all, their home base, as it were, was Atlantis, but they were also behind the other great civilizations of Egypt and Babylon. Unfortunately, the Cabalans left their pupils too soon. Babylon sank into wickedness, Egypt enslaved the Israelites, and as for Atlantis, a foolish experiment with nuclear power by arrogant scientists ended catastrophically, destroying its Cabalic civilization. A few citizens managed to survive, the Atlantans clinging to flotsam and drifting to Black Africa, the one corner of the world the Cabalic enlightenment had not even touched. They weren't at the level of the Cabalans by any stretch, but they were far above the Africans. They introduced metallurgy, counting, and law—albeit in simplified form, in deference to the limited capacities of the African people. They also introduced their spiritualist religion, which they called Umbanda after the fundamental vibration Om. Unfortunately, the Atlantans soon succumbed to disease, violence at the hands of the natives, and the sheer despair of being surrounded by such barbarism. As a result, the Africans never advanced very far, and even worse, the sublime Umbanda became mixed with fetishism, superstition, and generally barbaric practices. And that was what was brought to Brazil with the slaves. There was much truth and enlightenment in their religion—the parts from Cabal, by way of Atlantis—but much error and primitivism, from Africa. Our mission is to purge Umbanda of those impurities. So Umbanda, the real Umbanda, isn't an African religion; true Umbanda is Umbanda without Africa.

Mané's account and the myth of Zélio de Morais, while reporting rather different sets of events, represent variations on a theme. To begin with, both locate the fundamental truth of Umbanda in the rarified reaches of elsewhere, in some realm beyond the material, imperfect, sensual world—Cabal, far out in space in the one case; the Superior Astral plane, beyond even space and time, in the other. Both tales condescend. Zélio's new religion will use the spirits of humble old black slaves and rustic Indians to translate the sublime into a language the masses can understand. Mane's story suggests that the ancestors of Brazilians were too primitive and ignorant and corrupt to grasp the wisdom and that it is the mission of the enlightened few to use their superior intellect and culture to cleanse Umbanda and recover its Cabalic purity. That, in fact, is precisely what Mané's medium told me when I interviewed him after the session and on other occasions. Both equally privilege the esoteric and the intellectualized, implicitly associated with the elite, the white, the European—the Frenchman Kardec, and Atlantis, which the popular imagination constructs as a kind of Athens to the tenth power. And both endorse a project of "whitening," of de-Africanization; Mané's tale is explicit in identifying Africa as the stigma, the cancer, that must be excised from a pure Umbanda.[24]

Discussion

And what is it Mané would cleanse from Umbanda? Within Mané's medium's mind, within the minds of those at the House of Saint Benedict, repulsive images fester that are reminiscent of Macedo's feverish vision of savagery. When I first read Macedo in the national library in Rio, turning those musty, crumbly pages printed over a century ago, I was struck by how vividly and succinctly Macedo encapsulated the prejudices and fantasies and revulsion that drove—and drive—the aesthetics of white Umbanda. This is a vision thoroughly repulsive to the sensibilities of the would-be bourgeoisie, those working-class followers of Zélio de Morais who yearned for acceptance by the refined gentlemen of the Spiritualist Federation in Niteroi. It is a nightmarish trip (at least for Macedo, and his intended readers) into chaos and barbarism— and Africa, the other that is also within. The words are there. *Lunatic, demonic dances, contortions, savage festivals, brutal and burlesque, delirium, depraved imaginations, torpid lewdness.* There is even an obscene negress—like many nightmares, especially it seems those in which the threatening protaganists are black, this one gains force and *frisson* from a grotesque sexualization. It resonates with Renato Ortiz's account of the historical development of white Umbanda—this imagery is what its inventors were fleeing from. It resonates as well with caricatures of Afrobrazilian religion and culture—in the popular media and in the discourse of priests, police, and politicians. These presented, albeit not usually in such lurid fashion, a picture entirely at odds with the desired bourgeois self-image of an enlightened, clean, rational, scientific, proper, modern, and white citizen. Macedo, by the way, was an abolitionist, yet he continually identifies this demonic scene with dark others—Africa, African slaves, negress, Indian. As I read this, I was struck as well by the vivid, sensual imagery—Macedo's ideology is couched in aesthetic, experiential terms. He does paint a picture.

I was also struck by the feeling of having seen Macedo's picture, albeit through unscandalized eyes, eyes that could see this as an affirmation of Afrobrazilian identity, an organic celebration of sense and spirit and *communitas*[25] in opposition to the cold, esoteric, and hierarchical visions of white Umbanda. I wondered whether the scene that so offended his sensibilities was really so much different from what I had come to know and love at the House of Father John. I was certainly familiar with various infusions of roots and leaves. Dona Linda, a daughter of Ossaim, the god of medicinal and sacred plants, prepared a number of such "beverages" from plants she gathered from the steep wooded mountainsides that lay between her home and the House of Father John. One particularly foul-tasting tea—castor oil would be ice cream in comparison— cured me of chronic gastrointestinal distress. Another, made from a plant whose leaves were like miniature green vulvas, Dona Linda prescribed to women suffering various reproductive maladies. There were teas and poultices and herbal baths to calm, cure burns and cuts, expel worms, energize the tired brain, awaken deadened desires, lighten moods, bring wisdom, drive away colds, and clear away the accumulated psychic dirt of living in this world. "Unknown infusions"? Linda, and several of the other women, knew, in detail, each plant, what it did, when to collect it—what phase of the moon, what time of day—how to prepare it, what to expect. In her deep quiet voice, Linda would discuss each medicinal plant as she prescribed it, always reminding listeners of the African healers who brought this knowledge to heal their great-great-grandmothers and grandfathers here in Brazil. These "unknown infusions" in fact connect people with Afrobrazilian identity viscerally, through healing ingestion by suffering bodies.

So much for Macedo's nauseating roots. The "gross instruments" I recognized as the three drums, *rum, rumpi,* and *lé* (the big, medium, and little drums, respectively), sanctified annually in blood, that call down the Orixás and connect living people with living spirit through rhythms that pulse within and without. The men who play these instruments at the House of Father John have been frequenting terreiros since early childhood, brought by older relatives, internalizing hundreds of toques and learning and teaching the lore of the drums, the differences in design from the various homelands—the Angola style they play with their hands at Father John's, the West African drums played with sticks in Nagô houses. The drummers take musicians' pride in their playing and evince a musicians' fascination with knowledge of the musical traditions, and their fascination and pride, along with the deeply embodied playing itself, are explicitly related to Africa and Afrobrazilian identity.

The demonic dances? At the House of Father John, I learned to recognize the dances representing the African deities that rule the various domains of culture and nature, the elemental categories of fertility, fresh water, industry, ocean, death, justice, beauty, thunder, hunting, disease, truth, courage, lies, disease, childhood, and chaos. I learned to recognize and, more, to appreciate the metaphoric allusions and aesthetic structures, to be moved by the grace and power, of those "demonic" dances. "Appreciate" seems too weak a word for the powerfully sensual, embodied connection I felt through these performances, and of course my connection must in turn be weak compared to that of the dancers filled with the deities and spirits. Macedo's revulsion—the revulsion of the House of Saint Benedict, and by extension of bourgeois society—is turned on its head at the House of Father John, where Afrobrazilian identity is embraced in blood, sound, movement, drums, medicine, dance, and all that pulses in its sensual aesthetic.

It is not enough to suggest that the vibrant ritual at the House of Father John is a sign of allegiance, an affirmation of Afrobrazilian heritage, while the cool blue twilight at the House of Saint Benedict is a rejection of the same. That is certainly true—in the one case there is a passionate embrace of that African "blood" that Brazil's myth of racial democracy has flowing through everyone's veins, in the other a mean bit of racism that can only really be self-hatred over the knowledge that that tainted "blood" flows through oneself, and one's nation. But there is more. These are two fundamentally different experiential worlds, each the sensual, aesthetic, embodiment of a radically different ethos. One fairly bursts with life, energy, blood, sweat, movement, rhythm, smell, and emotion, scratching at the wet earth of life and death as Father John did. The other is controlled, restrained, cool, blue, lilacs and swelling strings, otherworldly; no dirt under those nails. One resonates with the middle class, the bourgeois, and those who would be so; the other with the margins, the poor, the victims of a whole history of oppression.

I hesitated to call this an exploration of aesthetics in Umbanda, because "aesthetics" seems to connote an air of frivolity, a concern with decoration and surfaces. There is nothing superficial about these aesthetics and certainly nothing superficial about their implications. In these surfaces we can see (and smell, and hear) registered a whole history of racism, shame, repression, resistance, affirmation, and ambivalence, revolving around unsettled questions of identity and ethics. And the drama played out on these surfaces penetrates, by way of the senses, the very bodies of the folks at the House of Father John, and the House of Saint Benedict. This is what I mean by a politics of the senses.

NOTES

My research has been generously supported by the Department of Education through a Fulbright-Hayes Doctoral Fellowship and by various fellowships from the Department of Anthropology, the Dean of Liberal Arts, and the Graduate School of the University of Texas at Austin.

1. Names of people and places, along with certain other identifying details, have been changed to protect privacy.

2. There is a rich and varied literature on Afrobrazilian religion, indicative of the diversity of the subject. Sources covering the major varieties of these religions include Monica Augras, *O Duplo e a Metamorfose: A Identidade Mítica em Communidades Nagô* (Petropolis: Vozes, 1983); Roger Bastide, *The African Religions of Brazil* (Baltimore: John Hopkins University Press, 1983); Diana Brown, Umbanda: *Religion and Politics in Urban Brazil* (New York: Columbia University Press, 1994); Maria Concone, *Umbanda, uma religiao brasileira* (Sao Paulo: FFLCH/USP-CER, 1987); Beatriz Dantas, *Vovó Nagô e Papai Branco: Usos e Abusos da África no Brasil* (Rio de Janeiro: Graal, 1982); Juana Elbein dos Santos, *Os Nagô e a Norte: Pade, Asese e o Culto Egun na Bahia* (Petrópolis: Vozes, 1976); Peter Fry, *Para Inglês ver* (Rio de Janeiro: Editóres Zahar, 1982); Chester Gabriel, *Cominicações dos Espíritos* (São Paulo: Edições Loyola, 1985); Russel G. Hamilton Jr., "The Present State of African Cults in Bahia," *Journal of Social History* 3 (1970), 357–373; Lindsay Hale, "Preto Velho: Resistence, Redemption, and En-Gendered Representations of Slavery in a Brazilian Possession-Trance Religion," *American Ethnologist* 24, 2 (1997), 392–414; Meyer Herskovits, "African Gods and Catholic Saints in New World Negro Belief," *American Anthropologist* 39 (1937), 635–643; Ruth Landes, *The City of Women* (New York: Macmillan, 1947); Patricia Lerch, "Spirit Mediums in Umbanda Evangelada of Porto Alegre, Brazil: Dimensions of Power and Austhority," in *A World of Men,* edited by Erika Bourgignon (New York: Praeger, 1980); Marco Aurélio Luz and Georges Lapassade, *O Segredo da Macumba* (Rio de Janeiro: Paz e Terra, 1972); Carlos Marcondes, *Oloorisha: Escritos Sobre a Reli-*

gião dos Orixás (São Paulo: Agora,1981); Paula Montero, *Da Doença à Desordem* (Rio de Janeiro: Graal, 1985); Raimundo Nina Rodrigues,*O Animismo Fetischista dos Negros Bahianos* (Rio de Janeiro: Civilização Brasileiro, 1935); Renato Ortiz, *A Morte Branca do Feiticeiro Negro* (Rio de Janeiro: Editora Vozes, 1978); J. Reginaldo Prandi, *Os candombles de São Paulo: A velha magia na metropole nova* (São Paulo: Editora Hucitec, 1991); Esther Pressel, "Umbanda in São Paulo: Religious Innovation in a Developing Society," in *Religion, Altered States of Consciousness and Social Change,* edited by Erika Bourguignon (Columbus: Ohio State University Press, 1973); Arthur Ramos, *O Negro Brasileiro* (São Paulo: Companhia Editora Nacional, 1940); Parry Scott, *Sobrevivencia e Fontes de Renda; Estrategias das Famílias de Baixa Renda no Recife* (Recife: Editora Massangana, 1983); Liana Trindade, *Exu: Poder e Perigo* (São Paulo: Icone, 1985); Yvonne Maggie Velho, *Guerra de Orixá: Um Estudo de Ritual e Conflito* (Rio de Janeiro: Zahar Editores, 1975); Pierre Verger, *Orixás Deuses Iorubás na Africa e no Novo Mundo* (Salvador, Bahia, Brazil: Corrúpio Edições, 1981); Paul Wafer, *The Taste of Blood: Spirit Possession in Brazilian Candomblé* (Philadelphia: University of Pennsylvania Press, 1991).

3. Chester Gabriel, *Comunicações dos Espíritos* (São Paulo: Edições Loyola, 1985).

4. A detailed discussion of the ideological significance of old slave spirits can be found in Hale, "Preto Velho." Diana Brown gives an overview of the different kinds of Umbanda spirits and their relationship to questions of national identity in *Umbanda.*

5. My longest stretch in the field was a year and several months in 1990–1991; I have made several other trips, each of about three months' duration.

6. Racial prejudice is undeniable to the objective observer. The middle and upper classes are disproportionately white; the poor, disproportionately black. Racial profiling is pervasive, and not only among the police, who are notorious for singling out young black males—for example, from my experience, doormen for upscale condominiums routinely deny access or give the third degree to unknown black visitors, while buzzing up white guests without question. Elite politicians, television stars, and other highly visible symbols of success and prestige are with rare exceptions white; the homeless children who struggle to live on the streets of Rio—and who not so rarely die at the hands of vigilantes—are with few exceptions black. The literature debunking the myth of racial democracy is voluminous; good places to begin are with Thomas Skidmore, *Black into White: Race and Nationality in Brazilian Thought* (New York: Oxford University Press, 1974); and Carl N. Deglar, *Neither Black nor White: Slavery and Race Relations in Brazil and the United States* (Madison: University of Wisconsin Press, 1986).

7. Renato Ortiz, *A Morte Branca do Feiticeiro Negro* (Rio de Janeiro: Editora Vozes, 1978). Readers familiar with Ortiz's book will recognize the influence of his argument that "white Umbanda" or "pure Umbanda" is in part a defensive reaction to the stigmatization of Afrobrazilian religion and culture by the dominant society, especially during the formative decades (early twentieth century) of Umbanda. Diana Brown makes a similar argument, while Luz and LaPassade recognize contestation and affirmation of Afrobrazilian heritage and "counterculture" at places like the House of Father John that I describe in this essay.

8. While this last, dramatic event would seem to be the climax and key to the whole business about the root, I do not recalling hearing of this until 1995—four

years after I first began hearing these stories of Father John. I had always heard that Father John planted his root there—but never until then just how that came about. In other tellings, the conclusion is equally dramatic: Father John is tied to the trunk of a tree to be tortured. As the whip comes down, with his last strength he lunges against the earth, uprooting the tree and propelling it, and himself, into the heavens.)

9. Assertions regarding the good works done for the poor and people of color at the House of Saint Benedict struck me as being frankly paternalistic. In her ethnographic study of a Spiritualist group in Rio, Maria Laura Viveiros de Castro Cavalcanti, *O Mundo Invisível: Cosmologia, Sistema Ritual e Noção de Pessoa no Espíritismo* (Rio de Janeiro: Zahar Editores, 1983, gives an insightful discussion of Spiritualist *cardidade* (charity) directed toward the poor, which resonated with my experience at the House of Saint Benedict.

10. Detailed and insightful accounts can be found in Renato Ortiz, *A Morte Branca do Feiticeiro Negro,* and Brown, Umbanda.

11. Two useful references are: Bastide, *The African Religions of Brazil,* and Paulo Barreto (also known as "João do Rio"), *As Religiões no Rio* (Rio de Janeiro: Novo Aguilar, 1976). Bastide was a sociologist and relies mainly on historical sources; Barreto was a journalist who wrote around the turn of the century; his work is based on his personal observations.

12. Bastide, *The African Religions of Brazil.*

13. *Terreiros* are centers for the practice of Afrobrazilian religion. The word generally refers to an open, leveled space—such as those that Afrobrazilian slaves would have used to secretly practice their religion. Terreiros in Afrobrazilian religious context are built spaces, with roofs but often with dirt floors, reminiscent of the clearings of the past, that allow a direct contact between participants and the earth.

14. Yvonne Maggie (also known as Yvonne Maggie Alves Velho, *Medo do Feitiço: Relações entre Magia e Poder no Brasil* (Rio de Janeiro: Arquivo Nacional, Orgao do Ministerio da Justica, 1992).

15. Joaquim Manoel de Macedo, *As Victimas Algozes* (Rio de Janeiro: Typ. American, 1869); my translation.

16. Barreto, *As Religiões no Rio.*

17. Mario Laura Vveiros de Castro Cavalcanti gives a detailed ethnographic account of Spiritualism in contemporary Rio, *O Mundo Invisível: Cosmologia, Sistema Ritual e Noção de Pessoa no Espíritismo* (Rio de Janeiro: Zahar Editores, 1983).

18. Israel Cysneiros, *Umbanda: Poder e Magia* (Umbanda: Power and Magic) (Rio de Janeiro: Sindicato Nacional dos Editôres de Livros, 1983); 99-100, my translation.

19. Brown, *Umbanda.* Ronaldo Antônio Linares Linares, "Como Conheci Zélio de Morães, O Pai da Umbanda," and "Mais um Pouquinho Sobre Zélio de Morães," in *Iniciação à Umbanda,* vol. 2 (São Paulo: Icone Editora, 1988), 15–20.

20. Brown, *Umbanda,* 39–40.

21. See for example Brown, *Umbanda,* and Lindsay Hale, "Mama Oxum: Reflections of Gender and Sexuality in Brazilian Umbanda," in *Osun Across the Waters,* edited by Mei Sanford and Joseph Murphy Bloomington: Indiana University Press, 2001), 213–229.

22. Mané also goes by the name of Benedito.

23. Mané also gives a somewhat different explanation of how the Cabalans came to earth. It seems that the people of Cabal were pure spirit. Over thousands of years, they grew so numerous that the planet's gravitational field could not hold them all, and many of them were spun off into space, wandering through the universe. Some of these wanderers happened upon planet Earth and founded the civilization of Atlantis. I never pursued with Mané which was the "correct" account.

24. While my discussion of Mané's tale(s) emphasizes its racist dimensions, Mané seemed most interested in the fantastic aspects of space travel, the advent of civilization, and Atlantis and its downfall—and, at the end of the story, the mission of restoring Umbanda to its pure, original form.

25. Victor Turner, *Dramas, Fields, and Metaphors; Symbolic Action in Human Society* (Ithaca, N.Y.: Cornell University Press, 1974), 45. Turner defines communitas as a "bond uniting . . . people over and above any formal social bonds" and applies this concept most usefully to religious rituals, pilgrimages, and other totally involving social performances that dissolve everyday hierarchies and powerfully unite people in a feeling of shared humanity—if only momentarily. That certainly is a frequent effect of the rituals at Father John's.

12

Projecting Blackness: African-American Religion in the Hollywood Imagination

Judith Weisenfeld

Religion, Race, and American Film

The process of articulating racial and ethnic categories in conjunction with discourses about Americanness has been an integral part of American film from the earliest years of movie-making in the United States. As Daniel Bernardi notes in his collection of essays on race and early film, "cinema's invention and early development coincided with the rise in power and prestige of biological determinism, with increased immigration and immigrant restriction laws, and with the United States' imperialist practices in the Caribbean and Asia." He further argues that these "sociopolitical practices" so profoundly affected the development of early cinema that processes of racializing can be seen across "studios, authors, genres, and styles."[1] The work of exploring, defining, and projecting concepts of race, then, were woven into the fabric of this industry that would become such an influential part of American popular culture. By the 1930s, when the Hollywood studio system had solidified what scholars refer to as the classical Hollywood style, race had become a central and unremarked component of silver screen images of Americanness.[2]

In a growing body of work on the social construction of race, a number of scholars have argued that notions of race emerged as the primary way to express belief in inherent and fundamental moral, intellectual, and social capacities of people, investing what seem to be simple, visible differences with evaluative and hierarchical significance under the authority of the natural sciences.[3] Lola Young's work emphasizes the profound consequences for people of African descent of the shift from merely observing difference to evaluating it. She writes that "the African's skin colour became the defining characteristic and 'black,' from operating at a connotative level shifted to a denotative plane: to be black was to *be* evil, to *be* hypersexual, to *be* morally debased, to *be* inferior."[4] Thus the process of constructing race in America has involved attributing what are understood to be visible physical differences with larger meaning and ultimate significance. The production and maintenance of racial categories requires "technologies"—legitimating mechanisms that help to structure our lives in public and material ways, as well as in more subtle and veiled ways we are sometimes hardly aware of. These technologies consist of the set of elaborated discourses, "implemented through pedagogy, medicine, demography . . . economics," for example, that produce, re-produce, and seek to regulate race.[5] Film, as a significant contributor to the discursive production of race, gender, and sexuality in America, certainly deserves an important place in any discussion of the technology of race.

Film and other aspects of visual culture prove very effective in helping to produce and maintain race because of the profoundly visual nature of racial construction. Those of us who have been formed in the cultural context of the United States, for example, are trained to look and, through looking, to discern the racial location of the people we view. And, for most of us, what we believe we learn from this internalized and often unconscious way of looking helps us decide how to proceed in relation to the people our eye evaluates. Even those who resist acting in ways that are expected in a racially stratified system (e.g. by accepting and internalizing racial hierarchy) are, nevertheless, aware of the power of the structuring mechanism of race. Once inside a racialized system, the gaze of some racialized people is necessarily empowered and empowering while others are not permitted to look, or to define the terms for visual interaction. Those empowered to look also assume the power to categorize and racialize. Because "race" as we know it is so fundamentally an epistemological product of the West, it certainly makes sense that it relies profoundly on the visual—generally taken to be the most privileged sense in the Western consciousness. Oyeronke Oyewumi argues that the West privileges the body (a move that is a prerequisite to the development of racial categories) because "the world is primarily perceived by sight. . . . The gaze is an invitation to differentiate."[6] But the centrality of the body in Western thought also stands alongside the insistence that Western rationality has subordinated the body, which then becomes the province of the nonrational other. " 'Bodylessness,' " Oyewumi writes,

> has been a precondition of rational thought. Women, primitives, Jews, Africans, the poor, and all those qualified for the label "different" in varying historical epochs have been considered to be the em-

bodied, dominated therefore by instinct and affect, reason being beyond them. They are the Other, and the Other is a body.[7]

The "film eye" has participated fully in this process of racializing through
differentiation and through the privileging of some perspectives over others,
and by valuing as aesthetically pleasing some bodies and not others.

Historians of American religion have only just begun to explore the impact
of the moving image on twentieth-century American religious life. Recent
scholarship on religion and American visual and material culture has focused,
for example, on Protestant iconography, on the functions of material culture
in the homes of religious individuals, and on understanding particularly religious ways of viewing. Film, which is such a profoundly affecting medium,
and one in which filmmakers have often engaged religious themes, has been
comparatively less studied. In addition to producing scores of Bible films and
religious epics, Hollywood studios and independent filmmakers have utilized
religious issues, characters, and conflicts as subject matter for American movies since cinema's earliest days. The variety of uses of religion in American
film, particularly in relation to the projection of racial categories, calls out for
serious attention. Margaret Miles has rightly argued that we must be careful
to differentiate between the power of the devotional image and that of images
from mass media, but at the same time she insists that we must take seriously
the ways the conventions of mass media influence viewers with regard to religious issues.[8] There are, in fact, many instances in the history of American
film in which filmmakers have produced movies with explicitly religious goals
in mind, presenting them as devotional images for use with confessional audiences. More commonly, the commercial film industry has deployed images
of religiosity as part of its "crucial role in [the] construction . . . representation/
re-presentation, and . . . transmission" of particular understandings of American identity.[9]

My broadest concern in this essay is with the ways American films have
represented religiosity through the technology of race, with particular emphasis
on the presentation of African-American religion. The close ties between particular ways of racializing characters in film (that is, using the privileged gaze
of the camera to invest skin color with moral meaning) and representations of
religion are striking in even any brief survey of American movies. The coupling
of religion and race at certain moments in film authorizes and naturalizes
American racial categories and works to describe and proscribe the boundaries
of the category of religion. In many cases, mobilizing race in relation to religion
helps to train the spectator with regard to what is and is not to be considered
appropriate religion for the American context. The drive to define insider and
outsider categories of religion, common in so many social contexts, has often
coincided with the power exercised in the United States by some racialized
groups over others. We must understand the contest for the very right to define

what constitutes religion as situated in a field of other categories in process, including those of "modern," "primitive," "American," "foreign," "man," "woman," and "white." Lillian Smith, in reflecting on growing up white in the Jim Crow American South, has described the impossibility of separating out the elements that have contributed to the formation of American identities and of understanding these categories in isolation from one another.

> Religion . . . sex . . . race . . . avoidance rites . . . —no part of these
> can be looked at and clearly seen without looking at the whole of
> them. For, as a painter mixes color and makes them new colors, so
> religion is turned into something different by race, and segregation
> is colored as much by sex as by skin pigment.[10]

Film has functioned as an important arena in which this mixing has taken place.

Constructions of blackness must, by necessity, be the starting point for my discussion because the black body is the ground on which racial hierarchy rests in the United States context and images of blackness in American film have proved very powerful legitimating mechanisms for racial hierarchy.[11] Hollywood traditions of representing African-American *religion* have been central to the formation of U.S. filmic images of blackness. Anyone familiar with American movies knows the commonplace strategies of marginalizing black characters in the narrative and in the visual frame (usually by including them only as faithful servants) and of deploying them as mirrors that help to construct whiteness.[12] Another common Hollywood projection of blackness positions black characters at the center by focusing on the performative aspects of African-American religious practice and by deploying an aesthetic that relies on constructions of the primitive. The majority of Hollywood's "all-colored cast" films produced from the late 1920s through the late 1940s use religious contexts to frame their stories. These "all-colored cast" films include: *Hearts in Dixie* (1929), *Hallelujah* (1929), *The Green Pastures* (1936), and *Cabin in the Sky* (1943), as well as significant segments of other films such as *A Night at the Opera* (1935) and *Tales of Manhattan* (1942), among others.[13] These films that focus on African-American religion stand alongside the legions of Hollywood movies (most of them "B" movies) that imagine African and Afro-Caribbean religions and use them to mark sites of chaos and terror.

In most cases, the "all-colored cast" films and the jungle films recognize and make use of the power of the aesthetics of African-American religious expression, so often grounded in utilizing the body's sound and motion as conduits to connect with the divine. Many of the actors involved in the productions did bring experiences with and commitment to a religious way of being that emphasizes modes of worship developed in African-American social contexts and that values oral and embodied performances of the word of God. In mobilizing black religious aesthetics, these Hollywood films did so in service of an essentialized understanding of African-American religion, presenting something the filmmakers understood to be the fundamental religious and racial nature of "the Negro race." In this view, African Americans do not experience the true power of the divine in their lives but simply imagine—through childish, emotional, and musical displays, devoid of theological inquiry—that they do.

In this essay, I use Metro-Goldwyn-Mayer's 1929 film *Hallelujah*—a significant signpost on the Hollywood landscape of representations of blackness and black religiosity in this period—to disclose and examine patterns in American popular culture traditions of racializing religion. *Hallelujah* marked both a solidifying and a transformation of a set of traditional approaches to representing blackness in American popular culture, moving away from using black religion almost exclusively for comedic or horror purposes and instead exploring its dramatic possibilities. Metro-Goldwyn-Mayer's strategy of presenting this narrative dramatic film as "authentic" and as containing documentary truth based on the observation of blacks by a Southern white man is indispensable to the pattern that it set. The aesthetic of primitive black religion that *Hallelujah* presents becomes immediately sanctioned by this discourse of authenticity. In significant ways *Hallelujah* conformed to the conventional ways in which American literature, art, and theater have figured people of African descent as "natural," as opposed to reasonable; childlike and therefore unfit for full citizenship; and inherently religious in ways that are inextricably linked to sexual expression. *Hallelujah* stands as an instructive example of the Hollywood approach to encoding religion as a central constitutive component of the construction of race. In this, and in the other "all-colored cast" films of the period, understanding African-American religion is fundamental to interpreting the moral valence of blackness in the United States. The film encourages viewers to believe that they cannot properly locate African Americans on the American social and political landscape without first consuming the spectacle of black religious practice. The conclusion toward which the film propels viewers insists that a true understanding of African-American religious expression requires that whites forever exclude African Americans from access to full citizenship.

Discourses of Authenticity

In 1928, King Vidor, one of Metro-Goldwyn Mayer's most successful directors, finding himself in between projects, decided to spend some time in Europe. Having directed a number of important and successful silent films for MGM—most notably *The Big Parade* (1925), a World War I epic, and *The Crowd* (1928), a study of the life of an average man set against the large urban environment of New York City—Vidor was excited when he heard that the studio wanted him to direct his first sound film. Synchronous sound, in which the dialogue or singing correspond with the movement of the actors' lips, had only begun to make its way into American feature films since the 1927 release of the landmark Warner Brothers film *The Jazz Singer*, itself very much about complex processes of racializing religion in America.[14] Just as the projection of constructions of race had been part of the development of the silent motion picture, so had the addition of sound been bound up in conjunctions of religion and race from the outset, and Vidor had in mind something that would contribute both to the new "talkie" technology and to the ideological landscape of racialized religion. He recalled in a memoir years later that the idea for this movie had been with him for a long time, writing:

> for several years I had nurtured a secret hope. I wanted to make a film about Negroes, using only Negroes in the cast. The sincerity and fervor of their religious expression intrigued me, as did the honest simplicity of their sexual drives. In many instances the intermingling of these two activities seemed to offer strikingly dramatic content.[15]

Having been unable to convince MGM to permit him to do such a film in past years, Vidor was excited that the availability of the new sound technology would strengthen his argument, and he began making concrete plans. Aboard ship returning to the United States he drew up a list for the studio of elements "suitable for an all-Negro sound film," foregrounding religion: "river baptisms, prayer-meetings accompanied by spirituals, Negro preaching, banjo playing, dancing, and the blues."[16] Vidor's desire to make this film was so great that, in attempting to overcome the resistance of the studio to the idea of an "all-Negro cast" film, he pledged to defer receiving his salary in order to defray the film's production expenses.[17] Once Vidor received permission to go ahead with the film, the studio allowed him to exercise a large measure of control over all phases of production and, as a result, the final product was largely the result of his wishes and decisions, with a few significant exceptions of intervention from the studio and the censors.[18]

The story that Vidor chose for his first sound film focuses on Zeke (Daniel L. Haynes), the eldest son in a large family of sharecroppers, his conversion following his brother's death, his rise to renown as an itinerant revivalist, and his fall resulting from the seductive lures of Chick (Nina Mae McKinney), a woman he converts and baptizes. Despite the attempts of his parents, both devoutly religious, to keep him from falling prey to temptation in the city, Zeke succumbs. After running off with Chick and murdering her former lover (who is responsible for Chick's death near the film's end), Zeke serves a term in prison, an experience that redeems him and permits him to return to the idyllic life of the rural South. In interviews leading up to the film's release Vidor insisted that he created the story from his own observations of southern black life, arguing forcefully for its authenticity. He told a reporter, "I used to watch the Negroes in the South, which was my home. I studied their music, and I used to wonder at the pent-up romance in them. . . . The story is based on events with which I was familiar as a boy at home in Texas."[19] When the picture was finally released, the studio's promotional material emphasized Vidor's qualifications to direct this "authentic" rendering of black life, focusing on his credentials as a native southerner and, therefore, his intimate knowledge of the "colorful race."[20]

Vidor understood MGM's fear that white southerners might interpret the release of an all-colored cast film as a political statement about African-American civil rights and respond negatively to the film and, subsequently, to other MGM productions. In numerous comments to the press during the production period the director articulated a set of limited goals for the film, insisting that he had no intention of making a political statement. Nevertheless, Vidor saw himself as providing some sort of service to African Americans by making them the subject of his movie and rendering them as "real." Louella Parsons, the Hollywood gossip columnist for the Hearst newspapers, reported: "Mr. Vidor hopes to make a race picture just as 'Nanook of the North' was a race picture, and above all, he wants to show Negro life as it really is and without a mission or problem to solve."[21] Vidor insisted that the film would be a small, focused, emotional study in contrast to the large-scale pictures he had done in the silent cinema, and he reassured the studio and potential white viewers that such a "factual" representation need not involve any statement for social change.[22]

Just as Vidor claimed to have no interest in politics in producing this film, he also asserted that he did not intend to make any particular religious statement, although he did understand the medium of film to be, in many ways, a mode of spiritual expression. "All my life I have been interested in the science of being: ontology," Vidor said many years later. "And this fascination has kept pace with my professional dedication: film making." He continued,

> perhaps films can help us learn about life and living. Does the
> chance to watch shadows of ourselves in the speaking dark of a
> movie house explain cinema's great attraction. . . . Must I, as a direc-
> tor, continue to see films and life as an antinomy? Why must I pain-
> fully shuttle back and forth between the real and the unreal? Life is
> one. I must try to meld the science of being and the aesthetics of
> cinema. Only by doing this can I hope to evolve a comprehensive
> and viable philosophy of film making. . . . How else are we to ex-
> press our humanness? How else are we to express God?[23]

Although Vidor did not put this discourse into play explicitly during the production and publicity phases of the film, his perspective on film as an expression of the divine must certainly have informed his approach to *Hallelujah*.

It seems clear that, from Vidor's perspective, multiple authenticating mechanisms combined to support and justify this production in which he would place African-American religious life at the center. First, he relied on his belief that film allows the filmmaker privileged access to profound onto-logical questions, to the very nature of being—necessarily, it seems, racialized. Second, he emphasized the importance of his own specialized "knowledge" of African-American life, acquired through his empowered position as a white male observer, to ensuring the authenticity of the production. The question of the authenticity of the film's representation of black religiosity would surface time and again as the censors evaluated the film, as various publics viewed and commented on it, and as many African Americans objected to its rendering of "Negro life as it really is"—that is, to the imaginings of a Southern white man who insisted that "the Negro" was a singular entity and that he had priv-ileged insight into something essentially "Negro."

African Americans who were involved in the production or were simply keen observers of American popular and political cultures expressed tremen-dous hope that the film might both reshape screen images of blacks and have a concrete impact on their social and political lives. Two aspects of the pro-duction stood out as particularly heartening for many African-American com-mentators. First, that it was to be a sound picture, and, second, that its story would focus on black religious life. In some cases, in fact, the black press linked the two issues, as in the conjecture by the *Amsterdam News* that "since Halle-lujah is to have dialogue and vocal sequences, it is quite likely that the actors will sing all the well known spirituals."[24] The coming of sound, many black observers thought, would finally allow black actors to appear on the screen in dignified ways. Attention to the vocal skills of black actors, one line of argument proposed, would necessarily shift focus from the physical, aggressively em-bodied, and comedic emphasis in representing blackness. Ruby Berkley Good-win, an entertainment writer for the *Pittsburgh Courier*, opined: "much depends upon the Negro pioneers in this field of art. Interviewing some of them, we are convinced that the race will be well represented. Their voices blend perfectly in the spirituals and folk songs of the Negro. Their voices, soft and intonating are suited perfectly for screen-sound reproduction."[25] Summing up the hopes that many African Americans held for the film's social impact, Daniel L. Haynes, the film's lead actor, wrote: "I cannot say what our race owes King Vidor and Metro-Goldwyn-Mayer—there are not words forceful enough for that. 'Hallelujah' will, as Moses led his people from the wilderness, lead ours from the wilderness of misunderstanding and apathy."[26]

Appearing in the context of the large-scale urbanization of African Amer-icans and the tremendous expansion of vibrant black cultures in Chicago, De-troit, New York and other cities, *Hallelujah* touched on issues of concern to many African Americans, most particularly the religious meaning of urbani-zation and modernization. Vidor seems to have understood that a great deal was at stake in the shifts—of population, ideology, and sense of self—that were brought on for African Americans by the Great Migration of the early twentieth century. Where the political, literary, and social movements of the period emphasized and facilitated self-representation and agency in picturing African Americans, however complicated and contested this process remained, the marginal status of blacks in these early Hollywood films necessarily meant that the images produced were largely out of their control. The way in which African-American religious leaders, expressions, and institutions would appear in the Hollywood imaginary would largely be the result of a series of negotiations among white men in Hollywood and in the various agencies that managed the products of the industry.

The Motion Picture Producers and Distributors Association (MPPDA), the body responsible for regulating the content of Hollywood films, found much of Vidor's story proposal, script, and then final film product far too explicit in its portrayal of the fall of a preacher. At this point in its history the MPPDA operated under the guidelines of the "Don'ts and Be Carefuls," which prohibited, among other things, "willful offense to any nation, race, or creed" and "ridicule of the clergy" in any film produced by members of the Association, "irrespective of the manner in which they are treated."[27] "Colonel" Jason Joy, the head of the MPPDA's Studio Relations Department at this time, wrote to his staff that he had informed Vidor and the MGM producer Irving Thalberg that the story raised a number of problems in relation to the "Don'ts and Be Careful's." Joy's initial discomfort with the scenario also had to do with Vidor's plans to include a scene of a crap game and the use of the word "nigger" but later included concern for the film's representations of sexuality. Joy singled out the problem of "a strong negro [Zeke] exhibiting passions" as having the potential to disturb white viewers.[28]

At the same time that the film's treatment of African-American sexuality raised questions for Joy, he also found its uses of religion discomfiting. That the film associated Zeke's work as a revivalist with that of "real" ministers might offend "the religious people of the country," he thought. Vidor's script made this association clear, according to Joy, in a scene in which Zeke preaches at a revival and begins by saying "The text of my sermon will be . . ." In addition, in the first scene in which we see Zeke as a preacher, he and his family arrive in a small town to conduct a revival. They disembark from a railroad car that has the words "Ezekiel The Prophet" painted on the side. Zeke, wearing a silk robe, rides on a donkey at the rear of a parade of children waving small American flags and singing "Great Day, the Righteous Marching." Joy found this image particularly disturbing, as it could easily be read as "emulat[ing] Christ's journey into Jerusalem."[29] Joy took Vidor's imagined childish reenactment of Jesus entering Jerusalem as an authentic performance of black religion but also held out the possibility that the story could be made acceptable to "the religious people of the country" and that black religion could be presented as approximating real religion if the film could mute its representation of the morally corrupt preacher.[30] Although Vidor never modified the story to displace Zeke as the central character, Joy would soon be appeased on a number of counts as Vidor revised the synopsis, emphasizing to Joy's satisfaction that the father remained an appropriate clerical model (at least, as I will show, for a black preacher) and later removing references to Zeke as "the black Jedus" (sic).[31]

Other people at the MPPDA who evaluated the script and, later, the completed film concurred with Joy's sense of the tenuous connection between the film's version of African-American religion and real Christianity and expressed similar discomfort with the possibility that the film might leave a more affirmative impression with viewers. Joy and others feared that white Americans would find the notion that they were to take what they saw on screen as an expression of Christianity offensive. Nevertheless, Vidor's representation of black religiosity partook of available stereotypes to a degree sufficient to make sense to and placate the censors. Although the MPPDA required minor changes in the script, the association ultimately approved the project on the grounds that it provided a "realistic" portrayal of African-American life. Lamar Trotti, one of the MPPDA censors and a southerner, made authenticity the focus of his evaluation of the project in a letter he wrote summarizing his initial impressions. Trotti wrote to his superiors that, had the characters of Vidor's film been white, the film could not be released, but because the characters were black he did not think the MPPDA should worry. No one, Trotti insisted, believes in the sincerity of black religious expression. He concluded his evaluation: "The story seems real enough. If the characters were white it might be likened to Elmer Gantry, but there is no thought that Zeke is a hypocrite. He is just a weak nigger in the toils of a black Deborah."[32]

Despite the initial resistance from the censors, as well as some from the studio, Vidor was permitted to proceed and, by many counts, succeeded in his attempt to produce a "realistic" story about black life and religion in the South. An evaluator for the MPPDA who saw the film at its premiere at the Embassy Theater in New York City wrote:

> this film is full of the religious customs of the uneducated negroes, camp meetings where they roll on the floor and wave their arms and do all sorts of crazy things, baptisms in the river, where they act like crazy people; and many other curious performances which although true to life will not be understood by anyone who doesn't know negro customs fairly well.[33]

In many cases, the alleged realism of the film's portrayal of African-American religious display served as the most potent justification of its racism. When, for example, the Canadian province of British Columbia rejected the film for distribution on the basis of its conjunction of religion and sexuality, a studio representative suggested that the MPPDA argue in the film's favor on its merits as a "sincere portrayal of negro religious rituals."[34] One of *Variety*'s reviewers argued that the film presented

> a camera reproduction of the typical southland with its wide open cotton spaces, where the good natured, singing negro continues to eke out a bare existence. . . . It brings realistically to the screen how he lives in nondescript surroundings with continual evidence of illiteracy that even remains unpolished when becoming hysterically religious.[35]

In *Hallelujah* Vidor sought to provide a definitive statement on the race, it's psychology, and its religious practices. His approach incorporated existing traditions of popular culture representations of black religion in picturing it not only as simple and instinctive, and therefore appropriate for the childlike Negro, but also as fundamentally sexual. The film's story focuses, ultimately, on the inability of its central male and female characters to distinguish between religious sentiment and forms of expression on the one hand and their sexual desire for one another on the other, and Vidor presents this religious spectacle as revealing of the essential moral nature of blackness, as well as one that charts the political and social possibilities of African Americans.

Religion, Race, and Sexuality

When viewers first meet Zeke (Daniel L. Haynes), Vidor's main character, he is not seeking to become a religious leader—a status he achieves in the course of a wake for his brother, whose death has resulted from Zeke's neglect—nor does he seem to desire anything other than simple pleasures and his family's happiness. Early in the film, Vidor establishes Zeke's family context as one in which daily life needs are simple and religion is important, as he shows the members of the family reading the Bible aloud after a long day's work in the cotton fields. The interactions among Mammy (Fanny Belle DeKnight), Pappy (Harry Gray), and their children in these early scenes situate the family as generally religious. Vidor establishes Pappy's position as a religious leader in a larger community when Adam and Eve, along with their eleven children, visit and ask him to officiate at their wedding. Pappy notes with some dismay that "the damage is all done" but relents, concluding that "it's never too late to do the will of the Lord."[36] When Mammy congratulates them on finally getting around to "doing the right thing," Eve ties the decision to marry to her sense of herself as a respectable woman, insisting that she has always been so and wants to avoid any implication otherwise (see figure 12.1).

In this opening framing sequence, Vidor appears to be particularly interested in the question of whether the moral character of blackness can be ac-

FIGURE 12.1. Adam and Eve (center) ask Pappy (left) to marry them. Zeke (right) looks on. From Photographs and Prints Division, Schomburg Center for Research in Black Culture, The New York Public Library, Astor, Lenox, Tilden Foundations.

commodated to American national identity. Zeke, Mammy, and Pappy become central to his exploration of this issue, and his conclusion requires the characters to remain located in the strangely utopic cotton fields of the deep South, which he understands to be the natural environs of the American Negro. In this view, urbanization and cultural transformations that move blacks away from the rural can only be damaging because these processes might lead African Americans to imagine themselves as other than a primitive subculture within American society. Mammy's response to Eve's assertion of respectability strikes one of the film's central themes for the first time and emphasizes the film's perspective that the character of blacks is fixed and irredeemable despite their best efforts to act in ways contrary to that fundamental racialized nature.

In the context of the wedding, Vidor first reveals Zeke's inexorable conflation of religion and sexuality. As Adam, Eve, Mammy, and Pappy prepare for the wedding, Zeke follows Rose (Victoria Spivey), his adopted sister, into the living room. When Zeke enters the room, Rose is sitting at a small organ and begins to play the wedding march. We see Rose from behind as she sways from left to right on the stool and as Zeke advances toward her. Rose, unaware that Zeke is behind her, completes the song and leans toward the window to listen to Pappy performing the ceremony. Vidor cuts to a close-up of Zeke's face as he approaches Rose from behind. He breathes heavily and the expression on his face is clearly one of desire. We see Rose listening, still unaware that Zeke is in the room. Then, in a particularly intense sequence, Vidor shoots from Zeke's point of view and we see his hand reaching out to Rose's shoulder. Innocently, Rose turns around and looks in Zeke's direction. At first she seems happy to see him but alarm soon registers on her face. As Vidor cuts to a wider shot of Rose sitting and Zeke standing, we hear Pappy outside explaining to the bride and groom that marriage is like the mystical union between Christ and his church. Just then Zeke insists that Rose kiss him and, as she stands up and begins to back away, grabs her and draws her to him. As Rose begs Zeke to let her go, he pulls her close and kisses her, and, while she is clearly uncomfortable, she does not struggle. Zeke suddenly backs away from Rose and clutches his chest, looking shocked at what he has done. When they are called to come outside to celebrate the conclusion of the wedding ceremony, Zeke apologizes to Rose, saying, "It looks like the devil's in me here tonight." Rose readily forgives him.

The wedding segment is characterized by a number of powerful juxtapositions between marriage understood as a sacred institution on the one hand and the desire for illicit sexuality on the other. As I have already mentioned, Vidor introduces the encounter between Zeke and Rose in connection with Adam and Eve's announced desire for a wedding ceremony, despite having been together long enough to have produced many children. Pappy conducts the ceremony under a tree in the backyard, no doubt a reference to the tree in the Garden of Eden, given the deliberate selection of the names Adam and Eve. The sanctification of the couple's relationship, one already marred by illicit sex, takes place in the shadow of the symbol of the fall of humanity. Vidor may also have made subtle reference to the ascendancy of sexual desire over the sanctity of marriage in his positioning of Zeke and Rose in relation to one another. When Rose sits at the organ with her back to Zeke, an inverted broom leaning against the wall divides the frame with Rose to its left and Zeke to its right. The broom is a potent symbol in African-American history. Denied legally recognized marriage ceremonies, enslaved African-American men and women frequently conducted a ritual to mark their commitment to one another that involved jumping a broomstick. Vidor's use of an inverted broom in the frame emphasizes his view that sexuality compromises these characters' religious commitment.[37]

Vidor does not remain at the level of simply *noting* an association between religious and sexual expression for African Americans—as in the wedding scene—but proceeds to locate a profoundly sexualized religion at the center of African-American ritual. For example, when Zeke baptizes Chick after she is converted under his preaching at a revival, she interprets her religious experience in sexualized terms and in terms of her relationship to Zeke rather than to God or Jesus. As she is being dunked in the river, she cries out, "I have been a wicked woman. Oh, I've been a wicked woman but I'm sanctified now. Hal-lelujah. All because of you, brother Zekiel. Keep me good, keep me good, don't let me sin no more." And later, when Hot Shot (William E. Fountaine), her former lover, ridicules her conversion, she tells him that her soul has been "washed in the spring of the Lamb." He responds that she's been "washed in fires of the devil," insisting that she mistakes sexual desire for spiritual trans-formation. Chick objects to Hot Shot's attempt to convince her to continue in the con game with him and insists that no one will "keep [her] from the pro-tecting arms of Brother Zekiel." At her baptism Chick becomes completely lost in religious ecstasy, and, to the dismay of his family and followers, Zeke carries her out of the water and into a nearby tent. He is clearly affected by his prox-imity to Chick and by her sexualized moans. Vidor cuts to the interior of the tent as Mammy enters. We cannot see Zeke and Chick but hear her persistent moaning. The camera cuts to Chick lying on a cot, moaning in religious and sexual ecstasy, and Zeke embracing her and wildly kissing her neck. Mammy sends Zeke off, ashamed of himself, and chastises Chick, calling her a hypo-crite and telling her that she's got more religion than is good for her (see figure 12.2). From this point on, neither Zeke nor Chick can seem to separate sexual expression from religious experience.

The most striking and profoundly articulated section of the film in which Vidor weds African-American religion to sexuality takes place at the evening revival following the baptism. The set for the revival is a large, open, barn-like structure with a stage at the front, on which Zeke and his family stand. The room is darkened, but the available light casts shadows on the walls. Zeke preaches a short sermon promising to fight the devil on behalf of his people. Following the sermon the people begin to sing, form a circle, and move slowly around the room in a counterclockwise direction. We hear the sound of women wailing with emotion as it becomes clear that Chick stands at the center of the crowd, deeply involved in the emotion and physicality of the worship. Chick bounces in time to the music, with her arms raised, moving up and down, bending her knees. Following a close-up of Chick dancing ecstatically, Vidor cuts to a medium close-up of Zeke looking down at Chick from his position on the stage, his eyes wide with desire. Vidor then repeats this exchange, fol-lowing with a close-up of Rose, and later one of Mammy and then of Pappy, all clearly suspicious of Chick's intentions. Chick moves toward Zeke, stands directly in front of him, and grasps his leg, as he attempts to control himself. Chick motions with her head for Zeke to join her, and he steps down from the platform, bobbing up and down in the same manner that Chick has been. Zeke and Chick are now at the center of the circle, bending their knees in time to the music and moving in a clearly sexual manner. At one point, Chick looks at Zeke intensely, takes his hand, and puts the base of his thumb in her mouth, emphasizing the sexual nature of this worship. Eventually, Chick leaves the

FIGURE 12.2. Mammy chastises Chick. From Photographs and Prints Division, Schomburg Center for Research in Black Culture, The New York Public Library, Astor, Lenox, Tilden Foundations.

building, with Zeke following close behind, and the two run off into the woods. This scene serves as the culmination of a number of scenes in which Zeke and Chick commit themselves to resisting sexual temptation and yet find that religious expression leads them, inevitably, to sexual expression.

Music is an integral part of the way the film insists on African Americans' conflation of religion and sex in ways that Vidor argues necessarily marginalizes them from American political and social power. Music inaugurates and accompanies much of the religious frenzy and, outside of the religious contexts in the film, helps to present the characters as carefree children. At the same time, however, the film's music is often extremely compelling and enriches the high-quality visual elements. As a folk musical, *Hallelujah* integrates music into the story in a seamless way, relying on contexts in which people might naturally sing—at work in the fields, performing household chores, at religious services, and so on.[38] With the exception of "At the End of the Road," written by Irving Berlin, most of the film's music comes from African-American contexts, particularly traditional spirituals and blues. Vidor hired Eva Jessye, a college-educated former teacher and former member of the editorial staff of the *Baltimore Afro-American,* as the film's musical director. In an article published some months before the film's release, Jessye argued that music would be central to the film's power and took special pride in the variety of "Negro music" included and in her work as arranger and conductor for Baltimore's Dixie Jubilee Singers, featured on the soundtrack.[39] Many black commentators on the film noted its effective use of spirituals. W. E. B. Du Bois, in his review in the NAACP's paper *The Crisis*, longed for even more traditional music instead of the Irving Berlin "theme-song" but conceded that "the world is not as crazy about Negro folk songs as I am."[40] Berlin's song "At the End of the Road," which tells of happiness and redemption in the future, anchors the film's presentation of music, and in some ways the film positions Berlin's interpretation of "jazz" or of black music as being just as authentically black as the spirituals.[41]

Spirituals and the blues function in expected ways in the film to draw a contrast between religious life and worldliness, as well as to authenticate *Hallelujah's* portrayal of black life. In addition, the film contains a number of extremely moving moments in which Mammy sings traditional folk songs or sings extemporaneously, both underscoring the potential of the folk musical to tap "the transforming power of memory."[42] Early on, Mammy sings "All the Pretty Little Horses" while rocking her small children to sleep, each in turn. Later in the film, she vocalizes her distress as she senses something amiss (and will soon learn of the death of her son), chanting, "Lord, have mercy on my soul."[43] At the same time that folk songs and spirituals lend an air of dignity to some of the characters, the coupling of the spirituals with "tom-tom" drums signals the danger of sexuality. Indeed, the first sound one hears as the film begins—even as the screen remains black—is that of a distant drum, marking the characters and narrative to follow as primitive and probably unable to be redeemed or elevated.

Conclusions

Despite the widespread acknowledgment that Vidor had accomplished a great deal with his first sound film and that the release of an "all-colored cast" film produced by a major studio was a historic event, many commentators and reviewers—black and white—remained deeply uncomfortable with what they understood to be the larger implications of this particular rendering of black religiosity. Agreeing in some measure with Vidor's belief in the possibilities of an "all-colored cast" drama, Earl A. Ballard, a "race writer," commented that

> while the photoplay has served to give vent to the innate ability as actors to the principal characters who have won favorable comments from the critics of the daily press, it is a flagrant and misleading mockery of the race's religion. Some say it is blasphemous and had

any other race been involved, never would have passed the Board of Censors.[44]

John T. Sherman of the *New York News* insisted that "while 'Hallelujah' gives great opportunity for the race artistry, it undeniably pictures the group as moral morons and religious barbarians."[45] One black New Yorker who attended the film's premier objected to the *Amsterdam News*'s support of Vidor's work and emphasized the disjuncture between the self-representation of many African Americans in the period and Vidor's representation. He railed:

> after the picture was well under way on its opening night, it was clearly to be seen that the superb acting of the cast was being over- shadowed by the amount of spirituals, meaning weeping and wail- ing, and the weak, the low [in] spirit were dominating the picture. When one sees "Hallelujah," stripped to the bone and laid bare it is not hard to imagine why Harlem is the largest Negro City in Amer- ica, why Chicago, Philadelphia, and Baltimore and the others are in- creasing in Negro populations. "Hallelujah" is the answer."[46]

This viewer interpreted the film as insisting on a fixed and unchanging moral state for African Americans, a position that would ensure perpetual margin- alization from "American" culture. The Great Migration and African-American cultural and political developments in the period would, the writer asserted, prove otherwise.

Regardless of the position that African Americans took on this film, it seemed clear to all those who entered the public debate that more than just a movie was at stake and that any representation of African Americans on film could have social and political consequences. Indeed, the fortunes of the "all- colored cast" film declined in the wake of *Hallelujah*'s release. In the North, exhibitors feared that large numbers of African Americans desirous of seeing these movies would go to theaters in areas outside "their own neighborhood houses," mingle with whites, and inflame racial tensions in cities newly burst- ing with southern black migrants. In the wake of the film's release, a conven- tion of film exhibitors in the Southeast voted to forego showing any Negro pictures, and participants devoted special attention to MGM for its production of *Hallelujah* and its plans to release other films with black characters.[47]

While some film exhibitors felt that the production by major Hollywood studios of these "all-colored cast" films would give African Americans an in- flated sense of themselves, the configuration of race and religion presented by such films seems designed to accomplish something quite different. The tem- plate that *Hallelujah* set for representing African-American religion involved insisting on a fundamentally simplistic and imitative theology, a relentless association between the imagined hypersexuality of blacks and their religious expression, and the deployment of religion to characterize African Americans as essentially carefree, morally irresponsible, and apolitical. Each of the "all-colored cast" films produced from the late 1920s through the mid-1940s that use religious contexts avails itself of many of these elements set forward in King Vidor's work. The intense focus on sexuality found in *Hallelujah* becomes muted and the later films instead emphasize religion as a window on the fundamental incapacity and permanent childlike status of African Americans. Sexualized black religion appears instead in films in which blackness serves simply to construct whiteness, with black sexuality functioning to tempt and to mark wayward whites (usually women) who must reject the dangers of embodied black religion in favor of rationality.[48] The filmic techniques of the later "all-colored cast" films did not, in general, follow the style of *Hallelujah*'s hyperrealistic, ethnographic approach but instead used stylized, fantastical settings that often relied on dreams and dreamlike contexts for their narratives, contributing to the emphasis on a vision of the immaturity of African-American religion.

Regardless of the particular stylistic or ideological approach, Hollywood imaginings of African-American religion, along with its representations in literature and music, became especially contested ground, as black intellectuals negotiated their varied relationships to black folk cultures and did so in light of mainstream popular culture's commodification and re-presentation of elements of that culture. Writing in *The Crisis*, Loren Miller, a Los Angeles based civil rights attorney, bemoaned the nagging presence of "Uncle Tom in Hollywood" in a system that resulted in black audiences cheering for the white hero who rescues the blonde heroine from "savage" Africans and consuming newsreels that "poke fun at Negro revivals or baptisings." Miller argued forcefully that African Americans should take very seriously the impact of media on American political and social life.

> The cumulative effect of constant picturization of this kind is tremendously effective in shaping racial attitudes. Hollywood products are seen in every nook and corner of the world. Millions of non-residents of the United States depend almost entirely on the movies for their knowledge of Negro life, as those who have been abroad can testify. Other millions of white Americans of all ages confirm their beliefs about Negroes at the neighborhood theaters while Negroes themselves fortify their inferiority complex by seeing themselves always cast as the underdog to be laughed at or despised.[49]

While *Hallelujah* did not inaugurate the American cinema's exploration of racialized religion, the film did help to define critical patterns for early sound film that have contributed to the medium's ongoing engagement of race and of religion. The complicated issues that many critics of *Hallelujah* raised with regard to film's impact on Americans' understandings of race remain with us

today, as American popular culture frequently uses religious contexts as primary settings for African-American characters.[50] As with *Hallelujah* and the
other classical Hollywood "all-colored cast" films, the religious context in these
modern iterations serves both to attempt to chart the place of African Americans on the U.S. political and social landscape and to explore the moral valence
of blackness. Such projections of black religion have participated in the maintenance of racial hierarchy and in the process of defining American religion
in ways that explicitly marginalize—politically, socially, and religiously—forms
of religiosity linked with blackness. Never simply inconsequential entertainment, American film has been a vitally important arena for inculcating understandings of racialized religion, both for Americans and for audiences of American films around the world.

NOTES

1. Daniel Bernardi, ed., *The Birth of Whiteness: Race and the Emergence of U.S.
Cinema* (New Brunswick, N.J.: Rutgers University Press, 1996), 7. I use the term *ra-
cializing* to insist on the ongoing process of constructing racial categories and to avoid
any implication of races as "natural" entities. Also see Daniel Bernardi, ed., *Classic
Hollywood, Classic Whiteness* (Minneapolis: University of Minnesota Press, 2001); Mat-
thew Bernstein and Gaylyn Studlar, eds., *Visions of the East: Orientalism in Film* (New
Brunswick, N.J.: Rutgers University Press, 1997); Lola Young, *Fear of the Dark:
"Race," Gender and Sexuality in the Cinema* (New York: Routledge, 1996); James
Snead, *White Screens, Black Images: Hollywood from the Dark Side*, edited by Colin
MacCabe and Cornel West (New York: Routledge, 1994); Randall M. Miller, *The Kalei-
doscopic Lens: How Hollywood Views Ethnic Groups* (Englewood, N.J.: Ozer,1980). Very
few of these works recognize religion as an integral part of the constitution of racial
categories in the movies, which is the major concern of my forthcoming full-length
study on African-American religion in American film from 1929 to 1950 (University
of California Press).

2. The classical Hollywood cinema is defined by both stylistic markers and particular practices of production and exhibition. Although the boundaries of the period
can be set in a variety of ways, Bordwell, Staiger, and Thompson argue that the classical Hollywood system was in place from 1917 until 1960. They assert that the system
involved a particular style of narrative that emphasizes character and motivation, cau-
sation, and the creation of a coherent world in the use of space, composition, sound,
and editing and that the style emphasizes a realistic presentation of the narrative. In
addition, the vertically integrated studio system in which studios controlled production, distribution, and exhibition of films prevailed. See David Bordwell, Kristin
Thompson, and Janet Staiger, *The Classical Hollywood Cinema: Film Style and Mode of
Production to 1960* (New York: Columbia University Press, 1985).

3. See Robyn Wiegman, *American Anatomies: Theorizing Race and Gender, New
Americanists* (Durham, N.C.: Duke University Press, 1995), for a sustained discussion
of the development of racial categories in the United States.

4. Young, *Fear of the Dark*, 40.

5. A. Teresa de Lauretis, *Technologies of Gender: Essays on Theory, Film, and Fiction* (Bloomington: Indiana University Press, 1987), 2. De Lauretis begins with Michel Foucault's understanding of the "technology of sex" but emphasizes the differential constitution of male and female subjectivity. She does not explore racialized subjectivity in relation to either sexual difference or the production of gender, here. I would emphasize the connection between all three but choose to begin with race and understand its connections to religion, gender, and sexuality.

6. Oyeronke Oyewumi, *The Invention of Women: Making an African Sense of Western Gender Discourses* (Minneapolis: University of Minnesota, 1997), 2.

7. She goes on to assert that, where sight is privileged in the West, in Yoruba, a multiplicity of senses, anchored by hearing, taken together operate to help Yoruba people in apprehending the world. Oyewumi, *The Invention of Women*, 3, 14.

8. See, for example, Margaret R. Miles, "Image," in *Critical Terms for Religious Studies*, edited by Mark C. Taylor (Chicago: University of Chicago Press, 1998), 160–172.

9. John Belton, ed., *Movies and Mass Culture* (New Brunswick, N.J.: Rutgers University Press, 1996), 1.

10. Lillian Smith, *Killers of the Dream* (Norton, 1949), 17.

11. In emphasizing the importance of blackness for United States constructions of race, I do not mean to conflate "race" with blackness. Indeed, a great deal of recent scholarship on the construction of whiteness has insisted in extremely productive ways that the structures of race position everyone in a racial hierarchy and contribute to the production of both group and individual identity. See, for example, David R. Roediger, *The Wages of Whiteness: Race and the Making of the American Working Class* (New York: Verso Press, 1991); Ruth Frankenberg, *White Women, Race Matters: The Social Construction of Whiteness* (Minneapolis: University of Minnesota Press, 1993); Matthew Frye Jacobson, *Whiteness of a Different Color: European Immigrants and the Alchemy of Race* (Cambridge: Harvard University Press, 1998).

12. We see these strategies in films such as *Blonde Venus,* directed by Josef von Sternberg (Paramount, 1932), *Imitation of Life*, directed by John Stahl (Universal, 1934), and *Gone with the Wind*, directed by Victor Fleming (Selznick International, 1939), in which the black maid, played by Louise Beavers in *Imitation of Life* and by Hattie McDaniel in the other two films, functions to demonstrate the qualities valued in whiteness—beauty, reason, autonomy, and so on—by representing the opposite. In all three cases, as well as in others, the black characters are not fully developed and exist primarily to serve at the margins of lives of the white characters.

13. *Hearts in Dixie*, directed by Paul Sloane (Fox Film Corporation, 1929); *Hallelujah*, directed by King Vidor (Metro-Goldwyn-Mayer, 1929); *The Green Pastures*, directed by Marc Connelly and William Keighley (Warner Brothers, 1936); *Cabin in the Sky*, directed by Vincente Minnelli (Metro-Goldwyn-Mayer, 1943); *A Night at the Opera*, directed by Sam Wood (Metro-Goldwyn-Mayer, 1935); *Tales of Manhattan*, directed by Julien Duvivier (Twentieth Century Fox, 1942).

14. See, for example, Michael Rogin, *Blackface, White Noise: Jewish Immigrants in the Hollywood Melting Pot* (Berkeley: University of California Press, 1996).

15. King Vidor, *A Tree Is a Tree* (New York: Harcourt, Brace, 1952), 175.

16. Vidor, *A Tree Is a Tree*, 176. An undated note handwritten on MGM Inter-

Office stationery and preserved in the King Vidor collection contains items for "a story of the South" and includes some of the same elements that Vidor describes in his recollections on directing the film, along with others not included in the memoir. It is not clear if these are the notes he wrote for *Hallelujah* or for an earlier attempt to convince the studio to allow him to do an "all-colored cast" film. See King Vidor Collection, University of Southern California.

17. Vidor, *A Tree Is a Tree*, 176. See King Vidor to Metro-Goldwyn-Mayer, February 25, 1930; Metro-Goldwyn-Mayer Producer/Participant Statement for Hallelujah to August 1, 1981, King Vidor Collection, University of Southern California.

18. See Thomas Schatz, *The Genius of the System: Hollywood Filmmaking in the Studio Era* (New York: Owl Books, 1988), on Vidor's authority over his films. Vidor's later directorial credits include: *The Champ* (MGM, 1931), *Stella Dallas* (Samuel Goldwyn, 1937), *Duel in the Sun* (Vanguard Films and Selznick International, 1946), and *The Fountainhead* (First National Pictures and Warner Brothers, 1949).

19. "King Vidor's Fondest Dream Realized by Clever Work of Performers in Hallelujah," *Chicago Defender*, June 8, 1929.

20. See Frank Davis, "Hallelujah," King Vidor Collection, Metro-Goldwyn-Mayer Archives, University of Southern California. In addition to relying on his own experience for the film's story, Vidor selected Wanda Tuchock, who brought no such personal experience to the project, to write the script. About a month before the production wrapped shooting, the studio engaged Ransom Rideout, a black playwright and studio writer, to add dialogue, some of which made it into the final cut of the picture despite Vidor's objections. The studio also listed Harold Garrison as assistant director on the film. Vidor described him as "a Negro bootblack at the studio. He had a stand set up and we called him Slickum. We made him second assistant director in charge of the Negro cast." Garrison's role seems to have been to act as an intermediary between Vidor and the large numbers of local extras engaged on location and, perhaps, to oversee the travel of the lead cast members on Jim Crow railroad cars to the location shoot in Memphis, Tennessee. Thomas Cripps, *Slow Fade to Black: The Negro in American Film, 1900–1942* (New York: Oxford University Press, 1977), 243. Robert Benchley, "Hearts in Dixie," *Opportunity: A Journal of Negro Life*, April 1929; Nancy Dowd, ed., *King Vidor: A Directors Guild of America Oral History* (Metuchen, N.J.: Scarecrow Press, 1988). J. J. Cohn to R. A. Golden, Peabody Hotel, Memphis, Tenn., October 15, 1928, King Vidor Collection, Metro-Goldwyn-Mayer Archives, University of Southern California.

21. Quoted in "Will 'Hallelujah' Be Slap at Race Pride Is Query," *Pittsburgh Courier*, December 15, 1928.

22. "King Vidor's Fondest Dream Is Realized," *Chicago Defender*, June 8, 1929. In comparing the scale of *Hallelujah* to past films, Vidor was referring especially to *The Big Parade* (MGM, 1925), his six-reel World War I epic.

23. King Vidor, *King Vidor on Film Making* (New York: David MacKay, 1972), 230, 231.

24. "Best Negro Motion Picture Coming in Hallelujah," *New York Amsterdam News*, October 3, 1928. See also *Pittsburgh Courier*, June 9, 1929.

25. *Pittsburgh Courier*, June 9, 1929.

26. *New York Amsterdam News*, February 27, 1929.

27. Martin Quigley, *Decency in Motion Pictures* (New York: Macmillan, 1937), 42.

28. Memo from Colonel Joy, October 4, 1928, February 22, 1929, *Hallelujah* file, Motion Picture Producers and Distributors Association Case Files, Academy of Motion Picture Arts and Sciences Library (MPPDA).

29. Memo from Colonel Joy, February 22, 1929, *Hallelujah* file, MPPDA.

30. Memo from Colonel Joy, October 4, 1928, *Hallelujah* file, MPPDA.

31. Jason S. Joy to George Kann, Metro-Goldwyn-Mayer, October 6, 1928; Lamar Trotti to Mr. M. McKenzie, October 19, 1928, *Hallelujah* file, MPPDA. Joy eventually relented on the crap game, convinced that "because this form of amusement is indigenous to negro life," the scene could be left in. Memo from Colonel Joy, February 22, 1929, *Hallelujah* file, MPPDA.

32. Lamar Trotti to Mr. M. McKenzie, October 19, 1928, *Hallelujah* file, MPPDA.

33. F. L. Herron, August 22, 1929, *Hallelujah* file, MPPDA.

34. John V. Wilson to Jason S. Joy, December 12, 1929, *Hallelujah* file, MPPDA.

35. "Hallelujah," *Variety*, August 28, 1929.

36. Quotations represent my own transcriptions of the dialogue from the film.

37. In a conversation with Adrienne Lanier Seward on May 1, 1981, Vidor claimed that he did not deliberately place the broom in the shot. In response to Seward's reading of the broom's significance in African-American history in relation to the film's story, Vidor referred to its presence in the film as "a lucky symbol." The interview was conducted a year before Vidor's death and more than half a century after the film's release. Vidor's memory about certain elements of the production history is faulty, and it is possible that he is also unreliable on this point. Adrienne Lanier Seward, "Early Black Film and Folk Tradition: An Interpretive Analysis of the Use of Folklore in Selected All-Black Cast Feature Films" (Ph.D. diss., Indiana University, 1985), 259.

38. Rick Altman writes of the folk musical as "project[ing] the audience into a mythicized version of the cultural past" and as especially interested in the family and home. Rick Altman, *The American Film Musical* (Bloomington: Indiana University Press, 1978), 272.

39. "Eva Jessye, Musical Director for Newest Sound Film," *Baltimore Afro-American*, February 16, 1929.

40. W.E.B. Du Bois, "Hallelujah: King Vidor's All-Talking Picture," *Crisis*, October 1929.

41. In an editorial in *Opportunity*, Charles S. Johnson reported on the absurd assertion by a white neurologist (in a speech before a group of psychiatrists) that Irving Berlin created jazz because his mother had an irregular heart and unwittingly conditioned him, prenatally, to understand syncopation. Johnson continued: "and so goes another of the preposterous assumptions that Negroes created jazz. There was, not so long ago, a feature article in one of the popular magazines, by a white music hall favorite with the caption: 'How I Created the Charleston.' . . . She was naive enough, however, to explain that she had learned the essential steps from her Negro maid, and by transferring them from the servants' quarters to the stage, presumably, supplied the element of creation"; "The Origin of Jazz," *Opportunity* (April 1928). See also Jeffrey Melnick, *A Right to Sing the Blues: African Americans, Jews, and American Popular Song* (Cambridge: Harvard University Press, 1999).

42. Altman, *The American Film Musical*, 272.

43. Here, according to Jessica Howard, "it is not the meaning of the words themselves, but their repetition and treatment, specifically as chanted and chant-sung, that allows the 'true' bodily expression of Mammy to emerge (i.e., piousness, grief)." Jessica Howard, "Hallelujah! Transformation in Film," *African American Review* 30 (autumn 1996), 466.

44. Quoted in "New York Critics See Race Insult in 'Hallelujah'," *Baltimore Afro-American*, August 31, 1929.

45. Quoted in "New York Critics See Race Insult in 'Hallelujah'," *Baltimore Afro-American*, August 31, 1929.

46. Thomas H. Dorsen to the editor, *New York Amsterdam News*, August 28, 1929.

47. "Attempt to Bar Negroes in Films," *New York Amsterdam News*, October 2, 1929.

48. Josef von Sternberg's *Blonde Venus* (Paramount, 1932) is an excellent example of this type of film.

49. Loren Miller, "Uncle Tom in Hollywood," *Crisis*, November 1934, 329–330.

50. Recent films rarely make use of a religious context for the entire setting but instead provide brief scenes, most frequently in churches or revivals. Robert Duvall's 1997 film *The Apostle* (Butcher's Run Films) is an exception. While it is a much more complex portrayal of race, religion, and the relationship between the two for white and black southerners than the classical Hollywood films gave us, *The Apostle* nevertheless relies on an understanding of African Americans as naturally religious and more genuinely so than most white people, and it is this natural and simple capacity for religious expression that redeems the film's central white character. Madonna's 1989 video for her song "Like a Prayer" makes a strong political statement against racial intolerance but again uses an enthusiastic black church choir to authorize the character Madonna plays.

Index

Abbott, Granville S., 139
Abbott, Lyman, 102
ABHMS. *See* American Baptist
  Home Mission Society
Adlington, Ellen, 141
affaire de Bizoton, 238, 240, 243
Africa, 33, 94
African-Americans
  Abbott (Lyman) on, 102
  Baptist missionary work among,
    133–56
  Father Divine and Daddy Grace,
    209–27
  as freedmen, 94–100
  identity, 9–11
  as "mud people," 10
  one drop rule, 181, 202n.6
  redefinition of race in New
    Orleans, 183–208
  religion in Hollywood
    imagination, 305–27
  See also Blacks; Creoles
"African-American Women's
  History and the Metalanguage
  of Race" (Higginbotham), 8
Afrobrazilian religion, 283–304
Afro-Caribbean culture, 6
afro mass, 111–30
Aho, James, 10
Alana, Father, 46, 52–53
Alonso, Ana María, 176n.5

Alzola, José, 160
America. *See* United States
American Baptist Home Mission
  Society (ABHMS), 134–36, 138,
    140, 141, 144–50, 153n.29
American Ladies Magazine, 86
Americas
  building of by preexisting
    religious communities, 17–18
  racial identities in, 33
  white supremacy in, 83
  See also native Americans; *specific
    nations*
A Morte Branca do Feiticeiro Negro
  (Ortiz), 285, 302n.7
analogic relationships, 9
Anderson, Benedict, 15–17
Anglo-Saxon race, 85–110, 268
  See also "Aryan" race; "Caucasoid/
    Caucasian" race; "White" race
anti-Semitism, 62, 80n.30
Anuciación, Domingo de la, 40
Apache Indians, 158, 159
Apalachee Indians, 39, 42–43
Apostle, The (film), 327n.50
appearance. *See* physical appearance
"Aryan" race, 261, 262, 265, 266,
    267, 272, 273
  See also Anglo-Saxon race;
    "White" race
Asad, Talal, 14, 19

Asian immigrants, 260, 262
Asiatic Exclusion League, 260, 273, 274, 277
assimilation, 268, 274
assimilative whiteness, 268–75
atabaques, 111
Atlantic Monthly, 86, 89
"At the End of the Road" (song), 319, 320
Axtell, James, 106
Azusa Street Revival (Los Angeles, Cal.), 224n.4

Baer, Hans A., 219
Baker, George. *See* Father Divine
Bakhtin, Mikhail, 263
Ballard, Earl A., 320
Baptist Church, 134–42, 143, 144–50
Barkun, Michael, 10
Bartholdi, Frédéric-Auguste, 105
Baudier, Roger, 187
"Beginning of a Nation, The" (Eggeleston), 88
Bercovitch, Sacvan, 9, 10
Berlin, Irving, 319, 320, 326n.41
Bernard, Daniel, 305
Bertin, Father, 249, 251
Bilbo, Theodore, 220
Bizoton (Haiti), 238, 240, 243
Black Codes, 133
Blacks
    afro mass in Brazil, 111–30
    alleged racial inferiority, 91, 138, 231, 306
    in Haiti, 61–70, 73–78
    religious aesthetics, 282
    sensuality and sexuality, 281
    See also African-Americans
blanco, 177n.21
Blenk, James, 194, 195, 196, 197
blood libels, 13
Bloomfield, Maurice, 270
Boff, Leonardo, 124
Boyer, Jean-Pierre, 232–35, 253n.5
Brambila, David, 162, 169, 171
Brazil
    Catholic afro mass in, 111–30
    Umbanda aesthetics in, 283–304
Britain. *See* Great Britain
Brown, C. S., 148
Brown, Diana, 296, 302n.7
Brumberg, Joan Jacobs, 140, 153n.36

Buddhism, 144
Bullones, Joseph de, 43–44
Bureau of Immigration and Naturalization, 261–62, 275
Burke, Edmund, 268–69
Bush, George W., 4–5
Buteau, Pierre, 243, 246, 249
Butler, Judith, 8

Cabalans, 297–98, 304n.23
Cable, George W., 96–97, 98, 204n.29
CABMC. *See* Consolidated American Baptist Missionary Convention
caciques, 39, 40, 41, 42
California, 260, 276
Calusa Indians, 39, 43
Cancer, Father, 45
candomblé, 111, 123, 126, 127, 128, 284
cannibalism, 238, 241, 256–57n.51
Canzo, Méndez de, 50
Cape Verde, 211, 212
capoeiristas, 126
Cárdenas, Lázaro, 172
Cartwright, Samuel, 94
Cash, W. J., 92, 96
caste system, 157–58, 261, 266, 269, 272, 275
Catholic Church
    and Afrobrazilian religions, 292
    afro mass in Brazil, 111–30
    in American colonial era, 85
    among Indians in northern Mexico, 159–75, 176n.9
    Creole faithfulness and identity, 198–201
    in Haiti, 64, 65, 73–74, 76, 232, 236, 238, 245–52
    and redefinition of race in New Orleans, 183–208
    in Spanish Floridas, 35–36, 49
"Caucasoid/Caucasian" race, 13, 261, 262, 265, 266
    See also "White" race
Celtic-Americans, 92
"Census and Immigration, The" (Lodge), 101
Century magazine, 86, 88, 96, 100, 103
chabochi, 163–67, 177n.27
Chacato Indians, 43
Challeux, Nicholas le, 47
Charles III (king), 52

Charles V (king), 37
Charleston (S.C.), 37
chattel slavery, 11, 33
Chihuahua (Mex.), 159–75
China, 141, 153n.38
Chinese-Americans, 102, 133–56, 260–61
Chinese Exclusion Acts, 133, 149, 150, 260
Chisca Indians, 43
Christ. *See* Jesus Christ
Christianity
   in America, 16, 83–110
   in Brazil, 111–30
   colonial, 19
   European, 17
   evangelical, 135, 136, 137, 139, 272
   as social science, 102
   See also conversion; missionary work; *specific denominations*
Christophe, Henry, 253n.5
Citizens Committee (Comité des Citoyens), 190, 193, 196
citizenship, 139, 140, 153n.29, 260–77
civilization
   legislating in postrevolutionary Haiti, 231–58
   policing racial and religious boundaries of, 229–30
   of White men and race of Hindus, 259–77
Clarke, James Freeman, 269
Code Noir, 62, 71, 186, 234
collective identities, 6–11
Columbus, Christopher, 62
Common Sense (Paine), 88
communitas, 304n.25
Compostela, Diego Ebelino de, 51
Confucianism, 142, 144
Consolidated American Baptist Missionary Convention (CABMC), 146
conversion
   efforts in Spanish Floridas, 35–59
   and imagined biological basis of race, 13
   of Jews and Africans, 68, 71–72
   of non-Whites to Christianity in Americas, 83, 102, 104, 106, 107
   See also Catholic Church; missionary work
Cordero, Manuel, 164, 168, 169–70, 174

Corpus Christi parish (New Orleans, La.), 195, 199–200
Cotton, Sally S., 91
Council of the Indies (1657), 50
Council of the Indies (1698), 51
"crackers," 92–93, 107
Cravens, Hamilton, 138
Creel, Enrique C., 166, 172
Creoles
   Catholic faithfulness, 198–200
   Catholic identity, 200–201
   decline of distinctiveness, 188–93
   in Haiti, 62, 64, 65, 72, 74
   origins of identity, 185–88
   redefinition of race in New Orleans, 183–208
   "triumph" of segregated parishes, 193–98
crime, 95, 96
critical theory, 6
Critics Not Caretakers (McCutcheon), 20
Crooks, George R., 104
Cruz, Juan la, 42
cultural imperialism, 16, 18
cultural studies, 6
culture, 6, 139
Cysneiros, Israel, 295–96

Daddy Grace, 209–17, 222–27
Daily Crusader, 190, 191, 196
dance, 118–22, 256n.43, 293–94, 300
Das Bagai, Vaishno, 276
Dash, J. Michael, 245
Dawson, Alexander S., 179n.63
Dayan, Joan, 72
deGraca, Marcelino M. *See* Daddy Grace
de Graffenried, Clare, 92–93
De l'égalité des races humaines (Firmin), 231
de Man, Paul, 244
Desdunes, Rodolphe, 191, 192
de Soto, Hernando, 35, 38, 45
Dessalines, Jean-Jacques, 236, 254n.17
Devil and the Jews, The (Trachtenberg), 70
dialogized heteroglossia, 263
Díaz, Porfirio, 166
Dictionary of Races, 275
Dill, Bonnie Thorton, 7
Dillingham Commission on Immigration, 275
Discipline and Punish (Foucault), 241

discourse, 263
Divine, Major Jealous. *See* Father Divine
domination, 7
Dong Gong, 145, 148
Dravidians, 265, 272, 273
Drexel, Katharine, 198
Du Bois, W. E. B., 320
Dudley, T. U., 90, 98, 99
Durkheim, Emile, 19

Easter, 61, 67, 68–69, 74
egalitarian promise of inclusion, 136
Eggeleston, Edward, 88
Egypt, 9
Emerson, Ralph Waldo, 89
Enlightenment, 15
Escamilla, Rufino, 173
Escobedo, Father, 49
ethnic absolutism, 139
ethnology, 140, 261
Eurocentrism, 111–30
evangelism, 107
Exodus, 9–11, 143, 155n.55

Father Divine, 209–11, 217–27
Fauset, Arthur Huff, 213, 214, 220
FBI. *See* Federal Bureau of Investigation
feathers, 45, 46
Federal Bureau of Investigation (FBI),
    220–21, 223, 225n.25, 227n.62
feminism, 7
Ferguson, Miriam "Ma," 17
Fernández de Oviedo, Gonzalo, 40
fetishism, 229, 231, 243
films, 305–27
Firmin, Anténor, 231
Fiske, John, 90
Floridas, Spanish, 35–59
Fontaneda, Hernando D'Escalante, 49
Fort Caroline (Floridas), 47
Foucault, Michel, 13, 241
France, 233, 241
Franciscan order, 49, 50, 125
Franklin, Benjamin, 88, 101
Fredrickson, George, 13, 14, 28n.28, 72
freedmen, 96–100, 138
Froude, James Anthony, 244
Fuller, Thomas O., 147
Fung Seung Nam, 148

Galván, Edmundo, 162, 163, 164–65,
    167, 168
García de Palacios, Don Juan, 38
Garcilaso de la Vega, 38, 46–47
gardecorps, 72
Garrison, Harold, 325n.20
Garvey, Marcus, 217, 219, 226n.37
Gassó, Leonardo, 166, 167
Gavins, Raymond, 150n.1
Gebara, Ivone, 123
Geertz, Clifford, 19
Geffrard, Fabre Nicolas, 232, 236–37,
    238, 241, 242, 251, 258n.79
gender, 7–8
genealogical whiteness, 264–68, 273
Ghadar Party, 260
Gilman, Sander, 13, 63, 69, 87, 91
Gilroy, Paul, 139, 153n.32
Gobineau, Joseph-Arthur, Comte de, 236,
    244
God, 102, 106, 107
Good Friday, 61, 82n.57, 168
Goodwin, Ruby Berkley, 312
Gordon, Avery, 20
Gould, Jeffrey L., 158
Grace, Charles Manuel "Sweet Daddy".
    See Daddy Grace
Grady, Henry W., 97–98
Great Awakenings, 9, 136
Great Britain, 89–90, 106, 107, 265
Great Revival, 136
gringo, 177n.27
Guale uprising (1597), 41–42, 46, 50
Guillaumin, Colette, 12

Haiti
    Catholic Church in, 64, 65, 73–74, 76,
        232, 236, 238, 245–52
    Jews in imagination of, 61–70, 73–78
    legislating "civilization" in
        postrevolutionary, 231–58
    penal codes, 232–35, 239, 240, 242–43,
        252, 253n.7, 254n.14
Hall, Addie L., 148
Hall, Oakey, 89
Hallelujah (film), 309–23
Harding, Sandra, 7
Harper, Frances Ellen Watkins, 102
Harpers New Monthly Review, 103
Hartzell, Joseph, 187

Harvey, Paul, 146
Haskell, Samuel, 138
hate crimes, 4
Haynes, Daniel L., 312
Hayti, or The Black Republic (St. John), 238
headdresses, 44
heathenism, 33–54, 141, 275
Higginbotham, Evelyn Brooks, 8–9
Hijas de María, 165
Hinduism, 259–77
Hoffmann, Léon-François, 239
Holmes, Oliver Wendell, 89
Hoover, J. Edgar, 220, 221
Horton, Jonathan W., 141
House of Father John (Brazil), 284, 286–89, 292, 294, 295, 300
House of Prayer. *See* United House of Prayer for All People
House of Saint Benedict (Brazil), 284, 285, 289–91, 292, 295–98, 300, 303n.9
Hundley, D. R., 92, 93, 95
Hurbon, Laënnec, 240
hygiene, 160
Hyppolite, Florvil, 249, 257n.58

identity
    African-American, 9–11
    American, 88, 107
    black movement in Brazil, 114, 120
    collective, 6–11
    Creole, 185–88, 200–201, 202n.6
    national, of U.S., 9
    race as modern form of, 14
    racial, in Americas, 33, 87, 107, 202n.6
    reification of, 7
    religion as ideological instrument for constructing social, 85, 87
Iglesias, Eduardo, 167, 170
images, 87
Imagined Communities: Reflections on the Origin and Spread of Nationalism (Anderson), 15
immigration, 101, 263, 274
inculturationism, 122, 129n.4
India, 259, 265, 266, 270, 271–72, 276, 277
Indian immigrants, 259–77

Indians, American. *See* native Americans
indigenous peoples. *See* native Americans
"In Plain Black and White" (Grady), 97–98
Inquisition, 62, 70
"Institutes of Manu," 266
intermarriage, 72
Iraq, 5
Irish-Americans, 92
Israel, ancient, 9–10, 33, 155n.55

Jackson, Carl, 142, 271
Jacobson, Matthew Frye, 138, 139
Jamestown (Va.), 37
Jan, Jean Marie, 248–49
Janssens, Francis, 189–93, 194, 197, 200
Janvier, Louis-Joseph, 231, 245
jazz, 326n.41
Jazz Singer, The (film), 310
Jean-Jacques, Thalès, 233, 253n.5, 253n.7
Jefferson, Thomas, 88, 91, 94
Jessye, Eva, 319
Jesuit order, 41, 49, 71, 159–75, 176n.9
Jesus Christ, 61, 67–69, 75–77
Jews
    blood libels leveled against, 13
    "demonic," 63, 69–70, 76
    in Haiti, 61–70, 74–78
    in medieval Europe, 71–72
    as "mud people," 10
    in Saint-Domingue, 71
    in Spain, 62–63, 74
    "stubbornness" of, 13
Johnson, Ceasar, 147
Johnson, Charles S., 326n.41
Johnson-Reed Act, 263, 276
Johnston, John, 91
Jones, Oakah, 176n.5
Jordan, Winthrop, 13, 14, 19
Jororo village/mission (Floridas), 43–44, 51
Josephites, 197–98
Joy, "Colonel" Jason, 313–14
Juárez, Benito, 174
Judaism
    medieval rabbinic, 17
    See also Jews
Judas, 67–69, 76, 80n.30, 168
justice system, 89

Kames, Lord, 88
Kardec, Allan, 294
Kardecismo, 294–95
Kersuzan, François-Marie, 232, 245–51
King, Martin Luther, Jr., 9–10
Kipling, Rudyard, 280n.55
Ku Klux Klan, 133, 221, 223

Lacrampe, Pére, 250
La Croix, 246, 247
ladino, 158
La Encarnación a la Santa Cruz mission,
    43
Lafon, Thomy, 192, 196
language, 87, 195
Lao Tze, 144
La république d'Haiti et ses visiteurs
    (Janvier), 231
Larose, Serge, 234–35, 240
Latin America, 157–58, 292
Laudonnière, René, 41
Laureano de Torres y Ayala, 43, 51
Le Conte, Joseph, 138, 142
Le Gouaze, Joseph, 237
Le Mystere de la Passion, 70
Les Chemins de la Croix (stations of the
    cross), 74
"Liberty Enlightening the World"
    (Bartholdi), 105
limpieza de sangre (purity of blood), 71,
    72, 158
Lincoln, Abraham, 94
literacy, 93
Lodge, Henry Cabot, 101
Lomnitz-Adler, Claudio, 174
"Lost Tribes," 33
Louis XIV (king), 71
Louisiana, 185–86, 188
Louisiana Purchase, 186
Lowell, Percival, 270
Luna, Tristán de, 40
Luther, Martin, 276

MacArthur, Robert Stuart, 104, 105
Macedo, Joaquim Manoel de, 293, 297,
    299, 300
magazines, 86, 107
Magic Island, The (Seabrook), 68
Maina, Pedro, 157, 168, 169
makandals, 72
Manaus, 284

Mané, Father, 297–98, 304nn.23–24
Manifest Destiny, 100, 133
"Manifest Destiny" (Fiske), 90
marriage, 42, 72, 160–61, 186, 254n.17,
    261, 271, 317
marronage, 72
Mary, Aristide, 192, 196
Massachusetts, 106
McCutcheon, Russell, 20
McKay, Claude, 217, 218
McPherson, Aimee Semple, 212, 225n.11
"Meaning of Africa in Haitian Vodu,
    The" (Larose), 234
medieval Christendom, 4, 62
mélange de sang (mixed blood), 72
Menéndez de Avilés, Pedro, 37, 38, 41,
    47, 49
Menéndez Marquéz, Juan, 42
Mennonites, 85
mestizo, 158, 177n.21
metalanguage, 8
Metro-Goldwyn-Mayer (MGM), 309–13,
    321
Mexico, 157–80
Mexico City (Mex.), 37
MGM. See Metro-Goldwyn-Mayer
Mier y Terán, José, 165
Miles, Margaret, 307
Miller, Loren, 322
Million Man March (1995), 20
missionary ethnology, 140
missionary work, 131–56
    among Chinese immigrants and freed
        Blacks, 133–56
    among Indians in northern Mexico,
        157–75, 179n.63
    in India, 272
    and Sikhism, 276
    in Spanish Floridas, 40–54
Mitchell, Elder, 215
modernization, 14
Monaco, Father, 46, 52–53
"Mongoloid" races, 13
monotheism, 229
Morehouse, Henry Lyman, 150
Moses (biblical figure), 10
Moss, Lemuel, 137
Motion Picture Producers and
    Distributors Association (MPPDA),
    313–14
motion pictures, 305–27

movies. *See* motion pictures
Mozoomdar, Akhay Kumar, 267
MPPDA. *See* Motion Picture Producers and Distributors Association
mulattoes, 64, 65, 73, 91
Müller, Friedrich Max, 265
multiracial feminism, 7
Munson, Arley, 271, 277
music, 319–20, 326n.41
Muslims, 72, 276

Nanak, Guru, 276
Narrangansett Indians, 106
Narváez, Pánfilo de, 37, 40
nation
    as cultural phenomenon, 15
    in Haiti, 63–66
    and race, 5–11, 18
    and religion, 5–11
    in Sierra Tarahumara, 170–75
nation-state, 15, 16, 229
national communities, 15–18
National Day of Prayer and Remembrance, 5
nationalism, 4, 139
National Repository, 86, 100
national security, 4
native Americans, 33
    Abbott (Lyman) on, 102
    alleged heathenism, 36–54
    behavior and rituals, 39–44, 54
    conversion efforts, 48–52, 106, 157–80
    "Indian problem" in northern Mexico, 157–80
    marriage among, 42
    physical appearance, 36, 44–47
    in Spanish Floridas, 35–59
    See also specific peoples
Naturalization Law (1790), 137, 139, 150
Nau, Léon, 233
"Negroid" race, 13
New Orleans (La.), 183–208
New Orleans Medical and Surgical Journal, 94
New Thought theology, 209, 216, 217, 222, 224n.2
Nicaragua, 158
Nicholls, David, 65
Noah (biblical figure), 13
Nord Alexis, Pierre, 247, 248, 250
Nuestra Vida, 161

Ocampo, Manuel, 163, 169, 173, 174
Olmsted, Frederick Law, 183
Omi, Michael, 86
one drop rule, 181, 202n.6
O'odhma people, 123
Oré, Luis Jerónimo de, 41–42, 46, 48
"Oriental" religions, 270
Ortiz, Juan, 40
Ortiz, Narciso, 162, 163, 167, 171, 173
Ortiz, Renato, 285, 299, 302n.7
Oyewumi, Oyeronke, 306
Ozawa, Takao, 262

Padilla, Agustín Dávila, 40
paganism, 38, 40, 43, 48
Paine, Thomas, 88
Papists, 88
Parliament of World Religions (1993), 20
parochial schools, 198, 199, 207n.76
Parsons, Louella, 311
Passion plays, 70, 74, 75
Peace Mission, 209–11, 217–23, 224n.5
Péan, Marc, 246, 248, 249
Pegues, A. W., 147
Pelé, Jeanne, 238
Peña, Father, 167
Pentecostalism, 224n.4
Pétion, Alexandre, 253n.5
Philip II (king), 38
Philip III (king), 50
physical appearance
    of "crackers," 92
    of Daddy Grace, 213–14
    of Father Divine, 219
    in Haiti, 64
    of native Americans in Floridas, 36, 44–47
    for racial categorization, 202n.6
Pichardo, Francisco, 167, 171
Piñan, Manuel, 163, 164, 166
Plessy v. Ferguson, 98, 190, 193, 196, 204–5n.37
political activism, 222
Ponce de León, Juan, 40
Portugal, 72, 157, 285
Posada, Alonso de, 38
positive thinking, 209, 218
Potter, Henry C., 102
Powell, Adam Clayton, Jr., 216
power, 7, 281, 307
Pratt, Mary Louise, 140

Price, Angelene, 93
Price, Hannibal, 238, 241, 245, 251
prostitution, 72
Protestantism, 104, 229, 276, 307
Puritans, 9, 85, 88
"purity of blood" statutes, 13

Quakers, 85, 88
Quiroga y Losada, Diego, 50

Raboteau, Albert, 9, 10, 11
race
  as biological fiction, 11, 13
  caste as preserver of, 272
  Father Divine on, 217–19
  and gender, 7–8
  genealogical whiteness, 264–68
  in Haiti, 63–66
  historiography of, 11–15
  instinct, 267, 270
  as metalanguage, 8
  missionary discourse and remaking,
    137–43
  as modern form of identity, 14
  and modernity, 11–15
  and nation, 5–11, 18
  "origins" of, 28n.28
  and religion, 5–11, 62, 72, 275, 277,
    307
  sense and sensuality in rituals and
    representations of, 281
  Smedley on, 12
  visual aspects of, 306
  See also African-Americans; Blacks;
    "White" race
racial democracy, 157–58, 285, 286
racial formation, 86–87, 158, 181
racial intolerance, 14
racialization
  in Haiti, 62
  in northern Mexico, 160–62
  in Spanish Floridas, 36–37, 39, 48, 54
racial profiling, 4
racism, 4, 14, 72, 138, 139, 285
Rangel, Rodrigo, 45
rape, 96
Rara festivals, 61–62, 65, 75–78
rational analyses, 4
rationalist secularism, 15
rationality, 281
reification, 7

religion
  African-American in Hollywood
    imagination, 305–27
  Afrobrazilian, 283–304
  and construction of White America, 85–
    110
  decline in 18th century, 15
  in film, 307
  in Haiti, 63–66
  and "Indian problem" in northern
    Mexico, 157–80
  materialist analyses of, 20
  and modernity, 4
  and nation, 5–11
  "Oriental," 269–70
  power to shape social world, 3
  and race, 5–11, 62, 72, 275, 277, 307
  and sexuality, 314, 316–19
  and society, 18–21
  under slavery, 143
  See also specific religions
"Religion as a Cultural System" (Geertz),
  19
religious communities, 15–18
religious universalism, 16–17
religous extremism, 4
restraint, 281
Rio, João do, 294
Rio de Janeiro (Brazil), 284, 285, 291
Risley, H. H., 266–67, 270
rituals, 281
Rivail, Hippolyte Denizard, 294
Robert, Joseph T., 141
Roberts, Mamie S., 148
Roberts, Nicholas F., 147
Robinson, E. G., 134, 142
Robles, Ricardo, 164
Rogel, Juan, 38, 41, 42, 45, 48
Roman Catholic Church. See Catholic
  Church
Roosevelt, Franklin, 221
Roumer, Thérèse, 67
RS2169 (statute), 260, 273

Saint-Domingue, 71, 72, 233
St. John, Sir Spenser, 238, 244
St. Katherine's church (New Orleans,
  La.), 189–97, 199
St. Louis Cathedral (New Orleans, La.),
  183, 187

St. Rose of Lima church (New Orleans, La.), 195
Salnave, Albert, 247, 248
Salvador (Brazil), 292
Sam, Simon, 246, 247, 257n.58
Santa Fe (N.M.), 37
Satan, 69, 73
sati, 271
Scotch-Americans, 92
Scribner's, 86, 102
Seabrook, William, 68
Second Great Awakening, 136, 151n.13
secularization, 3, 16, 17
segregation, 98, 181–201
self-identity, 3, 87, 107
Seminole Indians, 36
sensuality, 281
"separate but equal" doctrine, 190, 205n.37
Sessons, Mrs. Meander S., 148
sexuality, 8, 217, 281, 306, 313, 316–19, 322
Seymour, William J., 224n.4
Shaw, John, 194, 196–97
Sherman, John T., 321
Shoemaker, Michael, 272
Shuck, Henrietta Hall, 142
Siddiqi, Muzammil H., 5
Sierra Tarahumara (Mex.), 159–75, 176n.9, 177n.21
Sikhism, 259, 267, 275–76, 279n.21
Singer, Merrill, 219
Sisters of the Blessed Sacrament, 198, 207n.76
slavery
    of Africans, 36–37, 62
    of American Blacks, 9
    Brazilian, 292
    chattel, 11, 33
    dancing under, 256n.43
    emancipation in U.S., 94, 96
    in Floridas, 36–37
    in Haiti, 64, 73
    Hundley on, 95
    in Louisiana, 185, 186
    of native Americans, 50
    religion under, 143
    in Saint-Domingue, 71
Smedley, Audrey, 12, 44
Smith, Ezekiel E., 147
Smith, Jonathan Z., 18

Smith, Lillian, 308
Smith, Samuel Stanhope, 88
Smith, Theophus, 9
social construction, 7
Sodhi, Balbir Singh, 5
Sollors, Werner, 9, 86, 87
Song Sam Bo, 146
sorcery, 72, 232, 252, 253n.10, 293–94
Soulouque, Faustin, 236
sound films (talkies), 310
Spain
    acceptance of intermarriage, 72
    colonialism, 157
    Inquisition, 62, 70
    Jews in, 62–63, 74
    "purity of blood" statutes, 13
    and racism, 72
    slave codes in Louisiana, 185
Spanish Floridas, 35–59
Spanish Hispaniola, 70
Spencer, Herbert, 91
Spiritualism, 294–95
Stoler, Ann, 13, 139, 153n.32
Strong, Josiah, 104–5
Sunday, Billy, 212, 225n.11
Sutherland, Justice, 262–63, 264, 273

"Table of Nations" (Genesis), 13
Tainos, 62
tambor de mina, 123, 125
Tarahumara Indians, 159–75
tattoos, 45
Taylor, Isaac, 272
Taylor, Mark C., 4, 18
Ten Great Religions (Clarke), 269
Tepehuán Indians, 176n.9
Tequesta Indians, 39
terreiros, 292, 303n.13
terrorism, 4–5
Texas, 17
Thalberg, Irving, 313
Theosophical Society, 271
Thind, Bhagat Singh, 259–68, 272–73, 275–77
Thoburn, J. M., 270, 272
Thorne, Susan, 136
Tillett, Wilbur Fisk, 100
Timucua Indians, 39, 51
totemism, 229, 231
Trachtenberg, Joshua, 69–70, 76
Trautmann, Thomas, 265

Trotti, Lamar, 314
Trouillot, Duverneau, 245
Trouillot, Hénock, 235–36, 255n.35
Tylor, E. B., 19

Umbanda religion, 283–304
UNIA. *See* Universal Negro Imrovement
    Association
United House of Prayer for All People,
    209–17, 222–23, 224n.5
United Kingdom. *See* Great Britain
United States
    Indian immigrants in, 259–80
    justice system, 89
    national identity of, 9
    religion and construction of White
        America, 83–110
    in second half of 19th century, 101
    values, 16
United States v. Bhagat Singh Thind, 259–
    80
Universal Negro Imrovement Association
    (UNIA), 217, 226n.37

Vasconcelos, José, 172
vaudoux. *See* Vodou
Victorian era, 87, 91, 107
Vidor, King, 309–22, 325n.20, 326n.37
Virginia, 106
Vivekananda, Swami, 271
Vodou, 61–62, 64, 65, 71, 73–74, 76–78,
    231–58
voodoo. *See* Vodou

Warner, Charles Dudley, 89, 90, 104
Warner, Edward, 222
war paint, 45, 46
Watts, Jill, 219, 222, 224n.2
Wayland, H. L., 140
Weber, Max, 19
Weisbrot, Robert, 222, 224n.1
Weismantel, Mary, 158
Western civilization, 3
White Over Black (Jordan), 13
"White" race
    assimilative whiteness, 268–75
    and Christianity, 83–110, 277
    civilization of and Hindus in U.S., 259–
        77
    genealogical whiteness, 264–68, 273
    in Haiti, 64
    religious aesthetics, 282
    supremacism, 10, 62
Whiting, Albert, 214
Williams, Chancellor, 214–15, 225n.17
Winant, Howard, 86
Winthrop, Wait, 106
Wolverton, Judge, 259, 261–62
women, 7, 137, 152n.18, 153n.36, 165
Woo, Wesley, 148

Young, Lola, 305–6
Youxue Zhengdaohui, 148

Zélio de Morais, 296, 298, 299
Zinn, Maxine Baca, 7
Zuniga, Governor, 43